Exchanging The Past

Exchanging The Past

A Rainforest World of Before and After

Bruce M. Knauft

The University of Chicago Press
Chicago and London

Bruce M. Knauft is Samuel C. Dobbs Professor of Anthropology at
Emory University. He is author of four previous books, most recently
Genealogies for the Present in Cultural Anthropology and *From Primitive
to Postcolonial in Melanesia and Anthropology.*

The University of Chicago Press, Chicago 60637
The University of Chicago Press, Ltd., London
© 2002 by The University of Chicago
All rights reserved. Published 2002
Printed in the United States of America

11 10 09 08 07 06 05 04 03 02   1 2 3 4 5
ISBN: 0-226-44634-4 (cloth)
ISBN: 0-226-44635-2 (paper)

Library of Congress Cataloging-in-Publication Data

Knauft, Bruce M.
   Exchanging the past : a rainforest world of before and after / Bruce
M. Knauft.
      p.   cm.
Includes bibliographical references and index.
      ISBN 0-226-44634-4 — ISBN 0-226-44635-2
   1. Gebusi (Papua New Guinea people)—Social conditions.
2. Gebusi (Papua New Guinea people)—Social life and customs.
3. Acculturation—Case studies.   4. Hybridity (Social sciences)—
Case studies.   I. Title.
   DU740.42 .K52   2002
   305.89′912—dc21

                                                      2001006552

♾ This book is printed on acid-free paper.

Contents

Galleries of photographs follow pages 118 and 182

Acknowledgments

Some debts can never be fully repaid, and this book has many of them. They span two continents and several generations. Having sedimented over time, they grow all the stronger. My greatest thanks are to the many Gebusi who have been part of my life and to my wife, Eileen Cantrell Knauft. Eileen has been my constant partner and spiritual companion in field-work, even when, during this re-study of Gebusi in 1998, she could not be physically with me. Her support through corre-spondence, logistical help, and financial management has been at the core of this project. My debt to Gebusi is hard to express, since their experience has become part of me. The names of my Gebusi friends and acquaintances are many and go beyond list-ing; there is no easy dividing line between those who are more or less important to this book, and almost no list could avoid leaving someone out. A number of my cherished Gebusi friends will hopefully come alive to the reader in the chapters that fol-low. Sayu Silap and Didiga Imbo were my closest companions and helpers during my stay with Gebusi in 1998; my thanks to them is profound in many different ways.

For help and friendship in and around the Nomad Subdis-trict Station, there are several persons who deserve appreciation. Because of Nomad's remoteness, it is a thankless job to keep the station running despite financial constraints and government bureaucracy. Amid these difficulties, I was welcomed with warmth and support by many people. This support went beyond permission to document a wide array of records and observe a wide range of activities; it included thoughtful, friendly, and productive conversations about a great variety of topics. A very special thanks goes to the quiet and wise man who has been the mainstay of the Nomad Police Detachment for so many years, Senior Constable Ibuge Gobi. I also had warm and friendly support and conversation from Constable Nathaniel Haga and from the teachers at the Nomad School: Headmaster Ted Ano, Mr. Joseph Salangau, Mr. Jack Truman, and Mr. Wallan Kuwalihe. Nomad Subdistrict Affairs Manager Sam Gaiworo provided me not just official permission and initial housing on my first night but generous access to official records and valuable insights into the workings of the station. The Nomad business officer, George Asei, was also very helpful in these regards. The pastors of the Nomad churches—Catholic, Evangelical, and Seventh Day Adventist—were all accommodating and warmly welcomed my presence. I owe a particular debt of gratitude to Cyril Afenang, the lay pastor of the main Catholic church at Nomad, who, along with his family, has faithfully given many years of his life to his mission among Gebusi and others in the Nomad area. Thanks also go to the mission staff at the Montfort Catholic Mission in Kiunga, who accepted my presence at their youth development course and who continue to be my link for correspondence and packages sent to my Gebusi friends. In Gasumi Corners, I am grateful for the help collecting data on daily visitation and sleeping patterns from Didiga Imbo, Anagi Agi, Yamda Wasep, Keda Segwa, Howe Uwok, and Gilayo Dedagoba.

At Kiunga, I was graciously offered access to police records by Detective Sergeant Willie Mio and given additional information by Inspector Hariba Mamaea. My research affiliation for work in the Western Province was facilitated by Richard Mal-Aria, the province's Local-Level Government Affairs Officer in Kiunga. In Port Moresby, I had the great fortune to not only be officially supported but welcomed and provided with the best of intellectual stimulation by the indefatigable Dr. Colin Filer of the National Research Institute as well as by Dr. Mark Busse, then of the National Museum of Papua New Guinea. I would like to thank the National Research Institute of Papua New Guinea for my formal affiliation with it for the period of my research, and the institute's Research Liaison Officer, Michael Laki, for so quickly and painlessly negotiating approval of my research visa through the bureaucratic layers of the Papua New Guinean government.

Financial support for the fieldwork in 1998 on which this book is based has come generously from a range of institutions, and their support is gratefully acknowledged. These include the National Science Foundation, the Fulbright-Hays Faculty Research Abroad Program of the U.S. Department of Education, the Wenner-Gren Foundation for Anthropological Research, and the University Research Committee of Emory University. The then-chair of Emory's Anthropology Department, Peter J. Brown, supported my taking the research leave needed to complete the field research for this book. Write-up support from the Harry Frank Guggenheim Foundation was indispensable in allowing me to complete a rough draft of this project within a year of having returned from the field.

Comments on previous manuscript versions of this project are warmly appreciated from Joel Robbins, Eileen Cantrell Knauft, and especially my father Edwin Burt Knauft, who read and commented on a complete version of this book's penultimate draft. The anonymous publication reviewers for the University of Chicago Press also supplied extremely helpful comments. A special thanks also goes to the executive editor at the University of Chicago Press, T. David Brent, who has been not just supportive and helpful but intellectually nuanced in his suggestions. John Raymond provided superior copy editing and prose suggestions; remaining faults of language are my own. Beyond the specific persons who commented on a manuscript copy of this project are the many colleagues and students who responded effectively to portions of my argument in the context of seminars, professional meetings, and conference presentations. These venues and their constituents are too numerous to easily list, but special mention needs to be made of the students in the VM seminar of the Vernacular Modernities Program, which I direct at Emory; these students have stimulated me to develop many of the ideas expressed in the present book. For supporting the larger intellectual mission of which both the Vernacular Modernities Program and the present book are parts, I extend a sincere thanks to Howard A. Rollins, Jr., past Director of Emory's Institute of Comparative and International Studies; to Steven E. Sanderson, former Dean of Emory College; and, for generous program funding, to the Ford Foundation, Emory College, and the Emory Graduate School of Arts and Sciences. A great thanks also goes to the Emory Graduate School and to Emory College for their generous subvention to support indexing and the publication of color photographs in this book. Interim Graduate Dean Gary S. Wihl and interim college Dean Robert A. Paul deserve special thanks in this regard. Photographs 1 and 3 were taken in 1981 by Eileen Cantrell Knauft, whose permission to publish them is gratefully acknowledged. (The remaining photos used in this book were taken by me in 1998.) For intellectual stimulation and support, sincere appreciation is extended to my faculty colleagues at Emory. Special mention should be made of Professors Donald Donham and Ivan Karp, who have been instrumental in helping me refine my ideas, though they bear no responsibility for the weaknesses herein.

A final thanks goes to my present and former graduate students; they are my true colleagues both at Emory and beyond. They have given me the courage not just to teach anthropology from the heart but to go back to the field and learn it all over again.

The softest light is the morning's first, brushing the clouds to their faintest glow. It bathes Sayu as he slides ahead of me, down the trail and into the dawn. As we walk back to our village, I remember him from sixteen years ago in this same rainforest, when he was five years old. Sayu was the most charismatic child I had ever met. His impish smile would flood around him like the sun that pierced the forest canopy. He would wrap his small body in leaves, smear soot on his face, and put a feather in his hair. Swelling with whimsy, he would beat a length of bamboo as a make-believe drum and perform—a resplendent dancer at an imaginary feast. His play was as full of Gebusi custom as it could be. He would lilt a fetching echo to songs the men sang to the spirits at night. Or pretend to marry a five-year-old girl in sister-exchange marriage. Or cook some sago to divine and then accuse a make-believe sorcerer. More than any other child in the village, Sayu was constantly in and out of our thatched house. Women jokingly said that my wife, Eileen, had become his fictive mother or "side-mother." Eileen hugged him, cared for him when he was sick, and joked to the women that we would take him home with us when we left. That was in 1982.

A deep affection and pride washed over me when I first met Sayu again three months ago, in June 1998. Now, at a new dawn in this rainforest of memories, the dancer of childhood returns home with me. A fine young bachelor, Sayu has just enacted the spirits in full splendor. All night long, his crocodile drum has pulsed to their images emblazoned on his body in paint and plumage. His understated smile is as strong as the pearl shell just beneath it, his eyes as bright as the bird of paradise he has now become. I see him wonderfully transformed, his magnetic aura fully adorned. And yet, the fuller story of this young man is not at all what I thought it would be.

Sayu's young father, Silap, perished just three years after we left the Gebusi. His mother, a wonderful woman named Boi, died suddenly two years after that. She had been foraging alone with her two sons deep in the forest when the sickness overcame her. Far from the settlement, twelve-year-old Sayu and his younger brother cried and clutched their mother as she writhed and died in the night. A search party found the two terrified boys and carried their mother's corpse back to the village. Boi's second husband, Doliay, rushed home. Inquests were held and the sorcerer responsible for Boi's death was identified, a man named Basowey. Doliay was enraged and stalked his enemy in the forest. He split Basowey's skull with a bush knife. Then he cut off his head. The killing was too public for concealment; Doliay went to national prison for six years. There he became a model prisoner and then returned to the village as a respected man and a Christian. In due course, he was baptized. During his absence, however, Sayu had been left behind, orphaned, with no close guardians.

In 1994, following a dispute over his relationship with a young woman, Sayu walked eighty miles to Kiunga—through lands he had never seen and groups he had never known. With its three thousand inhabitants, Kiunga was a mining supply depot, a muddy gateway to the modern world, the emerald city to those in the forest. Quick and smart, Sayu finagled work in Kiunga as a domestic helper and "houseboy." He lived the kinless life of a teenage worker in town—washing dishes, doing laundry, cleaning house—and learning to ride a bike, dance to disco music, and watch his employer's satellite TV. Two years later, he returned home to the outskirts of Nomad, where his treasured boom box still warbles cassette music to everyone's delight. He has become a dandy, but he remains thoughtful and works hard. For the last three months, Sayu has been my companion, helper, and confidant.

The drama of last night recedes with the darkness as the muddy trail slides us toward our settlement. We are going back to Gasumi Corners, where traditional dancing is all but dead. Sayu's pearl shell is now crooked. His feathers are skewed and the red ocher paint is smudged and sweaty on his taut skin. He has been the red bird of paradise for the night, the lone visiting performer in a rare spectacle of fading tradition. He has danced until dawn for the first time, not to disco, as before, but in stately costume. Now past forty, I walk with Sayu as his friend and part-parent. I tell him what I feel: my eyes have seen his traditional dancing with the breath-spirit and pride of his dead father, his dead mother, and his side-mother, Eileen, who is back in America. I turn away so as not to cry.

Walking for another half hour, we approach the Nomad Station to wind our way home past the airstrip. Here is where the Australians established a patrol post in 1963. A school, health clinic, and tiny market have since grown up and survived alongside the government station despite the departure of the Aussies, who left in 1975 when Papua New Guinea became an independent country. The light is brighter now. Even on Saturday morning, Sayu is concerned that someone at the station might see him in the traditional grass skirts of the dancer. He has been the center of attention all night long, but that was in an old village of the forest, whereas Nomad is the place of educated teachers, officials, and pastors. Slipping behind a bush, Sayu slides off his skirts and quickly puts on his shorts. Now hybrid, he keeps the signs of the dancer above his waist but the security of Western clothes below. Around his neck, he now hangs the blue beads and cross that signify his Catholic baptism.

We shake hands firmly with others along the way before finally reaching home. There we are greeted by those who did not make the trek—most of the village. They ask whether they can hear the tape recording I made the previous night. As the spindle turns, we listen to the men's joking, Sayu's drumming, the sound of his dance rattles, the women's weak traditional singing. But we also hear the evening's flashy string band, its guitar and ukulele, the singing learned from the radio and from others' cassettes: bush modern music. The mix of musical styles reminds me of the enchanted listeners the night before in the old longhouse. They had drifted through shadows thrown by modern wick lanterns and traditional resin torches. Some had wreathed themselves splendidly in leaves, body paint, and bird feathers. Others had sported a colorful shirt or hat, or worn spiffy sunglasses in the night. Yet others mixed and matched cheerfully—a collage of body painting here, Western clothing there, a headdress on a hat. All of them had paused appreciatively, indeed, beckoned gratefully to pose for my flashing camera—as if to take modern photography into the heart of their changing traditions.

Tomorrow will be Sunday in Gasumi Corners. The church service will be long in the hot morning as we listen passively to the harangues of the pastor and the strictures of God. Then we will watch rugby and soccer on the government sports field until late in the afternoon or early in the evening. The children will go to bed early so they can be up and off before 7 A.M. on Monday morning—another weekday of instructional discipline at Nomad Community School. After dark, the men will again consider whether they can scrape together enough decorations to dress up in traditional costumes for the government contest next week. They would like to have some chance of winning a little of the prize money that officials hand out after judging the performances of the various local traditions. This happens on the lawn of the government station on Independence Day. Anything to gain a token of money at a place as remote and undeveloped as Nomad. Perhaps, as the men mused before, they will dress one of their uninitiated young men in the regalia of a traditional male initiate for this national rite of modern celebration. But he can never be initiated in fact, because initiations are no longer practiced by the people of Gasumi Corners.

Will last night's dance-until-dawn become a memory of nostalgic tradition? So I wonder as I melt into morning sleep and Gebusi lives, in September 1998.

◆ ◆ ◆

Where does it go, the past? Is it sloughed off as irrelevant? Ground up into a different way of becoming modern? Or does it survive intact like a spore, alive in the dwindling traditional dance, waiting to grow into someone's memory or book? Perhaps it spins new webs upon older ones that are never quite lost but never really found again. The past gives up some things and makes others its own; it becomes the same and yet very different from what it was.

This book follows the remarkable path of social and cultural change among the six hundred Gebusi of the lowland rainforest in the Western Province of Papua New Guinea. Like the rest of the world, the Gebusi confront modern agents and institutions. As Marshall Berman (1992: 33) puts it, modernity emphasizes progress and renewal through identification with the triumphs of Western-style economics, politics, material culture, technology, and aesthetics. But like the rest of the world, Gebusi configure these developments in their own distinct fashion and with their own idea of what it means to be progressive as opposed to traditional.

Before investigating the dynamics of this social and cultural change, some background is necessary concerning Gebusi in 1980–82, when I first lived with them, and in the ethnographic present of 1998. The following chapter sketches this introductory material and summarizes the analysis that follows in the rest of the book. Chapters 2 and 3 trace the path of Gebusi changes through intense sorcery beliefs and killings to the physical relocation of a prominent community next to the Nomad Station during the late 1980s. The focus then shifts to three institutions at the Nomad Station that have influenced Gebusi: the police, the Christian churches, and the community school. Gebusi experience with these institutions is explored in chapters 4 through 7. Chapter 8 then steps back to consider contemporary Gasumi Corners in the round, including the current interplay between forest, village, and the Nomad Station; the significance of market activity, sports, and new forms of singing; the new role of feasts; and the changing status of traditional dance and costuming. The final chapter draws these themes together and illuminates the subaltern status that Gebusi adopt as they self-consciously exchange their sense of the past for their hopes for the future.

Ethnographically, this book describes and explains striking changes in a society that had one of the highest homicide rates documented in the cross-cultural record. In particular, it explores the history and means by which an extraordinary rate of killing associated with sorcery accusations has dramatically declined. The cause of this decline bears scrutiny. In contrast to some of their neighbors, Gebusi have never been subject to significant levels of government coercion. In recent years, government intervention has declined to yet lower levels, especially in the rainforest areas where Gebusi communities forage, garden, and hunt. And yet the Gebusi rate of killing has continued to drop. To account for this and other social changes, we are drawn to alterations in Gebusi attitudes and values.

In recent years, Gebusi hopes for the future have diverged increasingly from the realities of their social and material life. This disjuncture between present conditions and future expectations informs the Gebusi's willing Christianization and, more generally, their willingness to submit themselves to institutions and agents associated with a larger world. In our own Western past, historians have suggested that European notions of modern progress emerged as an escalating divergence between people's actual experiences and their expectations of the future. This occurred during the late eighteenth century—the same period that is often associated with the beginning of modern Western societies.[1]

The discrepancy between experiences and expectations has intensified among Gebusi during the last fifteen years, and it shows no sign of abating. With an eye to a hopefully new and better future, Gebusi say that they are exchanging their old ways of life for new ones. And yet, this change occurs despite a painful absence of wage labor, out-migration, resource extraction, and other economic initiatives. These possibilities are intensely desired and imagined by Gebusi but are extremely difficult to achieve given their remote rainforest location. Development for Gebusi is at least as much cultural as it is economic or political; it foregrounds changes in values, desires, and fantasies. Even if Gebusi later reassert or reinvent their previous beliefs or customs, they will do so in a new way and in a context that has been irrevocably changed.

The changes described in this book are unique to Gebusi; they cannot be taken to represent changes in other world areas, other parts of Papua New Guinea, or even other parts of the country's Western Province. As the Papua New Guinean writer John Kolia (1980: 176) noted, "Nobody has visited more than a tiny fraction of the villages of any one province. No generalizations can be made therefore—but often are by foreigners . . ." Though anthropologists often feel that their findings have broader relevance, this relevance does not often generalize at the level of specific content. This is especially true in Melanesia, whose population of fewer than eight million people boasts an amazing degree of cultural diversity, with over one thousand languages and associated cultures.

For Melanesia, Gebusi are unusual for their small population, their geographic remoteness, and their violent history of scapegoating and killing sorcery suspects. During the last twenty years, groups of Gebusi have also become distinctive for the remarkable extent of their social transformation and their acceptance of outside authority—despite or perhaps because of their continuing remoteness and lack of economic development. Through particularities of history, Gebusi have long viewed themselves as subject to the influence of powerful outsiders. In the precolonial era, Gebusi were raided with impunity by their more populous and warlike neighbors, the Bedamini. During the late 1960s, very late in the colonial era, Australian patrol officers "pacified" the Bedamini, supplanted their influence, and established themselves as benevolent if ignorant authorities at the Nomad Patrol Post. More recently, Gebusi have accepted the influence of Papua New Guineans from other parts of the country who have administered the Nomad Station during the postcolonial era.

Uniqueness aside, what Gebusi do reveal is the way desire for modern wealth informs altered modes of subjectivity and new forms of subservience. In this respect, Gebusi crystallize and throw into relief features that are common but diffuse among many marginalized peoples in so-called developing countries. Though subject to many variations, desires and fantasies of becoming successful in a modern, material way are frequently combined with changed ways of relating to those in local communities and to outsiders. Among many marginalized peoples, these changes foster acceptance of modern institutions controlled or heavily influenced by people who come from other groups, other parts of the country, or other countries altogether. These individuals may include government officials, teachers, religious or economic proselytizers, health care workers, or employees of NGOs or other development programs. Interactions with such persons are of course highly relative and contextual: they depend upon specifics of cultural orientation and history, the type and degree of prior disenfranchisement, and the particular institutions or organizations that local people feel compelled to engage. Subordination to outsiders and their organizations may be reduced—for instance, when local populations are relatively large or have significant political or economic influence.

Whatever its context, outside influence is not just material or economic, it is social and cultural as well. In the contemporary world, the ways that outside values influence local people help reveal how rural populations intensify their desire for Western-style goods and commodities, on the one hand, and become subject to new forms of inequality, on the other. Of course, local communities have many different reactions to this situation, and their responses generate a host of new cultural developments. As a result of such developments, indeed, it can be argued that cultural diversity is expanding rather than shrinking in the world today. In this sense, cultural proliferation occurs at the same time and in some ways for the very reason that modern capitalism has become fully global—it influences social life in even the remotest parts of the world. In many of these areas, as at Nomad, cultural change operates through desires for modern progress that incite new attitudes and foster new types of inequity.

Because these changes depend on the interactions between local cultural orientations and global forces—rather than on either of them separately—they are often hard to understand through perspectives that expect global forces to produce cultural convergence or homogeneity between peoples that have different ways of life. Reciprocally, these changes are also hard to understand from perspectives that emphasize the continuity and atomism of local cultures, as if they persist apart from wider influences. Nor are these changes easily comprehended by approaches that stress the staunch opposition and resistance of local people to outside pressures.

Though economists, political scientists, and global theorists stress the worldwide march of commodity markets, the desires incited by these commodities reach much farther than their material and economic acquisition. In economically marginal areas, the backwash of so-called development often does not engage the material means of gaining wealth so much as it does the cultural imagination of progress in the context of local power relations. Especially among the young and middle-aged, desire to pursue a lifestyle of success associated with a wider world is blocked by lack of money, education, and access to government. If the means to satisfy aspirations are lacking, as they often are, it is not surprising that the values, meanings, and exhortations of agents and institutions that *are* associated with a wider world attain special status. Hence it is also not surprising that people in conditions of economic marginality may contextually submit themselves to the authority of one or another institution that they associate with the benefits of a larger world. Juxtaposed against the higher status and wealth claimed by educated persons or outsiders, local people can become relatively passive or subordinate when they attempt to associate with or learn from modern institutions—such as schools, churches, government, extra-local business corporations, or international development organizations.

Of course, social life among Gebusi and other marginalized peoples entails much more than passivity or a sense of falling behind. Creative and highly "agentive" countermoves are common at the local level. Among Gebusi, we find new forms of feasting, performance, and music that meld traditional practices with Western commodities, disco dancing, and "parties" (*fati*). In this sense, the desire to be successful in a modern, material way drives a spiral between the development of new traditions and the re-definition of old ones. As discussed in chapter 8, however, this process ulti-mately results in Gebusi mockery of their traditional beliefs and their cele-bration of being newly modern in the highly popular performances that culminate the festivities on Independence Day.

In theoretical terms, this study emphasizes alternative or vernacular ways of becoming modern based on changes in values, beliefs, and expecta-tions. Gebusi envision this as a process of direct exchange (*sesum degra*) in which customs and spirits that are backward or "backsliding" are replaced by those that are "new" and "come up on top." Socially and politically, this process entails submissiveness and passivity by Gebusi in those contexts that are most modern and most controlled by government officials, pastors, and other outsiders. The dynamics of what I call "recessive agency" in these and other contexts foster patience and acceptance of powerful outsiders while increasing local openness to external influence.

In recent years, anthropologists have paid increasing attention to how local people create new beliefs and hybrid practices as they resist the intru-sion of modern forces.[2] In complementary fashion, other anthropologists have emphasized cultural continuity through the persistence of distinctly nonmodern attitudes and beliefs.[3] As a result, our understanding of cultural dynamics in non-Western worlds is not in danger of neglecting either the persistence of cultural orientations or their hybrid changes. The competing sides of this awareness become prominent in the ongoing debate between anthropologists who emphasize transformation and those who emphasize continuity—between those who focus on the globally intrusive and those who focus on the culturally conservative.[4] Amid these complements, an-thropologists need to pay greater attention to the ways that local people actively and willingly engage cultural attitudes and expectations that derive from elsewhere. Since social scientists from other disciplines seldom shed critical light on the inequalities that result from this process, it is all the more important for anthropologists to develop such an awareness as we conduct research today.

The final purpose of this book is to combine a critical exposé of culture and power with an appreciative understanding of contemporary social life in an out-of-the-way place. The humanity, meaning, and richness of experience among peoples such as Gebusi is not undone by a cultural economy that includes reception and subservience. The responses of Gebusi are rich and varied. Accordingly, ethnography of social life in the present need not be any less intriguing, provocative, or rigorous than was the study of highly unusual or "exotic" customs—including those such as spirit mediumship, sorcery divination, and ritual homosexuality that I found to be so prominent among Gebusi in 1980–82. Anthropology needs greater understanding of the cultural means by which local people engage modern institutions and how these engagements inform local attitudes, social relations, and inequalities. Investigating this process need not preclude the presence of the author in the text or the details of the lives of others in the field. But it does require greater attention to how people actively seek out and engage organizations such as the local school, business, church, government administration, business, or development agency.

Chapter 1

A World of Before and After

In 1980, the Gebusi were far more traditional than I had any right to expect. And if the Gebusi were traditional, so was I. A fledgling researcher, I had bought fully into anthropology's classic lure: to study a people who were as remote and little-contacted as possible. With the help of my advisor, I picked an appropriately blank spot on the map of interior New Guinea—a terra incognita in the tropical rainforest. This ethnographic blankness was even more accurate than I suspected: my first expedition revealed the area to be as devoid of people as it was infested by mosquitoes. The nearest sizable group was an unstudied population of about 450 people who had been ethnographically designated as the "Bibo" but who in fact called themselves "Gebusi" (see map 1 and photo 1). Along with my wife and fellow doctoral candidate Eileen Cantrell, I lived with Gebusi from 1980 to 1982.

Though my first fieldwork was dated by its search for the primitive, I won't forswear its results. Anthropology will be poorer if it gives up on the diversity of cultural pasts. Even the study of social change seems impossible without documenting earlier conditions—the "before" that implicates the "after." In the present case, it was only upon writing and publishing the results of my first fieldwork that I began to realize how unusual it was for Gebusi traditions to have persisted so strongly into the 1980s. Courtesy of remoteness, historical circumstance, and luck, Gebusi had never been subject to missionization, wage labor, out-migration, expropriation of land, cash cropping, or much in the way of direct government interference. When they were first contacted—by Australian patrol officers in 1962—Gebusi were still using stone axes.

The first years of colonial influence were, from the Gebusi point of view, beneficial. In addition to receiving occasional trade goods, these benefits included especially the Australian pacification of the Gebusi's more numerous and militaristic neighbors, the Bedamini, who had raided Gebusi border settlements with impunity. Beyond the securing of their eastern flank, however, Gebusi received little colonial attention except for a yearly census patrol that passed through major settlements to count heads. In 1975, a scant thirteen years after first contact, the Australians left and independence arrived at the Nomad Station and for the new country of Papua

Map 1. The Strickland-Bosavi Area

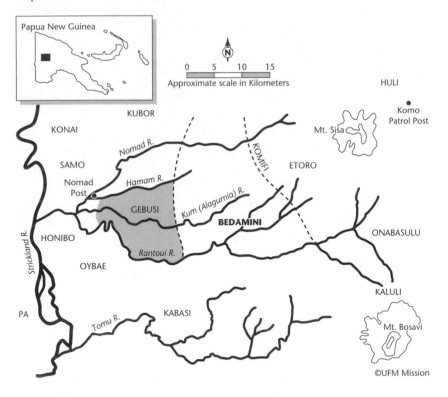

New Guinea. In 1980, children younger than five had never seen white skin and so fled when they first saw us.

At the time of our initial arrival, indigenous customs seemed robust as well as profound. Indeed, though I hardly realized it at the time, the pacification of the Bedamini along with the simultaneous introduction of steel tools—which enabled larger garden clearings and bigger houses— probably encouraged more feasting and ritual activity among Gebusi than had been possible before the Australians arrived. In 1980–82, all-night spirit séances led by one or more entranced spirit mediums were held until dawn an average of once every eleven days. At these songfests, lascivious spirit-women entered the medium's body and exhorted the all-male audience with tales of flirtation and sexual enticement (Knauft 1989). Public enactment of spirit-world beliefs abounded: ritual feasts, dances in stunning costumes, and initiations in full splendor at the communal longhouse. Ritual homosexuality was actively practiced: teenage boys sucked the penises and swallowed the semen of older men to acquire the life force of male adulthood (Knauft 1987a). Initiation ceremonies boasted elaborate rituals and a full complement of bawdy jokes, feasts, dances, spirit séances, and folktales.

Practices and beliefs concerning sorcery were equally striking. Gebusi deaths from sickness were invariably followed by spirit séances and divinations to identify the sorcerer responsible. Through a dizzying and ominous set of inquest procedures, sorcery suspects were forced to undergo divinations and risked being executed (Knauft 1985a). A mortality tabulation of 18 clans revealed that virtually one-third of Gebusi adults had been murdered. The rate of killing was among the very highest documented in a human society (Knauft 1987c). Most of these killings were executions of persons who had been accused of sorcery and scapegoated within their own communities. During the precolonial era, slain sorcerers were routinely cooked and eaten: the accused sorcerer was considered inhuman and was treated in the same manner as a game animal of the forest. These patterns persisted under colonialism and after independence; they were often effectively hidden from government awareness. In 1977, a man killed his half-sister on the spot after the corpse of his daughter "opened its eyes" and "looked at her" during a corpse divination. In 1978, a man and his brother were killed and eaten as sorcerers, and in 1978–79, two elderly widows were killed as sorcerers in separate cases. In one of these instances, the woman's body was stealthily exhumed and eaten in a neighboring village.

Immediate Exchange

For Gebusi and their neighbors, killing sorcerers was a normal part of the cycle whereby some persons were exchanged directly for others. Gebusi society and culture were firmly configured through what has been called "direct reciprocity."[1] This orientation is aptly illustrated by marriage practices. In contrast to many parts of the world, including significant parts of Melanesia, Gebusi strive to exchange women between different clans or lineages: the bride's true or classificatory brother should marry a true or classificatory "sister" of the groom. In effect, every marriage should be balanced—a double marriage. Accordingly, Gebusi lacked customs of bridewealth, in which a preponderance of valuables are given by the groom's side as an initial exchange for the bride to compensate her natal kin for their loss of her domestic and reproductive abilities. By contrast, a Gebusi woman should be compensated directly by one given in return—a woman-for-woman system of marital exchange. Analogously, among Gebusi men, sexual pleasure was received in direct and immediate reciprocity for the task of "growing" a young man to adulthood, that is, the pleasure of supplying semen in orgasm for homosexual insemination.

This logic of immediate and equivalent reciprocity also informed Gebusi feasting and killing. For major feasts, visitors hunted game deep in the forest while the hosts processed sago palm and readied one or more domestic pigs for slaughter. Major visitors brought net bags laden with dried meat and fish to the feast. At the conclusion of the ceremony, visitors presented these prized foods to the hosts, who reciprocated with large rolls of cooked sago and steamed pork. The exchange of valuable feast food was immediate and equivalent. By contrast, Gebusi lacked patterns of large-scale competitive exchange—found in highland and insular areas of Melanesia—in which large gifts of food or wealth indebt the receivers until they can repay or exceed the amount with a return gift at a later time.[2]

A logic of direct reciprocity also informed Gebusi exchanges of persons-for-persons at death. To them, each and every death from sickness was a murder—the killing of one individual by another through supernatural means (Knauft 1985a). The relevant beliefs will be discussed in due course, but the larger point is that each loss of life through sickness called for a compensatory death in exchange. This retribution was accomplished by executing the sorcery suspect held responsible for sending the sickness. In the same way that the sorcerer may have spiritually eaten and consumed the body of the victim, the sorcerer's body could be cooked and eaten. And in the same way that the sorcerer caused the victim to suffer prior to death, the accused sorcerer could be burned or tormented before being slain. Given this logic of direct replacement, it is not surprising that a man was far more likely to be attacked as a sorcerer following the sickness-death of another male, while women were more frequently killed following the sickness-deaths of females (Knauft 1985: 133–35). In one case in which a teenage initiand had died from sickness, the young male sorcery suspect was tied and dressed up like an initiate before being slain and eaten.

In principle, then, Gebusi believed that every sickness-death merited a sorcery execution. In practice, this principle was followed a bit more than one-quarter of the time; between about 1940 and 1982, 26.5 percent of known sickness-deaths (56 of 211) precipitated the killing of at least one alleged sorcerer or led to another sorcery-related homicide (Knauft 1985a: 124).[3] Correspondingly, not every marriage was completed as a direct replacement through sister-exchange. This reciprocity requires equal numbers of "brothers" and "sisters" in each kin group, but the small size of Gebusi clans led to unequal numbers of male and female clan siblings. In addition, some strong-willed young women resisted effectively and refused the marriage proposed for them (Cantrell 1998). As a result, the actual rate of sister-exchange was just a bit above half of all first marriages (Knauft 1985a: 169). When the marriage was not reciprocated, both sides were supposed, in principle, to simply accept that an exchange was not possible. But disgruntlement could easily fester over time. Indeed, one of the strongest findings during my initial fieldwork was that imbalance in marriage exchange was highly correlated with sorcery accusation. In-laws who were related to each other by virtue of an unreciprocated marriage were highly prone to accuse each other of sorcery (Knauft 1985a: chap. 7; 1987c). Though glaring in statistical terms, this pattern was largely denied by Gebusi themselves. They claimed both to me and to each other that the identity of sorcerers could be known only through spiritual means: "We don't know what makes sorcerers angry. We just see the divination and we attack the person who the spirits show us is guilty." In structural terms, however, lack of direct reciprocity in marriage was often a strong motive for reversing this imbalance by other means—through killing.

The cultural logic of exchange in Gebusi sorcery accusations helps account for the surprising fact that no Gebusi, as far as we know, actually tried to practice sorcery. The risk to personal survival of being known as a sorcerer was so great that it was one of the last things Gebusi would contemplate doing. Empirical evidence aside, however, the spiritual and physical "proof" of sorcery practice—derived from elaborate spiritual inquests and divinations—was self-evident to Gebusi. As a logic of projective belief and direct exchange, the execution of sorcery suspects provided its own justification.

In political terms, this system of violent scapegoating worked as a strong leveling mechanism. Compared even to the decentralized societies of the fringe New Guinea highlands, Gebusi had little in the way of leadership roles or centralized authority. To be aggressive or publicly self-interested was considered antisocial—similar to how a sorcerer might act. Potential male leaders as well as sharp-tongued widows were often accused of sorcery. The problem of unrequited sister-exchange also made it very difficult for a man to marry and retain more than one wife; he easily became the target of marital resentment or sorcery accusation. Though the spirit medium stood out as a figure of important spiritual authority, his influence was limited to his entranced state. Gebusi made a notably clear distinction between the medium's spirit familiar, which provided the voice of spiritual advice during séances, and the persona of the medium himself, which had no special authority in daily life.

In sum, direct reciprocity among Gebusi combined features of heightened political decentralization, sister-exchange marriage, male ritual homosexuality, domination of women, and a person-for-person model of killing and cannibalism that took the life of the sorcery suspect as compensation for the life of the sickness victim.

On the positive side of exchange, Gebusi who died of sickness were reincarnated as beautiful or powerful animals of the forest: the red bird of paradise, the hornbill, the egret, the cuscus, the cassowary, the lizard, the turtle, or a large fish. By means of this animation, the physical world became the spiritual embodiment of Gebusi ancestry as well as the home of those animals and plants that had never been human. Collectively, this corpus of spirits formed a parallel world that Gebusi could communicate with and enjoy through the entranced discourse and singing of the spirit medium. Voiced through the medium, the words of the spirits were echoed in deep song by the men of the community during all-night séances. During these songfests, Gebusi could interact with spirits who saw and understood things that Gebusi themselves could not. By this supernatural means, the spirit familiars of Gebusi mediums could locate and reclaim the "lost spirit" of many sick persons, thus keeping them from more serious illness or sorcery. The spirits could also help Gebusi locate lost pigs and forecast the success of fish poisoning or hunting expeditions. They could also help identify sorcerers.

In ritual dances and initiations, Gebusi celebrated the integrity of their rich and helpful spirit world. These festivities brought together beautiful images of the spirits—their feathers, fur, foliage, and other icons. These icons were arranged in aesthetic harmony and literally embodied on the dancers, who became the center of attention during the nightlong celebrations. As an enactment and celebration of this spiritual concord, groups of Gebusi from different settlements came together in a spirit of camaraderie and collective enjoyment to witness these spectacular dances. Along with a wide range of other Gebusi ceremonies, ritual feasts and dances were quite frequent in 1980–82.

Time Passing

What changes, by the late 1990s, had occurred in Gebusi society and culture? More personally, what had happened to the individual Gebusi I had known as friends and confidants? Only snippets of information had come to me in the interim, and none of it was very revealing. Some colleagues suggested that modern developments—Christianization, schooling, outmigration, and a trickle of economic development—would surely have brought major alterations. But others emphasized that the more things appeared to change, the more they actually stayed the same, based on deeper continuities of culture and meaning.

Even concerning homicide, different alternatives were possible. By 1982, I knew the killing rate had already declined to about half its precolonial levels—from a whopping 39 percent of all adult deaths to 23.3 percent during Australian colonialism and then to 19 percent between 1975 and 1982. Much of this reduction came from the cessation of Bedamini raids, which had decimated a number of settlements. But Gebusi scapegoating and killing of sorcerers within their own communities had continued. What had happened since 1982, however, remained a mystery to me. Given the continuing absence of Australian intervention, some colleagues thought that the rate of killing could have risen. In recent years, tribal violence has reemerged dramatically in parts of the New Guinea highlands.[4] In some areas, new forms of violence are associated with so-called "raskol" behavior of young criminals; violent gangs of raskols have arisen in cities or towns and then spread to rural areas.[5] Gebusi had always been able to hide most of their killings from government officials. Now, with Gebusi left on their own, patterns of the past could easily reemerge or find new expressions. This view was held by the missionary who had lived among the neighboring Bedamini people since the mid-1960s. But other changes were also in the wind, and these linked the scapegoating and killing of sorcerers with customs now associated with a backward past rather than with progress toward a hoped-for future. I was truly uncertain as to what I would find.

Added to my empirical uncertainties were personal ones. In 1980, I was an ambitious twenty-six-year-old neophyte anthropologist. The quintessential researcher-on-a-shoestring, I had nothing to lose and everything to prove. I still wonder at the enormous gap between my book learning about Melanesia, which was prodigious, and my personal experience, which was zero. I had never been west of Oregon, but I had the hubris of ignorance, endless energy for work, unbridled faith in intercultural understanding, and that limitless naiveté that is essential to keep one from assessing more objectively the difficulty of the task ahead. To this mix was added the challenge of reorientation for my wife, Eileen Cantrell, who had given up her own research interests in the Himalayas to be my partner in the lowland rainforests of New Guinea.

Although my first fieldwork yielded a wealth of ethnographic riches, these belonged to a specific period of Gebusi culture and of Melanesian anthropology. Viewed from the present, it does little good to think of culture as pristine, a belljar of yesteryears. As against this, the past and the present need to have the same tension in our work as they do in the lives of the people we study. The historical and the new are complements that provide the figure and ground for each other. Accordingly, the present book complements my first volume on the Gebusi by building on its detailed findings at the same time that it recontextualizes, historicizes, and transforms its approach.

My motives for fieldwork were different in 1998 from what they had been in 1980. I was both more knowledgeable and more worried than I had been the first time out. Already a full professor and author of four books, I could now busy myself with the life of being an academic. But for this very possibility, I was all the more nagged by the sense that my reading and writing and teaching—somewhat like preaching—had taken my thoughts too far from the lived experience of others. I needed to get back to the field. But fieldwork is always a humbling experience. Perhaps my finely honed sense of being a successful anthropologist would fall like a house of cards. And the rainforest knows that a body at forty-four is no longer what it was at twenty-six. I worried about the burden of my absence on my wife and son, behind in the United States, especially if anything serious should happen to me. (In fact, I did get bitten by a death adder and feared at first that it might be fatal.)

My uncertainties were also theoretical. Middle-aged sensibilities seldom retain the naive immunity of a younger mind. How would I combine my theoretical awareness of change with the importance of cultural continuity? Though going under many guises, debates in anthropology crackle between views that emphasize cultural tradition and those that stress global transformation. These disputes echo anthropology's other oppositions: Is cultural diversity stronger than regional or global connection? Are societies more strongly informed by historical values or by recent changes and new developments? Is human experience more strongly influenced by cultural meanings or by the workings of political economy?

These questions are often unanswerable, but they have spawned important developments in anthropology in recent years. At present, anthropologists often mediate these alternative points of view by recognizing that local tradition and modern change are both important. This has been described as a process of becoming "alternatively modern" or as producing a "vernacular modernity" or "parallel modernity" (see Knauft in press a).[6] These conditions borrow from but are different from those that influenced Euro-American societies and cultures over the last century and more. People in diverse world areas are increasingly influenced by broadening standards of material progress and cultural development. But they interpret and respond to these developments in different ways. As changes and commonalities race around the world, people appropriate and configure their responses differently depending on their cultural context and history. The tension between what is considered modern and what is considered traditional also keeps our thinking alive to contrary tendencies and urges us to view local and larger dynamics in the direct context of each other.

Given these benefits, the present work adopts what might be generally called an alternatively modern point of view. This perspective foregrounds experiences that pulse with ambivalent desires, contradictory goals, and conflicting images. Prominent among these, particularly for the young and restless, is that aching desire to be wealthy or otherwise have a prestigious lifestyle that increases one's stature in a larger world. This drive can push and constrain young men and women differently; alternative ways of being modern are often highly gendered.[7]

Why do so many people so actively want economic development? How does this aspiration connect with desires to adopt a different and more contemporary set of cultural values? Why do visions of becoming modern lead people to experiment with their lives even when there is little chance of tangible benefit or payoff? What impact do these processes have upon local traditions that people have grown up with? Anthropologists have found it difficult to confront these questions.

On the face of it, ethnographic re-studies based on long-term research would seem finely suited to this task: a rich understanding of "before" and "after" is crucial to comprehending social and cultural change. In fact, however, ethnographic re-studies are often less concerned with what people want in the present than in extending, updating, or reasserting the researcher's original findings. Seldom as detailed or penetrating the second time around, re-studies tend to bring the author's past perspective into the present without fundamentally altering it. As major changes are documented, they are often tinged with nostalgia for how things used to be, either by reproducing the past or lamenting its passing. Returning to the field after sixteen years, I found myself wanting to guard against nostalgia for the Gebusi past and for my initial work. This is hard to do: it makes one vulnerable, both personally and professionally. My younger colleagues warned me that my experiences in the field would now be very different from what they were in 1980–82. I wanted to accept these changes at their current face value. So I tried as much as possible—however impossible in fact—to clean my slate of prior expectations and see Gebusi life through their eyes as they now experience it.

I can start by summarizing the most prominent continuities and changes in Gebusi society and culture in 1998. The analytic and theoretical frame that helps us understand this mosaic will emerge in the process.

World of Continuity

Gebusi amazed me. Some of their customs and beliefs were the same as before. Fathers and brothers still asserted that daughters and sisters should marry through direct reciprocity in sister-exchange marriage. Basic patterns of social organization and kinship were intact, including multiclan settlements with high coresidence between in-laws and between maternal uncles and the children of their sisters.[8] Now residentially reconfigured on the outskirts of Nomad, the overall size and composition of my old community of Gasumi was similar to what it had been before.[9] Its new name was Gasumi Corners.[10]

The extensive gardens near Gasumi Corners still furnished the dietary staple, starchy bananas. The daily heat of 100 degrees and the steam of humidity were just as great as ever. Away in the bush, gardening and foraging and hunting remained largely as before. The slow pace of the rainforest was still wondrous in its quietude, and Gebusi retreated there when they wanted. Women still used stone adzes when they processed sago in the forest, not because they lacked metal tools but because the traditional implement pounds the pith better than metal ones. The forest is still the home of nuts and bamboo shoots and wild greens and bird eggs and river fish and fresh water prawns. It's still the place to gather string for net bags and body decorations and torch resin and leaf plates and sago leaves for thatched roofs and all the various woods and barks and vines that become the walls and floors and supports of Gebusi houses.

Those in Gasumi Corners consider themselves fortunate to have land that abuts on the government station. They are able to live near Nomad while being able to access their traditional lands, going back and forth as they please. The rainforest remains the Gebusi breadbasket and under their control. Unlike the situation in the Amazon, central Africa, remaining pockets of Southeast Asia, and increasing parts of Papua New Guinea, the Gebusi rainforest has not been subject to development schemes or outside extraction. Land is extensive and permission to garden or to hunt is still readily granted by the owners. Though the threat of commercial logging rumbles like an unseen storm over the expansive horizon, its deluge has not come to this part of the rainforest. Like their more distant neighbors, Gebusi could probably be duped by logging companies to sign their land away for the lure of phantom wealth. Such deals can descend like manna from helicopters that dramatically bring well-funded advance teams to rainforest settlements. But where Gebusi live—mostly within a day's walk of the Nomad Station—there has been enough clearing of large trees and corresponding secondary growth in gardens and settlements that the area is no longer considered prime land for largescale logging of hardwoods.[11]

Back in 1980–82, Gebusi patterns of movement and dwelling—daily, weekly, and monthly—were as fluid and shifting as the bends of their rainforest rivers. Families took extensive trips to hunt or forage or process sago in the rainforest. To these travels were added visits to other settlements for feasts and dances or simply to visit relatives or friends; Gebusi liked to congregate when they could. Most settlements were virtually deserted during the day and sometimes only thinly peopled in the evening as well. In 1980–82, Gebusi slept at their main residence only a bit over half of the time, 55.3 percent. During a typical week, the average adult would spend about two nights (29.7%) at a garden house or bush shelter plus another night (12.5%) visiting some other hamlet (Knauft 1985a: 26, 401 n. 16).

Though to a lesser extent, this same basic pattern persisted in 1998 even though the descendants of my original community now lived near the Nomad Station. Based on complete records from mid-July to late November, 1998, residents of Gasumi Corners slept somewhere other than their principal residence almost one-third of the time (30.3%).[12] About one night a week (13.5%), the average adult from Gasumi Corners was sleeping at another hamlet or village, and a bit more than once a week (16.8%) he or she was sleeping at a subsistence location in the forest. Mobility was most pronounced for unmarried young men, who slept away from their primary residence almost half of the nights (49.8%). Revealingly, however, those from Gasumi Corners very rarely stayed in a town or city more distant than the nearby Nomad Station; this occurred only 0.6 percent of the time. Out-migration and long-distance travel are still rare for Gebusi.

As had also been the case in 1980–82, politics in Gasumi Corners was less personally aggressive than in many parts of Melanesia. Now, however, it was focused around village moots peppered with assertive speeches and presided over by a local elected councillor. Major feasts were still held, and visitors still brought net bags of dried meat and fish to exchange for large rolls of steamed sago and cooked pork at the end of the festivities.

In aesthetic terms, Gebusi still enjoyed the traditional costuming of dances and initiations, if only to participate as visitors at one of the outlying settlements where these customs were still practiced. Or perhaps they might see the splendid costumes of old in traditional dance competitions now held on the parade grounds at the Nomad Station on Independence Day. Finally, sickness-deaths were still sometimes believed to be caused by sorcery, though, as will be seen, these beliefs were much less intense and much less likely to cause violence than before.

World of Change

Though they took place amid continuities, changes among Gebusi in 1998 were astounding. In the Nomad area, sixteen years is practically a generation. The descendants of my old village now boasted a whole flock of new youngsters and of adults who had survived childhood (see photos 3 and 4). By contrast, very few men of my own age or older were still alive; most of those I had known as adults had died. Of the six teenage bachelors initiated in 1981, only three were still alive. I mourned the passing of many friends and now saw their personalities, amazingly, in children who were pushing toward their own adulthood. Gebusi were, in demographic terms, a new people, and they were more numerous than before, having increased from about 450 to about 615 persons.

Change and turnover notwithstanding, I was remembered more than fondly and was joyously welcomed. Two children had been named after me during the intervening years. Once worn, the glove of friendship always

seems to fit. It felt absolutely wonderful to be back. Within one day of arriv-
ing, I was given a house that had been newly built in Gasumi Corners. I
quickly made this my base of operations and found myself living with
friends, going both to Nomad and to the forest, and conducting the intense
data-gathering of fieldwork from June to December, 1998.[13]

As I quickly found, the people of Gasumi Corners had not just a new
residence but a new way of life. Living on the outskirts of Nomad, social
life in Gasumi Corners often revolved around activities at the government
station that carried what Raymond Williams (1977) might call a new structure of feeling. The old village of Gasumi, where Eileen and I had lived for
two years, had been abandoned and reclaimed by the rainforest. Through
a series of splintered movements and reaggregations, the descendants of
Gasumi and its surrounding settlements had ultimately reaggregated as a
set of four hamlets on Gebusi land that was an easy half-hour saunter from
the Nomad Station and its airstrip. Previously a people of the deep rainforest, the 121 inhabitants of Gasumi Corners now live on the margin between the primary forest and the grasslands and tertiary forest that surround the Nomad Station. On one side is a life with an airstrip, churches,
a school, market, sports teams, an aid post (health clinic), and a government
office (see photo 5). On the other side lies the rainforest, with its main ar-
tery, the Kum River, just eight minutes from their doorstep (see photo 6).
Gebusi have relocated near Nomad quite willingly and voluntarily: they
want to live within easy reach of the government station and within its
circle of influences and activities.

Despite important continuities, the magnitude of this change is hard
to overstate. I am fully convinced that if I had studied the Gebusi only in
1998 there is little way I could have reconstructed the depth and character
of indigenous culture that was present just sixteen years earlier. Conversely,
there is no way I could have extrapolated the extent or character of change
based on my understandings of 1980–82, however accurate these were at
the time.

Singing to a New Spirit

Within a few days, I learned that a large proportion of adults at Gasumi
Corners—84 percent, as it turned out—were now baptized Christians and
regular churchgoers at one or another of the local denominations: Catholic,
evangelical Protestant, or Seventh Day Adventist. Reciprocally, Gebusi spirit
mediumship was defunct. Between 1982 and 1998, all twelve of the practic-

ing mediums in my two communities of original study had either died or "cut their tie" (*gisaymp*) with the traditional spirits. No new spirit mediums had been initiated or were being trained. Gebusi now sing to God rather than to their traditional spirits. For more casual entertainment, weekends now echo with the evening songs of male "string bands" that include guitars or ukuleles. This singing has been influenced by commercial cassette tapes of national singing groups and rock bands while being hauntingly beautiful in its own new way. Children and younger adults flock to the C-grade "video night" movies shown at Nomad every month or two. Amid these changes, the world of the old *to di* spirits—the "taken away" spirits of deceased Gebusi and of animals that were so vividly portrayed in Gebusi séances and dances—has almost ceased to exist. In the new world of God, on one hand, and of modern entertainment, on the other, the spirit people of old are simply not relevant. Traditional dancing when it does occur is less a celebration of spiritual cosmology than a decontextualized form of modern entertainment—as in the multiethnic competition of dance performers on the lawn of the government station on Independence Day.

The details of spiritual change will occupy us in subsequent chapters. With respect to sorcery, however, the main point is that in the absence of traditional forms of spiritual communication, sorcery inquests are practically impossible to arrange, carry out, or interpret. In 1980–82, Gebusi interacted directly with the spirit world through the sung discourse and dialogue of spirit séances. This has now been replaced by the peremptory dictums of an absolute God, disseminated by the Christian pastors. In the Nomad area, these pastors are educated men hailing from other parts of Papua New Guinea. Like the pastor, God may reward your faith, but not as an exchange among equals. You must wait until Judgment Day, until death, and then rely on the mercy of omnipotent grace. Despite this asymmetry, Gebusi have flocked to Christianity, and not because they have been forced. They have wanted to live near Nomad and go to the churches that are invariably associated with its more modern style of life.

In the face of Christian beliefs, death for Gebusi has become both more and less problematic than before. Though close relatives of a dying person may still suspect sorcery—and may harbor discontents against a possible target—these suspicions cannot be publicly explored or validated in the absence of a spirit medium. Given the collective support that has always been needed to take consensual action within the multiclan community, the inability to communicate with the *to di* spirits saps the impetus for retribution. In principle, sorcerers can still be executed and their death explained to authorities as a lethal illness deep in the bush. In fact, this occurred twice during the mid-1980s, and it could happen again. There is now little tolerance of such action by Gebusi, however. The primary aggrieved is much more likely to mutter vague suspicions than to take strong action.

As evident from their own discussions, Gebusi have internalized Christian beliefs concerning morality, sin, and the need to leave judgments about death in the hands of God. As a modern super-spirit, God holds the power to take retribution and damn evil persons to hell. Reciprocally, he wields the ability to grant unlimited wealth and happiness to those who believe in Him, that is, in the everlasting life of heaven. Ultimately, most Gebusi do not think they should meddle with the power of God. Following death, funerals are now Christian, with the pastor left to preside. Even if someone tries to orchestrate a sorcery accusation, the suspect can now countersue in a village moot by arguing that he or she has been subject to slander—false accusation without evidence. Increasingly, the Gebusi's own sense of spiritual progress makes old traditions such as taking retribution against sorcerers seem irrelevant.

Though the Gebusi's particular sense of becoming modern entails giving up sorcery beliefs and inquests, this pattern does not generalize easily to other peoples and cultures. In some societies, it is just the competition over modern gain—or over the projected stigma of being "backward"—that galvanizes power struggles between factions, ethnic groups, or those who are unequal in modern hierarchies of status and power. In significant parts of Melanesia, Africa, Asia, and Latin America, this antagonism can articulate with contemporary accusations of sorcery or witchcraft, sometimes including violent retribution. In his book *The Modernity of Witchcraft* (1997), Pierre Geschiere highlights the contemporary elaboration of beliefs in spiritual malevolence in postcolonial Africa, with special reference to south Cameroon (see also Comaroff and Comaroff 1993). Why this has not occurred among Gebusi is an important question that involves issues of political economy and history that we will consider in due course.

New Schools for Life

Both as a cause and as a result of the reduction in violence, changes have mushroomed in other areas of Gebusi life. In Gasumi Corners, boys and girls between the ages of about nine and fourteen go to the Nomad Community School. For the most part, they attend school quite enthusiastically.

As is also the case in church, school instruction is in Papua New Guinea English or in *tok pisin,* the Melanesian lingua franca. Schooling lasts seven hours a day, five days a week. As such, it provides a major new form of socialization. For men and boys, Saturday and Sunday afternoons are additionally consumed by watching and playing in a protracted series of rugby and soccer matches on the Nomad ball field. The male community of Gasumi Corners gives special attention and support to its home team, the Gasumi Youths, who play teams from rival villages or other ethnic groups, some of whom used to be tribal enemies.

For women and older girls, Tuesday and Friday mornings are now associated with selling food at the Nomad market. At first light, women from Gasumi Corners walk to Nomad laden with net bags filled with their best produce and foraged foods. Their hope, often unrealized, is to sell these items to the families of the government employees, teachers, and aid post workers who come to the market. This slim cadre of paid provincial and national workers forms the wage-earning basis of Nomad's paltry cash economy. Low stakes notwithstanding, selling food is one of the only ways for Gebusi women to make money. As a result, the desire of government workers for a variety of foods in this remote and ill-supplied area has spawned petty cash-cropping in local gardens, including at Gasumi Corners. Though nontraditional foods comprise only a small portion of their cultivated food, Gebusi now grow such crops as pumpkins, squash, pineapple, corn, or peanuts for sale at the market. Bananas remain the starch staple, supplemented by sago, but sweet potatoes are now also raised on a significant scale, both for local consumption and for market sale.

The Nomad scene has also altered the performance of traditional dances and initiations. In most Gebusi villages, including Gasumi Corners, initiation rituals have died out and traditional dancing has become vestigial. But men still enjoy getting dressed up and dancing in traditional costume on the government parade field on Independence Day. Including regular churchgoers, villagers may also attend as visitors at traditional dances in outlying settlements where these events are still staged. Even at these remote sites, however, activities are touched by Nomad's sphere of social and cultural influence. The traditional dances and initiations at distant locations are now generally held in late August or early September. This allows the main participants to re-present themselves in full costuming at Nomad just a few days or weeks later for the interethnic displays and traditional dance competitions held on September 16, Independence Day. Even at remote villages, traditional dances and initiations are now usually held on a Friday or Saturday night. These weekend evenings increase the scale and festivity of the event by drawing a larger range of visitors and school children, including people from the general Nomad area. As part of this increased spectatorship, visitors typically augment traditional dance entertainment with string band singing or commercial music played on cassettes from a boom box. Even at outlying settlements, then, the line begins to blur between a traditional dance or initiation and a neotraditional "party" (*fati*).

The Gender of Change

Most aspects of social and cultural change among Gebusi have been strongly gendered. On one hand, men's traditional patriarchy has weakened; women participate in a wider range of activities than before. On the other hand, men assert increasingly modern forms of masculine dominance. This dynamic of female agency and escalating male assertion spurs Gebusi men and women to engage and appropriate wider notions of progress, success, and development.

Gebusi men exercised primary control in the indigenous system of sister-exchange, though mothers had influence and strong-willed young women could sometimes refuse the man betrothed to them (Cantrell 1998). With the decline of sister-exchange, female marital agency has expanded; it is more difficult than ever to marry off a woman against her wishes. Male dominance has also weakened in other areas. Men used to define and control the image of the voluptuous spirit woman through the songs of the spirit medium and his male chorus. Likewise, the archetypal image of the spirit woman was appropriated by male dancers in ritual feasts. Female sexual power was likewise appropriated in the ability of Gebusi men to "grow" boys into men through homosexual insemination.[14] Men's social and political dominance was enforced by their preeminent control over violence, both in the accusation and execution of sorcerers and in husbands' ability to exert physical control over wives.[15]

Contemporary changes have compromised all these supports for male dominance (see Tuzin 1997). Spirit séances are defunct, violence against sorcery suspects is rare to nonexistent, and male ritual homosexuality occurs in only a few of the remotest villages. Whereas male homosexuality never appeared to be socially or culturally passive among Gebusi—even among the coy and coquettish recipients of men's attentions—the dynamics of male sexual attraction have now changed. Men and boys now exhibit little interest in homoeroticism. Those who have not been initiated know little or nothing of homosexual insemination (Knauft 2001). By contrast, young Gebusi men now worry increasingly about how they can attract a woman as a wife. This anxiety is fueled by the decline of prescriptive sister-exchange and other forms of marital pressure on women.

Before, women were in principle barred from spirit séances; now they are baptized, full members of Christian churches. Indeed, women and girls constitute at least half if not more of the church congregations on most Sundays. Almost all girls from Gasumi Corners now go to the Nomad Community School, where they are taught alongside the boys for as many years as they continue to attend. Schoolgirls are also beginning to play team sports, and within a few years, they will probably have several teams of their own in competition at Nomad. Among the adults and teenagers, women constitute 91 percent of the sellers at the Nomad market, which furnishes women an opportunity to earn money and an important venue for socializing both within and between settlements. Though market proceeds are paltry, women's market activity is symbolically important and makes them participants in a modern form of economic transaction.

All these changes push uneasily against patterns of male dominance that now seek more modern forms of assertion. Amid women's contemporary role in marital politics, market, church, and school, men appear to be developing more contemporary forms of masculine agency. Men tend to control money, both within the family and within the community—and the larger the sum, the more likely men are to control it completely. Husbands are much less likely to pay the nominal fees for their daughters to complete local schooling than they are for their sons. All twelve of those from Gasumi Corners who have completed grade six have been boys. In the Nomad sports leagues, boys and men have about twenty rugby and soccer teams; women have two teams, for soccer. These female team members are almost entirely the daughters and wives of government workers. The leaders of all the churches in the Nomad area are men, including the lay prayer leaders. Only 12 percent (4/34) of the women in Gasumi Corners know *tok pisin,* as opposed to 59 percent (20/34) of men. Overwhelmingly, it is men who have managed to visit the town of Kiunga, ride in an airplane, and work temporarily for one of the oil or mineral exploration teams that previously crisscrossed remote portions of the province. Significant cash income—although rare and sporadic—remains an exclusive male province. Women's accrued proceeds from the Nomad market are typically appropriated by or given to a husband or male relative.[16]

Men are also preeminent in the elaboration of traditional costuming and of what we might call neotradition. Women are reluctant to dress in traditional dance costuming for public viewing in villages, and they are not encouraged to do so. This aversion is especially strong for young women, who are deeply ashamed of exposing their breasts. Men also dominate the public reenactment of folk traditions at the Nomad Station for Independence Day and cultural shows, and they receive the preponderance of prizes awarded.

None of this makes women irrelevant to processes of change. If anything, the actions of women in marriage, in church, in school, and at market drive Gebusi men to ever-more-modern assertions. In the process, the very notion of what it means to be progressive or successful in a contemporary context becomes inextricably linked with new notions of masculinity and masculine dominance. This easily includes male control in matters of money, educational advancement, religious leadership, neotradition, and sports.

The Straightening of Time

The modern world of the Nomad Station presents new markers and standards of time, and these have become yardsticks for personal progress. By contrast, traditional notions of time among Gebusi—as in many parts of Melanesia—were largely circular.[17] The Gebusi word for "tomorrow," *oil*, was the same as the term for "yesterday." The word for "day after tomorrow," *biar*, also denoted the "day before yesterday." Likewise, *ewhar* was both "three days hence" and "three days prior." A man addressed his son as "father" and often named his eldest son after his own dead father as well. Ideally, this boy would grow up and live on this grandfather's land, which had lain fallow during the intervening generation. There, the boy-become-man would eat from the coconut palms and process the sago that his namesake had planted for him in a prior generation. As such, he would reproduce in name, place, and physical substance the temporal cycle that also regenerated the spirits of the forest and those of people. Generations recycled their identity.

So, too, each day followed the next in seamless continuity; there were no terms for specific days or for units of days. Even terms for season or year were vague and barely marked in the Gebusi lexicon.[18] In 1980–82, we absorbed this mentality of unmarked time; each day, week, and month blended imperceptibly into the next. If we forgot to mark a day on our calendar, it was easy to lose track. Gebusi lived within time that was at once endless and ever-present; temporal unfolding had little significance.

This past abuts on a modern sense of time that is straight and directional; time changes from a circle to a line. Nowadays in Gasumi Corners, time is strongly marked and measured to keep track of personal action and development. The days and hours are repeatedly named and monitored. Sunday is for church, plus ball games in the afternoon. Monday through Friday are for school, plus markets on Tuesday and Friday. Alternate Monday mornings are for collective community work in the village. Friday and Saturday nights are for relaxation or, if one is lucky, for a *fati* ("party"), the all-purpose pidgin word that combines any manner of feast, music, or dance and which has generally replaced the traditional terms for ritual feast (*gigobra, habra*). Saturday morning is for helping out the pastor in his compound or for fixing up the church grounds. Saturday afternoon, like Sunday afternoon, is for ball games at Nomad.

Almost all of these occasions are marked internally for time as well. The bell rings for church and to mark the classes of the school day, which is meticulously divided into 30-minute units and written up as such in each teacher's daily activity report book. The referee keeps track of time and sounds his airhorn to mark the halves and the end of each ball game. On Tuesday and Friday, marketers must arrive by early morning and be gone by noon. To not know time is to not be modern. All the men, it seems, want to have wristwatches.

The passage of measured time is now also central to personal development. School progress is marked against the passage of time. The years are numbered, and to be at all successful, you have to get at least to grade six. Fridays are for tests, and one must be prepared on that day in order to pass. The end of grade six brings the entrance examination for high school. It is a difficult test to finish on time. Almost all fail, while a rare few pass—usually the children of government workers.

Managing time is essential in sports as well—effort must be marshaled to top the score of one's opponent by the closing horn. (Traditional Gebusi sports and contests, by contrast, ideally ended in a draw.) Similar patterns of temporal management are evident in Christianity. Tomorrow may be too late to repent; Judgment Day can come at any time. You must give your life to Christ today if you want the benefit of everlasting life. It is not just being good that counts, but being good, clean, and moral at the final instant of time, the moment of your death—or the end of the world. The passage of time itself now becomes a moral problem. In the mix, progress in life becomes a race against time. And time—as the pastors, the teachers, and the referees all say—is running out.

Communities Muted, Subjects Disembedded

In 1980–82, the term that best captured Gebusi social relations was *kog-wayay*. I glossed this term as "good company" and juxtaposed it against "violence" in the title of my first book (Knauft 1985a). *Kogwayay* was an all-purpose term used by Gebusi to distinguish their customs from those of other people. Applied especially to traditional feasts, dances, spirit séances, and initiations, the term referred broadly to anything quintessentially Gebusi. During my first period of fieldwork, Gebusi never seemed to tire of telling me, "Our *kogwayay* is our way of doing things. Our *kogwayay* is different from yours." I learned the term on my very first day among Gebusi in 1980.

The three morphemic components of *kog-wa-yay* reveal its traditional significance and, by juxtaposition, highlight contemporary change (Knauft 1985a: chap. 3). *Kog-* is a root marker that means "together with," "similar to," and "friend" (*kog-ay*). In 1980–82, it indexed the strong Gebusi tendency to do things collectively in a spirit of friendship, be physically close to each other, go places and do things together, and dress similarly. During the early 1980s, it was almost tantamount to being insane for a Gebusi to go out from the village alone into the forest. It was also a huge invitation for sorcerers to attack. Gebusi at that time took extreme measures to travel in pairs, or remained behind together. Men liked to dress up like each other, and initiates or dancers were always dressed in identical costumes. Similarity, friendship, togetherness, collectivity—all of these were "*kog-*."

The second aspect of Gebusi good company, *wa,* indexed the casual, breezy, and freewheeling talk of the communal longhouse, which included good-natured stories, histories, events of the day, and banter. These were collectively referred to as casual talk (*wa-la*). In the course of these relaxed discussions, information would be traded, histories remembered, and community consensus eventually reached about matters of collective action, such as clearing land for gardens, building houses, hunting, or arranging a feast. I was always surprised how much Gebusi enjoyed talking and how seldom their collective gabfests caused ill will or animosity.

The third component of good company, *yay,* was the exuberant "heart-breath" (*solof*) of yelling or cheering in joy. Gebusi gatherings were filled with vivacious cries and yells, especially from men. Included here were the whooping *bup-kay* of men walking in the forest, the playful *yay-kay* of men sexually teasing each other, and the collective *waw-kay* of men straining together with a log or with a heavy sago cooking packet while placing it on the coals. Cries and yells often filled the longhouse at night.

Men exuded camaraderie, sharing smoke and food, conversing with visitors or those from other households, joking loudly, and telling raucous stories.

By 1998, however, most of this had changed. Collective friendship, communal talk, and exuberant yelling or joking were hardly characteristic of Gasumi Corners. Nor, on the other hand, was communal violence a common or continuing reality against persons scapegoated as sorcerers. The festivity as well as the collective anger of traditional culture had been muted and replaced by the calmer if no less firmly pursued pleasures of the neotraditional Melanesian *fati,* the string band, the boom box or disco, the sports field, the market or trade store, and the relentless wish for an airplane trip to Kiunga, where ships, roads, trucks, and stores could be seen. Amid these desires, social life had become differentiated and disembedded from its village matrix. Whether a person goes to this church or that, walks out to sit by the airstrip or the ball field, or just "takes a spin" around Nomad is an individual rather than a collective act, especially for men. Walking alone on the paths outside the village and even in the deep forest is now perfectly normal for older children as well as adults. There is little fear of sorcery, no fear of craziness from being alone. Conversely, togetherness is pleasant but not central to social life.

Patterns of communication have been crosscut as well. The casual talk of evening banter, *wa,* is now decentralized into numerous smaller houses. By contrast, public discourse musters an ever-larger place for hortatory monologue, *ta,* modeled on speech styles used by the pastor, the teacher, and the government worker. Monologues infiltrate village moots and oratory in the community, as when a senior man or old woman struts back and forth to intone stern discontent about the actions of someone in the settlement. Although Gebusi are deeply subservient to forceful monologues at Nomad and in church, new patterns of public speaking indicate the internal reproduction of this subordination through the authoritative styles of modern dominance within Gasumi Corners.

Against this dominance, joking in stylized fashion is now, increasingly, a thing of the past. I remember the grinning bemusement in Gasumi Corners when, during my first few days there in 1998, I initiated a bawdy joking sequence with one of my old friends. Now a Seventh Day Adventist, Yuway was clearly touched by my gesture and tried manfully to subdue his irrepressible smile. But the larger point was that old-time joking, although tolerated from a middle-aged outsider like me, was a bit anachronistic and out of place.

The hospitality that surrounds such banter has also been compromised, including the proud display of sharing smoke from large pipes stoked with traditional tobacco. Although still permitted among Catholics, tobacco sharing is much less general than it used to be. Evangelicals and Seventh Day Adventists will neither give nor accept a smoking pipe, since their churches taboo this practice. This restriction undercuts the etiquette of traditional hospitality, in which every man of the host village provided several hits of strong smoke sequentially to every visiting man.[19] Among those who continue to smoke, cigarettes are preferred to traditional pipes even though—or perhaps because—they are very expensive and tend to be smoked individually rather than collectively.

Changes in the physical structure and organization of Gebusi houses reinforce the decentralization of social life. It is as if the old community of Gasumi has spread out and scattered through Gasumi Corners like a spatter of ink on a glass table. The traditional longhouse has residentially "exploded": each of the walled living sections or "rooms" of the old longhouse now exists as a separate and independent building (see photo 7). Separate sleeping houses have been built for women and men. Often, there are yet more separate houses for household cooking. In all, each family or small extended kindred has its own cooking and sleeping structures.[20] In the process, the area of roofed living space has grown enormously. Measurement of house sizes revealed that the square footage of housing space per capita in Gasumi Corners in 1998 was effectively double what it had been in Gasumi during 1980–82.[21]

Amid this proliferation of structures and living spaces, settlements have no central dwelling where everyone can meet. None of the four hamlets in Gasumi Corners has a central longhouse.[22] Except for important occasions, the members of individual households rarely assemble under one roof for evening conversation. Visitors may stay in one or another family dwelling, but they are seldom hosted en masse by the community at large, in contrast to 1980–82. Although people pass through Gasumi Corners to and from Nomad for many reasons—including those from distant villages with different ethnic affiliations—there is little notion, as there used to be, that every visitor should be formally hosted with a finger snap and sharing of smoke from each adult man, followed by offerings of food and water and then by extended collective conversation into the night.

Gasumi Corners is flung out in a larger sense as well. Whereas Yibihilu had spread along a single clearing, the present community meanders through four distinct hamlets or "subcorners." Each is a two-minute walk from the others, typically separated by a hillock, stream, or grove of trees, and barely within earshot of a loud yell. People from all four hamlets consider themselves members of "Gasumi Corners," but each subcorner has its own name and functions independently as a feast-giving unit. Though in a sense compressing the old rainforest community of Gasumi into a single unit, the spatial result is that people from each hamlet often treat each other more impersonally, as passing acquaintances rather than as either coresidents or welcome visitors.

The collectivity, talk, and exuberant joking that were so distinctive of Gebusi culture are now more muted. That traditional dances and initiations are no longer held in most Gebusi settlements reinforces this trend. What Gebusi used to designate as distinctive about their culture has changed significantly. By 1998, the word *kogwayay* was largely an anachronism; its principle of reciprocity and equivalence has been supplanted by a new, more modern, and more asymmetrical social ethic.

Challenges of Self-fashioning

How do life choices change as social life becomes more differentiated and contextually disembedded? Especially for men, there are now new options to choose from, leading to different outcomes and spawning a new awareness of alternatives—a new self-consciousness about creating one's life. Do you want to be a dedicated churchgoer? A conscientious student at school? A top-rate sportsman on the community team? Perhaps aspire to be a storekeeper? Or simply be a good traditional hunter and house builder? Though a variety of skills were always cultivated by Gebusi—hunting, singing, house building, spirit mediumship, and so on—none of these took them outside the range of community social relations. In school, at church, at the market, or on the ball field, however, things are different. Nomad is a cultural and linguistic polyglot. The nine thousand persons in the Nomad area comprise eight language and ethnic groups: Gebusi, Samo, Kubor, Bedamini, Oybae, Honibo, Pa, and Kabasi. There are also *tok pisin* and Motu speakers, the English of school and government officials, and the diverse cultural backgrounds of national and provincial workers. Most of this diversity is amply represented at the Nomad School, on the ball field, in the market, and in government and church activities, which quickly bring people from different backgrounds into contact.

Across this spectrum, social relations become contextual, slanted to one or another role and less closely bound with networks of village kin. Teachers purposely sit students from different ethnic groups next to each other so they will be forced to communicate in pidgin or English. Members of sports teams and churches, clients at the aid post, and women at the market are all exposed to cross-village and cross-ethnic relations to an unprecedented degree. Although villagers tend to cluster among themselves, crosscutting networks of acquaintance and friendship have wide ramifications, especially for young men.

For the more decentralized societies of Melanesia, anthropologist Maurice Godelier suggested that traditional politics was characterized by diverse leadership roles for men: gardener, fight leader, shaman, ritual leader, and so on.[23] In a sense, one can see this system as now expanding to encompass the more differentiated roles of contemporary life in places such as Nomad. And yet, a distinct change emerges in the process. None of the traditional roles involved subordination to outside values, nor, as a complement, aspirations for class distinction (see Gewertz and Errington 1999). By contrast, all of the newer roles—church leader, school leaver, storekeeper, sportsman, marketer, and so on—engage values of progress and distinctions of hierarchy that emanate from beyond the local community. As Gebusi differentiate into this world, they experience their own equivalent of the historic European transition from community to society, from *Gemeinschaft* to *Gesellschaft* (Tönnies 1957).

Amid these changes, personal choice rises to a higher key. The decision to pursue this or that kind of social relationship takes one down different paths that engage different types of people and different standards of success and lifestyles—on the sports field, at school, in church, at the market or store, in the forest, or at the feast. Self-fashioning has a greater variety of risky outcomes and becomes self-conscious in a new kind of way. As Foucault (1984: 39–42) pointed out in his analysis of Baudelaire's essay, "The Painter of Modern Life" (1970 [1863]), one of the distinctive features of being modern is the mandate to explore how one might become a different kind of person in the future than was possible in the past. For Gebusi, this exploration increases one's openness to influence by outsiders who control the institutions at Nomad and who are identified with the power and success of a larger world.

The Christian ethos of moral self-examination easily steps into this breach; it becomes a natural part of the modernizing process for the aspiring subject. Christianity intensifies the process by which one's choices are made self-conscious and problematic—an ongoing choice between good and evil, between personal discipline and being subject to personal damnation. If the stakes associated with these choices are high in religious terms, their respective costs and benefits loom especially large for remote peoples such as Gebusi, for whom the material benefits of more secular progress remain largely illusory. And yet, how is one to know what new choices to make and how to make them? The resulting uncertainty primes people to accept direction from powerful outsiders who are in charge of locally modern institutions such as the church, school, market, aid post, and government station.

Solicitors of Change

Despite or perhaps because they are geographically remote, Gebusi have actively sought out social and cultural change. Gebusi are generally pleased with and thankful for their present lives; they have few regrets about what they have given up. Though life in the traditional village had its high points—its feasts, dances, initiations, and spirit séances—it also cloned a long series of look-alike days in which nothing much seemed to happen. Between the poles of subsistence work, on the one hand, and relaxed socializing, on the other, stretched a large intervening space in the late afternoon that seemed to beg for more interesting and novel activity. Whether at the communal longhouse, visiting at our house, or simply sauntering around the village, Gebusi in 1980–82 frequently appeared to be in search of something to do.

It is against this traditional background that places like Nomad exude a distinct aura of newness, power, intrigue, interest, and activity. The habitus of life in the village did not include the ability to see a sports match, go to the market, be in a schoolroom with forty children close to your own age, attend video night, spend a few small coins for a package of crackers at a tiny Nomad store, be exhorted in church on Sunday to follow the Bible, or saunter to the airstrip to see a plane land or take off. Beginning as what we may call "entertainments of modernity," these activities and events now emerge as important as well as interesting to Gebusi. They enliven social life and provide a large new realm of conversation, gossip, speculation, information, and interest. Against the intrigue of modern activities and events, the traditional laissez-faire of the hamlet or village easily becomes negatively marked as a symbol of inactivity or backwardness. In the rural imaginary, towns and cities have often been sites of action, energy, and entertainment, of cultural as well as material power (see Williams 1973). This is certainly true, in its own tiny way, of the relationship between Gebusi and the government station at Nomad.

For Gebusi, the cultural and social magnet of Nomad is not clouded by a history of colonial violence or oppressive coercion. Gebusi were beneficiaries rather than targets of colonial intrusion against the neighboring Bedamini people—and Gebusi were left largely alone in the bargain. As far as I know, no Gebusi has ever been killed by a bullet. The communities in the Nomad area have not experienced forced labor, taxation, land alienation,[24] or dependence on cash-cropping. The Australians did introduce steel tools, cloth, and money, and, among Gebusi, they half-heartedly encouraged peaceful means of resolving disputes. As we will see in chapter 4, the postcolonial police detachment at Nomad has in many ways been even more benign in these respects. The Catholic lay pastor, who came to Nomad in 1988, likewise began his ministry in a low-key manner.

Reciprocally, Gebusi have welcomed rather than shunned the presence of Christian churches, along with teachers, health clinic workers, and government employees. They have moved into the modernizing orbit of these outsiders willingly, actively, and often enthusiastically. They are pleased that their children can go to school. They enjoy the fact that exposure to modern activities has leapfrogged their beliefs and practices over larger and more traditionally powerful groups that are father away from Nomad. Given their regular practice on the Nomad ball field, they can often beat the visiting rugby and soccer teams of their rivals as well.

Of course, it is always possible that Gebusi are now on a temporary turn of a cultural wheel. Maybe they will eventually become disenchanted or disillusioned with Nomad's version of becoming modern. They could become cynical, move back to the bush, rejuvenate traditional customs, or resuscitate the killing of sorcerers. Maybe, despite almost forty years of continuous service, the Nomad Station will fall into disrepair and see its national workers and pastors depart to other areas.[25]

Any of these scenarios are possible, but even if one or more of them eventuate, the change that Gebusi have lived during the last two decades is impossible to eradicate. The histories of peoples are littered with sedimented changes and continuities—waves of change, resistance against what is new, rediscoveries or reinventions of what is old. But amid these cycles and punctuations are key periods when people willingly decide to deviate from their past, chart a new direction, adopt new ways, and hope for a future that is somehow better. In the course of these alterations, culture changes. No matter how much of the past later resurfaces, it invariably does so in a new key and against the yardstick of more recent aspirations. Even in their rediscovery and reinvention, traditions become relativized, historicized, and made self-conscious in a new way. This is an important part of modern self-consciousness, of questioning the relationship of the past to the future.

Exchanging the Past

Gebusi say they are exchanging their past for their future. In saying this, they use the same concept that they use for direct and reciprocal exchange in marriage, feasting, or killing (*sesum degra*). Throughout Melanesia, practices of exchange are widespread and deeply rooted. Likewise, the notion of exchange has claimed a large conceptual and theoretical place in the anthropology of Melanesia.[26]

When Gebusi say they are directly exchanging the customs of their past for those of their future, however, we are presented with a different order of exchange. This not just a reciprocity of people or valuables across time, but an exchange of very different styles of life. It is not just an exchange *in* time, but an exchange *of* time itself—an exchange between different ways of relating to time, different modes of temporality. In the process, this exchange entails new ways of relating to oneself, to others, and to material goods.

One of the criticisms of exchange and exchange theory in anthropology is that it too easily assumes that things "balance out over time." From a systematic point of view, one marriage or death or gift may balance out with another. From the point of view of individual actors, however, there can be important and indeed glaring imbalances. From this perspective, the reciprocity that is intrinsic to the system as a whole covers up or effaces the fact that some individuals or groups gain or lose significantly, and sometimes disproportionately, relative to others. This point has been strongly emphasized by Pierre Bourdieu (1977, 1990), who stressed the practical inequities that emerge in the process of exchange. We have seen this quite dramatically among traditional Gebusi when a person was killed and eaten in reciprocity for the death of someone who died from sickness. Likewise in sister-exchange marriage, some women were pressured or coerced into marriage to satisfy the dictates of equal exchange.

This insight helps shed light on the Gebusi dynamic of exchanging past customs for future ones. For one thing, it suggests that the exchange of the past for the future may not be equal or reversible for all persons. In the context of this momentous exchange, we should consider how and why some people benefit more than others. Further, it suggests that the resulting inequalities may be of a higher order than they used to be—in the same way that the exchange of temporality is of a higher order than the exchange of individual people or goods. In short, the cultural stakes involved in this new exchange may be higher than previously: exchange is undertaken not to maintain a cultural system but to transform it.

As might be guessed, Gebusi do not state things in these terms—or

at least they didn't to me. What they do say is that they have directly exchanged their traditional spirits, dances, and many other practices, including even their personal spirits/souls/life-breaths (*fin* or *solof*) for new ones.
This way of describing change is highlighted in the Christian conversion
experience (as we shall see in chapters 6 and 7), but it also occurs more
mundanely in the direct replacement of various customs and practices.

Whether the exchange of the past for the future is a contravention
or a continuation of Gebusi patterns of equivalent reciprocity emerges as
an intriguing question. On the one hand, it may be possible for Gebusi to
later "switch back"—to reexchange past practices for future ones in selective ways. On the other hand, exchanges in real life can seldom if ever be
undone to re-create the conditions that preceded them. Because transactions occur *in* time, as Bourdieu suggested, they irrevocably alter the relationships among people. These changes can be yet more pronounced when,
as among Gebusi, the structure of exchange is itself being transformed.

Recessively Modern

Success in matters of money, schooling, Christianity, or government is ex-
ceedingly difficult for Gebusi to attain. The Nomad area is beset by economic
marginality, geographic remoteness, and government bureaucracy. In social
terms, the very attempt to be successful in a contemporary way requires of
Gebusi a willing passivity—a willingness to wait long and patiently in church,
at school, in the market, by the government office, or at the health clinic.[27]
In all of these contexts, Gebusi confront outsiders—Papua New Guineans
from other parts of the country—who are more wealthy, educated, and connected to an outside world than Gebusi. Officials, teachers, preachers, and
other outsiders at the Nomad Station have a relatively modern style of life
oriented around jobs, government wages, and the store-bought goods that Gebusi desire. They are fluent in pidgin or English, which few Gebusi feel comfortable speaking. They come to Nomad to do their jobs and to enlighten,
teach, heal, develop, or govern local people from a position of assumedly superior knowledge and authority. They also run and in practice dominate
the institutions important to Gebusi in and around the Nomad Station.

In practical terms, Gebusi hopes seem geared to catching fragments of
outside success or at least associating culturally with its general style of life.
In the process, Gebusi men and women, boys and girls, have learned to sit
passively and to accept the authority and knowledge of others. Gebusi now
hope and listen and wait, patiently, for the fire-and-brimstone pastor who

exhorts them to spiritual progress; for the schoolmaster who compels them toward educational progress; for the government buyer at the market who may dole out a few small coins of economic progress; for the government official at Independence Day who passes judgment on the efficacy of their own indigenous dances; for the sports officials to enforce the rules of the ball games. In the midst of this de facto hierarchy, what is indeed new is Gebusi's willing patience and subordination, their acceptance of strictures from a larger world of power and hoped-for progress, largely without resistance or irritation. What this entails for the way people perceive themselves is striking, and yet Gebusi tend on the whole to be appreciative rather than resentful of those in power. This struck me immediately on my first Sunday: I watched incredulously as Gebusi sat so patiently through the long church service.

This is not the traditional pattern of endless community "talk" (*wa*), in which banter and stories and jokes were traded communally and reciprocally in the longhouse community. Epitomized by the church, the school, and the government, this is a new world of audience silence held in place by the monologic speech (*ta*) of outsiders. Authoritarian and preachy discourse was disparaged and resisted by Gebusi sixteen years earlier. But here they were, waiting to be exhorted by government workers or pastors from other parts of the country.

At Nomad, the path to becoming modern is paved with a particular kind of active passivity that we may call recessive agency. Recessive agency may be defined as willingly pursued actions that put actors in a position of subordination, passivity, and patient waiting for the influence or enlightenment of external authority figures. This type of agency runs against the grain of our Western assumptions concerning what it means to be a social agent—the notion that agency entails assertive action to actualize personal desire through energetic intervention.[28] In theories of so-called modernization, this assumption is often joined with the notion that local people become active agents to engage and exploit objective possibilities for economic profit and material gain. But the situation among Gebusi is different and somewhat reversed in this regard. In situations such as the Gebusi's, what modern contexts present are not objective economic opportunities to be exploited through active agency but a model of modern cultural subjugation accommodated by local people in the hope, often futile, of achieving a more materially successful style of life. At issue is a recessive agency or "active passivity" that increases cultural and social engagement with modern institutions and activities by means of subordination.

This subordination is contextual—it is particularly prominent in local people's interactions with modernizing institutions and agents. Given Gebusi's particular culture and history, the subaltern nature of their agency in and around Nomad is distinctive. Peoples who have greater local force and authority are less likely to accept outside influence so willingly. In the Nomad Subdistrict, this includes the Bedamini, who resisted government influence in the past, scoff at it in the present, and, not coincidentally, continue to practice a wide range of indigenous customs that Gebusi have mostly given up.[29]

Though variations are legion, peoples in many marginalized areas find themselves ultimately and contextually engaged by modern organizations and authority figures that treat them as subordinate and unenlightened. In these particular contexts, the task of becoming modern tends to compromise rather than cultivate local entrepreneurial agency—that agency that looms so large in Western ideologies of rural economic development. Instead of a rational process of economic improvement, the so-called modernizing process easily becomes a cultural dynamic whereby local people become subordinated in the relative absence of material success.

Under these conditions, the path of local aspiration can have poignant and ironic consequences. In particular, local aspirations may unwittingly encourage conformity to modern notions of social hierarchy based on differences of lifestyle and achievement in a world of money and manufactured goods. Direct or reciprocal interaction can be increasingly supplanted by the unilateral authority of the government official, pastor, teacher, market buyer, or development officer. At Nomad, this authority is totalized in the notion of an all-powerful God. God does not "interact." He may choose to listen to your prayers, but only at his discretion. You have to wait a long time, and even then you can rarely be certain he has heard you.

Though these changes tend to be most marked in the social context of modern institutions and activities—school, church, government activities, and so on—over time they can influence social relations within communities as well. Local inadequacy or failure in public and institutional contexts may be compensated for by asserting the trappings of modern male dominance more firmly at home. This results in the emergence of what we may call "displaced dominance." Displaced dominance emerges in homegrown fashion as a compensatory style of modern assertion and relationality pursued within the community and in domestic contexts, typically by men.

From Direct Reciprocity to Modern Hierarchy

Against the hierarchy of God, government, school, and money, traditional orientations are hard-pressed to maintain themselves. Some dimensions of direct reciprocity continue to exist in Gasumi Corners. Reciprocal interaction is promoted through the continuing ideal of sister-exchange in Gebusi marriage and by direct reciprocity of food-giving at feasts. But these customs are increasingly encapsulated by and subordinated to larger asymmetries. The Gebusi world of direct reciprocity has changed from what Marcel Mauss (1967) would call a system of "total exchange" to a relativized practice, a small sphere of delimited transaction that is under increasing threat from larger, less reciprocal, and more modern interactions. Traditional sociality has become just one kind of interaction among others, and not the most aspired to or most influential one. In some ways, as with sorcery retribution, direct reciprocity is now seen as the most backward or lowest form of social relationship. As against this, it is important to be somewhere on the scale of outside status, even if near the bottom, than off its civilizing scale entirely. In this context, direct reciprocity can be orthogonal if not inimical to a hierarchy of modern advancement.

To some degree, these two worlds stay in tension. At major feasts, hosts bring wild game and are reciprocated with the meat of domesticated pigs and processed sago. But increasingly, pigs and sago are supplemented if not replaced by rice and tinned fish. These store-bought foods, which are the prestigious results of monied purchase, have a qualitatively different status that is superior in desirability and cultural capital to those that they replace. This difference turns a reciprocal exchange of domestic and wild food into a relationship of superiority between feast-givers, who are successful in a modern way, and visiting hunters, whose role is burdened with customary tradition.

In marriage, although fathers and brothers still assert that their daughters or sisters should marry through direct exchange, such intentions become mute in the face of reality. Only two of the twenty-two ever-married men in Gasumi Corners were married through sister-exchange—and these two men were the oldest in the community. None of the sixteen marriages that occurred in Gasumi Corners between 1982 and 1998 was transacted through sister-exchange. Although the ideal of sister-exchange persists, the results of attempting to actually arrange one were dramatically evident in Gasumi Corners while I was there in 1998. One of the intended brides refused to accept her intended husband. Despite intimidation and even a scolding by a police officer, the young woman insisted that no one could force her to marry and that it was her right to choose her partner. Villagers acknowledged there was little they could ultimately do, and within a short period of time, the marriage as well as the other marital union that was "exchanged" for it were both dissolved.

Failing direct reciprocity, fathers and brothers of a bride often say they will demand an exorbitant bride-price in money—many hundreds or a thousand kina.[30] No Gebusi can supply this amount. In fact, the actual rate of marital compensation is very small. In ten first marriages in Gasumi Corners since 1982, the average bridewealth payment was 56 kina (U.S.$28), and in six of these marriages, no bridewealth was paid at all.[31]

Where does it go, the disgruntlement that accompanies lack of reciprocity in Gebusi marriages? Traditionally, of course, it was funneled into sorcery accusations and executions, but that's no longer the case. The details of sorcery belief and its vestiges are explored in subsequent chapters, but the short answer is that the power of modern hierarchy—the symbolic authority of God and the Government—has usurped the agency of Gebusi retribution. That this external authority is, as we shall see in chapter 4, not backed up with coercive force underscores its symbolic and subjective dimension.

The Culture of the Nomad Station

In the world of Nomad, direct reciprocity is subservient to modern hierarchy. This hierarchy is distinguished by the wealth, knowledge, and lifestyle of outside pastors, teachers, aid post workers, and government officials. The great majority of those in authority at Nomad are men, a modern male hegemony. They have what the people of Gasumi Corners achingly desire: Western houses, racks of clothes, shoes, boom boxes, plane tickets to fly back and forth to Kiunga, money for tinned fish and rice, and maybe even luxuries like a VCR or refrigerator. They speak fluent pidgin if not English, are literate, able to read the Bible, and—for the most part—are prominent members or leaders of the local churches. Gebusi hold up these people as role models. When I asked the boys and girls of the Nomad school to draw pictures of what they wanted to be in the future, they drew policemen, soldiers, pilots, teachers, construction workers, nurses, a doctor, a rock singer, a TV technician, a stage actor, and so on (see photos 8 and 17). Some had been copied from drawings or photos in schoolbooks. Only six of the 104 children drew pictures of themselves in a village setting or indigenous context, including a traditional dancer, a fisherman, a woman fetching water, and an old woman with a net bag.

Few if any of the national or provincial employees are self-consciously distant or condescending to Gebusi; most of them are pleasant and, to my own sensibilities, quite friendly and conscientious. Even the pastors tend, on the whole, to be thoughtful and understanding in their expectations. It is hard to ascribe their superiority to a sense of willful domination or exploitation; most have a strong sense of duty to their jobs, respect for local people, and make personal sacrifices to live in such an out-of-the-way place. They do not denigrate local people in an explicit way, and they are tolerant, in practice if not in belief, of local cultural practices. Indeed, their general sense of good will and duty went decidedly against my stereotype of Third World functionaries. If anything, then, their orientation underscores the cultural and structural dimensions of change among Gebusi and surrounding peoples as opposed to the force of government oppression or economic coercion. Indeed, had the officials and others at Nomad been more high-handed, their cultural impact might well have been significantly less.

Relative to Gebusi, however, all these workers have lifestyles of distinction and material access. They maintain a confident sense of themselves when dealing with an outside world of towns or cities. Their style is assured and legitimately assertive in meetings and modern discourse, making decisions, writing, speaking a national language, acquiring and managing money, and traveling by air to other parts of the province and the country. Their capacities are self-evidently superior, and their access to the benefits of a wider world is patent (see Wanek 1996). However, this world and their place within it do not promote reciprocal exchange with Gebusi. As pleasant and earnest as they are, national and provincial employees are at Nomad to govern, instruct, and enlighten rather than to learn or to engage local people on their own terms. The same could be said of NGO and development workers in many if not most Third World contexts.

At issue here is not force or coercion in a direct sense but a modern sense of self and personhood associated as if naturally with the hope of a new kind of cultural success. This success is based on new forms of authoritative knowledge and informs a new moral hierarchy that inculcates contextual subservience in those who are not already distinguished. As such, modern hierarchy draws upon the ostensibly best and most earnest strains of modern liberalism to create new forms of cultural hegemony actualized through subjective domination.

Politics of Marginal Economy

At places like Nomad, contextual passivity and displaced domination are clearly related to external influences. But the materiality of a larger world is at least as important for its absence as for its presence. Here one feels the

irony of a situation in which the image and fleeting presence of manufactured goods—airplanes, refrigerators, VCRs, boom boxes, a fancy house, a
wardrobe of clothes, and the like—creates desires by the very fact that they
are so typically removed from effective possession or access by villagers (see
Foster 1996/97).

The political economy of the Nomad Station underscores this paradox
of modern presence through material absence. Nomad has no roads to anywhere; it can only be reached by air. The Nomad Station is at pains to attract
money or development; its tiny cash economy depends on the paltry wages
of government officials. Back in 1980–82, the station boasted one sparkling
bright yellow truck. The officer-in-charge drove it proudly around the station and even coaxed it up the one bouncing road that the Australians had
constructed from Nomad to one of the Bedamini settlements a few miles
away. By 1998, however, the truck had long since broken down and had
not been replaced. There was little reason for a new one to be airlifted to
Nomad in any event, since the one existing road had been washed out by
rainforest floods and erosion.

As a monument to Nomad's backwardness, the rusting hulk of the
old yellow truck has been intentionally buried upside down, tail in the air,
on the front lawn of the main government office. There it stays—at the very
center of Nomad Station. It provides a fitting symbol of Nomad's precluded
modernity—a hope for development that is marked most of all by the presence of its failure.

The plight of rural Papua New Guinea, as in many so-called developing countries, includes basic infrastructure that has deteriorated, crumbled, or simply disappeared. It is staggeringly difficult to maintain roads or
airstrips, schools, stores, health posts, and civil administration in rural areas. Exportable resources that could bolster the local economy are typically
in short supply or, more commonly, as at Nomad, nonexistent. The problems of poor transportation and communication are compounded by a
mountain of inefficiency as well as the complicated paperwork that often
barely literate officials are expected to complete. Ironically, as at Nomad,
local officials may be well meaning and conscientious. But corruption and
bureaucratic largesse in the top tiers of the national and provincial hierarchy create a slew of budgetary shortfalls along with a mass of technical regulations to ostensibly enforce financial rules. This creates a clerical and bureaucratic nightmare for those trying to maintain or staff local facilities and
programs.

In the absence of resources or incentives, it is extremely hard to attract
qualified personnel to staff schools, aid posts, or development projects at

places like Nomad. Candidates with the best education invariably gravitate to the larger towns and cities. Unless a local area has been fortunate enough to educate its own homegrown officials, infrastructure can easily decay from understaffing as well as from physical neglect.

These strains are more than a side issue to the way local populations live—they are at the heart of what influences and interests them. So, too, the workings of local administrative institutions are increasingly central to the ethnography of local circumstances. However, these are usually given only brief mention in anthropological accounts.

Providing at least a small counterweight to rural difficulty in the No-mad area is the station's status as a subdistrict headquarters in Papua New Guinea's expansive Western Province. The Nomad Station boasts a long, flat airstrip that has been in continuous operation since 1962. On a larger scale, a different district of the Western Province boasts one of the country's largest and oldest gold and copper mines, on a mountain at the headwaters of the Ok Tedi River. The Ok Tedi mine has been owned and run by a multi-national mining conglomerate, Broken Hill Proprietary (BHP), in conjunc-tion with the Papua New Guinea government.

The mountain of gold at Ok Tedi has supplied Papua New Guinea with a major share of its gross domestic product over the past two decades— as well as causing large-scale environmental destruction along the Ok Tedi River and the Fly River more generally (Kirsch 1996). It has yielded a sizable yearly royalty for the national government and, to a lesser extent, the pro-vincial government of the Western Province. Though the vast bulk of this financial windfall is siphoned off long before it reaches remote stations in other provincial districts, such as Nomad, a small trickle of budgeted funds manages to seep into Nomad through cracks in the edifice of graft and in-efficiency. As a result, the Nomad Subdistrict Station, which is supposed to oversee its extensive territory of nine cultural groups, continues to have a working airstrip, a school staffed by four teachers, a police detachment with two constables, a health clinic with nine irregularly paid nurses and aides, and a government office with a number of busy officials.

Thus, despite continuing budget calamities, outrageously high prices, expensive air transport to Nomad, and chronic shortages of both personnel and matériel support, the most basic functions of government and national presence do, despite frequent breakdowns, bump along at the Nomad Sta-tion. Along with occasional outside support for church activities, this allows Nomad to retain its slim trappings of modernity in the absence of economic promise, expanding infrastructural development, or routinized commerce in the heart of the rainforest.[32]

In overall terms, however, the economic impact of Nomad upon its surrounding peoples—besides introducing a few more Western clothes—is not much different in 1998 from what it was in 1982. Our aerial photos reveal that the size and physical composition of the Nomad Station is about the same now as it was before (see photo 5). However, the cultural impact of the Nomad Station over this period has been nothing short of remarkable. In the process, a large range of people, including those from Gasumi Corners, have hitched their lives to its institutional world.

Change in the Anthropological Wind

Anthropology has few good models or theories for addressing the willingness to change that Gebusi present, but such patterns are increasingly common in the world today. People in many if not most world areas actively reach out to engage features of cultural, political, or economic modernity as they imagine or interpret them to be. The degree to which new standards of value and worth are accepted can be all the greater when, as among Gebusi, local people have a great desire for material success but little in the way of political, economic, or demographic clout even within their local region.

In the many places where economic marginality persists, as at Nomad, an increasing volume of outside ideas, images, and fantasies of wealth easily accentuate a local sense of hope, on the one hand, and deprivation, on the other. Given this perception, it is little wonder that marginalized people like Gebusi are receptive to outside authorities—economic, political, or religious—in hopes of achieving a small boost up on the ladder of modern success.

At places like Nomad, this process is at least as much cultural as it is economic. Without roads, resources, or anything to export, the idea of economic development at Nomad is little more than a pipe dream. Yet just because of this real impossibility, the motivation to develop a local modernity in *cultural* terms becomes all the stronger. Spiritual progress through Christianity is an important substitute for more materially modern rewards. Conversely, the sin and backwardness that are continually attributed to the wayward flock provide an explanation for the striking lack of economic development in the local area. These moral failings further enforce local subordination to figures of external power and authority. The cycle of aspiration, disappointment, and deference easily repeats itself (see Smith 1994).

Understanding this cycle helps explain exactly why it is that local ideas and fantasies of modern power may not spur organized resistance among local populations in response to conditions of disempowerment (see Gramsci 1971). To the contrary, deprivation can increase self-doubt, subordination, and even self-disparagement (Sahlins 1992; see also Epstein 1984). This drama becomes culturally specific and cannot be explained by the rational assessment of the presence or absence of economic opportunities. Rather, it thrives on new forms of expectation that cathect, imagine, and aspire to unattainable wealth and status. The core issue is: What motivates people, even in the absence of objective opportunity or coercive pressure, to engage a wider world and willingly give up parts of their own?

Anthropologists and critical theorists have often been slow to recognize and address this problem. The issue is easily sandwiched between theories of cultural stasis and continuity, on the one hand, and those of resistance to political and economic intrusion, on the other. Beyond such models, groups like the Gebusi quite willingly put themselves in positions of acceptance through an appetite for progress that far outstrips the objective possibilities for its material fulfillment. Neither economic determinists nor culturalist theorists are very good at explaining this phenomenon.

Progress as Ideology

What have been the empirical results of modern development and so-called progress? It is easy to adduce contradictory patterns. Nations chart their GDP, while industries and regions strategize their economic niches, development zones, investment opportunities, and payoffs. But in many rural areas, particularly in developing countries, the dismal results of development schemes, state planning, and economic initiatives are too obvious to be ignored (e.g., Escobar 1995; Gupta 1998; Scott 1998; Ferguson 1999). In the backwash of progress, however, people's hopes are often fanned while their lives are not improved. This pattern afflicts many parts of the so-called Third World, and it intensifies each year as the wealth gap widens between the world's richest and poorest countries.

If the problems of being or trying to become modern are not new, they have certainly not escaped prior analysis. These issues were foregrounded during the development of the social sciences in the late nineteenth and early twentieth centuries. Classic social theory was highly attuned to the social problems of a modernizing world, as evident in the works of Marx, Durkheim, Weber, Simmel, Veblen, Tönnies, and others.

Adding to the fraught nature of the modern world has been the social and cultural calamities of the twentieth century: two world wars, colonial oppression, a major economic depression, the horrors of the Soviet state, and the ghost of colonialism in the revolutions that hoped to replace it and in subsequent terror and repression. Neither the green revolutions in agriculture nor other well-intentioned modernizations worked very well. It is little surprise that the current strategy of the International Monetary Fund and the World Bank to intervene and set standards for economic and political development in so-called developing countries is at once so neocolonial in nature and so compromised in outcome.

And yet, ideologies of economic betterment and progress survive all this. Indeed, they often seem to reign supreme on the global as well as on the Western stage as we begin this next century. How can it be that the desire for progress and betterment in commodities and technologies has not only continued but deepened its hold on human imagination in the face of so much counterevidence, particularly in underdeveloped countries and rural areas? Can this cultural process indeed be explained—much less justified—by the objective changes that becoming modern has brought, or is it rather a relative absence of material change that fuels the growth of cultures of modernity in these contexts?

Over the decades, anthropologists have been skeptical of seriously engaging the impact of modernization as ideology. But as James Ferguson points out in his book *Expectations of Modernity* (1999), this trend deserves to be reversed.[33] In one or another guise, ideologies of modern progress and economic betterment associated with the West are increasingly the standards against which local developments are evaluated. This often results in economic and political disempowerment masked by the success of modernization as a cultural ideology. Although quick to celebrate the continuities and the hybrid resistances that people generate, ethnographers are only beginning to analyze the cultural depth of the ideologies of becoming modern.[34]

At issue is the "calling" posed by local desires to become modern under circumstances of economic marginality and relative decline. These circumstances bristle with ironies that a Max Weber might appreciate, but in a radically new key. The process of becoming alternatively modern need not reflect a capitalist ethic that ties hard work to objective conditions of financial investment and economic maximization. What we often find in remote areas is not material productivity underpinned by an ethic of endless work but a relative *lack* of economic development accompanied, ironically, by a mounting ethic of responsibility and culpability for not attaining modern success under conditions that are not conducive to its achievement.

Sandwiched between the misplaced triumphalism of positivist social science and anthropology's uncertainty about the global march of modernity, our eyes should open to how many people actively internalize new tropes of progress and success. We can draw upon Marx to say that people make their own sense of progress, but they do not always make it under conditions of their own choosing.

Emerging notions of what it means to have status and success in a contemporary world encapsulate what Marshall Sahlins (1985) calls the cultural structures already in place. Old cultures do not die, but they often become relativized, relegated to pieces of a larger puzzle (LiPuma 2000). This process of becoming relative makes cultural features self-conscious in new ways. Individuals are confronted by choices and decisions about traditional and nontraditional activities and lifestyles. Indigenous cultural practices easily become associated with the past and with a new sense of history. This historical awareness also recasts or reinvents past practices against local configurations of progress: the direction of the future is intrinsically contrasted with a notion of what is backward and to be left behind (see Hobsbawm and Ranger 1983).[35] Local notions of being "backward" or "developed" are in this sense mutually defining. As a result, the process of becoming "modern" is not homogenizing and does not reflect cultural convergence. Rather, it is as locally different as the beliefs and practices against which becoming "developed" or "modern" are configured. One culture's emerging modernity is not the same as another's any more than the practices and perceptions of its past are identical.

The task of understanding diverse paths of cultural change amid larger fields of power articulates well with anthropology's longstanding emphasis on the appreciation of cultural diversity, on the one hand, and its critique of inequality, on the other (Knauft 1996). It can also help us understand the apparent paradox whereby the peoples of the world become increasingly diverse and differentiated at the same time that their engagement with larger fields of economic and cultural power has more and more in common.

In the absence of concrete study, these issues are difficult to describe "in general." The present book presents a case example of this dynamic and attempts to explore its larger implications.

Chapter 2

Sorcerers of the Past

The trends of the present only have depth against the trends of the past. For Gebusi, this past entails a life-world of sorcery. Consider a world where crocodiles can sneak up and devour you. The image pricked my imagination when I was new to the tropics and to Gebusi. Wilted, I craved to swim in the deep bend of the river where it curled around our village. I enjoyed this respite a couple of times when bathing. Warned about the crocodiles, I asked how big they were. Yuway drew his facing palms a foot and a half apart. Breathing a sigh of relief, I wondered whether I should continue my daily dip amid the small-fry I had never seen—until I found out that, for economy, Gebusi measure crocodiles by width rather than by length. Yuway's measurement could have been for a twelve- or fifteen-footer.

Gebusi died in terror all the time. Sometimes they died from the spirit of a crocodile, the reincarnated form of a nasty old man who can attack when one is unguarded in the river. Fear can be greater when the spirit makes you forget that the attack has happened at all. He covers up the attack by sewing up your wounds, making you appear whole, and sending you wobbling back home, where you become violently ill and die. In anthropological literature, this is referred to as "assault sorcery;" in Melanesia's lingua franca, it is termed *sangguma*. Gebusi call it *ogowili*.

Most ogowili were terrifying warriors rather than crocodiles, but our own images of reptilian terror resonate. The warrior sneaked up on a surprised victim in the forest, brutally murdered him or her, and cut out and ate his or her insides. Then he covered up the attack with magic, made the victim forget, and sent him or her home to die. We might protest that this is empirically impossible, but Gebusi developed elaborate ways of investigating assault sorcerers "objectively," as we shall see.

The other main kind of Gebusi sorcery, more common and yet more insidious, has been *bogay,* or "knot," which falls in the ethnographic category of parcel sorcery. Parcel sorcerers are believed to harm the victim by damaging a bundle that includes some tiny stolen part or residue of the victim—a piece of his or her fingernail, saliva on a crumb of leftover food, a fragment of clothing with his or her sweat. Among Gebusi the bogay sorcerer is thought to take a fragment of the victim's feces from the forest floor and tie it up in leaves on a stick. As long as the fecal matter is bundled in the knot, the victim cannot easily digest food or excrete, loses all appetite, and wastes away. Relatives may make public appeals for any suspected sorcerers to relent, to untie the "knot," and to throw it away so the victim can recover. But bogay sorcerers are believed to be heinous: they typically hide the crime and their identity, wait until the victim has suffered greatly, and then burn the parcel to produce an awful death. As with ogowili, there is no evidence that Gebusi ever practiced bogay sorcery—that anyone actually gathered excrement, tied it up, or attempted to kill someone by burning it.[1]

Finding the Sorcerer

Our young friend Hiali died in 1981 during our fieldwork. Who was the sorcerer responsible? Swamin, one of the village spirit mediums, held all-night spirit séances attended by the men of the village. In the darkened longhouse, Swamin's human spirit left and its place was taken by spirit persons (*to di os*). The spirit people lived in the trees and in the rivers. They saw what Gebusi could not, and if you befriended them, they could help you find out what you wanted to know. Swamin's tiny spirit voice sang, and the men of the community chorused the words in beautiful harmony, song after song through the night. They also asked the spirits questions or roared their approval. They joked salaciously with the invisible spirit women, inviting them to stay and have sex with them. Later in the night, the spirits gave clues about Hiali's death. In bits and pieces, they suggested that the sorcerer was from Hiali's own village, that it was an older woman who was angry with Hiali's brother, Silap. The men realized that Tosi was being indicted as a sorcerer. She was a surprise suspect, but suddenly her guilt made perfect sense. Among other things, her daughter had been married nonreciprocally to Hiali's true brother, Silap, and then their marriage had dissolved in enmity.[2] But the positive spirit of the occasion persisted, not only with the spirits but also among the men, including Tosi's own relatives. The séance singing continued. Then, toward dawn, the spirits instructed Swamin and the rest of the men to go into the forest and search by a particular tree for Tosi's *bogay* stick—the murder weapon that they said she used to cause Hiali's death. As the séance ended, the men filed out to the designated spot. They dug around and eventually pulled up a twig with detritus around one end. They asked Swamin if this was the bogay. He inspected it and explained that if they looked carefully, they would see how the sorcerer had magically transformed the twig and detritus: it was actually a bundle of burned excrement that had been cleverly disguised to look natural. To Gebusi, this "bogay stick" was like a smoking gun with fingerprints. Tosi was confronted and accused.

Who is the sorcerer? The spirits told Gebusi and showed them evidence. But other steps were taken to confirm the spirits' indictment. If the death was from ogowili—a sudden, quick illness—men dressed in battle gear and went into the forest at the conclusion of the spirit séance. Armed with bows and arrows, they cautiously and silently stalked the ogowili down the forest paths that the spirits had identified. The spirit medium helped direct them and sometimes announced that they had lost the ogowili's path. In some cases the trail disappeared into unfriendly territory and the search was given up. In others, the ostensible residue of the assault was found, magically transformed to make it look almost natural. An odd dark area in the clay soil became the blood of the dying victim. A wad of bark under a river stone became the victim's flayed skin. A strange stick became the broken arrow or bow of the ogowili attacker. It was amazing to me how real these discoveries seemed to Gebusi and how seriously they treated them. Men took the magically transformed "remains from the assault" (*buluf*) or "sorcery knot" and confronted the suspect. The accused was thus presented with a fait accompli—the tangible evidence of his or her guilt.

Trial by Divination

It is hard to forget the smell of a rotting corpse; it burns through your nose and into the pits of your brain. Neither can you forget the body of your friend, bloated, disfiguring so slowly, awfully dripping, grotesque beyond recognition. His or her closest females relatives "keen"—that term that covers wrenching wails, red-eyed despair, hoarse-throated sobs, groveling in the dirt. They tenderly stroke the bloated, stinking body and rub its putrid essence on themselves. The cadaver's ooze mingles with their tears and sweat. We remember this well from Gebusi deaths in 1980–82.

The sorcery suspect can be forced to confront this monstrosity and undergo a divinatory test. He or she must shake the decomposing corpse as if to wake it from disfigurement—to show his or her true grief that the person has died. In response, the jostled body can identify the sorcerer. The dead spirit could make cadaveric juice drain or gush dramatically from its bloated torso. It could make its eyes bulge or even burst from their swollen sockets. We might say this was ocular extrusion caused by the intracranial pressure of gases from decomposition in the brain and eyes. But for Gebusi, it was a clear sign that the suspect was guilty. If this happened when the suspect was shaking the corpse, he or she could be killed on the spot—axed through the skull—with little objection from even his or her closest kin. In late 1980, we watched Aywaymus, an elderly sorcery suspect, shake a corpse in divination while he trembled like a tattered leaf. Fortunately for him, the corpse made no sign. Two years previously (as well as a few years later) other suspects were not so lucky.

As another method of divination, the sorcery suspect would be told to cook a leaf-wrapped mound of sago starch with a fish or a pig heart placed inside. The sodden mass was carefully arranged on the heated hearth of the person who died, and additional small fires were built around its periphery. This unusual and difficult cooking technique was never used except in sorcery inquests. The accused man or woman would nervously tend the cooking fires all day until the packet was removed at dusk to see whether it was cooked. If the spirit of the dead person wanted to exonerate the suspect, it could reach out to receive the packet; the warmth from its unseen hands was believed to supply extra heat to ensure that the sago and its contents would be fully cooked. But if the spirit was angry and wanted to indict the suspect, it was believed to withdraw its hands so the packet would be undercooked. The suspect could then be killed, cooked, and eaten in place of the uncooked food. Not infrequently, this execution would take place after the collected kin of the suspect had gone home; the accused would be attacked in the bush while foraging with only one or two close family members.

Our friend Tosi was accused of bogay for the death of Hiali and was forced to undergo a sago divination in 1981. Tending the cooking fires for the divination, she coupled her nervousness with a dignity that spoke volumes about her determination to prove her innocence. When the cooking was over, she sat patiently and gave the sago she had cooked to Silap, Haili's brother, and to his sister, Mus. A few in the community thought the sago and fish were sufficiently cooked, but many thought otherwise. Within a few days, Tosi moved permanently out of the village and set up a small new hamlet with her closest kin. An accused sorcerer is not always killed, but he or she is never completely free of guilt. Such persons are ripe for reaccusation after someone else in the community gets sick and dies. The chances then go up that a previous suspect will be reaccused and executed.

Life in the Face of Death

Of the nearly four hundred deaths we investigated in 1980–82, including those from all the remembered lineages of two major communities, not a single one was attributed to what we would call natural causes. Even the man who had plummeted from the top of a palm tree and broken his back had died from sorcery: an ogowili had caused him to lose his grip and fall. The man who committed suicide had been driven mad by a female sorcerer: Why else would someone go off alone and drink fish poison?! Another sorcerer had taken the form of a death adder and bitten a young man so that he died. Whatever the cause of natural death, a sorcerer was behind it.

Gebusi life has always been precarious. If we look at sorcery from our own end of the telescope, it was the risk of death from sickness that fueled sorcery rather than the other way around. Persons could be struck down by disease and death at any age, and half of all infants died of sickness before surviving a single year (Knauft 1985a: 20). As we would see them, the real enemies in this tropical lowland have been a vicious combination of malaria, pneumonia, filariasis or "elephantiasis," tuberculosis, and diarrhea. Gebusi are gradually and then totally depleted by microbes, parasites, clogged lungs, contaminated blood, and swollen spleens. Almost all adults have had at least one brush with death from illness; their bodies wizen as they approach what we call middle age. Acute sickness cycles with poor nutrition, helminthic (parasitic worm) diseases, skin funguses, lesions, tropical ulcers, the pulmonary impact of smoke-filled houses, the smoking of native tobacco, and, since the 1960s, the introduction of influenza. In 1980–82, the chances of a Gebusi boy of five living to age forty was only about one in six; that of a girl, one in three (Knauft 1985a: 81). Many Gebusi died from illness, and those who were killed merely increased the toll.

Adding to sickness and sorcery, disgruntled Gebusi sometimes asked their tribal enemies, the Bedamini, to come en masse and execute a Gebusi sorcerer, especially when the suspect belonged to a different Gebusi settlement from which armed resistance was feared. The information and safe passage afforded to foreign warriors in these death contracts (*to map*) encouraged Bedamini raids to extend into Gebusi territory during the precontact era. Unconstrained by Gebusi beliefs that only the sorcerer should be killed, Bedamini war parties would sometimes surround the targeted longhouse at night, set fire to it at dawn, kill as many fleeing inhabitants as possible, and carry off these human trophies for eating in their own land. In the 1940s and 1950s, a number of Gebusi settlements were decimated in this way.

From all these causes—sickness and disease, the killing of sorcerers, and the invited raids of enemy groups—Gebusi of the precontact period were subject to great demographic stress. In border areas, they were being absorbed into the Bedamini population. Robert Edgerton (1992) has even nominated Gebusi for the notorious label of being a "sick society" in the colloquial rather than the medical sense of the term. But unusual as they were, Gebusi cultural dynamics were quite viable. This is underscored by the fact that marriageable young women—the key segment of the population for purposes of demographic reproduction—were almost never killed by Gebusi.

This exception is thrown into relief by the generally high rate of killing in other age and sex categories. Between about 1940 and the end of my first fieldwork, in 1982, virtually one of every three Gebusi who lived beyond childhood died by being killed: 32.7 percent (129 out of 394) of all adult deaths were homicides.[3] Killing claimed a sizable percentage of young men as well as older men and women; only young women and children were spared (Knauft 1985a: 124–125). Related to this and partly explaining it, the bulk of killings, 87 percent, were executions of sorcerers, also including persons executed in association with the sorcerer (ibid.: 119). The intricate accounts of these killings were as central to the drama of Gebusi social lives as their violence was frequent (ibid.: chaps. 5, 7–8).

The extent of Gebusi sorcery executions is thrown into relief when we realize that the maximum rate of homicide vis-à-vis Gebusi sorcery beliefs is 50 percent, that is, the execution of one sorcerer for every sickness-death. A killing rate of 33 percent is two-thirds of this rate. In 1981, 65 percent of senior Gebusi men had individually executed at least one person during the course of their lives (ibid.: 132). Most men were not aggressive or threatening in daily life, but under conditions of sorcery inquest even the most mild-mannered man could easily become a killer.

How does the Gebusi rate of killing compare with that of other societies and cultures? Criminologists answer such questions by determining the number of persons killed in a known population per year and extrapolating this number to a standardized population of 100,000. In these terms, the Gebusi rate of killing has been among the highest yet documented and is equivalent to some of the worst slaughters known.[4] For comparison, we can take World War II, which is generally described as the most destructive war in human history. In Europe, the six years of war between 1939 and 1945 took between 15 million and 20 million lives, including the Holocaust, and resulted in a homicide rate of between 455 and 600 per 100,000 population per year. Even the higher of these two estimates is exceeded by the Gebusi rate of precolonial killing, which was equivalent to 683 per 100,000 per year.[5]

Yet higher figures have been recorded for other groups in the Gebusi's larger culture area within Papua New Guinea. These include a homicide rate of 778 for the Hewa of Papua New Guinea, to the north of the Gebusi, and a rate of over 1,000 among the Etoro, to the northeast.[6] These societies also killed the majority of their victims as sorcerers or witches. In other parts of New Guinea it was not uncommon for between 20 percent and 35 percent of adult men to be killed in warfare during the precolonial era.[7] There is hence ample evidence that the high rate of killing among Gebusi was not anomolous vis-à-vis some other areas of interior New Guinea during the precolonial era.

Lethal Disconnections

What is the tenor of social relations in a society in which more than half a percent of the population is being killed each year? To a surprising extent, this depends on local cultural circumstances.[8] Gebusi lived in relatively self-contained settlements that averaged just 26.5 persons. This means that Gebusi homicide averaged one execution per settlement every seven and a half years. The persons killed were typically men or women believed beyond question to be malicious sickness-senders. More than that, they were considered to be heinous individuals who were so deviously and ruthlessly murderous as to be virtually inhuman. Their elimination from the community was taken as a collective benefit, and even the closest kin of the person who had been executed ultimately tended to accept the identification of their relative as a convicted sorcerer. The general perception among Gebusi who were *not* practicing sorcery—which was practically everyone—was that they had little to fear from other Gebusi, except from sorcerers.

As such, the high rate of Gebusi killing did not produce a social perception of catastrophic violence or homicidal risk. Social relations within settlements and communities seemed remarkably congenial and genuinely friendly. Hence the title of my first book: *Good Company and Violence*.

With the benefit of hindsight, I now realize that my information from 1980–82 foregrounded a slice of Gebusi history after the decline of Bedamini raiding and before the demise of Gebusi sorcery inquests altogether. Though I had little perspective on this at the time, this framing helps explain how Gebusi from the late 1960s to the mid-1980s could maximize their intersettlement friendship, ceremonial life, and good company—with little threat of external attack—while continuing to conduct internal sorcery executions, which remained largely outside the awareness of government officials. As Renato Rosaldo (1980) demonstrated in his landmark history of Ilongot headhunting—and as I documented in my history of Melanesian warfare (Knauft 1990)—the historical context of so-called tribal violence can shift dramatically over time.

The Politics of Understatement

Many anthropologists have characterized highland peoples of Papua New Guinea—and especially the men—as aggressive and intimidating in personal demeanor.[9] Sternness, pride, and hostility are often stressed, especially in public encounters. But if such portrayals have truth, they are greatly inaccurate for Gebusi and others who live in the southwest lowlands on the other side of the mountains that separate them from the highlands. Descendants of a different cultural and historical stock—and even of a different language phylum—Gebusi are, if anything, deferential. To me in 1980–82, their daily emotional tone resonated more with the depictions of politeness and avoidance of conflict common for parts of Southeast Asia than it did with the bullying tactics described for New Guinea highlands big-men. Simply put, Gebusi went to great lengths to be nice to each another. In the multiclan longhouse, men talked and joked in collective camaraderie for hours upon hours (see Knauft 1985a: chap. 3). Most spirit séances were all-night songfests of laughter and festivity among men from the multiple clans in the village and the wider community.[10] This ethos was punctuated by all-night dances and feasts, complete with spectacular body costuming, piles of food and drink, singing by women, dancing by bird-of-paradise men, and festivity until dawn. Such gatherings were expressly designed to bring people together in good company, and they were devoid of the competitive gift giving prominent in some other parts of Melanesia. Our old village of Yibihilu had hosted or attended one of these fests as guests an average of once a month between 1980 and 1982.

Gebusi discord was largely limited to the specific context of sorcery accusations following serious illness and death. Even then, Gebusi were highly circumspect about antagonizing suspected sorcerers. Since a sorcerer was thought to have hidden and lethal anger, the last thing Gebusi wanted was to provoke him or her. Even for an aggrieved relative who was trying to rally men from several clans against a sorcery suspect, it was better to appear reasoned and "objective" about the accusation—rather than angry or impetuous. When a sorcery suspect was finally accused, the tone was amazingly accommodating—on the surface:[11]

> Accuser [in a soft voice]: Well, I don't know who could have sent this sickness. I really don't. And, well, I just don't know. None of us knew. But we had this séance and, well, the spirit medium said that it was a man from this settlement and, well, he pulled the [bogay] leaves here [holds the bogay in his hand]. And, well, there's no one else [he named you]. I'm scared [to talk to you]. I don't know what to do. I just don't know anything else. But if you want to cook just a bit of sago [do a major sago divination], well, then, everything would be better [you would have a chance to prove yourself innocent].

Beneath the euphemisms and the mask of friendship, the accused had little choice except to perform whatever divination was requested. To refuse would not only be a clear sign of his or her guilt but show a lack of remorse. When the divination was eventually conducted, the primary accusers helped the suspect make the sago packet as a sign of ostensible support. It was as if they were trying to convince the community that "we have nothing personal against the suspect" and that they would accept whatever "objective" results were obtained from the divination.

Reciprocally, if the accuser was understated but the suspect denied the accusation angrily, it only sealed his or her guilt in the eyes of the community. As Wasep once told me in 1981, "When it's said, 'I didn't do it, I didn't do it,' then we know they're just going to secretly lay on another [bogay] again." Imbo then added, "One shouldn't be angry and deny it.

People will call you no good." The best thing to do if accused of sorcery was, first, be humble and remorseful; second, neither confirm nor deny the accusation; third, conduct whatever divination was required; and, last, simply hope for the best. Though there was no way the accused could really shake off a presumption of guilt, a humble and cooperative demeanor increased the chances that he or she would not be killed or that the violent retribution would ultimately be redirected onto another, less fortunate target.

Even if divinations confirmed the accusation and the original suspect was killed, the community typically rebounded within a few months or a year. Clans were too small and the larger web of kinship through aunts, uncles, cousins, in-laws, and friends was too powerful to be resisted for long. People ended up living once again in longhouse communities with those who had killed their relatives. Even in our own culture, the battered wife often goes back to her husband, the child often defends the very parents who abuse him or her.

Learning to Accept

When there is no other choice, people make the best of unfortunate circumstances. I experienced this myself when Sayu's father, Silap, occasionally became possessed by evil spirits. Sometimes he would run about the village tilting at windmills—shooting arrows at houses, driving off imaginary spirits, or carrying an ax to chase down any person who might appear to him as a threatening specter. Though Silap would eventually emerge from his delusion and have no memory of what he had done, we worried that he would injure us or someone else when he was possessed. After Silap returned to normal, no one got angry at him, including those he had injured. What good would it do? There was no way to restrain or punish Silap; you just had to tolerate him.[12] The only other alternative in a society with no jail or prison was to kill him. And no one wanted to put an end to Silap; on the great majority of days when he was normal, he was one of the main men in the life of the village. So we simply lived with the danger of his occasional delusion.

I had my closest brush with Silap after my wife and fellow researcher, Eileen Cantrell, lost a tooth filling and left for Port Moresby to find a dentist. Late one day in a winding-down dusk, the slow-witted young man in our village, Mogasoyl, came to my house and lisped that Silap's "ear has become blocked" (*dul taboy-da*). It was a stock phrase: "He can't hear us." "We can't get through to him." "He's gone crazy." It all meant the same thing. Not wanting to explore this with Silap himself near the main longhouse, I hunkered down for an evening at home alone—carefully placing my bush knife by the wavering flame of my kerosene lantern and putting my flashlight nearby.

Just after I had taken off my glasses and blown out the lantern for the night, a thud hit my porch. I froze, my heart pounding wildly, and strained to hear. Silence. Another footstep fell on my porch. My bottled-up fear burst into action: I lurched for my knife—but instead knocked over my lantern, which crashed and broke. Reaching next for my flashlight in the dark, I knocked it away as well. When I heard the next step, I bolted through my back door into the blackness—and fell off the three-foot stump that separated our raised house from the pig wallow below. Completely muddy, scraped, and blind without my glasses, I was terrified. Lacking light or a weapon, I sprinted wildly up the village path, stumbling but not stopping, sensing Silap must be behind me. I collapsed against the door of the last house before the forest, beating on it and gasp-shouting, "Let me in! Open up quick! Silap's crazy and he's right behind me!"

It is not hard to imagine, on reflection, what response I should have expected. The occupants were inside a securely closed home, with a murderous crazy man certain to rush in along with their local anthropologist. As it happened, the men in the house were all away and there were only women. Would you open up? Of course not, and neither did they. Stymied and scared, I raced off further afield and, exhausted, threw myself in some bushes, hoping to hide. I prayed that crazy men with ears blocked to humanity don't hear gasping breathing.

After awhile, nothing happened. The moon rose higher. Nothing happened. Finally I snuck slowly back to that last house and attempted my best semblance of normalcy. "Silap has gone," I averred. "You can let me in and I'll tell you what's up." The log barricade was pulled away and I scrambled inside. Finally safe, my tension broke free, as if every pore could cry. I thanked the women again and again for letting me in. It never crossed my mind that they had first refused me, that I could have been killed for their lack of aid. Any port in the storm, even if late, and I didn't ask questions or mention their previous refusal. The past was forgotten in the safety of the present.

So, too, for Gebusi whose brother or sister or husband or wife has been killed as a sorcerer. In a world in which everyone is either dead or part of society, it is impossible to stay separate for long, much less forever. If people accept you back, you take them back, too—on whatever terms they offer. We knew one woman who willingly married the man who had killed her own mother as a sorceress. He was a strong protector. What better insurance could she ask for?

Gebusi have accepted what they must, like most of us when forced to do so. They protected their sanity by admitting as well as accepting that, well, their relative might have been a sorcerer after all. Better to live with your remaining relatives and get the most out of life while you can. It does little good to exhume the horrors of history if your goal is to live your life in a multiclan community. People can even learn to laugh at themselves in the process—as I did when I found out that the slow-witted Mogasoyl had misspoken and that I had misheard. Silap hadn't been blocked in his ear, his *dul;* he had had some problem with his *canoe,* his *du.* The slippage between my understanding of the language and my slow-witted acquaintance had made all the difference. It must have been the village cat who had dislodged the roofing stick I later found on my porch. The "footsteps" were probably her own thudded jumps on the porch when she startled from having knocked the piece of wood off in the first place. Primed for attack, I had certainly heard it differently. But while I was thrashing through the bush and screaming outside Sefomay's house, Silap and his housemates were calmly asleep at the other end of the village.

Though bad things happen, including in imagination, you ultimately accept them—which is what I also would have had to do if Silap *had* been delusional and driven me from my house. As it was, I only had to laugh at my own paranoia and terror, along with the Gebusi—for whom the whole story was too sidesplittingly funny to be forgotten. If it had been them, they would have laughed at themselves in the same way they expected me to do—which I quickly did, by way of catharsis. Even those bruised by Silap in previous episodes had joked about it afterwards. It was a bonding kind of humor. In my case, I had finally revealed in full dramatic splendor my own vulnerability to unseen malice—just as Gebusi do when they confront the image or entailments of sorcery. Like Clifford Geertz's (1983) famous brush with cockfights and police, which so endeared him to Balinese villagers, my spontaneous reactions of fear and frenzy made me more of a real person to Gebusi. And if my response reflected my own insecurity, theirs has reflected their experience of uncontrollable forces that are much more hurtful and pervasive: debilitating disease, premature death, killing by tribal enemies—and sorcery.

Life Reasserted

The only novel I read during those first years of fieldwork was John Irving's *The World According to Garp* (1978). I thought it fit Gebusi to perfection. Call it happy fatalism, that ability to laugh through the worst of life, make its cruel ironies your best jokes, assert your will to care and live on despite all the bad and weird twists, even among those who have caused you and your closest relatives the greatest harm. Like Garp's story, Gebusi lives were endlessly fraught with danger and ended unblinkingly in death—but they still managed an appreciation of life and an enjoyment of people. For them, a positive social world was both undeniable and irrepressible.

Against real and projected realities—sickness, death, and sorcery—Gebusi pursued lives of zest and vitality. Their social connections were genuine and perhaps stronger for having to tolerate so much. Carousing in the longhouse made collectivity intense—hours upon hours of talk, stories, joking, laughing, eating, and smoking among those from different clans. It helped that we lived in Yibihilu village, which was linked through festivity to the celebrations of joyful climax for the initiation of young men and women in late 1981. The details are a different story, but its heightened ethos brought the expression of Gebusi culture to full flower.[13]

Friendship and fun in a community that can kill its members are hard to convey; they go against our sense that violence contaminates the rest of life. But foreign cultures (and sometimes those close by) are renowned for not fitting our image of how human lives are supposed to operate. What remains common to humanity is the resilience of human spirit in the face of its own worst enemies. Through spiritual incarnation, ritual effervescence, song, dance, and daily talk, Gebusi asserted the vitality of life and of social living as if to counteract their violence and death from sickness.

Though Gebusi lived life to the hilt, they had little illusion about prolonging it. Notwithstanding the anger that ultimately congealed against sorcery suspects, Gebusi accepted illness, debilitation, and suffering with remarkably little complaint. We were amazed by their ability to live with pain. I remember a woman with a foot swollen permanently to twice its normal size. Her leg would shake in torment but her face would remain calm or even have a soft smile. The woman might joke that her "leg was rotting," but her spirit was not. The deaths we saw came with quietude and acceptance; the dying were comforted by the warm hands of friends, and they gave way to piercing wails only at the end.

Gebusi were poised to enjoy life rather than cheat death. Notwithstanding their crusades against sorcery, there was little they could do to reduce risk, either from disease or from each other. Their answer was to savor simple social pleasures, smile easily, laugh often, and celebrate when they could.[14]

The Decline of Violent Death

If attitudes and practices concerning death can change over time, what about changes among Gebusi? My findings from 1998 are striking. From interviews, mortality surveys, discussions, and cross-checking, I documented that the 59 adult Gebusi deaths that had occurred since 1982 included only three homicides, 5.1 percent. This marks a sixfold reduction in killing from the previous combined rate and an almost fourfold reduction from killing during the years just prior to and during our first fieldwork. The homicide rate for the sixteen years between 1982 and 1989 extrapolates to 89 per 100,000 persons per year. Though thirteen times the current U.S. homicide rate, this still marks an enormous decline relative to previous levels. Moreover, there have been no killings at all in my communities of study during the last ten years; the homicide rate there has dropped to zero during that time. Though the future cannot be known, the overall trend is clear.

A similar pattern is evident in the Nomad Subdistrict, with its population of approximately nine thousand persons.[15] The police records that will be considered in chapter 4 reveal ten adult homicides among the peoples of the Nomad area over the past ten years—from June 1988 to June 1998. This extrapolates to an annual homicide rate of 11 per 100,000 persons, which is in the same general range as the U.S. homicide rate during the past 30 years.[16]

How and why has the rate of killing declined so remarkably? What has happened to the belief in sorcery and the scapegoating and killing of sorcerers, which were so culturally entrenched and pervasive in previous years? Several possible explanations present themselves. First, police intervention and government coercion might have intensified. Although this has happened in some developing countries in postcolonial times, state violence and coercive control are not at all prevalent among Gebusi or in the Nomad area, as discussed in chapter 4. Second, illness and disease might have declined due to improved health care; this could plausibly reduce the rate of natural death and weaken the drive to eradicate sorcerers. This idea cannot be directly tested, but available evidence points against it. While Gebusi in 1998 had greater access to a medical aid post than they did in

1980–82, medical intervention has little effect beyond distributing standard-issue antimalarial pills in a region where resistant strains of malaria are endemic. The haphazard assortment of antibiotics handed out irregularly by aid post workers are seldom taken in full course. In the long run, these are less likely to cure illnesses than to provoke resistant strains of infection. Mercifully, the rate of infant death has been somewhat reduced due to standard inoculations, and this has fostered a slow and consistent increase in numbers that has augmented the Gebusi population by about a third over the last twenty years. But malnutrition remains high and may have risen because greater numbers of children depend on limited protein supplies that have not appreciably expanded. In any event, the deaths of young children were not traditionally attributed to assault or parcel sorcery and rarely prompted sorcery inquests or accusations. As such, reduction in child mortality does not emerge as a likely cause for the decline of Gebusi sorcery beliefs and inquest practices.

Finally, Gebusi may have realized that the killing of sorcerers has posed a demographic threat and so solicited the help of outsiders to reduce this cause of death. Though a hopeful interpretation, this does not appear to fit the facts. As noted above, the Gebusi rate of killing did not compromise their reproductive viability as a population. Indeed, a functionalist explanation of homicide reduction is practically the reverse of Gebusi's own logic concerning sorcery. For indigenous Gebusi, the execution of an accused sorcerer was undertaken as a principal way to *reduce* the suffering caused by illness and sickness-deaths in the community.[17]

The Present of Sorcery Past

Sorcery beliefs have not disappeared; Gebusi still harbor the general notion that adults and teenagers can die from sorcery. Belief in sorcery also persists among the icons of modernity at Nomad: teachers, aid post workers, government officials, and even police officers and pastors believe that sickness and death can be caused by sorcery. Increasingly, however, sorcerers are associated with a backward lifestyle that both villagers and officials say they are leaving behind. Likewise, spiritual inquest, public divination, and the taking of collective vengeance against sorcerers is infrequent and frowned upon as being part of the antiquated customs of the past. Sorcery is not "past" in the sense of being an absent belief. Rather, it is "past" in the sense of belonging to a disparaged history that is resisted as reality and seldom responded to with certainty or concerted action. As we shall see in chapters 5–8, sorcery beliefs now have a shrunken status that exerts a decreasing pull on community imagination or social agency, especially among those who live within several miles of the Nomad Station. A few sorcery inquests still erupt in outlying areas, as we shall see in the following two chapters, but they are increasingly the exception rather than the rule.

If these patterns index what has happened to Gebusi violence, they beg the question of why. In one respect, the decline of Gebusi sorcery retribution seems linked to the rise of a vernacular sense of becoming modern in this remote corner of the world. But this cannot be taken for granted. A wide array of anthropologists have documented the persistence of sorcery and associated occult beliefs and retributions in a range of Melanesian societies, as well as in Africa, South and Southeast Asia, and Latin America. Many examples could be used by way of illustration.[18] Among the Duna people, north of the Nomad area, Strathern and Stewart document the killing of a woman as a witch by her own son in 1998.[19] The contemporary killing of witches is reported in parts of South Africa, the Congo, Java, and Bali, to name just a few locations.[20] Nor is the continuation of occult beliefs and associated retributions limited to rural regions or uneducated persons. In a recent article, the late A. L. Epstein (1999: 292) noted,

> William Kaputin, who I believe was one of the first Papua New Guineans to be called to his country's judiciary, leaves one in no doubt that he accepted the reality of sorcery, as did his fellow Tolai, Allan Marat, who was the first student from Papua New Guinea to be accepted for a doctorate in law at the University of Oxford. The subject of his thesis was the official recognition of customary responses to homicide in Papua New Guinea. One of the proposals put forward in his thesis was that "the only way to rationalize the law and the customary belief in the existence of sorcerers and perceptions of causality is to rationalize the law and legalize the killing of reputed sorcerers" (Marat 1987 [pages uncited]).

In postapartheid South Africa, cycles of suspicion and attack against witches prompted an official "1995 Commission of Inquiry into Witchcraft and Ritual Murders in the Northern Province" (see Comaroff and Comaroff 1999). Concerning the Congo, Wyatt MacGaffey (2000: 16) writes:

> At the National Constitutional Assembly, a former minister of justice, a MuKongo, who in 1980 had suggested admitting diviners as expert witnesses, recommended that all judges be initiated in *kinganga* [knowledge of

spiritual powers] so they would be able to evaluate evidence of witchcraft themselves.

In Congolese popular opinion, MacGaffey notes, "the death of a prominent politician is never 'natural,' but always the result of some kind of sorcery" (ibid.: 225). Indeed, "[w]hen Laurent Kabila's miscellaneous army displaced Mobutu in 1997, some of its units conceived their task as that of rounding up witches to purify the country of corruption" (ibid.: 226). Contemporary execution of witches is also reported for parts of Indonesia, consistent with the continuing significance of sorcery and witchcraft beliefs in many parts of Southeast Asia.[21] Dramatic cases that attract widespread public attention are only the tip of the iceberg. Indeed, a range of scholars have suggested that witchcraft and sorcery are best seen not as relics of the past but as themselves a "mode of modernity, a theory and practice of power in societies of the twentieth century" (MacGaffey 2000: 227; see Geschiere 1997).

The persistence of sorcery and witchcraft in diverse societies and world areas sharpens the question of why such a precipitous decline of violence against accused sorcerers has occurred among Gebusi and in the Nomad area more generally. How is it that the process of becoming locally modern has sapped rather than spurred this violent enterprise? How does this pattern contrast to the rejuvenated sorcery and witchcraft beliefs that are linked to the "malcontents of modernity" in many parts of Melanesia, Africa, and other world areas? How are Gebusi alterations likely to change, and in what ways do they seem irreversible? We can approach these questions by examining those Gebusi killings that *have* taken place since 1982 and by considering their legacy to Gebusi today.

Chapter 3

The Severed Head and Other Affairs,
1982–98

Yibihilu, the "place of the deep water," was a small footprint in the rainforest. On a bluff above a large bend in the Kum River, some fifty people hacked a clearing from the bush and lashed together a longhouse community in the mid-1970s. In 1980, we found it to be one of the larger settlements and were welcomed to live there.[1] The village's government name, based on its prior and ancestral settlement, was "Gasumi."

Gebusi at that time were widely dispersed over 170 square kilometers of rainforest in seventeen settlements. From the airstrip and patrol post at Nomad, the track to Yibihilu burrowed for five hours through the rainforest and across two substantial rivers. Our village and the Nomad post remained worlds apart; neither Gebusi nor we visited Nomad very much. After we left in 1982, the village of Yibihilu persisted, but only for a few years. Bush timber and sago thatch don't last long under fourteen feet of annual rainfall and daytime heat that regularly tops one hundred degrees. People themselves decay at a quick rate; the pile of deaths accumulate; sorcery accusations boil over; and the remainder recombine in new assortments of clan-mates, in-laws, and maternal kin.

The central longhouse at Yibihilu had been forged around the friendship of Uwok and Silap—two men who were energetic but unrelated to each other. They were "bush rat" to one another—their special gift-exchange name. Yibihilu sprouted around Uwok and Silap like grass in a clearing, and it came to full bloom in 1981 when the initiations of the community were held there. But things had changed by the time Silap died, in 1985, three years after we had left. The divinations held for Silap's death yielded little conclusive result and Uwok grieved for his bush rat. He told me in 1998 that he just couldn't live any longer in the aging longhouse they had helped build together. So he and a diverse group of relatives moved out of Yibihilu and trekked far south beyond the Sio River to a place with no settlement but lots of sago and game animals. After a few months of foraging and relative isolation in the bush, however, Uwok and his group were enticed by an invitation to come and live to the northwest, not far from the Nomad Station, where one other family had already built its house. In a big step, he decided to accept.

It is something of a distortion to describe the shifting movements of Gebusi as determined by a few leading men—even though these household leaders do have their influence. Each family votes with its feet and makes its own choices. The idea of "changing residence" is itself flexible and sometimes partial, like the fruit bats of the forest that flock here and there among favorite places to roost.

Eventually, during 1986 and 1987, about half the people who had lived at Yibihilu joined those who had moved with Uwok to that portion of Gebusi land near the Nomad Station. They did so in dribs and drabs and have continued to forage and to keep some of their gardens deep in the bush. By contrast, the other half of the village gradually drew away and clustered deeper in the bush at the distant site of Harfolobi. The place has always been preternatural, just above crystal pools that thread shimmering cascades to the waterfall that Eileen and I frolicked in a few years before.

Dispersed by place, the erstwhile Yibihilu community continued to have friendships and kinships that stretched between Harfolobi and the small new settlement on the outskirts of Nomad. While forest dwellers at Harfolobi occasionally came to see what was happening by Nomad, those already there could be reciprocally drawn bushward to visit Harfolobi and the tranquility of the forest.

It was to this elongated community that Christianity first came. Cyril Afenang was a Catholic lay pastor from the Mountain Ok area, whose peaks are well beyond the Gebusi's northwestern horizon. The priest from the Diocese of Kiunga had sent Cyril to prospect for souls in the Nomad area. He reconnoitered sporadically in 1986 and set up a small house and chapel between the government station and Uwok's little hamlet a year later. Christian beliefs will occupy us later, as they did Gebusi, but for the moment they had little influence beyond curious and sporadic churchgoing by Uwok and a few others. At that time, the Gebusi settlement by Nomad was associated with a homestead called "Agiwa Corner," named after its rugged resident. A Pa-speaking man from across the Strickland River, Agi had been the manservant or "houseboy" of the patrol officer, but after his work was over he had stayed at Nomad, become a translator, married a Gebusi woman, built a house, and founded a settlement with his in-laws on their nearby land. Agi and his Gebusi wife and children had lived near Nomad in a family homestead since at least the late 1970s. It was they who had invited Uwok to come and live close to Nomad.

Sorcery's Revenge

Amid these budding changes and the first tiny trickles of Christian influence, a number of sickness-deaths in Uwok's hamlet and up at Harfolobi occurred without retribution. But pressure ultimately built for more decisive action. Spirit séances and divinations were carried out at Agiwa Corner as well as upstream at Harfolobi. Cyril the Catholic, not knowing their significance, even sanctioned the beautiful singing that drifted his way from the rainforest. Community concern deepened when one of their main spirit mediums, Hogoswimam, became seriously ill in 1987. Though Hogoswimam lived near Harfolobi, his in-law and friend Swamin, the community's most active spirit medium, had his own hamlet downstream and was spending more and more time at Uwok and Agi's settlement. So Swamin held a spirit séance near Agiwa Corner with the hope of rooting out sorcery before Hogoswimam died from sickness. During the séance, Swamin's spirits named two women as bogay sorcerers. Both were old widows living up at Harfolobi and thought to have had grudges against the stricken spirit medium. Perhaps Swamin or his spirits also realized that the accused old women had few kin to support them; one or both could have been killed in the bush without alerting the government.

Swamin himself had already executed one old woman in just such a manner a few years before our initial arrival. In about 1975, Uwok had himself stalked and killed a whole family of reputed sorcerers. He clarified the accounts of others with his own description. Finding the family, he snuck up on the husband, Wawa, from behind. He split this main suspect's head with an ax, splattering his brains. Uwok then jabbed the sharp end of his bow through the temple and into the skull of the man's terrified wife, Wabe, who was also considered a sorcerer. Finally, he grabbed a sharp piece of bamboo and chased down their young boy, Giwiay, who had fled. He didn't suspect Giwiay of any wrongdoing, but he knew that if the boy lived to tell the tale, Uwok faced a long jail sentence from the government officers. So he pierced the young boy through the base of his skull: the third killing of the gruesome day was completed. Uwok then tied the arms and legs of the bodies together and dumped them into the river, where they floated downstream for others to see. The rest of the community did nothing, since even the close clan brothers of the slain family, Yaba and Yokwa, had sanctioned the killing. It was only the government officers that Uwok and others had to deceive, and this was easily done. No action was ever taken against him.

A dozen years and living closer to Nomad had brought other changes, however. Hogoswimam was not yet dead, and though things started out as planned, the accusations of 1987 took on a life of their own. When the inquisitors arrived from Agiwa Corner, the Harfolobi residents did not repel or contravene them. Hogoswimam was their main spirit medium, and the old women who had been accused were not centrally integrated into their settlements. The two sorcery suspects were tied up, beaten, burned with scalding water, and threatened with execution. Under duress, the two women admitted to practicing sorcery. In a key twist, however, they also named three others who they said were also sorcerers living next to Nomad—in Agiwa Corner.

It was true that a mounting number of sickness-deaths in Agiwa Corner had gone unavenged. And the three persons named by the accused sorceresses had each been suspected and in some cases formally accused of causing previous deaths. Contrary to what one might have thought, then, the two groups that had gone their separate ways from old Yibihilu did not polarize over accusations of sorcery from each other's new settlements. Instead, they unified to take common action against the suspected sorcerers in both locations. In the process, yet another woman of Agiwa Corner was also added to the list of suspects.

The four new suspects from Agiwa Corner were rounded up, tied to stakes, beaten, and forced to confess that they were sorcerers. This widened the field of inquiry while also making it harder to cover up the inquest; the scale of these sorcery accusations was unprecedented and posed a dilemma. The inquest had spread from two old women deep in the forest to four more people living closer to Nomad. All had confessed. The situation had grown to proportions that bordered on government awareness. Killing all these suspected sorcerers was unrealistic, but how and why to execute some and not others? Given the circumstances, news of any murder would spread—but taking no further action against so many admitted sorcerers in the community would be more literally suicidal from the community's point of view. From a Gebusi perspective, then, lack of more decisive action against individual sorcerers for several years had led to their accumulation and now to their massed emergence. Sorcerers had typically been killed one at a time (or in pairs if closely related) but rarely purged en masse.

The final piece in this puzzle was the changeover at Nomad from Australian patrol officers to Papua New Guinean national police. Whereas Australian officers had scoffed at sorcery and refused to take it seriously, the national officers at the time—who had natal ties to other parts of New Guinea—were quite willing to assist Gebusi in their inquest, including intimidating or beating suspects to obtain confessions and then putting them in jail.[2] In an ironic twist, this action produced a degree of humanitarian improvement. Gebusi had seldom brought their sorcery disputes to Australian officers. Instead, they hid their inquests from government awareness and simply killed the suspects when they were off in the bush, as Uwok had done. With the acceptance or complicity of the victim's own kin, it was relatively easy to kill the suspect and keep the matter from official attention. With the national police as allies rather than enemies, however, the balance shifted.

In the end, then, Gebusi brought all six suspects to Nomad and forced them to restate their confessions in front of the national police officer. They were not executed but put in the Nomad jail and sentenced to several months of hard labor. This change was important: it had become better to use the strong arm of government against sorcery suspects and avoid the risk of mounting an execution altogether. Although the national police were willing to intimidate or jail sorcery suspects, they were nonetheless quite clear that a local killing would saddle the executioner with a long and arduous prison term outside the Nomad area. At least during the late 1980s, then, the result was the official prosecution of sorcery, as reflected in the following Nomad police record concerning the trial of Sefomay on September 30, 1987.

> *30-9-87, 9:00 am   Sefamai Hogwa (F) aged 53*
> *Village Gasumi*
> *S/P Nomad*
> *Prov. Western*
>   *CHARGED:*
> *That between the months of January and September 1987 you did unlawfully*
>   *administer to another person namely Kokei Sasuwo [Hogoswimam] a*
>   *substance namely Homogap, that has been subject to the act of sorcery.*
>   *Thereby contravening section 9(2)(a) of the Sorcery Act, Chapter 274,*
>   *volume 10.*

Witnesses:

   A) Agewa Gerabi, Agewa Cona

   B) Huga Huako, Nomad Station

Jail time ultimately completed, all six convicted sorcerers were released and returned to their settlements in 1988. It added to the credence of this action that Hogoswimam, the ailing spirit medium, started to feel better and ended up recovering completely from his illness.

In a twisted sort of way, the entire episode was almost a good-news story. All believed that the suspected sorcerers, submissive and chastened, would not quickly resume their evil ways. To this day, suspicions of sorcery against these persons are tempered by their own exhortations and those of their kin: having been almost killed and then officially punished, they are much too scared to ever practice sorcery again.[3] In 1987, of course, they were subject to brutality, pain, and humiliation. But they had not been killed and were even considered rehabilitated in the aftermath. All six were reabsorbed by their community and have not been beaten or attacked as sorcerers in the eleven years since. In 1998, the five women were still alive and the man had died a natural death.

Looking back, irony in fieldwork can surpass that in fiction. The Papua New Guinean police—though confined to the Nomad Station, believing in sorcery, intimidating and punishing those unfairly accused, and siding with their attackers instead of the victims—ended up short-circuiting lethal violence against the accused sorcerers. They kept them confined and safe from attack by angry villagers, underscored that villagers should not take matters into their own hands, and gave the suspects a new lease on life. By contrast, the Australian officers before them had patrolled in the never-ending bush, tried to order people about, harangued against all manner of fighting and killing, and put offenders in jail whenever they could—that is, whenever they could find out what was happening, who was attacking whom, and where they could be tracked down. With national independence in 1975, the Australian departure had been widely lamented by those, including some locals, who feared that savage killing would reemerge without the Australian practice of patrols in the bush. But the Aussies had never given credence to sorcery beliefs, and they were seldom consulted, much less trusted, by Gebusi. They never realized how much consensual killing was going on behind their backs. Gebusi had kept it that way. But a new page was turned as Nomad became a national rather than a colonial outpost.

Despite this trend, the hopeful ending of 1987 did not last long into 1988 for Gebusi.

The Severed Head

Boi had been the best friend of my wife, Eileen, at Yibihilu, and I think she was the most intelligent Gebusi we have ever known. Though she fought continually with Silap, her impetuous husband, Boi had a middle-aged beauty that was at once serene and calming to others. Her relaxed laugh, sparkling eyes, and friendly disposition warmed those around her like a bark cape on a drizzly night. Boi was a natural at schmoozing with the women, spinning tales, sharing gossip, and occasionally—though it got her into trouble—flirting a bit with one or another of the men. She got to know Eileen and confided plentiful stories to her of people and spirits through which community histories and forest places came alive.

We left the Gebusi in 1982, and after Silap died in 1985, Boi moved up to Harfolobi, near her natal land and back with her closest kin. In 1987, she was enticed to become the second wife of Doliay, one of the youths we had helped initiate to manhood six years before. Doliay, who tops out at four feet and seven inches, was (and is) the smallest adult Gebusi man we have seen. But he has always been a tiny Atlas, as if every fraction shaved from his height was put back into brawn. And Doliay has always had burning energy.

The marital and residential arrangement between Doliay and Boi ended up being significant for later events. When still quite young, Doliay had first married the beautiful young Hadeagum. After Yibihilu split up and disbanded, Doliay lived with Hadeagum near her relatives in Agiwa Corner, even though Doliay's true brother lived, like Boi, up at Harfolobi. When she became his second wife, Boi moved in with Doliay at Agiwa Corner, but she also spent time a good bit of time at Harfolobi, where Doliay would come and visit her and be with his own true brother. In effect, when Doliay took Boi as a second wife, he stretched his immediate family across both ends of the erstwhile community of Gasumi.

Taking two wives has never been common or easy among Gebusi; the co-wives resent their husband as well as each other. The men of Agiwa Corner and Harfolobi were also piqued at Doliay: still a young man, he was launching a two-ring circus of marital and domestic expansion while keeping two attractive women for himself. In fact, it was unclear whether his polygamous union with Boi would last when she went with her kin past

Harfolobi to process sago deep in the forest in early 1988. For the moment, Doliay stayed with Hadeagum in Agiwa Corner.

Boi's expedition started out well enough. Though an ulcerating sore had developed on her leg, she shrugged it off. After a day of processing sago, she felt a bit woozy and returned from deeper in the forest to a bush house. The next day, Boi said she felt better and went back into the forest to collect sago grubs with her two boys. She never returned.

Perhaps it was septicemia—blood poisoning from her infected leg— that caused Boi to die so quickly. By the afternoon she couldn't walk and by evening she was fading in and out of consciousness. She died alone in the night, accompanied by the sobs and terror of Sayu and his younger brother, Huwa. Eventually, their cries were located by a party of torch-bearing searchers. Stunned and disbelieving, they returned to their settlement wailing and carrying Boi's corpse.

News spread like a rainforest flood: Boi, healthy just a few days ago, had been brutally murdered by an ogowili sorcerer. Adding insult to death, people were incensed at Doliay. Why had he let his wife go into the forest accompanied only by her two young sons? Why had he elected to stay so far away that he didn't even know she was getting sick, much less protecting her while she was ill, so exposed to a sorcery attack deep in the forest? This acrimony was compounded by the rage of Boi's natal relatives from the adjacent community of Kusabl. They arrived en masse and shot arrows at Doliay (who had rushed to the scene), shouting that he had married their "sister" as a second wife and then left her alone to die. Everyone swelled with anger, but the arrows missed their mark.

In Gebusi inquests for ogowili, the location of the spiritual attack— that is, the place in the forest where the victim was exposed and un-guarded—is an important site of investigation. As it happened, the distant forest place where Boi had taken ill was near the main path toward a third community. In this direction, the track first went through a tiny hamlet inhabited by the tall and easy-going Basowey and his deaf-mute brother, Gosayl, along with their wives and children. Sandwiched in the border zone between two communities, Basowey had sometimes affiliated for major feasts with Gasumi and sometimes with his natal community of Sirigubi, further north. This arrangement had left the people of Gasumi ambivalent about him. Was he an ally or merely an outsider?

Boi's corpse decomposed in the Harfolobi longhouse for several days while the women keened. Finally, the corpse was ripe for gruesome divina-tion. The six Gebusi who had been convicted of sorcery just a few months earlier were still suspects, but not as much as one might have imagined. All six had been accused of parcel sorcery (bogay), but a sudden death deep in the forest is almost invariably attributed to the warrior attack of a male assault sorcerer, an ogowili. The only man among the previous six, Kasubia, had been far away in Agiwa Corner and was ruled out as a suspect. With no other ogowili suspects in either Harfolobi or Agiwa Corner, the community directed their suspicions as if naturally against Basowey and Gosayl. Both men were told to come and do a corpse divination. Boi's body was by now in an advanced state of decay. When Gosayl, the deaf-mute, shook the corpse, it gurgled. But when Basowey shook the corpse, its eyes reportedly burst from their sockets. Whether they actually burst or not I will never know—the incident could have become more intense as it was told to me. In any event, Basowey made immediate excuses and desperately tried to explain how the definitive sign the corpse had made against him could have been caused by someone else. Along with Gosayl, he practically bolted back to his settlement before any action could be taken against him.[4]

Shortly thereafter, Hogoswimam held two spirit séances that confirmed the accusation and provided further details.[5] The spirits narrated in vivid detail how Basowey had kept anger strong in his heart, how he had mercilessly stalked Boi, how he had had no pity on her children, and how he had killed her with an arrow, eaten her, covered up his deed, and left her to die. The spirits also announced that Sayu, Boi's son, had seen the attack. Though it had been dusky, he had caught a glimpse of the ogowili and could substantiate the spirits' account. The spirits suggested that Boi's relatives and Doliay ask the boy what he saw in the forest as his mother turned deathly ill.

Sayu had seen both his parents die and was now called upon to identify the sorcerer who had killed his mother. At first Sayu was uncertain and vague, but, yes, he said he had seen a shadowy figure or essence near his mother as she got sick. In answer to the anxious and coaxing eyes of the adults who asked him, yes, the figure had looked something like Basowey.

This was all the additional proof that Doliay and the others needed. But as is often the case, and especially in cases of ogowili, no immediate action was taken. As both Boi's husband and clan brother to her deceased first spouse, Doliay had primary responsibility to engage support and lead the attack, but the time was not ripe. Basowey had retired to the large village of Sirigubi and could not easily be targeted. So Doliay paid compensation to Boi's natal relatives to soften their anger against him. Then he returned to Agiwa Corner and bided his time.

As Doliay described it to me, the image that he couldn't shake was that of Sayu and his younger brother sobbing alone over the corpse of their mother. Doliay's *fin*, his spirit, told him not to tell his plans to anyone. But the pressure on him to act came from several sources, in addition to his own natural intensity. Much anger had been heaped on Doliay. He had pushed the customary boundaries in order to marry Boi, and now she had died without his even knowing she had been sick. Along with losing his second wife, he had been blamed and shamed. It was now time to focus his anger on Basowey.

Feigning normalcy, Doliay cut grass at the Nomad airstrip. He waited until the talk and worry over fighting had died down and kept a keen ear for news of Basowey's movements. When the time was right, Doliay borrowed a good metal file from an official and sharpened his bush knife to its finest edge. He then went off toward Basowey's little hamlet.

On the way, Doliay tested his anger and focus by spear-fishing in a passing stream. He skewered a nice large fish—a good omen. What happened next can be told by Doliay:

> I looked around in the bush near the settlement. I found Basowey spear-fishing at a stream with his young daughter nearby. Basowey didn't see me, but I watched him. He still didn't see me. Then I struck a tree hard with my bush knife. How he jumped with surprise and fear! "Why have you come?" he asked. "I came 'just because,' " I said. Then I shook his hand/snapped his finger. I rolled tobacco and put it in my tobacco pipe and shared smoke with him. Then I reached in my net bag. I got out some of the sago with my fish in it, and I gave it to him. We cooked it on the fire there and he ate it. After a while, he said, "I think we should take the trail so I can go back to my house." He went first.
>
> As he walked ahead, I got so very angry. I took my bush knife and hit/struck him as hard as I could on the back of his head. His skull was cut and blood flowed. He turned around and I hit him again in the forehead, cutting through his forehead and face. He reached for his bow and fired an arrow at me, but I dodged it. We fought. He struck at me with the sharp end of his bow, but he missed. I hit at him again with my bush knife; he put up his hand to block the blow and my knife cut deep into his forearm. He was bleeding all about. We fought and fought until he laid down and died. I lifted up his head by the hair; he was dead. I cut and cut around his neck. I was so angry. I kept cutting until his head was cut off. I left his head and his body there. Then I went back to Harfolobi.[6]

Doliay made no attempt to cover up his deed. Indeed, he gave his bloody bush knife to the Catholic pastor and then turned himself in to the police at the Nomad Station. He was quickly flown to Kiunga at government expense—before he could be attacked by Basowey's relatives. He was then tried and sentenced to six years at Bomana, the Port Moresby national prison.

Doliay never resisted his prosecution or imprisonment. Indeed, he gained the respect of police and prison wardens for owning up to his actions and accepting the consequences of having avenged his wife's death. In the process, Doliay became a model prisoner. In his account, he was consistently befriended by police, prosecutors, and later by the prison wardens. He was rewarded for his honesty, his willingness to serve his time, and his hard work. First made prison cook, Doliay was later promoted to chief of the commandant's kitchen. He prepared special meals for the top prison staff, and he ate them, too. He was given the key to the food storehouse. Guards smuggled him cigarettes and an occasional beer. When his six-year sentence was up, Doliay was given a letter of official commendation and reference as a cook—a credential he proudly showed me and which he keeps to this day as a sacred possession.[7] Seven years after his return, Doliay still wears the shirt given him by one of the wardens as a present upon his release. After returning to Nomad and to his wife, Hadeagum, Doliay named his first son, Willie, after one of his jailers.

While in prison, Doliay learned to speak *tok pisin,* the nation's lingua franca. He learned government ways and principles of order and discipline as well as how to cook. He remains the only one of Gasumi's residents to have seen Port Moresby, the nation's capital—even if only through the windows of a prison van and an airplane. Based on his religious experience while in prison, Doliay become a dedicated Christian upon returning to Nomad.[8] He said to me, "My old spirit has been exchanged in direct reciprocity for Jesus."

Following Doliay's description of his conversion, he and I had a long talk about how and where sorcery still exists in the Nomad area. He emphasized that people in Gasumi Corners, including those like Sefomay, have completely given up sorcery. He stressed that Gasumi people were good people who went to church and believed in God. Yes, people still die from sickness, but that is a matter we simply have to leave up to God. People in other settlements might still practice sorcery. But in Gasumi Corners they are too scared to practice sorcery—because of what Doliay himself did to Basowey. Even if his own children died from sickness, Doliay said he would simply let "the big fellow," God, take care of it. Doliay's own spirit, his *fin,* had really been completely exchanged, he said, and he could no longer fight or kill, no matter what. He described to me the gradualness of his spiritual conversion. He wanted to be completely sure he had no desire to fight or do bad things before he was baptized. Even when he is deep in the bush and can't be in church on Sunday, he said, he bows his head and prays.

I am not religious myself, but I was struck by the sensitivity, thoughtfulness, and earnestness of Doliay's account. He is deeply aware of the magnitude of his crime in killing Basowey, and he is humble about the divine grace that forgave him when he was baptized by the visiting Catholic bishop. On the morning of our conversation, I couldn't find Doliay at first; he wasn't at his homestead or anywhere in Gasumi Corners. When I finally found him, he was helping the pastor cut grass in the church compound. He has never to my knowledge been among those who have tried to wheedle the pastor or benefit from his presence.

If Doliay's time in prison transformed him, his killing of Basowey also transformed his home community. With one blow, he changed their social and political landscape. Shortly after Doliay's imprisonment, his village mates at Harfolobi realized that their small settlement was vulnerable to a revenge attack from Basowey's relatives. In part because of this, those from Yibihilu who had previously moved to Agiwa Corner invited their erstwhile companions at Harfolobi to move downstream and join them once again. In short order, this is what they did. The Harfolobi residents still travel back to their old homestead on occasion, and they keep some gardens and maintain small houses there. But since 1988, their main residence has been with their old compatriots a mere half-hour walk south of the Nomad Station. In effect, the old village of Yibihilu that split apart in 1985 has reaggregated by the same river but downstream near the Nomad Station. The name of the reconstituted settlement is "Gasumi Corners."

Culminating Mosaics

Looking back, it seems obvious that sickness-deaths and sorcery retribution were a key cause both for the breakup of Yibihilu and then for its reamalgamation at Gasumi Corners. The death of Silap, the accusations against six bogay suspects from both upstream and downstream, the ensuing death of Boi, and the killing of Basowey—all these were pivotal events.

One other violent spasm can also be added to this mix to complete the residential history of Gasumi from 1982 to the present. This episode involved the frightened flight of an old woman named Sayame from further east into Gasumi Corners—followed shortly thereafter by her closest kin.

A spinster with no children, Sayame had been accused of sorcery. She had been beaten and burned until she was almost dead, then left to flee for her life. Miraculously, she recovered after coming to Gasumi Corners in 1990.

Why did the people of Gasumi Corners let Sayame stay among them, followed by her three clan brothers and their wives and children? Her kinship ties to them were not particularly close. Part of the answer, residents said, was that the dispute against Sayame and her brothers was back in her natal settlement and did not apply to Gasumi Corners. Why wouldn't she practice sorcery in Gasumi Corners? First, they said, she was too scared from the previous attack against her to become a sorceress again. Second and relatedly, she was grateful to them for accepting her and had no motivation to harm them. Third, she was accompanied by three clan brothers and their wives and children. The addition of these families was seen as a benefit rather than a cost to people in Gasumi Corners. With plenty of garden land and a sense of pride and vitality in having a large and active group, Gasumi Corners accepted rather than rejected this willing addition to their community. Finally, Sayame became a Christian and attended church faithfully every Sunday.

The accretion of Sayame and her relatives was the last case of sorcery retribution—and the last major demographic change—to impact the descendants of Yibihilu at Gasumi Corners.

Patterns in Time

We may summarize the history of the Gasumi community from 1980 to 1998 as follows:

1980–82	Bruce and Eileen live at the village of Yibihilu, known by government officials as "Gasumi."
1981	A major initiation is held at Yibihilu.
1981–82	Yibihilu begins to split up following the death of Hiali, shortly after the initiation. Tosi and eleven of her relatives move out.
1985	Silap dies, Yibihilu breaks apart. Roughly half of Yibihilu's residents end up moving upstream near Harfolobi; the other half move downstream to Agiwa Corner, near Nomad.
1987	Six persons are accused of bogay sorcery—two from Harfolobi plus four from Agiwa Corner. They are accused, beaten

	into confession, convicted by Nomad police, and labor at Nomad as jail mates for one to three months.
1987	The Catholic pastor, who has had sporadic contact with Gebusi for a year, builds a house between Agiwa Corner and the Nomad Station.
1988	Silap's wife, Boi, dies at Harfolobi; Basowey is accused of ogowili; Doliay kills Basowey; Doliay is charged and sentenced to six years in the national prison; the residents of Harfolobi move in to Agiwa Corner, which becomes known as "Gasumi Corners."
1988–90	Via the local Catholic church, Christianity begins to have a significant impact.
1989 or 1990	Sayame is accused and beaten as a bogay sorcerer at Yulabi. Sayame is burned; nearly dead, she flees to Gasumi; she and her kin are accepted in Gasumi Corners.
1989–98	No one from Gasumi Corners is attacked or killed as a sorcerer.

This last entry is particularly important. It is as if the dying gasps of sorcery retribution lapsed with the killing of Basowey and the recovery and conversion of Sayame shortly thereafter. Doliay's gradual conversion to Christianity while in prison was echoed in his community while he was absent. The initial context of this process, however, was a continuing belief in sorcery and retribution against sorcerers. Yibihilu had broken apart over death and sorcery. Further death and sorcery and an execution brought them back together again—and then added another segment to their community. When I asked my Gasumi friends and others if there was still sorcery in the community, their answers were negative: "We no longer know much about sorcery." They admitted that some sorcery still persisted in other communities, especially those that had no church, and that some of those sorcerers could make people sick in Gasumi Corners. But this was not a major concern, and they were largely content to leave such matters to God.

Eleven sickness-deaths had occurred in Gasumi Corners during the ten years since Basowey had been killed, including the deaths of important senior men, wives, marriageable women, girls, and boys. None of these deaths had been avenged, and no further sorcery cases had been brought by the people of Gasumi Corners to the Nomad police. Nor did there seem to be mounting pressure to find a scapegoat, including for the death of Uwana, the senior man who died at Gasumi Corners when I was there in 1998. Deaths were increasingly attributed to spiritual evil or to generic forms of sorcery but with little groundswell for public inquest or revenge.

This pattern is not as simple to explain as it may first appear. Sorcery beliefs have persisted or reintensified in other world areas, including in other parts of New Guinea. Gebusi still spend large amounts of time in bush settlements and deep in the forest. Particularly in these contexts, it is still quite possible for them to attack and kill a suspected sorcerer. Especially if the suspect is an unsupported older woman, there is little chance that such killings will be discovered by government officials.

The sorcery accusations of the 1980s help put this possibility into perspective. During this period, five of the six persons accused of bogay within the Gasumi community were women, and all but one of these were old widows. Sayame, who was almost burned to death for bogay at Yulabi, was also an old widow. This pattern dovetails with what I found at the neighboring community of Yehebi, to the south of Gasumi. Over the sixteen years since my first visit, this community had killed two people as sorcerers. In both cases, an old woman was accused of bogay sorcery and executed deep in the bush. In one case, the old woman was an aged spinster who, like Sayame, had never married or had children. The people of Yehebi had successfully concealed these killings both from the government and from their resident missionary. In each case, they simply told outsiders that the old woman died of sickness during an extended foraging trip and hence had been buried in the bush. No report of the slayings was ever made, and no killers were identified or apprehended.

Given the impunity of these killings, it is clear that Gebusi could still execute old women if they wanted to do so. Contrast Doliay, who killed a suspect who was not only a married man but a member of another community. There was no chance this killing would go undetected or unreported; it was known throughout the area within hours. And yet, in the wake of this homicide, the rate of Gebusi killing has declined dramatically. The slayings of Basowey and the two old women mentioned above are the only three killings among the 59 deaths that occurred in the communities of Gasumi and Yehebi since 1982. No killings at all have taken place in these communities during the 1990s.

These findings sharpen rather than dull the question of why Gebusi do not continue to accuse and kill suspected sorcerers. Of course, Gebusi and others in the Nomad area know about the police. They are well aware of the six years that Doliay spent in prison for killing Basowey. And they know the longer history of colonial-*cum*-government prohibitions against fighting and killing. To what extent has the reduction of Gebusi sorcery retribution been caused by the threat or fear of government intervention?

Gebusi know that the Nomad police believe in sorcery, and that the police have been willing to prosecute cases of village sorcery in the past, particularly when the suspect was made to confess. Even if Gebusi are no longer killing sorcery suspects, why haven't they been making public accusations, extracting confessions, and bringing suspects to the Nomad police, as they did in 1987? More generally, what is the legacy of government influence? To answer this question, we need a better understanding of the Nomad police.

Chapter 4

The Guards of Nomad

It looks so grand from a thousand feet up, that glow so deep green and vast. The broccoli-top trees crowd together as if there's nothing beneath—an emerald skin hiding worlds of life within. A blue-brown ribbon etches through the growth, snaking toward its partner and merging in gentle delight. You look at the nestled crook of these two rivers, closer, where the green shifts from dark to bright, from old forest to new—continually cut and always sprouting. Within this lime green patch you see a score of small white squares arranged neatly at attention. Ten line up evenly on one side while their partners face them across the lawn, their metal roofs glinting. You think about how these houses were built for homes by those early officers, so colonial and rugged, trekking in from far away. Just beside them is the rectangle they laid out and made even, so flat and very long, its grass still short and trim. Your plane will swoop down on it now, the gilded spine of that book you have come so far to read. But the text is not what it was, nor text at all. It has become the faces that line the airstrip, bright and eager as their skin is dark, watching expectantly while you land. You open the door to receive the blast of heat and humanity. Welcome to Nomad.

Colonial Incursions

Back in 1962 when the world seemed simpler, a few Aussie stalwarts and many groaning New Guinean carriers trudged through rainforest and swamp and managed to cross the Strickland River. They came to a cultural watershed: the last great area of Papua New Guinea—and one of the very last in the world—to be "unpacified" and still beyond the range of civilization. So it was said. Not just warfare but cannibalism still thrived, and especially among the Bedamini, Gebusi's eastern and aggressive and populous neighbors. Humans eating humans fit the "savage slot" and the colonial headlines on the Aussie doorstep down under. The same was even more true of its opposite icon: the dashing patrol officer who singlehandedly brings peace and order to the last dark savages. I do not scold their accomplishments but merely put them in context. Like their many "police boy" Papuan men from other parts of the colony, these young soldiers braved heat and malaria and undersupply and loneliness. Piled on top of that was stress from ignorance, uncertainty, suspicion, and fear of attack in a place more than foreign. But all this begged the higher mandate of white rule: to always show confidence, to always lead decisively, and to never show weakness or doubt, especially with the so-called natives.

To local people, these strange creatures with big hats were, as Edward Schieffelin put it for an earlier patrol, "like people you see in a dream."[1] For both sides, however, the dream quickly got real. After the Nomad post and the airstrip were set up in 1962–63, saturation patrolling of the Bedamini began. It was not an easy operation. The Bedamini stayed resistant, hard to get to, and, as a group, "one of the most arrogant ever encountered." Over a ten-year effort, Australian officers spent over 2,000 patrol days among them and announced that the Bedamini had been pacified.

The effect on the neighboring Gebusi was wonderful. Gebusi in eastern border settlements had always been fodder for Bedamini raids. Even to the west, where I worked, Gebusi had sometimes experienced a long-distance raid when other Gebusi let attackers cross their land. In 1982, Gebusi remained nervous and deferential with Bedamini, alternately fearful and subordinate on those few occasions when they encountered them. This same Gebusi attitude applied to patrol officers, and it not hard to see why. The Australians had not only supplanted the Bedamini as the military force, their power had shriveled the threat of enemy attacks. These new overlords could be bossy; they demanded respect and fostered fear. But they hadn't come to intimidate Gebusi and seldom even came in direct contact with them.

Compared to Bedamini, Gebusi became "quiet tractable people who have seldom given the Administration any difficulty" (Barclay 1970–71: un-paginated). Even the earliest explorers had found them "most friendly," as opposed to their hostile neighbors. As a result, Australian officers spent only 151 patrol days among Gebusi and their western neighbors during the same ten years that the Bedamini were so massively "pacified." During the thir-teen years of colonial presence, from 1962 to 1975, Gebusi received just one patrol per year on average—the annual census patrol that spent a single night in just the larger villages. Its main goal was to count enough people to report some progress in sizing the local population. The resulting en-counters come up as "friendly" and "cooperative" in patrol reports, includ-ing one rare case in which the patrol stumbled upon a Gebusi sorcerer tied up for execution and arrested the would-be attackers.

Gebusi accommodation did, however, bring an economic downside: they never got nearly as much Australian attention as they would have liked. Australian officers had all manner of miraculous and wonderful things, from axes and matches to soap and salt and clothing, not to men-tion the rifles they could shoot and the airplanes they could fly. Like the mouse that roared, however, Bedamini got the benefits as well as the boot of colonial intervention. At first, almost all the good things of Western design flowed like the patrols to Bedamini and by-passed Gebusi. Patrol Officer R. E. Randolf described the result in his area study report for 1973:

> The Gebusi receive far less attention from the Administration and re-main politically, socially and economically deprived, while the Biami [Be-damini] are in receipt of constant Administration attention, rural develop-ment grants, mission services and the full time services of a great proportion of the Nomad Staff. The Gebusi are certainly nowhere as aggres-sive as the Biami, but that apart, the Biami have had far more publicity, more attention, and are more politically aware as a result.

Along with lack of political awareness came relative autonomy, and Gebusi made much of it. In fitting incongruity, Gebusi continued not only their spirit séances, dances, and initiations but also their sorcery inquests and divinations and executions. As massed violence, Bedamini warfare had attracted a surfeit of colonial force, but it also diverted attention from a higher rate of continuing homicide among Gebusi. The strong warriors who resisted the government were patrolled while their weaker neighbors were left to kill on their own. Gebusi killings came in ones and twos with the consensus of most in the community. As mentioned before, these execu-tions were relatively easy to conceal from the government. Fear of the Australians did slacken the murder rate somewhat; it also led Gebusi to target more women as sorcerers and kill them deeper in the bush.[2]

From a practical point of view, the patrol officer—or "*kiap*," as he was known—was a benign if ignorant despot. Policeman, judge, and jury rolled into one, he could berate, detain, or jail offenders at will. It is said (but never in official records) that he could also hit people or have them beaten up. He was supposed to follow rules, and usually did, and this helped those around him follow his game. But at least as importantly, he kept the airstrip and the radio maintained and received the occasional planeload of trade goods, supplies, and medicine. These provisions were paltry by his standards but incredible to those around him. He hired carriers and laborers and paid them, moved around a lot, cleared paths, bridged a few rivers, and constructed the stub of a road—all on a shoestring budget. He made things happen. Through payments and gifts and trickle-downs, a smattering of goods reached local people. By 1971, officer Fitzpatrick noted that about half the people had some Western clothing, which they wore whenever they could in the kiap's presence: "Generally speaking every household also boasts an axe with possibly metal plates, mugs, spoons, and the odd billy can." (Fitzpatrick 1970–71:10).

The right arm of the kiap—both arms, really—were the native police or constables.[3] Recruited from coastal and long-contacted parts of the colony, they tended to be smart, tough, well trained, and shrewd in knowing the latitude and the limits of their white boss. The color bar was very thick: more rigid in New Guinea than in Asian or Latin American colonies, and probably similar to that in South Africa. But with a good dose of police training, lots of practical experience, and the pride of being civilized, the constables shared as much or more background with the kiap as they did with the local people, whose languages and specific customs were different from their own. Stuck in limbo between a desired world they could never attain and a local one they didn't desire, the Papuan constables harbored the classic and conflicted psychology of the postcolony before its inception. But it didn't take long for their own time to come. By the end of 1975, independence had arrived and the patrol officers were leaving. At Nomad, they had reigned just thirteen years.

Remotely Postcolonial

With the Australians gone, the Nomad airstrip and its post remained, along with its aura. New officers-in-charge came to fill the void, Papua New

Guineans with some education and often with prior experience as constables. Their style was different, their steps less sure, their literacy deficient, but they had a better understanding of local community issues and problems than their white predecessors.

In short order, the infrastructure of the new country both expanded and deteriorated, especially at bush stations such as Nomad. Supported by generous grants-in-aid from Australia and more recently by a trickle of royalties from the Ok Tedi mine 125 miles to the northwest, government services ostensibly expanded. By 1998, the Nomad Subdistrict Station harbored a health clinic, a community school with three buildings and a water tank, a government office house, a separate building for elected local officials, a long metal storage shed for equipment, and a power house with a diesel-run generator that was, as in the colonial days, still supposed to provide electricity for three or four hours a night to the rows of Australian-built houses. With no roads or vehicles, every stick of everything is still flown in to Nomad—at inflated prices. Added to this are the wages, transport, lodging, and supplies required for any trained workman or official who does a job at Nomad. If supplies are missing or forgotten, the workman waits and collects pay in the interim. It cost K 14,000 (about U.S.$7,000) to reconnect a house to the wire that leads to the Nomad generator.

Official functions have both proliferated and been decentralized. In 1998, the Nomad government roster had four teachers, nine aid post workers, one executive government liaison officer, one paid local government president, one full-time and one part-time bookkeeper, two cash office managers, one postal clerk, two radio operators, one full-time and one part-time department of primary industries officers, and various other local aides. To these were added the constable, the senior constable, and the man who used to be called the kiap or OIC (Officer-in-Charge) but whose position had since become the "Acting Subdistrict Area Affairs Manager."

The whole scheme of local government, finance, management and mismanagement has become so complex and interesting that it really merits a book of its own. Not that the existing system of governance needs any more scattered papers or forms or reports piled and written but rarely read and sometimes never sent but kept in cockroach-eaten stacks that signify most of all the fact of their production rather than their content. Even at Nomad, budgetary machinations pretend to engage hundreds of thousands of kina per year. But amid financial convolutions, requests, denials, delays, shortfalls, and freezes, there is precious little actual receipt of government funds. All dealings must be in cash, in piles of small bills and coins. All monies must be obtained in person in Kiunga, which means paying round-trip airfare, flying to town, waiting for official permissions and signatures, staying at the town's one hotel (at K 190 = U.S$95 per night), waiting at the bank, and personally bringing back bags of cash in appropriately small denominations. Added to this are social and transportation delays and the incidentals and amenities that are important for the Nomad officer who has temporarily escaped from his bush station to enjoy a paid trip to town. Due to its record of financial improprieties, the Western Province now requires completion of thirteen official steps, signatures, forms, and so forth, before a check for government expenses can be obtained and cashed.[4] This all transpires *after* the budgetary allocation has finally been authorized and funds actually located in accounts, both of which are also byzantine processes.

Like so many other structures and functions, those of the police and the old kiap are now subdivided and kept in separate spheres. The area affairs manager at Nomad—a hard-working and paper-ridden Christian man from Popondetta—receives what he can of the promised but seldom forthcoming government allocations. He is responsible in a diffuse way for the well-being and operation of the station as a whole, but he has few funds to dispense and no authority to enforce compliance, much less to charge or punish offenders.

Police have the right to arrest and detain criminals, but only if there is clear and legally valid evidence of a crime that breaks a specific national law. As government employees, police cannot legally intervene in locally defined problems but only in those that break a national law, such as stealing or murder. Offenders can be brought to trial, but only if evidence is collected, unforced confessions gained, testimonies taken, and records of interviews and antecedent reports written up on appropriate forms and properly signed and submitted. The police have no right to judge, so they must wait for the visiting magistrate (something like a circuit judge) to fly to Nomad. Problems pile up on this system so quickly that it is best if we step back and consider what actually happens at the Nomad police office on a typical day. At first blush, this seems close to nothing.

Station at the Center

The Nomad government office is an unimposing whitewashed building the size and shape of a small-to-medium-sized suburban house. Shabby by our standards, it remains the most modern and important building for miles in all directions. You climb the half-dozen steps to the open porch-corridor that consumes a third of the house's space, snapping the fingers of the men along the way. On weekdays younger and senior village men hang out in small groups and talk in the polyglot of five major languages plus pidgin and Motu that make up the casual welter of Nomad's language environment. Often they just sit or stand or smoke or do nothing. For the unemployed, time is not a precious commodity, and at least the porch is shaded. The villagers' presence is fine with the government employees. Officials occasionally emerge from offices to chat or to talk to an elected ward councillor or someone else. They blend in with not much more formality or clothing than those around them—with the exception of their hard-soled shoes and the fact that their shirts and shorts are unmarred by stains or tears. The scene is a far and welcome cry from the command authority of the Australian kiaps.

Of the seven rooms in the government station, the biggest is for the police. If the door is closed you are out of luck and might as well gaze at the tattered board of official memos for the umpteenth time, since it hasn't changed, or just sit with the men and decide what to do. Informal rule number one is that a functionary takes his office key when he leaves and nothing at all can take place concerning his duties in his absence. When the postal clerk is absent from Nomad—which is much more than half the time—no regular mail goes in or out from the station, though he continues to receive a regular wage. When the cash office manager is gone or has lost the key or there is no money received, the cash office is closed. (I was never able to change money or buy stamps at Nomad during my stay.)

The two constables are also gone some of the time, but less than most of the others. Mr. Haga twisted a knee while playing rugby at the station and needed medical attention in Kiunga. Between that and other business and delays, he was gone about two and half months of my own six, plus a couple of other shorter departures. The senior constable, my good friend Mr. Gobi, was more dependably in, except for departures such as his monthlong refresher course in police procedures and constitutional law, which he was honored to take north of Kiunga at the mining town of Tabubil. When both men were gone, there was no police presence or legal authority in the Nomad Subdistrict. But Nomad has been lucky, since many of the yet smaller outstations have no police; the positions stay vacant and there may be no government presence for years at a time. Mr. Gobi and Mr. Haga are from the Pare region just across the Strickland River; they know the Nomad area and have relatives in the region.

This pattern is common in Papua New Guinea: the few from rural areas who get educated and gain employment as literate workers in a major city or town often end up returning to a government station or town in their natal area. At Nomad, most of the government workers come from one or another part of the Western Province, though not from Nomad specifically. Their government travel helps keep them in touch with kinfolk elsewhere in the province and makes it tolerable for them to have their official job at a place as remote as Nomad. In the country as a whole, this pattern reinforces itself. Those rural areas that provide literacy and training for their schoolchildren sport a few who go to provincial high school and eventually get national training. These people come back for visits and eventually—after years of gaining experience in bigger places—to run things locally in one or another official capacity. As such, they form a small but important homegrown middle class that connects the local area to the bureaucracy and politics of the rest of the country.

At Nomad and many other outstations, however, attracting officials is an uphill battle. No Gebusi from Gasumi Corners has ever enrolled at Kiunga High School and none seems destined for this opportunity in the foreseeable future.[5] Small outstations have few local people to come back and little to attract educated workers or officials from elsewhere. In the absence of kin or personal connections, why would anyone want to work at an isolated and undersupplied station such as Nomad? And yet, stations like Nomad constitute the bulk of government outposts in Papua New Guinea.

Of Constables and Crimes

In 1998, the Nomad constables had a palpable sense of duty toward their jobs. Police in Papua New Guinea have a proud tradition that stems from the colonial past of the Royal Papuan Constabulary Service (Kituai 1998). All uniformed police officers in Papua New Guinea are trained at the national police academy in Port Moresby. They are paid regular wages directly by the national government, which bypasses provincial vagaries and chronic delays and budgetary freezes.

Almost every day that he was at the station, Senior Constable Gobi would enter the police office by 8 A.M. or very shortly thereafter, stay until noon, break for lunch, and then return until 4 P.M. In an official world where little can be depended on, and with little reinforcement, this dependable presence should not be minimized.

The daily register of the Nomad Occurrence Book typically appears as follows:

ON DUTY
241/98 [day #241 of 1998]
24/6/98 [June 6, 1998]
RPSC S/C [Royal Papuan Senior Constable] GOBI is now signing on duty at 0800
  hrs. The situation reported all quiet for the working hours.
    For your Information Only

OFF DUTY
400 PM 29/6/98 S/C Gobi is now signing off duty at 400 PM. The situation
  reported all quiet as normal.
    For your Information Only

The Occurrence Book is the official log of all police activity, complaints reported, and actions taken. On most days, nothing much is recorded. I hung out many mornings in the police office, copying records and kibitzing. The twenty-by-twelve foot sawn-timber room has a paint-splotched work table, two old desks, a couple of rude benches, an office chair with crumbled foam flaking like ancient Swiss cheese, a tall bookshelf that lists from haphazardly stuffed papers and old report books, and a desk-bound forty-pound Underwood typewriter with no top, a broken "e," and a ribbon that Mr. Gobi rewinds by hand as he painfully produces a typed report or correspondence. On one of the desks stands the two-way police radio to Kiunga, which actually works and is a prized and guarded possession, used *only* by police. Mr. Haga is less commonly present but he can be seen if not talking on the radio then reading a magazine or sometimes a law book. People occasionally float in and out to chat, and the constables may get tired of fidgeting and go out to the porch and strike up pass-the-time conversations with those who are glad to oblige. On the surface, whole strings of days go by with nothing official happening. The Occurrence Book echoes this lax rhythm with paired entries of "On Duty" and "Off Duty" and little else in between.

Occasionally, of course, an offense is reported. Someone walks in with a grievance to tell, an accusation to make, a problem to spin out. Mr. Gobi is all ears and the tone is casual and conversational in both directions. He gives advice and explains what he can and can't do, what the options are. He takes notes and listens and responds for as long as it takes—that is his job. Then he unfailingly writes up a summary of the issue in the Occurrence Book in the standard nonstandard English that is the language of government in most of the rural country.

The Occurrence Book is rigorously kept. Indeed, it is the official record that the police are doing their job. A prominent right column is left blank for an agent of the police superintendent, at some distant time, to visit Nomad and check-mark and initial every page of the book. These marks are the official recognition that the constables have been at work and doing their jobs.

Though seemingly infrequent, substantive entries dot the Occurrence Book like occasional dandelions on the government lawn. Given that the book is systematic and well kept, I decided to tabulate all entries over the previous five years—from November 4, 1993 through November 3, 1998. These incidents radiate out in all directions from Nomad, including disputes right at the station as well as reported crimes and incidents among the roughly nine thousand people of the Nomad Subdistrict.[6] Gebusi offenses and complaints are but a fraction of the total, though many patterns, including those concerning sorcery, are roughly similar throughout the Nomad area.

The 282 occurrence entries during the five-year period reveal broad information and some amazing cases. Full descriptions were courtesy of Mr. Gobi, who, being such a pleasant man with so little to do, gladly told me information many times longer than the cryptic entries themselves. I grew to like him quite a bit. A short, balding, and trim gentleman with twenty-three years of police service, seven children, and an affable smile, Mr. Gobi was a rural intellectual, a social analyst and critic, afficionado of police work and its limitations, relentlessly honest, completely unpretentious (with others as well as me), soft-spoken, often wise, highly knowledgeable about local disputes, compassionate about human failings, and genuinely concerned about the Nomad community. He was ever willing to talk, including with someone like me who he felt could understand the fine points of his job and the bureaucratic and logistical impediments under which he labored. Mr. Gobi had been the senior constable at Nomad for several years and had written most of the book's entries over this period. As if I needed further encouragement, he not only allowed but encouraged me to plop down at one of the vacant desks, take out my tiny Libretto computer (which visitors loved to observe), transcribe whatever I wanted from his books, and pick his brain about any cases that struck my fancy. I was also allowed to stay for police interviews and complaints that came up while I was in the office, including one brought by my friends from Gasumi Corners. The vast bulk of the time, however, it was just the two of us.

His English was better than my *tok pisin*, but neither of us was entirely fluent in the other. So we conversed in a mixture of both, depending on the topic and vocabulary. We spoke that distinct genre of speech, style, vocabulary, and intonation that I call "Papua New Guinea English." It braids together pidgin and English and has about the same relation to Webster's lexicon as black ghetto speech does to Peter Jennings. Speaking pure English, on the other hand, made me feel like I was trying out for a job as a dictionary. Though the alternative wasn't pretty or crisp, it got the job done, like most multi-tongues. As needed, we would slide registers back and forth between purer *tok pisin* and purer English, to reiterate and double check our meanings. The result, to speak professionally, is that I have fair confidence in my "police data" for the Nomad Station. This is noteworthy, since accurate information about grassroots police work in most developing countries is sparse and typically unreliable.

The first thing to be said, empirically, is that the 282 complaints and incidents over the five-year period average out to one occurrence every 6.48 days. During the typical week, then, the Nomad police have one complaint or incident to write up or deal with during part of one day, while they have none during the other four working days.

Among the complaints or occurrences or crimes that are reported to the Nomad police (or that they otherwise become aware of) the top seven, which account for three-quarters of the total, are as follows:

Stealing	23.8%	$N = 67$
Threatening words/behavior	13.1%	$N = 37$
Assault	10.6%	$N = 30$
Illicit Sex/Adultery	9.9%	$N = 28$
Sorcery	6.4%	$N = 18$
Fighting	5.7%	$N = 16$
Willful Damage to Property	5.0%	$N = 14$

To these are added other less frequent offenses, including several cases of homicide.[7] The types and extent of these complaints and "crimes" are highly variable, as is the degree of police action. We can start at the top of the list by considering a representative sample of the most common Occurrence Book entries, working from the more frequent to the less frequent varieties. (Some readers may prefer to read these initial entries selectively and proceed with the discussion of them further below.)

25/2/98 BREAK ENTER AND STEALING
The Break and Enter and Stealing was at Jonah Wigibi's residence. The goods stolen were not known. The suspects were not known, and also the stolen

goods. Police are waiting for the owner of the house to give full details of the
stolen items.

For Your Information Only

22/9/98 THREATENING WORDS

Complainant Mr. Uruba-Dohi reported that he was threatened by his brother. His
    brother was angry because the complainant goes around with his wife.
    For Your Information Only.

10/4/98 ASSAULT

Complainant or Informate of Assault Mr. OMU GAG of Benedina village reported
    that the suspect was the complainant husband. The defendant Mr. Nekuwe hit
    his wife with stick and bush knife. The women was admitted to the hospital
    at Debeperi Aid Post. The serious or condition was not available. The matter
    is still pending.
    For Your Information Only.

19/8/98 SEXUAL OFFENCE

Complainant Mr. Tulo Yima reported that his wife's brother the suspect had
    sexual intercourse with his daughter namely Miss Ronna Tulo. While the
    suspect had sexual intercourse with his daughter, her mother went after her
    daughter and she found her daughter Ronna and Jonah were having sexual
    intercourse. They saw her and ran away without clothes. Police advised
    complainant to wait for the defendant before we'll investigate the matter.

14/4/98 SORCERY

Complainant Mr. Solemon TOBI reported that his brother got sick and he blamed
    Mrs. Gyasimi Nanei and Mr. Daniel Saina used magical power to make his
    brother sick. The woman admitted that she used magical power and she get
    sick hold dirty clothes and she used magical power to get man sick. The
    council brought the leader of magical power and she admitted. Police advised
    Council to bring Mr. Daniel to Police for more investigation.
    For Your Information Only
[In the left column, in red ink, is a subsequent addition: No Police action. No
    Proof of Offense.]

28/10/98 FIGHTING

Fighting during the Youth Show between Samo and Biami. It was started when
    Mr. Toropa Duya ran without good reasons. The people worked hard for road

project and they did not get pay. They saw that the Project officer is running away, so they got angry and fight break out.
For Your Information Only.

28/10/98 WILFUL DAMAGE
Complaint Mr. Howadiai Sagili of Soyu village, Nomad subdistrict reported 12 coconut trees, yam suckers and one pig was killed by the suspect namely OLI of the same village. The suspect got married to two wives and of second, went to her father. The complainant got angry and destroy. Police are still investigating.
For Your Information Only.

Like lead-ins to larger stories, these snippets provide points of entry to elaborate social and dispute histories, many of which are known by Mr. Gobi. Even as bare-bones records, however, these entries index a key point of transition: from a verbal dispute to a formally written record of complaint. With this comes official recognition of the dispute, crime, or accusation, and public knowledge that the occurrence is now a matter of government record. In the process, local delicts become legible to the state (Scott 1998). They also provide the basis for future official action.

On the surface, it might seem that there is plenty to keep the Nomad police busy. Even if only one "occurrence" comes in during the typical week, the average month sees: one case of stealing; one case of either assault or threatening words/behavior; one case of either illicit sex, sorcery, or damage to property; one case of fighting, firearm violation, murder, trespass, or insult; and a fractional case of a more unusual complaint or offense.

In most cases, however, including the most severe, official action remains minimal or nil. Only three of the twelve reported murders and infanticides (some from sorcery) ever came to trial. Why? This situation is supremely frustrating to Mr. Gobi. Perhaps the best way to understand this disjunction is to trace the course of investigation that the constables confront.

The Path of Prosecution

The first problem is the difficulty of travel and fact-finding. The constables see themselves as largely unable to leave the Nomad Station to investigate complaints. There are no motor vehicles at Nomad, and even if there were, the station is cut off by three unbridged rivers that curtail easy access beyond a kilometer or two in any direction.[8] The colonial "patrol in the bush" is dead. The so-called government rest houses—which the Australian kiaps had built in each major settlement—have fallen down and have not been replaced. The police have no tents or camping supplies, and even if they were to hike and sleep with resident families in villages, they would feel it incumbent to pay for food or otherwise reciprocate. They have no funds for this.[9] And they are not accustomed to the social awkwardness and physical discomfort that such an arrangement would entail—perhaps any more than our own policemen would if we told them to ask a random household to put them up for the night.

Police are not paid much to begin with. According to the official pay scale listed in the 1998 Papua New Guinea Police Gazette, constables receive between K 5,534 and K 7,494. In 1998, these amounts averaged a yearly salary of U.S.$3,250. In 1999 and 2000, plunging currency rates reduced this amount to about U.S.$1,950. Most of the goods bought with money depend on international manufacturing and transport; as the exchange rate falls, prices go up. One short trip to buy supplies in Kiunga costs K 200 for round-trip airfare plus elevated air freight charges for each kilogram of cargo, in addition to the high price of the goods themselves.

As a result, the police at Nomad are largely confined to the government station. When a serious complaint arises, they request that the defendants and witnesses come to the Nomad Station to provide statements. But they have little way to enforce these requests, much less apprehend suspects hiding in the bush. As stated in the "Transportation" section of the Nomad Annual Police Report for 1994 [spelling unaltered]:

> Most complains are received at the duty office [Nomad police office] by the complainants or victim and village committees/councillors. In most cases the suspects could not be brought to the Station or refuse to come, and as a result those reported complaints are left pending or unattended to and sometimes forgotten. This makes the work very difficult for Police and could not perform duties effectively. This Station requires 1 × river transport of Outboard Motor with Dinghy attached. 1 × land transport should also be considered later when the road system is improved or maintained. To cater for all these, above requirement should be considered seriously.

Those Who May Have Seen: Sorcery on Trial

Witnesses are the next hurdle. Even when individuals are persuaded to come to the police office at Nomad, they may be unwilling or too scared

to testify—or they may lie. A publicly witnessed crime can easily go unpros-
ecuted, just as in our own cities, when no one is willing to provide names
and eyewitness testimony. Interviews must be written up—a laborious process for police given their writing skills, the task of getting vernacular statements translated into pidgin, and the difficulty of conceptualizing and
spelling everything in formal English. Physical evidence is not easily produced. Even in cases of suspicious death, police rarely see the body.

Given Mr. Gobi's knowledge and contacts, he typically knows what
happened, but he can't prove it legally. The following case is exemplary:

> 26-4-94 Report of Wilful Murder at Hafimi village
> The informant, namely Cr. Fofowa Oroma Ward 8 Biami census division Nomad
>   reported to police that the deceased namely Baruba Pema of Hafimi village
>   was allegedly murdered on 20/4/94 at about 4pm in the bush. His body was
>   found on 21/4/94 at about 5pm, took the body to the village and buried on
>   next day, 22/4/94. Suspect is not know at this moment, however, there are
>   some leading information to this case from these listed witnesses follows: [four
>   persons listed, all of Hafimi].
>   [Red-ink note in margin]: No information was given to police to follow up.
>   Police attended but no one give information of deceased death who killed him.

The follow-up statement, three weeks later, reads as follows:

> 18/5/94 Wilful murder Hafimi.
> In reference to the above, two suspects namely Burula Kosai and Labo Omabo
>   and witnesses brought to the station for questioning. However, when
>   questioned by police, suspects denied into the murder of the deceased, Baruba
>   Apema. As a result, police could not proceed further investigation to this cases
>   due to no proper witnesses or eye witnesses. Investigation unsuccessful both
>   parties complainant and suspects sent home. This matter now ends here.
>   Situation quiet.

Mr. Gobi's verbal account, rendered in my own English, runs as follows:

> Back in 1994, Baruba, a senior man of Hafimi [Bedamini], was executed
> as a sorcerer. He had been Mamus [i.e., village liaison to the Australian ad-
> ministration] and had been a government interpreter and fight leader dur-
> ing the 1960s and '70s. But the Mamus position was given up when the
> Australians left, and he became just an older man living with no authority.
> So he was resentful. He was accused of killing a young unmarried man in

Hafimi through sorcery. At the funeral feast for the young man, the suspect's family went to collect firewood, but they went off and left him to come back by a different way [that is, they made sure Baruba would be unaccompanied when he was attacked]. Baruba came back alone and was confronted by people of his community, who killed him and cut up his body. They left the pieces on the trail. The next day, Baruba's close family went out and found the parts of his body.

The matter was brought to police. But no one would admit to the killing and no witnesses or real evidence could be found. So the case couldn't be prosecuted and was dropped. This is what happens when sorcery cases don't end in conviction. People say that courts will not convict people of sorcery, even when they admit it. And they see that standards of evidence and witnesses favor those who take revenge against the suspect by just going ahead and murdering him or her.

This case is as forthright as it is dramatic. There is no attempt to cover up the killing of a major figure in the village—his body is dismembered and left for close relatives to discover. But everyone denies being one of the killers and no eyewitnesses are willing to testify. So the death is recorded as an unsolved murder. Mr. Gobi is keenly aware of this problem. His upset, however, is distinctive: he fully believes in cases of sorcery but believes they should be prosecuted so the sorcerer can be punished and put in jail. This would be just retribution for the sickness-death and also help satisfy the villagers' demand for vengeance. It would also encourage local people not to take matters into their own hands or execute the suspect, which he definitely thinks is wrong.

Mr. Gobi's reasoning has a strangely compelling logic. Its hybrid blend of modern and traditional would reduce the rate of murder and protect the suspect even while it punishes him or her. This is just what happened in Gasumi Corners when the Nomad police jailed the six sorcery suspects back in 1987, as described in chapter 3.

But the Faustian bargain, as we might see it, contains another consequence—that police tolerate the beating of sorcery suspects. Although sorcery suspects are no longer beaten up by the Nomad police (which national officers freely admitted to back in 1982), there is still a presumption of guilt and allowance for local inquisitions against those accused of sorcery. This is evident in Mr. Gobi's ambivalent acceptance rather than outrage at the kicking to death of his own clan-brother for sorcery, in a remote settlement across the Strickland River, at the close of 1997.

More uncertain cases emerge as police are told about and investigate violence against a sorcery suspect before he or she is actually killed. Nomad police do warn villagers that they will be considered murderers if they execute a sorcery suspect. However, they are hamstrung by the technicalities of prosecuting attackers as well as by their informal sense that the sorcerer deserves some degree of punishment. The police chafe at their inability to conduct this punishment "fairly," that is, through the trial and imprisonment of the sorcerer.

In some cases, Mr. Gobi is quite convinced of the sorcerer's guilt but is stymied by the legal and logistical bureaucracy. In one dramatic case, a Bedamini assault sorcerer who had already confessed described to Mr. Gobi how he had sliced up the victim's flesh, eaten the meat, and then put ants, which he had put under a spell, on the body to heal the wounds and make the victim appear whole—whereupon the victim returned to his village and died. Convinced of the man's guilt, Mr. Gobi pursued the case through legal action:

> Since he killed this man and admitted it, I wrote up the case and we took the suspect and went for trial in Kiunga. At the trial, he again admitted all that he had done, as written up in his statement. But his lawyer was a new man from Port Moresby that knew all about law. He asked where the independent witnesses of the crime were, and there were none. He asked where the physical evidence was: "Where are the stones that the man's thighs were cooked with?' "Where are the leaves they were wrapped in?" And there was no evidence. So the magistrate became a supporter of the lawyer and the case was dismissed.
>
> We came back to Nomad and the sorcerer was set free. His people were angry because the sorcerer had won the case, and they came and got angry at me. I told them that our country is not communist but a democracy, and that the accused had rights. I said that even though he was guilty and we all knew it, the court still protects his rights. Sorcery is very difficult to prove, so he was set free.
>
> [BK] Were you upset that all the work you did to take this case to Kiunga went for nothing, that he was set free?
>
> Yes, I was really upset. All that work for nothing. It shows how hard and frustrating it is to prosecute sorcery. [. . .] People are relying more on sorcery so they won't have to go to jail, because killing by sorcery is so much harder to prove than outright murder. They know that if they kill the person outright, they may go to prison. But if they kill through sorcery, even if

they admit it, they probably will go free. So this is hard because people are killing more through sorcery. If we handle these cases at the local level, traditional custom can be followed and some action taken, but if they are formally prosecuted, they may get thrown out.

Mr. Gobi's reasoning is quite to the point. In one case, admitted sorcerers were acquitted by the government, so the next time around, villagers went ahead and murdered the suspect themselves. To Mr. Gobi, this is the worst result of all. He believes in sorcery, but also believes that murdering the sorcerer is quite wrong. Sorcerers should be prosecuted and deterred from sending sickness, but through proper means and without recourse to violence. Local vengeance only results in further killing and disrespect for the law.

As a nod to social science, we can note that despite and perhaps in some ways because of the lack of prosecution, Mr. Gobi is remarkably well informed about the details of sorcery cases in the Nomad area; people see little need to keep information from him since he is so unusually scrupulous about distinguishing legally admissible evidence from informal accounts. His understanding is further increased by his temperament as an interested, compassionate, and impartial party.

In Case of Confession

As I listened to Mr. Gobi, I was sympathetic to his plight. He was the cop who can't put the offender behind bars. Practicing sorcery remains a legally punishable offense in Papua New Guinea. The sorcerer on the loose, ready to strike again, is a real criminal. Then I thought about the sorcerers' supposed confession, and the fact that killing a person by slicing up his thighs and then sewing the skin back together with ants is, well, impossible. Mr. Gobi's accounts were so realistic that I had to pinch myself to remember that they were based on confessions obtained under duress if not under torture in the village and then readmitted to Mr. Gobi at the police office with witnesses present. Under such conditions, it is hard to know how much the victim may internalize or embrace the stigma projected onto him.

Admission to impossible acts of sorcery emerges dramatically in a case brought to my attention by Detective Willie Mio at the Kiunga Police Station. Mr. Gobi had kindly referred me to Detective Mio since all the paperwork at Nomad concerning witness statements, evidence, and trials is sent to Kiunga—with no copies saved. Mr. Mio explained to me that even at Kiunga, records are kept for only a few years and then burned; there is no place to keep them and no regular filing system. He was most cooperative, however, and rummaged through jumbled stacks until he found three cases from the Nomad area. One was the kicking death of Mr. Gobi's clan-brother as a sorcerer, which had been duly reported with no action taken. The second was the sickness-death of a Nomad School teacher's brother, who lived near Kiunga; his demise had been followed by a long and detailed legal investigation of the sorcerer believed responsible. The record of the third and final case exemplifies in remarkable detail a seamless connection between legal scrupulousness and empirical impossibility.

> Court File, Kiunga Police Station. Prosecutor Sgt. Kim. CID section, Investigator
> Sgt. Mio, Crime report NO. 32/95 Charge book no: 381/1995

> **The Police vs. Hahowai Mosimosia**
> Papua New Guinea District Courts Acts Chapter 40. The information of Willy
> Mio of Police station Kiunga in Papua New Guinea, a Sergeant of Police, laid
> this 22nd day of November, 1995, before the undersigned, a Magistrate of
> a District who (upon Oath) says that between the 16th and 25th of June
> 1995, at Togohai Village, Nomad, Western Province in Papua New Guinea,
> Hahowai Mosimisia, 40 years old, of Togohai village, Western Province,
> Nomad Sub-Province "**DID UNLWARFULLY** [sic] **KILLED ANOTHER
> PERSON NAMELY DABAYO MOSIMISIA YOUR SON**" thereby
> contravening Section 219 of the PNG Criminal Code ch. 262 of the PNG
> Revised Law vol. 9.
>   Signed (Magistrate)

> **Statement of fact:**
> Police alleged that on 16th of June 1995 between 6am and 6pm, at Togohai
> village in the Suabi area of Nomad, Western Province, the defendant now
> before the court namely Hahowai Mosimosia was with his deceased son
> Dabayo Mosimosia at their old garden collecting banana suckers for their new
> garden.
> While there the defendant knocked his deceased son unconscious with a stick over
> the shoulder, the deceased fell unconscious on his side and the defendant cut
> out a piece of flesh from the deceased's right bicep. The defendant who is noted
> for his sorcery woke the deceased after healing the wound with his sorcery.
> After this the defendant went home with the deceased and the defendant roasted
> the flesh which he had removed from the deceased arm and ate part of it and
> threw part of it away. The deceased fell ill straight after this and remained in

the house until the 25th of June 1995. While the deceased was sleeping in the house near the fire place the defendant took an axe and hit the deceased with the back of the axe on the right side of his head near the ear, causing the deceased to fall unconscious the defendant again using his sorcery power to wake up the deceased.

The deceased's condition then worsened soon after this and died two days later on the 27th of June 1995. The deceased was buried on the 29th of June, 1995.

The defendant who was known for his sorcery was then interviewed for his son's death by the village elders and was referred to the Police regarding his son's death and was conveyed to Kiunga.

When interviewed to by Police the defendant willingly and knowingly admitted causing his son's death by sorcery and was formally arrested, cautioned, charged, told of his rights under section 42 (2) of the PNG Constitution Act and was placed in the cells for this alleged matter.

Signed

District Sergeant W. Mio

Interview record of Mark Sai Jiarobi:

The pastor went to Togohu village to conduct funeral service before the burial but he discovered that the deceased did not die of illness but was murdered because his bones were broken. [Note: if the corpse's joints seem loose or "disjointed" prior to burial, this is taken as a sign that they were magically broken prior to death by an assault sorcerer.] When Pastor refused to conduct funeral service, I told all the village people that we have to find out [who the sorcerer is].

We questioned everyone individually regarding the incident. We then questioned the old man Hahowai, who is the deceased's father. He told us all his story but some how towards the end of the story, he got confused and did not know what to say so he straight away admitted everything. He admitted to us that he murdered his own son on the 16th Friday of June 1995, when two of them went to plant banana suckers in the new garden. He used a stick to kill him, cut and removed all the meat in the body and woke him or made his son alive again, then they came to the village. He also admitted to us that his son's fresh meat that he brought to the village, he cooked them on the fire and ate them. We did not force or threaten him but we were questioning him and he admitted to us freely and willingly because he was really sorry for his son Dabauo (deceased).

We told him to show us the scene or place where he killed his son. So he took us to the scene of crime and showed us that place. I really saw the blood stains [dark marks] on the ground and dead leaves [in which the human flesh was *allegedly cooked]. I also saw the footstep marks and place where he [the deceased] struggled when his father hit him on the head with the strong stick. We also saw the same stick lying there so we grabbed hold of it. He also admitted that after one (1) week on 25th of June, he murdered him again a second time using axe at the house when he was sick and lying. As a result his son Dabauo died after two (2) days. As far as we know and I can tell is that this is a very clear type of sorcery murder. All the community we know that he is the only sanguma man [assault sorcerer] in our village. That's all I saw and can say.*

Here we can note with proper wonder the fully legal prosecution of sorcery based on magical attack, including ostensibly unforced admissions by the sorcerer that he sliced open the victim, ate out his insides, healed him, and even "murdered him again a second time," using an axe and again healing his skin over the wounds. It is only on examining the body carefully prior to burial that the pastor realizes the underlying "evidence" of the killing, such as loose limbs taken to be "broken" from assault sorcery.

These are the same procedures that have been used to divine sorcery attack among Gebusi. The confession that was forced upon the sorcerer melts away in the resulting account, melding with the old man's grief and perhaps his sense of guilt over his son's untimely death. The place where he and his son stopped in the forest now becomes a murder site, with evidence adduced to confirm the account. The link between local custom and the legal prosecution is sealed by the repetition of evidence and of the old man's confession, first to Mr. Gobi at Nomad and then again in front of the Kiunga magistrate. (How could the old man do otherwise without contradicting his own earlier statements?) In the process, it is not unlikely that he actually embraces the possibility of prison—as opposed to being executed and having his body dismembered back in the village.

Here we easily recall the witch trials of Salem or those recorded so vividly in the medieval legalism of Germany or Italy (Erickson 1966; Kunze 1987; Ginzburg 1980). Alongside these examples, the present case begs a Foucauldian perspective on the postcolonial inscription of legal incitement, official categorization, and state punishment for witchcraft as an impossible crime (see Foucault 1979).

As if to bring irony full circle, however, the present case concludes with the fact that despite all the evidence against him, Hahowai never served a prison sentence. The magistrate never reached a formal verdict because Hahowai couldn't pay for his food as a prisoner at Kiunga and the jails were full in any event. He also had a bad cough, and there was concern

that would die in prison or infect other prisoners, and that his closest relatives would cause trouble or demand compensation if he died in police cus-
tody. So he was paroled instead. Lacking plane fare, Hahowai simply walked
all the way back to Nomad. This is a noteworthy feat, especially for someone
thought to be deathly ill. When he returned to Nomad, Hahowai could not
be put in jail because the local lockup had been shut down by the provincial
public health official. Hahowai was simply told to report back to Nomad
periodically as a condition of his parole, but he has not done so. The case
is still technically pending, but for all practical purposes, it is over. Hahowai
has simply gone back to his village.

Mr. Mio says, "Sorcery cases always end the same. They are based on
circumstantial evidence, and there is no money to pay for them to stay in
jail, so they are released and go home. That is why we need better and
stronger laws against sorcery."

Statutes and Limitations

Sorcery is not the only crime that is difficult to prosecute. Infractions such
as bodily injury, murder, or damage or theft of personal property also require eyewitness testimony and evidence. In addition to these are underlying disputes concerning adultery, divorce, marital compensation (which
Mr. Gobi refers to as "pride price"), and a range of other infringements that
pertain to customary law. None of these latter matters can be officially addressed by the police at Nomad. Unless a national law has been broken,
constables are told that cases involving customary practices should be handled by the "welfare officer" rather than the police. However, the welfare
officers are in Kiunga and can only be contacted by flying there in person
and hoping they are on duty and in their office. Unless the circumstance
is exceptional, this is impossible, especially for those who live in the Nomad
Subdistrict. In contrast to the days of the kiap, when government action
could be strong even if ignorant, there is now a perception, at least at Nomad, that police know what is going on but cannot take action.

In principle, charges can be heard at Nomad by the visiting magistrate. But given the impediments involved, the few entries in the "Charge
Book" are only a tiny fraction of all complaints. Charges require a charge
sheet; a statement of facts; a witness list; witness statements; an exhibit list;
a record of interviews; and an antecedent events form. Each of these items
has its own protocols. Mr. Gobi notes suggest the practical result [spelling
unaltered]:

Why police loses of their cases? In many cases police loses their cases because of incomplete files or part of the file is missing. The court should not be blame for that, becuse it is the police carelessness or negligence.

Police everywhere chafe against the demands of paperwork, legal requisites, and bureaucratic tedium. But given the educational and logistical constraints in a country like Papua New Guinea, especially in outstation areas like Nomad, the demands of such paperwork can easily be staggering. These are accentuated by the difficulty and time it takes to write in formal English, and that old Underwood with the broken "e" and faded ribbon that won't rewind.

Then there is the trial. Though the magistrate travels as a circuit court judge, he appears to have visited Nomad just three times between 1988 and 1998. By the time he arrives, many of the witnesses are away deep in the bush or have had second thoughts about coming to testify before an outsider. Defendants may decide to go into hiding. Even when everyone is present, the magistrate, schooled in law, may decide there are problems with the case or that the evidence is insufficient, that the rights of self-incrimination have been violated, and so forth.

Finally comes the sentencing. If the magistrate does come to Nomad and tries the case and finds the suspect guilty, what next? It is too expensive to fly the person to Kiunga and pay for the offender to be imprisoned there. And there is no jail at Nomad: the local Nomad lockup was shut down in the early 1990s and has not been replaced. Those convicted can be fined, but if they have no money, or claim they don't, there is little that can be done. So they are let go. The following letter was written by Senior Constable Gobi to his superiors in the wake of the visiting magistrate's visit to Nomad in 1995:

Provincial Police Commander; North Fly Command; Kiunga; 25th June, 1995
SUBJECT: CONVICTED PRISONERS
Sir,

I have refered to Senior Magistrate memo on dated 24th April 1995, he had made a good point about certain prisoners convicted and sentenced have never served their terms imprisonment. It is very true that many prisoners were still in the villages enjoying themselves in their villages. I, as a Senior N.C.O. in-charge of this Police station at Nomad-District, I have tried many ways, but it is very difficult, due to financial problems to Transport them to their various places of detention.

Nomad-District Rural lock up building is uncompleted since 1993 and convicted prisoners from 1993 to 1994 are enjoying themselves in the villages. The same suspects are making same problems in the station and villages. The suspects knew that police will not do anything. Police can arrest them and magistrate can hear their cases but they will not go to prisoner. That's why people are not worrying about committing offences.

   [. . .]

(Signed) S/C I. GOBI; Police Detachment; Nomad WP

Locking Up the Jail

The status of the Nomad lockup reveals much about the way government works and the problems of legal enforcement. Shortly after the Nomad jail was closed by health authorities, budgetary requests were made to construct a new one. K 20,000 was allocated, received, and spent, but problems resulted in only the frame and roof of the structure being built. A salary request for two wardens was also made and approved, and the funds were received along with uniforms. However, the Nomad constables cannot fill these duties, since jail wardens now require specialized training different from that received by police. Separate wardens were hired, but since the jail could not be used until it was built, they lived largely in Kiunga and continued to draw their pay while doing no work for about a year. Mr. Gobi ultimately complained about misuse of funds and the wardens' paychecks were finally suspended. In the meantime, another K 10,000 had been allocated to finish building the jail. By mid-1998, seven years after it was begun, the lockup building was finally complete. But the barbed wire fence surrounding the area remains to be constructed, and it has been difficult to get villagers to supply hardwood fence posts for this extensive perimeter. Another concern has also arisen: because the jail has been built on the far side of the Nomad airstrip, it will be hard to attract nationally trained wardens to work there unless housing is built for them on site. This also relates to the likelihood that prisoners would escape at night in the absence of some guard. So in 1998, another K 11,000 was pieced together to begin building a large house next to the jail to accommodate the wardens.

If and when this housing is completed, Mr. Gobi says it will still be unlikely that the lockup can begin operation. Getting professional wardens to stay at Nomad will be difficult, and prisoners will have to be let go when the jail is not staffed. Perhaps the biggest problem, however, is that food will have to be supplied every day to feed the prisoners. These provisions will quickly get expensive. There is no money in the local government budget for this ongoing expense, and spending scarce resources to feed prisoners while law-abiding citizens get no such food is politically infeasible. And with no food, the prisoners must be let go. Until these and other problems are resolved, the seven years during which no offenders have been jailed in the Nomad area will extend indefinitely into the future.

National Failure, Local Success

Given such difficulties, what effect have the police had on crime in the Nomad area, and the rate of murder in particular? Mr. Gobi feels confident that the great majority of homicides in the Nomad Subdistrict come to his attention. At least for Gasumi Corners and the neighboring community of Yehebi, I have been able to verify his assertion that no homicides have either occurred or been reported in these communities during the last ten years.

It could be argued, however, that surreptitious killings still occur in more distant areas and are kept from police awareness. Of the three Gebusi killings that occurred between 1980 and 1990, the two that took place in remote locations were successfully hidden from government awareness, as discussed in chapter 3. What if this previous pattern still persists in some fashion in more remote parts of the Nomad Subdistrict? We can maximize our homicide estimate by taking the 1980s rate of hidden killings among Gebusi and projecting its continuation among every area of the Nomad Subdistrict for all of the 1990s. Since ten killings are known to have occurred in the Nomad Subdistrict over the last ten years, we might project a maximum of twenty additional killings, for a total of thirty. This extrapolates to a homicide rate of 33 per 100,000 annually, which is still quite low for an area that had an extremely high rate of violence until recently.

We are thus left with a curious conclusion: though the Nomad police are hamstrung, though they bring only a fraction of homicides to trial, though killings may still take place and be unreported, the overall level of killing has still dropped precipitously. This decline represents a manyfold decrease from preceding levels of lethal violence, including those documented between 1975 to 1982. Even Bedamini tribal fights, so renowned in the early days of colonialism, seldom generated significant casualties in the 1990s. The last pacified area of Papua New Guinea—with its endemic warfare, sorcery execution, and cannibalism—has become a relatively safe place to live.

Notwithstanding a very few dramatic cases to the contrary, government officers as well as villagers consistently say that the Nomad area is now a calm and peaceful place to reside. By all accounts, this part of Papua New Guinea is far safer than the vast bulk of the nation's towns, cities, and more heavily populated rural areas. Indeed, Nomad has achieved something of a national reputation for peacefulness.[10] Though violence may still occur intermittently in villages, especially those more distant from Nomad, this violence is but a pale reflection of its former intensity.

Why? Answering this question engages other issues, including villagers' emergent sense of how disputes should be dealt with and how these procedures dovetail with their desire to adopt what they see as a more modern style of life. These factors interact with the informal job of the Nomad police on a daily basis—taking complaints, trading information, giving advice, and empathizing with those who have local grievances.

Village Interface

Mr. Gobi and Mr. Haga provide the villages of Nomad a sympathetic and uniformed ear for their complaints. Unlike earlier officials, neither of them uses violence. Even if no action is officially brought, the concerned attention of a national constable can give solace and dignity to the person who feels wronged. The officer explains the options available and gives advice about their likelihood of success. He calmly but firmly tells his interlocutors that it is wrong and backward for local people to take matters into their own hands.

In many cases, the constable discusses the complaint informally with the ward representative for the village in question. The Nomad Subdistrict has twenty-four wards, each of which has it own elected councillor. The councillor can call a local moot (which is hardly formal enough to be called a village court—see Gordon and Meggitt 1985). At this gathering, the aggrieved parties publicly state their cases. Any accused person or bystander is entitled to respond or add information. In my experience, speeches are listened to respectfully, with the assurance that the meeting will continue as long as it takes until everyone is heard. This method of hearing grievances is indigenous to Gebusi and has long been central to the formation of consensus among settlement or community members who come from different clans and are related through a welter of crosscutting marital, maternal, and extended kinship ties. But in contrast to 1980, when decisions were not binding and everyone was free to go his or her own way, the councillor is now ultimately in charge: he ends the moot by rendering a judgment and, when appropriate, assessing a fine or compensation payment. Though the councillor has little means of enforcing his judgments, the sense of his authority as well as the stigma of refusing to settle disputes in a nonviolent way are typically strong enough that parties abide by his decision. Their alternative is to risk contravening the weight of community opinion and also of prompting the opprobrium of the Nomad police.

On some occasions, of course, one or another respondent gets particularly angry—but they try to control their irritation. As has always been true in Gebusi sorcery cases, it is better to be seen as reasonable and judicious rather than hotheaded and vitriolic. And to refuse the collective will is tantamount to ostracizing oneself from the community.

Most moots concern highly local matters, which are adjudicated informally and never come to police attention. But when a village dispute is too intense for local resolution, it is brought to Mr. Gobi's or Mr. Haga's attention. They, in turn, can advise the councillor on ways the case might be informally negotiated or handled. From the cases I have seen and heard about, the Nomad constables work actively with rather than against the councillors. When the ward leader goes back to his community, his advice has the implicit imprimatur of the government and its authority. Finally, an official record of a complaint, written up by police in the Occurrence Book when the matter is brought to their attention, carries the formality of official government recognition, displeasure, and demand for resolution—even if no police action is subsequently taken.

In most cases, then, Mr. Gobi and Mr. Haga do not function as criminal detectives or prosecutors but as legal aid counselors. They counsel in a social and psychological as well as a legal sense of the term. Though they are both Pa speakers and are sometimes accused of bias on behalf of their ethnic group, they tend on the whole to be remarkably respected for impartiality.[11]

When the Guns Are Unlocked

That the Nomad constables seldom take coercive action underscores their actions when they feel that force is justified and unavoidable. Mr. Gobi owns a police shotgun as well as rubber bullets, regular cartridges, and tear-gas canisters that can either be fired from the gun or thrown like a grenade to disperse an unruly crowd. Regulations concerning police use of firearms are strict, and the constables at Nomad follow them carefully. In particular, they cannot shoot ammunition unless someone has already been wounded or slain in armed conflict and the officer judges that counterforce is necessary to forestall further death or injury.

When I discussed the matter with Mr. Gobi in August of 1998, it turned out that the last time he had fired his police shotgun was five years previously, at the time of the 1993 Independence Day celebrations. A large fight had broken out between Bedamini and Kubor. They were shooting arrows and running to get more; general warfare threatened to break out at the Nomad Station. Mr. Gobi fired tear gas from his shotgun to disperse the warriors. Thinking they had the upper hand, Bedamini were enraged at being deterred. Mr. Gobi told me the rest of the story as follows:

> I was at Biami Corner with my shotgun, and they were all there with spears and arrows ready to fire at me.
>
> BK: What did you do?
>
> I told them, "You can go ahead and kill me; I am not afraid. But if you kill me, then the government will compensate my family; they will have plenty of money. I am here as a government worker, and the government will pay for my family if you kill me. But if you shoot me, then I will make sure before I die that I shoot and kill you back. If you shoot me [points gun at the one man with bow aimed at him] then I will shoot you dead. And you too [points at another man]. When I shoot you and you die, the government will not pay any compensation to you. I am not afraid to die, but if I die and you die, my people will get all the compensation and you won't get any at all. You will just die for nothing." When they heard that, they decided it wasn't a good idea to shoot me. They said, "Okay, we'll just let it go." And so that was the end of it.

Mr. Gobi is very restrained in his use of weaponry, but he is no patsy. His soft-spoken style throws into relief the propriety of his actions when he knows they are appropriate and justified. He has the temperament I associate most of all with a concerned social worker in the United States but he is as tough as a cassowary's casque when needed. Though the latitude he gives local custom may seem to—and does—allow unacceptable violence against sorcery suspects, and also against women generally (from my point of view), he is respected and his actions carry weight despite his typical lack of legal or coercive means to enforce them. This means that people are likely to inform police of disturbances and bring grievances to them—certainly more so than they ever did to the Australian kiaps.

Though he has his own interpretation of local custom and its relation to national law—and to the financial and legal constraints on his office—

Mr. Gobi is genuinely concerned about safeguarding the rights of local people as he sees them. He has been in the Royal Papuan Constabulary for twenty-three years and has never had even a minor disciplinary offense (MDO) lodged against him. That he is still performing his duties consistently after nine years at Nomad indicates much.

I was somewhat surprised that Mr. Gobi supports the right of local people to rebel against local officials when their legitimate concerns go unheeded. This was driven home to me when Mr. Gobi had to use his police shotgun for the second time in five years, when I was at Nomad, in October 1998. Again it was to quell an intertribal conflict at the Nomad Station. Since Mr. Haga was gone at the time, Constable Gobi was working alone.

The fracas started as an uprising against one of the Nomad government officers. The officer had contracted eighty laborers for a month to clear a roadbed, but once the work was over, he had no money to pay them. Disgruntlement quickly spread, and the official in question was prevented from buying an airline ticket and hence from leaving the station. Eventually, however, he managed to get aboard an aircraft after it had finished its loading and was waiting to take off from the Nomad airstrip. Just before the door was closed he rushed aboard and shoved cash at the pilot. The latter promptly revved the plane's propellers to drive off the would-be attackers—who were massing at the door of the plane, just fifteen feet from the roaring propellers, and trying to extract the official. The propeller blast gave the edge to those inside, who wrestled the door shut against those pulling on it outside. The plane quickly taxied and took off.

Very quickly, the men on the ground redirected their anger against the other Nomad officials, who happened to be gathered in a small grandstand watching a rugby game at the station. The angry crowd ran to the grandstand, surrounded it, and pelted the officials with rocks they had grabbed from a nearby pile in the schoolyard. The officials leaped from the grandstand and scattered in all directions, several having been hit. At this point, the conflict was swiftly redirected once again—from the officials to an ethnic fight (complete with bow-and-arrow fighting and a shotgun blast into the air) between the Samo people, who had worked on the road project and wanted payment, and their traditional enemies, the Bedamini, who made light of their discontent. To quell the disturbance, Mr. Gobi, who had fled the scene along with the other officials, fired tear-gas canisters from his police shotgun. He maneuvered the warring factions apart, until one side crossed the Nomad River to one side of the government station and retired for the evening. Fortunately, no one had been seriously wounded. The lone constable then went back to the police office, radioed Kiunga, and told the Nomad community through his bullhorn that the riot squad would be flying in, along with their machine guns, to take action against anyone at Nomad who renewed the fighting. It was something of a bluff, but the tactic worked and the situation calmed down.

Almost a week later (after the Nomad local government agreed to fund their trip), three members of the Kiunga police riot squad flew in to the Nomad Station, toting their machine guns. Their primary task, however, was to guard the cash and coins that they had also brought in, at the urgent request of the Nomad officers, to pay the disgruntled road workers. The money had somehow been pried loose from someone's government budget. While they were guarding the money at Nomad, the Kiunga police also conducted their own investigation into the fight, with advice from Mr. Gobi. Their findings, which confirmed Mr. Gobi's own original brief account of the events in his Occurrence Book (see above, pp. 95–96), were as follows: The fight was not caused by the angry mob but by the government official who had contracted the road-clearing work without having money to pay the workers once the job was done.

The official became something of a persona non grata at Nomad. He came back briefly to settle his affairs, but left again. It was widely said that he would never return. Mr. Gobi, like most of those at Nomad, thought this was a fair result: the laborers got paid, the negligent officer was ousted, and the police—both Mr. Gobi and those from Kiunga—did their jobs objectively and properly. The government officers at Nomad did not take offense at having been pelted with rocks as targets of displaced hostility; in fact, they laughed about it afterward.

Jeffersonian Democracy

Thomas Jefferson reportedly opined that small local rebellions against the government were probably a good thing every once in a while. Mr. Gobi would have agreed. And it is partly because of this sentiment that Mr. Gobi and Mr. Haga were effective officers despite their limited official accomplishments. They were not coercive but remarkably restrained in their use of force, promoters of radical democracy, and cautious about imposing law on local customs. In a sense, Mr. Gobi is a Jeffersonian democrat. His definition of defensible action is different from a Western standard, and he does not always feel he can intervene when people take their own revenge, but he is very committed to the right of individuals to be free of illegal government force or prosecution.

The moral and cultural authority of Mr. Gobi and Mr. Haga reaches much farther at Nomad than their official actions. They rely, sometimes too heavily, on local belief and custom, but they are strongly committed to both legal constraint and the force of national law when clearly justified. More generally, they articulate custom with a moral and legal vision of local modernity—what it means, at Nomad, to be civilized and progressive in a principled way. Mr. Gobi and Mr. Haga are both literate, educated, professional, uniformed, armed when necessary, and regularly paid. They are seen as at once highly successful and eminently responsible in a disciplined modern fashion. Though far from flaunting the fact, they were also wealthy by local standards. It was the combination of their modern status and their local sensitivity that made these constables so important and respected as members of the Nomad community. Mr. Haga gave free video showings for the community from his house in the evenings. Mr. Gobi was a regular churchgoer and a member of the Nomad Community School board.

Toward the end of my stay, I sponsored a draw-a-picture contest for students at the Nomad Community School. They each drew a picture of what they wished to be when they grew up. Forty-eight percent of the boys (31/64) and 12.5 percent of the girls (5/40) drew pictures of themselves as a policeman or as a soldier of the Papua New Guinea Defense Force (see photo 8).[12] Not all of this youthful aspiration stems from the personal status of Mr. Gobi and Mr. Haga as individuals. The forceful image of the Kiunga police is also influential, as are tales about the Papua New Guinea Defense Force and the C-grade war movies and action videos that occasionally make their way to Nomad.

The idea of having force and authority melds as if naturally with being modern and successful and having the perks and the force of an outside world that money, outside training, and modern weapons can give. They are an attractive combination for school children attending classes in a remote rainforest outstation. Even if Mr. Gobi and Mr. Haga are exceptional individuals, the cultural salience of police and of uniformed force can be important in places like Nomad. Well beyond the limited force of coercion, this influence exerts itself by being locally comprehensible but also forcefully modern in style and expression. As such, it provides a strong link between what is wealthy, masculine, powerful, and yet moral in a progressive way. The image of modern authority in places like Nomad is both much greater and much different from the ability of police to bash heads or put people in jail.

Excessive Force in Towns and Cities: Nomad Police in National Context

Not all police in Papua New Guinea are as understanding, locally sympathetic, and restrained as Mr. Gobi and Mr. Haga. Reports of police brutality, corruption, and illegality are not uncommon in Papua New Guinea. Police from the Awin area of the Western Province freely told me that they beat, threatened, and cruelly tied up Irian Jayan refugees who were suspected of distributing or manufacturing homemade guns. Members of the Papua New Guinea Defense Force who chased down bank robbers from Tabubil in 1998 reportedly killed four of them on sight, shooting one at least ten times.[13] The one robber who was captured was apparently tortured and the bodies of the others sliced with razors before being released to relatives. Previous bank robbers who had been captured near Kiunga were said by eyewitnesses to have been paraded in public with scars and disfigurements from police beatings and burnings.

One article in *The National,* one of Port Moresby's two daily newspapers, documented police killings of four civilians during one month in the nation's capital (Nicholas 2000). One man had been shot and killed while trying to hitch a ride on a police vehicle, and another was beaten to death after being caught in a robbery. A third man was also beaten to death, and as the police drove back from the scene of the beating, a fourth man was shot to death for seeming to drive alongside the police van.

Conversely, criminal theft and assault are a major and chronic problem in the larger towns and cities of Papua New Guinea.[14] The prevailing logic seems to be that harsh police action is justified by the severity of criminal disturbance and its risk of causing more widespread social disruption or imitation of the crimes. "Modern" crimes, especially those involving guns or robberies of stores or banks, are most severely persecuted and punished. By contrast, more "traditional" crimes and disputes are often treated more leniently by police and settled through compensation or left to village courts or local elected leaders to adjudicate.

Yet more ominously, on June 26, 2001 heavily armed members of the Port Moresby police riot squad opened fire with live ammunition on demonstrators in the capital. Police had earlier used tear gas and automatic gunfire in the air to disperse protestors who had staged a five-day sit-in at the central government offices to protest government austerity and economic retrenchment measures. In the shooting that followed, three student demonstrators were killed while peacefully protesting near the University of Papua New Guinea. A number of others were wounded as they fled (Marshall and Head 2001).

By contrast, in some other parts of the country, such as the New Guinea highlands, police may be seen as highly ineffectual or even as pesky obstacles to the continuation of clan fighting and warfare. During her first day in Tari, in the Southern Highlands Province, ethnographer Holly Wardlow was escorted by a young man who had arranged for an illegal shipment of alcohol by plane. In his opinion, as she describes it, "Bribing the police—who are ineffective and too frightened to do anything about the truly dangerous criminals anyway—was just working the system" (Wardlow 2000: 64).

The renowned diversity of Papua New Guinea, with its hundreds of peoples and cultures, does not melt into a coherent mass just because it is postcolonial and increasingly modern in its own way. The persona of individual authority figures—with all their personal strengths or weaknesses—can have a large impact, especially in rural areas. Correspondingly, it would be wrong to imply that police in cities are generally brutal—many are restrained and dedicated—just as it would be inaccurate to suggest that police in rural areas are typically virtuous.[15]

Diversity notwithstanding, the role of Mr. Haga and especially of Mr. Gobi at Nomad from 1989 to 1998 is noteworthy. Their influence rests more on modern cultural and moral authority than on coercive force. They are not able to prosecute many cases, especially of sorcery, and they have no effective means of preventing persons from taking the law into their own hands, including the killing of sorcery suspects. And yet, their impact is palpable.

A practical result of the situation at Nomad is that official records, and informal police awareness of severe violence, are surprisingly complete between 1988 and 1998. Indeed, the constables are often privy to information for the very reason that they do not take precipitous or heavy-handed action. This information increases our ability—unusual in developing countries—to gauge the incidence and character of legal offenses in the Nomad area over this ten-year period.

Modern Safety in a World of Sorcery

Despite occasional exceptions, Nomad and its villages are now very safe places to live. This generalization may be slightly less accurate for Bedamini, whose history and greater distance from the Nomad Station put them further from its influence. But it is all the more true for those nearer to Nomad, including Gebusi and especially the people of Gasumi Corners. Their emergent sense of propriety—their sense of what it means to be good, bad, successful, and backward in a world that is both local and contemporary and that still has sorcery—has been strongly influenced by the vernacular modern attitude presented by figures such as Mr. Gobi and Mr. Haga and more generally by others in and around the Nomad Station. In the context of a nation that often appears from newspaper accounts and scholarly writings to be rife with postcolonial criminal violence and intermittent warfare, Nomad provides an important counterexample.[16]

Before concluding this discussion, an obvious paradox needs to be addressed. Belief in sorcery remains alive and well in the Nomad Subdistrict. On a sporadic basis, violent retribution against suspected sorcerers still occurs. Such violence is now comparatively rare, however, especially in places that are near the Nomad Station, such as Gasumi Corners. Even in outlying areas, the rate of sorcery retribution is only a dim reflection of its earlier self. As we have seen, however, the ability of police to exercise active control is practically nil. This is widely evident in the overall paucity of incarcerations, convictions, or prosecutions at Nomad, including against suspected sorcerers and against those who choose to murder them. Given this lack of coercive force, it is not surprising that an elderly person alleged to be a sorcerer may still be executed in one or another remote part of the Nomad Subdistrict every few years. The much more surprising result, however, is that the rate of lethal violence has so dramatically and persistently declined.

Sorcery at Nomad is not past in a social or sociological sense, but cases of sorcery accusation and execution have declined markedly. Moreover, sorcery is increasingly *associated* with the past; it is seen as part of a lifestyle that increasing numbers of people in the Nomad area are self-consciously choosing to leave behind. This process reflects a widespread cultural change in the Nomad Subdistrict and among Gebusi and the people of Gasumi Corners specifically. To conduct traditional sorcery inquests puts one on the disfavored side of the relation between what it means to be traditional and what it means to be modern.

Changes in Gebusi sorcery do not reflect the anthropologically celebrated condition in which local people resist the forces of modernity by attributing sorcery or its equivalent to malicious agents of modern success. Gebusi do not stigmatize the possession of commodities or attribute sorcery to the greed of conspicuous consumption (see Taussig 1980; Comaroff and Comaroff 1993). Rather, changes among Gebusi present what may well be a more common but neglected pattern in which people see traditional beliefs such as sorcery as the shackles of their own history. This relates to a key feature of what it means to be locally modern, namely, the drive to assert some new measure of progress against the shortcomings of the past. In the Nomad area, the desire to be modern is a key reason why people willingly bring their suspicions about sorcery and their disputes to the attention, official recording, and adjudication of Mr. Gobi and Mr. Haga. This very act marks sorcery and retribution against it as moral problems that require modern forms of judgment and response. The rise of this ethic is intimately related to why vengeance against sorcery suspects has declined so radically over the last ten years despite the relative absence of police coercion against either those accused of sorcery or those who murder them. As discussed in the next two chapters, this pattern is thrown into relief by the religious changes that Gebusi have experienced in recent years.

1. Traditional etiquette: the author snaps fingers in a welcoming line of adult Gebusi men, 1981.

2. Local parishioners and the author outside the Nomad Catholic church, 1998.

3. Sayu Silap in 1981, with toy bow and arrows.

4. Sayu Silap as a young man in 1998.

5. The Nomad Station from the air, 1998—very similar to its appearance in 1980.

6. A customary practice: men bring back bananas from gardens by the Kum River, a short walk from Gasumi Corners.

7. Gasumi Corners hamlet clearing and family houses.

8. Nomad schoolboy's drawing of his desire to be a policeman in the future.

9. Pastor Cyril Afenang leads Sunday worship at the Nomad Catholic Church.

10. Church poster of the heathen heart, closed to God by Satanic beliefs associated with forest spirits.

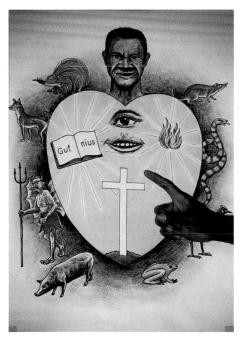

11. Church poster of the good Christian heart, open to the "good news" and opposed to pagan spirits.

12. Church poster of the death of a sinful man: God takes retribution against sorcerer-like individuals.

Chapter 5

The Demise of Sorcery's Revenge

A certain depth comes from the eyes of a man who knows his death throes are starting. Uwano was not old by our standards, probably in his late forties. Perceptive and a convivial joker, Uwano had shared with me the gift-exchange name *arga,* "breadfruit," since back in 1981. I liked him, and we always greeted each other heartily. But now he was only his shell, having given up his tiny reserve of strength to fight his death. Unlike Gebusi, I didn't think about assault sorcery that night as I crept into Uwano's last room. The swelling that would soon be his corpse had already taken his right arm and back. He gazed out with a mixture of knowledge and confusion. As he turned and seemed to recognize me, a shadow of a smile flickered across his face, a parting fragment of human connection.

I knew better than to tell him he would get better. I could only kneel down with a friendly and helpless smile, look softly through his eyes, and say *"Koya, koya"* ("friend, friend") as tenderly as I could. I took his hand in mine and stroked it. It was cold, already dead. He looked at me with that slight shake of head and eyes that is the Gebusi expression for "There's no way, it's impossible." Then he was gone from me, eyes drifting into space. His little frame shook with a small spasm that was all his life could muster. He did not look back to me as I waited there. After a while, I went to talk with his relatives. The stark glow

119

of the fluorescent bulb in that aid post room, which was furnished solely with people, cast them all in ghostly stillness bare on the floor.

We always project at death, I think, Gebusi with their sorcery and me with my thoughts of final human connection. And hopefully Uwano, too, reaching out from his doorway on death's divide. He died a few hours later, on October 9, 1998.

My breadfruit had been sick off and on since I had arrived the previous June, though no more so than his older brother or some of the older women. But whatever spirits there are in the world chose him for death. Just weeks before, he had been fairly energetic, but when his closest relatives took him to the aid post, the other men of Gasumi Corners were already confiding softly that he would die. In the same breath, they combed through his last week and tried to find when the assault sorcerer could have struck and brought his end so quickly. I inadvertently hit on the key moment when I asked whether Uwano had been to church the previous Sunday. I had merely been wondering if he had been well enough to attend, since I didn't remember seeing him and he was usually a churchgoer. No, he hadn't gone. Moreover, he had gone out alone to work in his garden that Sunday morning, accompanied only by his young child. His clan brother claimed to have warned him not to go alone. The assault sorcerer, they reasoned, had taken this opportunity to attack him and deliver a lethal blow.

The men's conversation then turned to dramatic stories of assault sorcerers, *ogowili,* who had killed in the past. In one brutal death of the early 1990s, the ogowili turned himself into an angry wild boar and lured his victim, Korlis, a young hunter, deep into the bush. In 1980–82, Eileen and I had known Korlis as an angelic child and the pride of his parents. But Korlis the young man shot an arrow and wounded a pig that was actually an ogowili. It turned and charged him. Korlis scrambled up a tree, but it was just a young sapling and broke under his weight, throwing him down. As he lay dazed, the enraged boar pierced his side. It had gnawed through his left thigh and much of his buttocks by the time his father and brother arrived to chase it off. Korlis lived just long enough to realize that he had been eaten and was dying. His father was inconsolable and refused to eat; he died "out of sadness" a few weeks later. The story was retold and the men responded, "I am scared. I am scared." The stories continued into the night.

The next morning, we went to see Uwano's body carried from the aid post and laid in state at his home. The morning was a hot one, the grayest and stillest I can remember. With death in the air, Kilasui summed it up, "Even the leaves are too scared to move."

I was worried for Uwano's orphaned children, but also for what else might happen. I remembered the brutal anger over assault sorcery in 1981—the men dressing in battle gear and stalking through the forest, ready to shoot anyone they encountered who might be an ogowili. I remembered how Doliay had murdered Basowey. But I had also gathered enough information about sickness-deaths since then to know that there had hardly been any spirit séance inquests, divinations, or public sorcery accusations during the 1990s. I was still a doubting Thomas; I needed to see the change in order to believe it.

We sat in the house waiting for Uwano's more distant clan relatives to come from a remote village. We worried that they might be angry and arrive in a show of force. But they didn't arrive. After several hours, I went to my own house over the hill for a bite to eat. Almost all the men and boys were gone when I returned; they had left to track the ogowili in Uwano's garden, where they believed he had been attacked. Fortunately, one young man had stayed behind, so I cajoled him to go with me and catch up with the others. What was it like to track an ogowili in 1998? The two of us raced and ran—so quickly that I scraped myself badly on a jagged fallen tree before we caught up with them. But there was nothing serious to catch up to as we entered Uwano's garden—no tracking the ogowili, no weaponry for stalking, no tense determination, no demand that young boys be left behind. The men had simply been as bored as I was waiting for Uwano's distant relatives and so decided to poke around in the place where Uwano might have become sick.

Their demeanor reminded me of overaged Boy Scouts with their kids looking around for a canteen or something that had been left behind in the woods. They didn't expect to find anything and said it didn't matter much anyway. I followed this group and that to see what they might find. Someone finally said with a shrug, "Maybe if a spirit medium was around we would have a chance of finding something. But since there isn't . . ." No evidence was expected, and none was found; they simply paid their respects to Uwano's memory by checking out the place where they thought he might have become sick. The kids were scratching and the mosquitoes were biting, so we went back to the village. Not wanting to waste the trip, some of the men searched the garden and pulled up weathered logs to carry back as firewood.

There was more talk about Uwano's death later on. One man said he had advised Uwano to go to church the previous Sunday. Others ruminated more fully on his activities the day he had gotten sick. But I was surprised to find more emphasis on Uwano's own culpability—his carelessness in going off alone to his garden—than outrage at any act of sorcery. Their attitude seemed curious since most Gebusi now feel quite comfortable going off alone or with small children to their gardens or into the forest; this is no longer considered a glaring invitation to sorcery attack, as it had been in the early 1980s.

The other surprising thing, at least for me, was the Catholic pastors' lack of concern about the possibility of sorcery divinations, accusations, or violence. They knew about the death, of course, but stayed largely to themselves except for the funeral. They gave no exhortations against fighting, no homilies against sorcery inquest or accusation. They assumed there would be no disruption, and they were right. As such, they simply waited to be told when to come and officiate at the funeral.

Uwano's burial was Christian in style. His body had lain in state for a day but no longer. (In fact, he would have been buried after just a few hours if the grave diggers hadn't been stymied by a downpour.) There was no corpse divination—no suspects yelling and shaking the cadaver, no concern that the body would open its eyes or spill its fluid. Only minor irritations lingered. Before the burial, Uwano's old sister whispered to me and a few others that the bones and joints of his corpse had been "broken" by the ogowili. She loosely wriggled Uwano's dead arm by way of demonstration. In further revelation, she lifted the cloth that covered Uwano's waist and uncovered his ulcerated testicles. A nearby relative grumbled in casual disgust: "The ogowilis must have cut and eaten his balls when they attacked him." That was all. There was no public speech making, no innuendo of accusation, little projected anger, and nothing to be worried about. Uwano's body was dressed in his white Sunday shirt, and he was carried by hand and put in a rectangular grave. Colored leaves were arranged around his head. Two of the Catholic pastors read a brief passage from the Bible and prayed routinely in front of the assembled community. The grave was filled, the service was over, and people returned to their hamlets.

For so many of the sickness-deaths in recent years, Gebusi had confirmed the same to me: "No one was accused." "We don't know who the sorcerer was." "We didn't do any divinations." "He just died and was buried." I cross-checked the accounts independently with friends and knew they were accurate. These trends presented a great departure from the deaths and death inquests we had witnessed at Yibihilu in 1980–82, not to mention the funerals and séances in other communities and my cross-checked accounts of earlier mortalities. But now, following the burial of Uwano, I finally felt as well as understood the full extent of this cultural change.

Lost Mediums, New Messages

The largest single factor in the decline of Gebusi revenge against sorcerers has been the demise of spirit mediumship. Sixteen years earlier, Gasumi and its neighboring community had boasted a dozen spirit mediums. Every few days, the desire to commune with the spirits would congeal like forest mist into an evening deluge of poetic culture. These all-night séances pulled together and then released the men's energy—in a lusty male chorus precipitated by the spirits through the chants of the medium. The spirit people or *to di os* could see and communicate many things Gebusi wanted to know. Like Greek gods, though, they also were filled with lust and caprice. During the spirit séances, Gebusi men enticed spirit women to stay and reveal yet more during the night. These *to di* people "animated" the Gebusi world in the Disney as well as the Shakespearean sense. They gave it slapstick and silliness and fantasy and impossible romance as well as drama, pathos, and deep meaning. Though they spoke to most Gebusi only in séances, the *to di* spirits informed local cosmology and could appear to Gebusi as birds, fish, possums, lizards, or dramatic large trees. They were co-inhabitants of the Gebusi world.

By 1998, however, the *to di* spirits were no more. In six months, I never heard them spontaneously referred to or communicated with. There was reported to be one older spirit medium in a distant Gebusi community who still gave an occasional séance, but he was clearly the last of a dying breed. The exception closer to home proved the rule: the previous spirit medium from the adjacent community of Yehebi made fun of his own craft by staging a mock ogowili hunt for public viewing on the lawn by the airstrip during the festivities on Independence Day. He sang off-key and then searched clownishly in the grass until he found an odd assortment of trifles that he comically claimed—to the laughter of his audience—to be the remnants of an attack by assault sorcery.

During the 1990s, young men in Gasumi Corners have been much more interested in the slim opportunities for development and modern advancement—schooling, sports, church, and the hope of wage labor—than they have been in spending nights in darkened houses singing traditional songs with the *to di* spirits. Some now believe that traditional sprit mediumship was roundly misguided. This view was expressed by Ubole, who in 1980–82 had been a young, smart, and up-and-coming spirit medium from Yehebi. In the first years after 1982, Ubole had remained quite traditional. In fact, one of the two women executed secretly for sorcery in the mid-1980s had been dispatched in part for making Ubole seriously ill. He recovered after she had been killed.[1] A short time later, an American missionary came to Yehebi. Ubole began going to church and gave up his practice as a spirit medium. When Ubole's two elder brothers both died of sickness, he believed they succumbed to sorcery, but he also faulted his brothers for not going to church and thereby inviting the sorcery attack. (This reasoning parallels the explanation of Uwano's death.) When the white missionary returned to the United States and was not replaced, Ubole worried that those who had killed his brothers with sorcery would turn their anger against him. By this time, Ubole had been baptized, and he trusted more in Christianity than in his own previous powers as a spirit medium. So he moved away from Yehebi to Gasumi Corners, with its nearby churches. He has lived in Gasumi with his in-laws and attended the Evangelical church since the early 1990s. Ubole summarized some of his personal history as follows:

> My elder brothers died from sorcery in Yehebi, so I didn't want to stay there. They never sang [at church] and so died. When the white missionary came, I went to Yehebi [to sing in church], but when he went to America, I came here near to Nomad, where there was a church. I didn't want to be in a place where there was a lot of bogay (parcel sorcery). I wanted to be in a place where people were good and where I could go to heaven.

> [BK:] You said your clan brothers never sang [went to church]. Do you think they could go to heaven, or not?

> I don't think so. I think you have to go to sing [in church] in order to go to heaven.

The Unmaking of Sorcery Retributions

The head pastor of the Nomad Catholic Church told me earnestly and convincingly that he never outlawed spirit mediumship or séances among Gebusi. Practically speaking, though, it was almost as if he had. Some residents of Gasumi Corners said that death inquests were given up because the pastor would have been angry if a spirit séance had been held. When Gebusi were baptized, there were told quite clearly that they must worship no other spirits except for God. Gebusi themselves have seen a clear conflict between singing to the *to di* spirits in séances and singing hymns to God in church. Even if not by decree, then, holding spirit séances and going to church have become mutually exclusive activities. Though church services were initially attended by only a smattering of Gebusi, it quickly became difficult to hold spirit séances and to keep their results binding without the collective participation and consensus of the settlement at large.

Underscoring this problem was the obvious fact that spirit séance inquests promoted violence against sorcery suspects—practices strongly condemned by the pastor. This violence was considered the epitome of unchristian and sinful behavior—an icon of spiritual backwardness. Ironically, however, the key role of spirit séances in mandating or galvanizing this violence went unrecognized by the Catholic pastor. After a dozen years living near Gasumi Corners, he was visibly surprised to find out (from me) that traditional killing had been legitimated in spirit séances. Indeed, the pastor laughed, he had enjoyed the traditional singing and had not thwarted it, including in the early days of his stay when spirit séances were still easily heard. His primary objective had been to stop the blustery and ultimately ritualized fights that surrounded funerals. My statistics, however, showed that these displays of violence had almost never resulted in killing, even prior to the colonial presence (Knauft 1985a: 250–52). Nonetheless, as with spirit séances, the Christian injunction against fighting was internalized by Gebusi, and the funeral fights have died out in recent years.

Virtually from the start, the demise of spirit inquest séances and of violence against sorcerers provided Gebusi a hoped-for link not just to Christianity and spiritual progress but with the modern style of life and wealth adopted by the pastor and others at the Nomad Station. The Gebusi desire to adopt this lifestyle, or at least to emulate it in some small way, has been a powerful motive for change. It has also informed their active desire to give up parts of their past. The relocation of Gasumi near the Catholic church on the outskirts of the Nomad Station underscores their commitment and desire for a new way of life.

Within a few years of the pastor's arrival, Gasumi Corners' most active and senior spirit medium, Swamin, began going to church, cut his tie with the spirits, and stopped holding séances. And with the decline of Gebusi spirit mediumship, the frequency and severity of sorcery inquests, accusations, and action taken against sorcery suspects all plunged. A senior man explained how it had been during the years that I had been gone: "We would still get angry over sorcery when a kinsperson died. If we had been able to find out who the sorcerer was, we would have killed him or her more often, like Doliay killed Basowey. But we didn't know for sure. Without a spirit medium, it was hard to find out."

The numerical data are worth reviewing here. I was able to document the full circumstances of burial and funerary rites for forty adults who died after 1982. Prior to that time, it was rare for a sickness-death to occur without at least one death-inquest séance being held. In the years immediately following our initial departure, in 1982, these death-inquest seances continued, along with their associated divinations and accusations, but at a somewhat lower rate.

As shown in figure 1, between 1982 and 1988, twelve of the sixteen deaths (75%) were followed by one or more death- inquest séances. Over half of these deaths (9/16) precipitated a formal divination and the public accusation of one or more sorcery suspects. In the following period, however, the rate of inquest séances following sickness-deaths dropped to 25 percent—or just four of sixteen deaths. Correspondingly, the rate at which divinations were conducted and a suspect accused dropped similarly, to 25 percent (4/16). This time period, 1989–94, corresponds with the effective influence of the Catholic Church at Gasumi Corners, where

Figure 1. Changes in sorcery inquest following adult sickness-death, 1982–1998

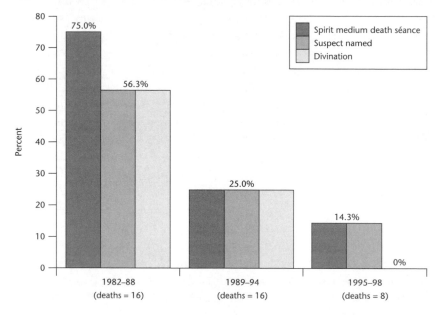

the community of old Gasumi had reaggregated. During the most recent period, from 1995 to 1998, only one of eight sickness-deaths—that of Imbo, the longtime community leader—was accompanied by a sickness-death séance. There was only one accusation and no divinations at all during this period.

We see the causal effect of declining spirit séances when the cumulative sickness-deaths since 1982 are divided into cases in which a death inquest séance was held or not held (see figure 2). Of the seventeen deaths followed by a spirit séance, almost 60 percent (10/17) were followed by a divination and accusation of a sorcerer. When no death-inquest séance was held, however, only three divinations were held and four suspects accused in twenty-three cases.

Nowadays, those few cases in which a sorcery suspect *is* named and accused can themselves have unanticipated results. Police records at Nomad document several incidents in which persons who had been accused of sorcery complained to police that they were being accused falsely and without evidence. A similar case occurred in 1998 at Gasumi Corners after the widow of the late community leader died. Although there was no séance or other divination, the woman's son became convinced that one of the

Figure 2. Death inquest séances, divination, and sorcery attribution following sickness-death, 1982–1998

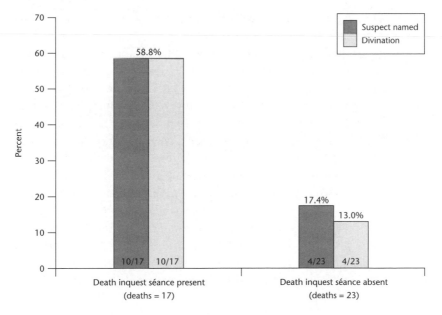

older women in the community was the bogay sorcerer responsible. He confronted her and waved a bush knife in her face. The targeted woman was incensed at his affront; she and her kin accused him of threatening behavior and slander. The case was taken to the Gasumi councillor, who called a village moot. Because there was no firm evidence to back up the man's accusation, he had to pay K 25 to the woman as compensation for falsely accusing and publicly threatening her. The weight of public stigma was shifted from the woman he had accused of sorcery to the accuser himself. The consensus was that the old women had not died from sorcery and that her son was acting in a misguided fashion.

As this case reveals, sorcery beliefs and a desire for vengeance can still persist following the sickness-death of a close relative—but there is little way to cohere consensus concerning the sorcerer's identity or what action to take without spirit séances and divinations. A suspected sorcerer might still be confronted by a grieving kinsman, but this action lacks a collective mandate and is increasingly stigmatized as an affront to the Christian propriety, civility, and well-being of the village. The accuser also risks having countercharges and fines levied against him or her.

The Shifting Sorcerer: from Parcels and Assaults to Deceptions by Satan

Being a churchgoer is now considered the antithesis of being a sorcerer. This is particularly important for old widows or those previously accused of sorcery; for them, attending church is a public testament that they have relinquished sorcery. The Gebusi term for "old widow" (*kogwasiap*) connotes a hag who is unproductive, unsociable, and irascible—irrespective of the person's actual persona. In Gasumi Corners, half of the women in this category (4 of 8) have been previously accused of sorcery. Not coincidentally, however, all of these old women have been baptized and regularly go to church—and none of them have been reaccused since they became churchgoers. More generally, active participation in church is one of the few ways that old women can associate with a modern institution and relinquish the stigma of tradition without being perceived as unseemly or out of place. Indeed, of all the age and sex categories in Gasumi Corners, older women form the only group that is 100 percent baptized.[2] This underscores a point mentioned in chapter 2: even as the risk of being victimized by violence has fallen dramatically, the *proportional* risk to older women has

Figure 3. Homicides as a percentage of male and female deaths, c. 1940–1998

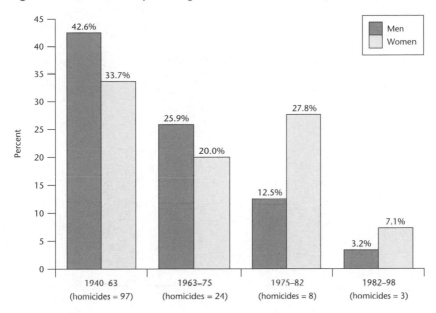

risen (see figure 3).[3] It is against this potential threat that older women from Gasumi Corners immunize themselves by going to church.

If going to church protects against being accused as a sorcerer, it also is believed to provide protection against being attacked by one. This was evident in the statement of Ubole, the former spirit medium, who avoided being attacked by sorcerers by moving to a settlement where there was an active church he could attend. This protection increases yet further if the individual goes to church on a regular basis. The death of Uwano, described above, underscores this point. As one of the men said while Uwano's corpse was laying in state, "If he had gone to church, he would be alive." Another man then added, "If Sebety [his teenage son] had gone with him to the garden, he would be alive."

Going off alone without someone as company used to be considered an unthinkable invitation to *ogowili* attack—avoided, as we might say, like the plague. Nowadays, however, social life at Gasumi Corners is increasingly differentiated. It includes individual trips to church, school, market, and sports events, as well as to gardens and the forest. Individuals are off on their own more often than before. It is hence not surprising that when a death *is* attributed to sorcery in Gasumi Corners, it is usually explained

Figure 4. Changes in sorcery assessed following adult sickness-death, c. 1940–1998

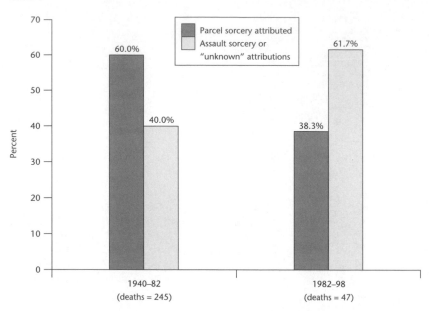

as an attack by an assault sorcerer on an individual who has gone off alone. This contrasts to dwindling attributions of parcel sorcery, that is, sorcery based on the tying up and burning a sick person's excrement or other "leavings." Whereas 60 percent of sorcery attributions used to be parcel sorcery, now over 60 percent are attributed to either assault sorcery or the growing "unknown" category (see figure 4).

The relative increase of Gebusi belief in assault sorcery (*ogowili*) as opposed to parcel sorcery (*bogay*) may seem like a technicality. But it further reduces the likelihood that vengeance will be taken against the sorcerer. Even in the old days, it was often hard to verify and take action against assault sorcerers, who tended to live in more distant settlements. Gebusi attributions of assault sorcery have thus carried a statistically lower risk of violence than those of parcel sorcery (Knauft 1985a: chap. 5). In contemporary circumstances, this means that when sorcery *is* attributed, it is now more frequently conceived as a type of sorcery that is difficult to punish and easier to dismiss.[4]

Lingering beliefs in assault sorcery now blur with Gebusi uncertainty about whether sorcery is the cause of death at all. In my information from 1980–82, all 202 sickness-deaths known from genealogies plus 10 deaths from accident or suicide were attributed to sorcery (Knauft 1985a: chaps. 4–5). For deaths between 1982 and 1998, almost one in five (9 of 47, 19%) were described by Gebusi as having a completely unknown cause: "We just don't know what caused the death, maybe it was ogowili or something else. We have no way of knowing." In many of the deaths that *were* attributed to ogowili, this designation was tepid—a kind of default characterization for cases where there was little evidence or knowledge about what had caused the death.

This trend connects with further changes in spiritual belief. In a number of cases, an informant mused that a person's death might have been caused by either an ogowili or an *osaw* spirit associated with Satan. In traditional Gebusi belief, osaw spirits were mythical underworld creatures that were never really lethal to Gebusi; they functioned in folktales as scary bogeymen and were not feared in daily living. Nowadays, however, osaw are increasingly "alive" and are linked to a general sense of trickery, evil, sin, and death. As such, osaw have become a point of articulation between the forces of Satan and those of the traditional sorcerer.

In 1998, osaw emerged at several points as new icons of spiritual malice. One older man was widely disparaged for having beaten his wife—an older woman—when she planned to go off with other women to the Gasumi pig-house feeding site. One man opined that an evil osaw spirit had come up inside the angry husband and caused him to be brutal. Because of this, they said, he had forgotten the Christian injunction not to fight or hit. In another incident, I asked one of my friends why the dutiful servant in one of the pastor's sermons was portrayed as undeserving of gratitude or thanks: "He must have been a bad servant boy after all. Maybe he had an osaw coming up inside him." In both of these contexts, the contrast between the osaw and Christian propriety is clear. The osaw acts with malicious intent that is similar to but not as lethal as that of a sorcerer. One of the older men, Hogayo, explained: "Osaw still live underground in the forest at night, but now they can also come up and appear like an ogowili during the day. When they do this, the osaw and the ogowili are kind of the same." In practice, osaw have become evil spirits who can "come up in people" and cause them to act in unchristian ways. Prior Gebusi beliefs in sorcery have begun to blur with those concerning malicious and unchristian behavior more generally.

A specific link between osaw and Satan was pointed out by Hogayo when the men gathered to discuss the deepening illness of Walab, a woman in Gasumi Corners. Hogayo started by saying that everyone hoped Walab's sickness would get better—she was the widow of his clan brother. Some of the men briefly lamented that "if we had a spirit medium, then we could investigate [the true cause of the woman's sickness], but we don't, so we can't." Hogayo then suggested that maybe it was actually only a small sickness that an evil osaw spirit was making *look* big—using deception to get people angry and worked up. The osaw could be doing this, Hogayo said, to fool people into believing that the sickness was full-blown sorcery and thus goad them to accuse and fight one another for no reason. Rather than causing lethal sickness, he continued, the osaw might be acting as an agent of Satan to "test" Gebusi—to see if they could be tempted to accuse and fight each other over false sorcery accusations. The implication was that if the people from Gasumi Corners tried to divine the cause of Walab's illness or take action against a suspect, they would be turning away from God and backsliding into needless animosity among themselves. He concluded by suggesting that everyone should talk about the illness further if it got any worse.

Public discussions and displays of sorrow are highly traditional and they continue in Gasumi Corners; they indicate community concern and provide a forum for encouraging kind intentions toward the sick person. But the increasing ambiguity over whether severe sickness is caused by sorcery, by osaw, or as a test by Satan dovetails with the absence of concrete "evidence" from spirit séances or divinations and undercuts the impetus for collective retribution against a sorcery suspect.

In place of retribution is the Christian notion of the Second Coming, when God will assume responsibility for cleansing the world of all evil persons, including osaw and sorcerers. In the interim, God is believed to judge people and can in principle take vengeance against sorcerers at his own discretion. When someone dies, God judges the fate of the person; his or her life is assessed as being ultimately good or evil. Good souls go to heaven, while those who have been sinful are damned to torment and everlasting death in hell.

Some church teachings portray the burning of evil persons in hell in ways that are highly reminiscent of Gebusi's own traditional practices of torturing and executing sorcery suspects (see photo 12). Correspondingly, Judgment Day is God's own sorcery inquest and Jesus is like his super spirit medium. But all of this is taken out of the hands of Gebusi. In contrast to the traditional spirit medium, God exercises absolute knowledge and power at his own whim. God does not tell Gebusi what will happen when. Unlike the *to di* spirits, his style is stern rather than salacious; he does not converse casually or joke with Gebusi. God's actions do not involve negotiation or calibrated reciprocity; they are based on unilateral control.

Spiritual Replacement

In recent years, Gebusi have been supplanting their beliefs in sorcery with generalized images of sinful malevolence and Satan. In complementary fashion, the image of God the Father, *"Papa Got,"* has replaced the *to di* spirits that were the centerpiece of their religious cosmology and the focus of their singing in spirit séances. As Gebusi say, there has been a direct exchange (*sesum degra*) between their previous spirits and their belief in God.

In some ways, nevertheless, going to church is structurally similar to traditional spirit séances. The spirit medium sang his songs line by line for the chorus to repeat; likewise, the pastor line-sings new hymns until the congregation has memorized them. The spirit medium was the sounding board for the word of the spirits, arcane and repetitive; now, the pastor is something like a medium for the word of God, even more arcane and repetitive.

There are also huge differences. The spirit medium was a community member who served as an icon of continuing tradition, while the pastor is an authoritative outsider strongly associated with God, on the one hand, and with the changes of a larger modern world, on the other. Spirit séances were held during the night in a darkened traditional longhouse when the spirits were active. They were highly eroticized and humorous. Church services, by contrast, are held in a metal-roofed building devoted to the worship of God, and they take place in the brightness of morning with an ideology of sober enlightenment for all. Spirit séances were held haphazardly, when people felt like it. Church services, by contrast, are held in modern time and are as regular as the week, beginning at 9 A.M. every Sunday morning. More generally, church is associated with the ways of the future, spirit séances with the ways of the past.

These structural differences dovetail with social ones of gender. During spirit séances, women were generally barred from the room and were relegated to the women's sleeping area of the longhouse (though they could listen to the proceedings). In the church congregation, by contrast, women are co-participants and often outnumber the men. More generally, as noted in chapter 1, the old spiritual mandate to Gebusi men to control women's sexuality, on the one hand, and to exert authority through violent force, on the other, has been compromised (see Tuzin 1997).

In raw cosmological terms, the power of Christianity is simply greater than that of the *to di* spirits. Though the old spirits had been able to tell Gebusi of things unseen, their suggestions had to be verified by Gebusi themselves. They seldom wielded determining force, they rarely got angry, and there were few taboos or sacrifices needed to placate them. By contrast, God has total control over all aspects of life—and afterlife as well. Correspondingly, God has a larger plan for everything and is not simply whimsical. However, his will cannot be known in detail. Though his word is not obscure by nature, awareness of it is restricted by ignorance and recalcitrance. Despite and even because of these impediments, God's will is universal and intended for everyone, just as God is all-knowing and omnipotent.

The difference between *to di* spirits and God is not just one of content but of ontology—it signals and commands a different way of being. God isn't just an unseen being, but the Creator of Everything. This idea was probably as new and unbelievable for Gebusi as the airplanes and trade goods that ushered it in and which then made it all the more plausible. Imagine it—the idea of a magnificent, dangerous, and wonderful world on a totally new scale and yet unified under a single spiritual command bursting with undreamed-of force and power. It confronts Gebusi as it came to them: an externality bigger and more powerful than anything they could have imagined. And it promises a new world of change and the possibility of ultimate progress.

By contrast to God, the *to di* spirits lived in a kind of mirror world that reflected Gebusi's own and interacted with it. The *to di* men were handsome, their women were beautiful and flirtatious, and they all enjoyed the festivity of spirit-world feasts and dances. Gebusi men could communicate with the *to di* during spirit séances: they could talk and joke with the *to di,* establish camaraderie, and entice their women. By singing with an established spirit medium, a young Gebusi man could intensify his ties with the spirit world and perhaps become a lover of a spirit women, who he pursued at spirit séances and in his dreams.

As arranged by the senior medium, a young Gebusi singer could be chosen to marry his spirit-world lover. After undergoing a series of rites and taboos, the young man claimed the women as his spirit wife, was inaugurated as a spirit medium, and gained kinship and social ties with the spirit world.[5] His own spirit could go and experience this world while visiting his spirit in-laws during spirit séances or in dreams. Reciprocally, the *to di* spirits entered the medium's body and replaced his own spirit at séances when they talked and joked with the Gebusi audience. Among the most important of the medium's familiars were his spirit wife and the spirit children she bore him. The medium's relatives and friends in the spirit world could also help Gebusi in their inquests and entreaties. As such, there was regular communication and interaction between the human and spirit worlds. Durkheimian reflection or not, the relation of *to di* spirits to Gebusi was, like Gebusi's own social interaction, based on exchange and reciprocity.

God is different from the *to di* spirits in almost all these respects. He exists in a world of absolute power and authority. Gebusi can try to engage God with their prayers, and they know that God sent his Son, Jesus, to live and die in the human world a long time ago. But their social relationship to God is tense and highly asymmetrical. God holds all the cards, has all the power. His word is not a conversation, and it has little humor, fantasy, or give and take, regardless of Gebusi desires for reciprocity.

Some of these asymmetries are shared as well by the Catholic pastors. Coming to Nomad from the Mountain Ok area of Papua New Guinea, these pastors have dedicated themselves to teaching Gebusi a new religion rather than learning about their old one. Though some of them have now lived among Gebusi for many years, they speak to Gebusi in tok pisin rather than in the vernacular, and they are more likely to give directions or suggestions than to interact with villagers on their own terms. In church, the pastors hold forth in a haranguing, dominating style of speech that Gebusi associate with shouting (*ta*) rather than conversation (*wa*). As Bakhtin (1986) might put it, Gebusi spiritual discourse has changed from dialogue to monologue, from being interactive to being didactic.

Gebusi have listened to the pastors. And listened and listened. They have been drawn to the spiritual side of a more modern and wealthy world. What is striking is not the fact that Gebusi haven't understood all of what has been told to them. Women and children never really understood much of *to di* talk in spirit séances, or at least so the men believed. Even the younger men frequently couldn't follow the innuendos and arcane metaphors of *to di* speech. Spirit séances had, in a sense, been conducted in their own indigenous 'pidgin' that bridged the unusual language of the spirits with that of living Gebusi.

Much more dramatic to me was how quietly and passively Gebusi now sit in church, for so many hours, patiently being talked and yelled at. Put simply, their agency has changed from assertive to recessive. This was the single biggest change in their social life: Gebusi sitting still, disciplined, subordinate, for so long, accepting the authority of others. Here they were on the hard church benches in the supreme duty of inactive activity as the morning sweltered. And it was their own choice.

Christian Fundamentalism

In some parts of contemporary Melanesia, Christian agency melds with the social action of parishioners. In a range of societies, indigenous Christian leadership is seamlessly bound with the politics of village life.[6] In other cases, spiritual agency becomes dramatic when members become possessed by the Holy Spirit.[7] Gebusi, however, do not have this direct experience of Christian agency. Their church leaders tend to be outsiders who dominate with scriptural authority and exhortation.[8] Parishioners are suffused with the authority of Christian fundamentalism rather than the charisma of divine grace.

It is useful here to distinguish fundamentalist Christianity from more charismatic or Pentecostal religious beliefs. Though these alternatives form a continuum across world areas such as Melanesia, their variants carry significant social differences. The fundamentalist end of the continuum stresses a stern and literal reading of the Bible. As Spittler (1994: 111, emphasis in original) puts it, *"The ideological definition of classical Christian fundamentalism refers to an unbending literalism in biblical interpretation coupled with a theory of inspiration close to dictation."* Historically, Christian fundamentalists have strenuously attacked as unorthodox if not heretical the direct experience of divine grace through the very personal and emotional experience of falling into a trance or speaking in tongues. By contrast, the experience of spirit possession and speaking in tongues is a key index of charismatic or Pentecostal religious practice. As a result, as Spittler (1994: 108) puts it, *"Far from being fundamentalist insiders, Pentecostals became one of the targets of fundamentalism."* By contrast, fundamentalism has been increasingly associated with "militant conservatism" (ibid.: 110).

In terms of spontaneous activity, then, we might say that Christian fundamentalism suppresses the spontaneous social agency of parishioners, while charismatic and Pentecostal Christianity encourage it. This difference has significant implications. Particularly in non-Western contexts, the scriptural authoritarianism of Christian fundamentalism privileges church leaders who are literate and who command some knowledge of the Bible. This favors those preachers who have had a Christian education in a town or city. At Nomad, this dynamic combines as if naturally with the status of the pastors as powerful outsiders who are relatively wealthy and perceived as paragons of a modern way of life. The religious authority of these persons is at the core of their identity and local purpose. The gap between their knowledge and that of the villagers is underscored and reinforced by the fact that they seldom know the vernacular tongue or have a full grasp of local customs. In complementary fashion, their authority is reciprocated by the relative passivity and acceptance of their harangues by members of the local congregation. Accordingly, there is little place for the active, spontaneous, and creative agency of spiritual experience for parishioners.

In reality, of course, the contrast between fundamentalist and charismatic Christianity is complicated by a range of intermediate types and complex hybrids. This is especially true in a world area with as much cultural diversity and variation as Melanesia, where local churches and denominations proliferate, sometimes with a vengeance. In this sense, the distinction between fundamentalist and charismatic or Pentecostal Christianity is a contrast of ideal types. Nonetheless, this conceptual difference can help clarify the relationship between religious devotion and social action in places like Melanesia—as Max Weber could have suggested.[9] Those churches toward the charismatic or Pentecostal end of the spectrum are more apt to be locally effervescent and to privilege villagers' self-expressions and religious interpretations.

This side of the coin is strongly evident, for instance, among the Urapmin people, studied by Joel Robbins (1995, 1997, 1998a, 1998b, 2001b). Urapmin have never been subject to missionization or Christianization by outsiders; their Christianity is entirely self-generated. Their practices are highlighted by frequent possession of villagers by the Holy Spirit at "spirit discos" as well as by a strong concern with the ending of the world and widespread prophetic disputations based on individual interpretation. The Urapmin's brand of Christianity has agency with a capital "A"; it is entirely homegrown and is controlled by the experiences of local adherents. Robbins (2001b: 88) concludes that for Urapmin, "The agency of the Holy Spirit lends local leaders (and others) the authority to take over their own churches. It is by positing a Spiritual authority that bypasses the mission to communicate directly with local people that charismatic and Pentecostal revivals make of themselves such 'handy and effective means' of localization."

At the other end of the spectrum is the Christian fundamentalism at places like Nomad. Gebusi have been repeatedly exposed to the harangues of fundamentalist outsiders; over time, they have become a religiously obedient flock. If God's word is arcane, like that of the *to di* spirits, it is presented by the pastors as a hard set of rules that must be diligently followed to ensure spiritual success. The stakes are high. At issue is not just everlasting life versus eternal damnation but, as we shall see in chapter 6, the material support and moral acceptance of the pastors, who are linked to an all-important larger world. To have hope of accessing the benefits of this world requires compliance to basic demands: don't fight, don't kill, don't do sorcery, don't drink kava (a native intoxicant), don't worship other spirits, and don't be "bigheaded" (*bikhet*). This last is a catchall category that includes prohibitions against being assertive or personally willful, self-possessed, arrogant, resistant, or prone to anger. These and the rest are solidified under the overall category of being "sinful."

Whereas Gebusi's indigenous category of evil was epitomized by sorcery—despicable malice sent deceitfully against others—the new category of sin is written much larger. It encompasses many more aspects of anger, willfulness, and, especially, resistance to Christian teaching and not going to church. In this regime, the proper complement to being "bigheaded" is to be withdrawn and appropriately respectful, passive, and obedient. Other prohibitions are also added: don't steal, don't be possessive, don't have illicit sex, and so on. But these are less marked or onerous, in part because close versions of them were already traditional for Gebusi. There also are some "do's," of course: do go to church, do pray, do trust in God, do labor in the pastor's compound, and do help out with the church.

Within this new cosmology, belief in sorcery forms an important subcategory, as we have seen. As in much of Papua New Guinea, Christianity in Gasumi Corners does not deny the existence of sorcery—it does not dispute that some people can make others sick. Rather, it subsumes sorcery under the category of sin and the practices of Satan. It commands people not to be sinful. Conversely, because God is the Almighty, he reserves the right to judge those who sin. It is hence not up to Gebusi to root out or attack the sorcerer: Who are you to think you can know about sorcery? Only God knows whether the sickness is from sorcery or who the sorcerer might be. As one man queried, "Who are we to cut someone and make his blood flow?"

More deeply, what is the place of sickness and evil sickness in God's larger plan? How does it relate to his will or to the workings of Satan, who can appear in the form of an evil spirit or a sorcerer? Gebusi say they have no way of knowing; only God knows, as proclaimed by the pastors. The proper answer is simply to accept fate and turn the other cheek. Even if this means an awful death caused by Satanic evil, by a human sorcerer, or by some vague combination of both, only God can respond; only God wields ultimate retribution.

What Gebusi know about God is limited. And this is fixed as text in the Bible as interpreted by the pastors. The pastors have the literacy, training, confident agency, and material support to come to Nomad and preach the power of God. This power seems greater because Nomad is such an out-of-the-way place. In a context devoid of economic development and with no roads to elsewhere, Christianity betokens a world of wealth, knowledge, and success as well as spiritual goodness and everlasting life. If God is the Almighty, he is also the deity of those who are themselves powerful and wealthy in places such as postcolonial Nomad. This larger package—material and economic, sociopolitical and spiritual—blends together and is hard to separate, but its spiritual dimension can be preeminent in places where there is little to attract economic development or other outside interest. The souls of people become their ticket for drawing a larger sense of progress to themselves. As such, the church becomes a primary vehicle for engaging the hoped-for benefits of a wider world—and for explaining why these benefits are so very difficult to obtain.

Gebusi have changed from being passively indifferent to Christianity to being its willing subordinates. This change reflects the process whereby the diatribes of others become gradually internalized. The mandates of external constraint merge with the stirrings of self-censure. Late in his career, Michel Foucault, that creative historian and philosopher of the human sciences, plumbed analogous ways that the Greco-Roman and early Christian world planed our Western subjectivity into individual self-judgments governed by fixed and absolute if not universal categories of Christian morality and conduct.[10] His story is not the same as ours, of course, even though there are more than a few similarities. Like Foucault, we should approach this issue through specifics: the details of Christian doctrine and its tangible impact on Gebusi subjectivity and social relations. These issues provide the focus of the following chapter.

Chapter 6

The New Spirit

We have been like little children with no mother or father, orphaned. The small child stands beside the highway, all alone.
The child asks for money and begs for things. The child asks
and the trucks go by and don't give him anything. He is hungry and asks for food or a little money, but all the trucks go by
and he has nothing. Then a truck stops. The person is nice and
gives the child a two-kina bill. But the child looks at it and says,
"What is this? I don't know what this is." And so the child
throws it away. He throws it away because he doesn't understand. This is like us. We have been hungry and searching and
wanting God to hear our requests. But when we get God's
word, when we get this big present that is so good for us, then
we throw it away like money that we don't understand. Now
that we know about God's word, we need to accept it.

At first [in years gone by] people were sick, we did spirit
séances, and there was lying and people accused each other of
sorcery. You were a parcel sorcerer (*bogay*), we said, and we
made you do a sago divination. But now Cyril has come here
and God has given his talk, and there is none of that [sorcery
accusations are finished]. All the stealing and fighting and bad
things are washed away for us when we are wiped clean with
the good water [when we are baptized.]

We are like corn. When the seeds of the old and dirty corn are planted, a fresh new corn plant comes up. Friends, this is like us. At first, we were like old corn that had been burned and we were just living like that, dirty. Okay, now Cyril came down here and washed us clean, look, like old corn that was replanted. Then, being planted, a good spirit (*fin*) rises up, a truly good spirit. When we were washed, we got a new spirit, we exchanged our old spirit for a new one. We took the old sins and buried them in good soil to come up new. The missionary here has shown us how this is done, how to do this. This corn comes up new. As it comes up, we have thrown away our old customs like the corn that was dirty, and we have planted ourselves in new ground.

—Homily by Keda Segwa, Nomad Catholic Church, July 26, 1998[1]

The Catholics' God

Christianity has generic impact at Nomad. As we shall see, the Evangelical, Seventh Day Adventist, and Catholic denominations at Nomad express different permutations of a common and highly fundamentalist Christian emphasis. The Catholic Church has the most direct influence on those in Gasumi Corners; almost 60 percent of the community's adults and teenagers are baptized Catholics (see photos 2 and 9). Lay pastor Cyril Afenang, later accompanied by his wife and children, has lived on the outskirts of the Nomad Station near Gasumi Corners for more than a decade. His nearby church is now an old building with a crumbly dirt floor. The walls are lashed with black palm panels, but some have broken loose from their moorings and are skewed like a spoiled Venetian blind. The metal roof is the church's architectural claim to glory but the ridge poles that support it are sagging. They are infested with a small bug that produces a cellulose compost that falls and forms piles as tall and narrow as a matchstick on the uneven rail benches below. Sweeping these tiny stalagmites from the pews is one of the Sunday morning chores, along with gathering colored leaves and a few planted flowers for the altar display. The decorations are put in brightly colored empty food cans or bottles. The most revealing of these to me was the white bottle of "King Bleach" labeled in red and gold next to the crucifix.

Gebusi dress up as they can for the Sunday service, and a lot more impressively in shirts and shorts and blouses—even if here and there torn and stained—than they ever could have in 1982.[2] The service follows a modified version of the Catholic liturgy, with many hymns and a few prayers, a scripture reading or two, an offering collection that yields a very few small coins, and the main pastoral message, followed by prayer and a concluding period of community announcements or *"tok save."* With a few exceptions, the structure of the service isn't much different from that of the other denominations at Nomad.

Hymns are sung in pidgin or English—variable in oomph and vitality, but usually in the low-to-moderate range, at least in the Catholic service. Songs are led heartily by the main pastor, however, and singing is a major part of his spiritual leadership. New melodies are gradually learned by parishioners through repetition. Songs entirely in English were the most difficult in vocabulary and meaning, with untranslated words like "kingdom," "redeemer," "immaculate," and "reign."

> Immaculate Mary, your praises we sing; You reign now with Christ, our Redeemer and King; Ave ave ave Maria ave ave Maria
>
> We pray you, O mother, may God's will be done; We pray for his glory, may his kingdom come; Ave ave . . .

For me, the message or sermon was the most interesting and important part of the service, revealing key features of belief and ideology. Except on rare occasions, these were presented in a mixture of pidgin and English by one or another of the Catholic pastors. The message was long and repetitive but interspersed every two or three minutes with a succinct and accurate translation into Gebusi by one of the young men from Gasumi Corners.

The sermons' content varied, but Mr. Afenang told me that the larger aim, over a period of time, was to convey the teachings and beliefs required for baptism. Regular or semiregular churchgoing for three years qualifies a Gebusi to be baptized; it is assumed that Christian belief has been sufficiently understood and internalized over this period.

As is common across Papua New Guinea, sermons in Gasumi Corners braid the rope of Christianity through repetition and pull it tight through exhortation. The balance between a loving God and an exacting and punitive one is skewed decidedly toward the latter. Potential joys pale against the threat of death and everlasting damnation—as if the loving Jesus is a bit too softhearted and complacent to part the darkness in such backward conditions. This said, none of Nomad's churches and particularly not Mr. Afenang or the other Catholic pastors have gone out of their way to disparage local customs. In this sense, they are different from the white missionaries among the nearby Bedamini, who reportedly collected and burned indigenous drums and dancing paraphernalia because they were considered sacrilegious. Among the Catholics at Nomad, by contrast, the trappings of traditional dancing were welcomed even by the Catholic bishop from Kiunga, who visited early in 1998 and was given a traditional bird-of-paradise headdress as a gift from the people of Gasumi Corners.

Mr. Afenang was the main preacher but sermons were also presented by one of the other three Catholic lay pastors. All of these men came from the Mountain Ok area of Papua New Guinea, though the others were principally stationed in other outpost villages rather than near the Nomad Station itself.[3] A sampling of sermon passages by the Catholic pastors, abstracted from longer and more digressive narratives, convey the most prominent themes. Imagine each homily swelling and ebbing in overlapping flows of elaboration, exhortation, an example or two of varying relevance, and random digressions.

> The theme for today is that we must try *hard* to be disciples of Jesus Christ.[4] The door to heaven is narrow. Not all of us are going to get in! We will have to try *hard* to get into heaven. If you have good things inside your house, you lock your door. You lock your door so people won't just come in your house and take your things. Well, God is the same way. If you knock on his door, it is locked and you will have to ask him if you can come in and have the good things of heaven. If you have turned your back on God, if you have been backsliding into bad ways, you will *not* go to heaven. God will have a *choice*. Now, if you have been *bikhet* [stubborn, noncompliant] he will say, "Do I know you? *No,* I don't know you. You can't come into my place!" He will leave the door locked and you won't be able to get into the kingdom of God. Not everyone can get in. God will let only a few people into his house. The rest will be shut out.

> You can't just have the *name* of being Christian. No! You must come to sing every Sunday. You must work on the mission station, you must help out and cut grass by the pastor's house, you must keep the church trails clear, you must help fix the church. We must pray. We must pray every day. If you give excuses to God, when his judgment comes he will say, "I don't know you. Who are you? I won't let you into my house." It will be too late for you to enter when judgment time comes!

Such exhortations can seem so self-evident in terms of Christian ideology that the analyst may hardly know what to say about them. But beneath this veneer emerges a world of contrastive meaning as soon as one steps back to consider the preceding lifestyle of the neophyte Christians to whom these homilies are directed. In the comparative study of Christianity, it is easy to lose sight of the specific significance that religious teachings may have vis-à-vis prior patterns of social and cultural orientation. In the present case, the differences between the details of Christian sermonizing and the Gebusi world of 1980–82 highlight the significance of Christianity in Gasumi Corners and in the Nomad area more generally. For the sermon above, we can note the following:

On Hospitality and Gaining Entrance

Gebusi longhouses used to be communal; anyone could come in or out. Dwellings now tend to be private family houses. In contrast to traditional hospitality—in which almost anyone who entered the village was hosted—who should be "recognized" to come into your house has now become problematic in Gasumi Corners. Passersby and visitors from other areas often walk through Gasumi Corners on their way to or from the Nomad Station. Decisions about whether to admit a given visitor into one's home reflect an increasing sense of social differentiation, individuality, private property, and decentralization. In 1980–82, Gebusi had little fear of theft. Items were domestically produced and their location when borrowed was easily traced within the community. Now, however, there is great demand for chains, locks, and metal boxes to protect the clothing, money, and other tokens of manufactured value that Gebusi have accrued over the years.

The divine practice described in the sermon draws upon and extends these modern changes. God exercises his choice to lock up his house; he restricts entry and is selective in admitting supplicants to everlasting life. Who should be accepted and who should be turned away is no longer determined by kinship or family relations or histories of friendship. Rather, it depends on the individual goodness of the supplicant and the personal disposition of the host. This orientation contravenes the traditional expectation that persons should be automatically accorded aid and resources—or refused them—based on their kinship and residential status. More broadly, the Christian world supplants automatic commitments based on social relationship and historical connection with assessments of internal worth earned through individual discipline and personal will. Reciprocally, a person's commitment to God does not produce a collective good and does not gain favor for anyone except the individual. Likewise, God's choices are determined by his own will and cannot be second-guessed or known in advance.

On Christian Work and the Production of Goodness

In the Christian message, personal virtue is manifested through concrete acts of supporting the church—this is how Christians can be recognized by God. Going to church regularly, learning and singing songs that praise God, and praying—all are important measures of Christian commitment. Prayers are particularly significant since they reflect an internal state of Christian belief: one's communications to God are individual, personal, and private. In this respect, prayer emphasizes an interiority that contrasts with traditional spirituality, which emphasized the transaction of ritual status through elaborate costuming worn for public display.

The internal nature of Christian commitment is complemented by social injunctions not only to attend church but to labor for God and his agent, the pastor—for example, to clear grass in the church compound, help repair the church, help the pastor work his land and weed his gardens, and so on. Working for the pastor becomes an index of one's dedication or negligence with respect to God. Parishioners are supposed to devote Saturday morning every other week to work for the Catholic pastor in his compound and on the adjacent church grounds. When conducting this work, pretense to know better than the pastor becomes, by implication, an affront to God. In the sermon above, the congregation is exhorted to follow directives and not be self-willed or "bigheaded." This general notion—of working under the personal direction of a boss rather than following one's personal desires or those of a larger collectivity—is distinctly modern at a place like Nomad. Government work is similarly directed in this authoritarian way. Both forms of labor provide their own hope of modern remuneration. If government work is supposed to be paid for with money, labor for the church is supposed to accrue spiritual well-being that may, potentially, be redeemed on Judgment Day.

> God does not promise in vain. But we must be prepared to wait. Sometimes God answers his promises quick, and sometimes a long time later. But God will fulfill promises, and the biggest promise is to live forever after you die if you are good now. God is no liar; he will keep his promise. But we must be ready for this. [. . .] Here is an example. When you fish, you don't know if you will catch a big fish. You wait and wait and maybe only get bitten by mosquitoes. But you wait and are ready, you stay prepared. God is the same. But God has made a promise—that Jesus will come back. And we know from this promise that Jesus will come back on the last day and give goods, wonderful things, to all he has chosen. We don't know when this

will be but we have to wait and be ready. Because we don't know, many people think they can live their whole life and nothing will come. But they don't know. They could die tomorrow. Jesus might come soon. So we must be ready *now*.

On Waiting, Chance, and the Unexpected

Amid yawns, stretches, those dozing in the back pew, and kids whining, the church service itself is a microcosm of patient waiting, deference, and self-denial. In 1980–82, life was enjoyed with self-conscious fervor against the ever-present possibility of sickness and death. In Christian doctrine, however, life becomes self-disciplined so that the greatest gratification is deferred until after death. In the Nomad area, this patient deferral is the ultimate extension of the secular need to wait in limbo for modern development—to wait for wage work, for market purchasers, for learning at school, for trade goods, and for the economic progress that is so desperately desired but always over the horizon. Later, later, maybe some day. In this sense, Christianity at Nomad expands the modern hope of material satisfaction by enlarging it to an ultimate reward for enduring patience in the face of perpetual frustration.

> We must believe that God will answer our prayers. We believe this. But we must not be like little children who always whine and ask for things. Children ask for food or things all the time, they cry and cry and whine and won't stop. What does the good parent do? The good parent doesn't always give the child what he or she wants. If the little baby wants to play with the sharp knife or play with fire, do we let the child do what it wants? *No!* The parent knows what is good for the child and doesn't give it everything and let it do everything.

> Well, when we ask God for things, we shouldn't be like little children, always whining and asking for things that aren't good for us. [. . .] God knows what is in our hearts, why we are really asking. He knows what our true needs are. When we pray, we may have to wait a long, long time for God to answer our prayers. We need to grow up as Christians and not just ask for things from God like little children would.

Of Fathers, Children, Judgment

Gebusi parents used to let children play with knives and literally play with fire. Often, they still do; children learn what harms them and become agents of their own safety. In a memorable incident one evening in 1998, an unsteady toddler about two and a half years old picked up a flaming bamboo torch. The torch was about four feet long and she staggered about the village brandishing it for about five minutes while it streamed flames and smoke. Her actions were watched intimately by a range of adults but no one intervened until she came close to a flammable roof of sago thatch. At that point the firebrand was quickly but gently taken from her hand, and she toddled off without admonishment.

By contrast, modern hierarchies of control and of judgment—at church, at the government office, and at school—are authoritatively regulated and directed by the person in charge. In traditional spirit séances, Gebusi spoke with the *to di* spirits and then with each other until consensus was reached. Now, God commands the pastor, the pastor commands the parishioners, and parishioners should command their children. Reciprocally, adults are childlike before God—subordinate, irresponsible, and ripe for judgment. In this Christian world, social interaction based on equivalence and direct reciprocity is replaced by a hierarchy of authority granted through the recessive agency of obedient recipients.

> We must be thankful for those who come to give us God's word and good things to us. But we must be able to carry on without them; we cannot rely on them so much. You have to learn to carry on by yourself, without help. The white missionaries came and showed us in Papua New Guinea about God's word. We learned from them but now they are gone and we have to carry on by ourselves.

> You see this poster of the bishop and the sister pushing and pulling this boat with Papua New Guineans inside? What is wrong with this picture? We are just along for the ride while outsiders are pushing us! Now we have to get in the water and push ourselves along to Christ. [. . .] You will have to give to the church yourselves, support it with your own offerings. Following God is not something others can do for you; it is something you must do for yourself. You have to start making development come up. This means turning your heart around, turning your spirit around to God. Here is a Bible poster of a man fighting another and cutting off his ear. Look at it! When I was first here, that was you. You used to fight like that. You would cut each other up. How bad that fighting was! But now we stop it. It becomes a thing of the past. You turn around when you come to know God's word.

On Modern Divisions and Authorities

Christian exhortation at Nomad tends as if naturally to authorize beneficial agents who come from elsewhere. In the passage above, these positive external influences include God, missionaries, and pastors. The other side of this bipolar world is occupied by local villagers, who emerge as backward, passive, and dependent. But as the sermon passage above points out, this makes it difficult for local spiritual development to be self-sustaining in the absence of outside tutelage and support. In a larger sense, then, the inadequacy and moral failing of local people is continually produced and re-projected onto them by the contradictions of a Christian-*cum*-modern ideology that privileges authoritative agency but requires the passive obedience of subordinates.

In remote places like Nomad, the local politics of religious belief provide connection to the Christian nation of Papua New Guinea. This connection is accentuated because local government officers and teachers at Nomad are prominent churchgoers and preachers. Conversely, the Nomad pastors teach "Christian education" as a subject to children at the Nomad Community School. The government supports Christian churches directly by allocating local program funds to maintain and improve church buildings and facilities. The relationship between religious and political authority emerged as a focal theme in one of the Catholic pastor's sermons:

> Before we learned of God, we in Papua New Guinea were all *separate* people. We argued and fought and killed each other, but now we are all *one*. Jesus is our number-one leader. When Jesus died on the wooden cross, his blood flowed for *all* of us. Before we were separate and fighting all the time, but now we are all together. Jesus died for all of us, so we all can go to the kingdom of God. We must all unite together.

> Before you used to fight. Fight, fight, fight. And you drank kava in your villages.[5] Now we have peace and are good with each other. But some of the bad things inside are still with us. Sometimes you don't come to church. You have a party in the village [the night before] so you don't come to church. Some people in our country keep asking for judgment and keep going to court. They argue and fight in court and keep asking so they can try to get something. But if we want to have everlasting life, we must always be *ready*. [. . .] God's judgment will come. Not like before, when it was only the Queen of England [who we looked up to as our leader, when we were an Australian colony]. Now it is the king who gives life for *all* of us. Jesus is the king and we want to go to his kingdom.

This passage extends and reinforces the polarity between good and bad in the contemporary world. On the "bad" side are traditional customs, fighting, drinking kava, not coming to church, traditional feasts or "parties" in villages, and not being ready for Judgment Day. On the "good" side are the Bible, unity, peace, churchgoing, being good citizens, and being prepared for Judgment Day. These oppositions have a marked historical dimension; they move from the historical darkness of traditional fighting to a period of colonial beneficence and thence to God as omnipotent king. In the process, the country of Papua New Guinea should be unified; diverse local customs and arguments should be superseded by unifying the nation's peoples under the authority of God's kingdom.

◆ ◆ ◆

Christian cosmology at Nomad links adherence to God's word with the moral progress and beneficial goodness of a modern world. This world is decidedly bipolar. Sinister forces of tradition and divisiveness are pitted against Christian devotion, obedience, and the goodness of self-discipline. The bigger the authority, the better, more powerful, and more unified the result. Against this is the childlike local individual who is laden with a dark past, doesn't really understand God's word, and is undeveloped and anarchic in the broadest sense of the term.

Confronting this reality, the local villager is configured as having individual choice. Good things result from the choice to follow Christian teaching, while bad things result from failing to abide by its directives. There is hope, but responsibility rests entirely with the person at the bottom of the hierarchy. The imperative to choose and maintain goodness in the face of all frustration is construed as a resolutely individual responsibility rather than as a collective or interactive one. The implication is clear: if things don't go well, it's your own fault.

In 1912, Durkheim argued that religion reflects society. What better reflection than Nomad Christianity of a hierarchical world in which outsiders are imbued with the authority of modern agency while villages carry the onus of failure and individual inadequacy?

> There was a master who had a work-boy [shepherd] who he asked to work in the garden and tend the sheep. He came back and he cooked food for the master and the master ate it and ate until he was full, sitting in his chair, and sat back but didn't give food to or thank the boy. And this is the way between bosses and servants. Nowadays, God is our boss and we are his servants. We must work for him and not expect thanks. We cannot ask

God to give us too much, we are his servants. We must work out of love, and not just expect things. We should not ask to be given too much. We must believe strongly in God. It must be in our heart. Our work is to make this seed of belief in God grow big, like the mustard seed. If things don't go well, we can't blame God or call it bullshit, we must believe because we are servants of God. We have to accept things as okay.[6]

A Gebusi Interpretation

While walking back to Gasumi Corners after the above sermon, I asked one of my friends why the master in the story didn't give food or even thanks to the servant boy who did chores for him. "He must have been a bad servant boy after all. Maybe he had an osaw [bad spirit, like an assault sorcerer] coming up inside him." In this view, if the underling works but goes unrewarded, he or she is intrinsically bad: it is his or her own fault. From outside powers, Gebusi have been subject to Bedamini decimation, Australian colonialism, postcolonial nationalism, and Christianity. They have become increasingly aware of their subordination, and their low status is increasingly considered to be their own fault.

These themes pervade the other denominations of Christianity at Nomad as well—Evangelical and Seventh Day Adventist—as well as informing the dynamics of schooling and government authority. Given that church sermons are explicitly ideological, however, how much do those from Gasumi Corners internalize their messages? How much impact does Christian teaching really have?

Degrees of Christian Commitment

As might be expected, Gebusi adherence to Christian doctrine is variable. At the high end of the spectrum are young men from Gasumi Corners with strong Christian beliefs. Near the top of this heap is Keda Segwa, who we knew as a ten year old in old Gasumi village. Keda has since attended the Catholic vocational school at Kiunga and is now a regular churchgoer and prayer leader in Gasumi Corners. While in Kiunga, Keda became schooled in the world of trade stores and purchasing. When he came back to Gasumi Corners, he founded the Gebusi's first tiny trade store, which he managed to keep running for several years until disputes over money closed it. During this period, Keda used some of the proceeds from the business to fly back and forth to Kiunga and bring back goods to resupply the store. As a result, he has flown on an airplane more times than any other Gebusi.

Fluent in pidgin but not strong in reading or writing, Keda is one of the Catholic church's staunchest members and has a distinctive sense of scriptural relevance. He is commonly tapped by the pastors to translate their sermons into the Gebusi vernacular during the Sunday service. On one occasion, Keda was also allowed to compose and present the Sunday sermon (in Gebusi). This message can be taken as a strong public view of Christianity from one of its strongest adherents in Gasumi Corners. Part of Keda's message was presented as the opening text of the present chapter.

As the text suggests, Keda denounces Gebusi traditional practices at least as forcefully as the pastors themselves. He singles out sorcery and fighting and talks explicitly about the waywardness of Gebusi in not being more receptive to Christian teaching. Keda has a strong grasp of baptismal cleansing and emphasizes how Gebusi directly exchange their old souls for new ones through the process of Christian conversion. He likens this exchange to the replanting of corn: an old seed of corn is planted in the ground so that a new, clean, and healthy plant can emerge in its place. Not coincidentally, corn is a recently introduced crop that agricultural officers showed Gebusi how to plant and raise; though no corn was grown at the old village of Gasumi, it is now raised at Gasumi Corners for sale at the Nomad market. Corn, like Christianity, is intended to yield a harvest of modern progress.

Keda's message underscores how the process of developing, or "coming up," is both spiritual and economic. In this view, as he puts it, Gebusi who don't know enough to accept God's word are like children who don't know what money is and so throw it away as worthless. To receive good things from God, he suggests, one must pray to God and continue to pray for rewarding results. What God promises is spiritual life, of course, but the word Keda uses for "good things" (*bip*) has the specific meaning of Western trade goods.

The church has provided Keda his own route to success, including his training at Kiunga and his opportunity to run the Gebusi's first little store. All this "coming up good" is a contrast to a childlike ignorance of money and the backward ways of the past. In Keda's view, this contrast connects intimately to the replacement of sorcery beliefs and traditional violence with the strictures of Christian propriety.

At the other end of the spectrum from Keda are a few non-churchgoers in Gasumi Corners—16 percent of the adults. Some of these persons are unmarried or newly married men who are more likely to become churchgoers in future years, that is, as they claim full adult status. It remains surprising, however, that there is little explicit stigma against non-Christians in Gasumi Corners. Most in the community have gone to church fairly regularly for several years and have been baptized and consider themselves full Christians. But those few who have not, or who attend only infrequently, do not form a social or political or kinship constituency. It is simply taken as their personal choice to stay outside the orbit of church. The elected leader of Gasumi Corners, who owns the community's only metal-roofed house, does not belong to any church and never goes to services.[7]

Little polarization has developed between those who go to church and those who do not. Most in Gasumi Corners go to church with some regularity, participate as actively as they are able, and accept the authority of the pastors. Though most do not actively reflect on Christian doctrine beyond the context of the church, Christian devotion forms an important aspect of personal identity as well as an active feature of weekly activity—as is also the case for many Christians in the United States. Perhaps similarly, the presence of non-Christians in Gasumi Corners is also accepted without demonstrable stigma or public disparagement.

Teaching Christian Development

The Catholic Church at Nomad is a highly important institution of spiritual-*cum*-economic development and modern progress. The church has outside financial support, facilities at Kiunga, gives support to pastors and prayer leaders, and has had a major religious and social impact in Gasumi Corners.[8] Most importantly, the church pays the plane fare and provides food and lodging at Kiunga for its prospective prayer leaders from outstations like Nomad. These adherents are flown to Kiunga and attend Catholic prayer and education courses. This is one of the few ways that those from Gasumi Corners may presently see and experience a world beyond the Nomad area.

The Catholic Diocese in Kiunga strives to be progressive in the most neoliberal sense of the word. Nowhere was this more evident than in the "political awareness" and "development awareness" courses offered at Nomad's Catholic mission station by diocesan personnel visiting from Kiunga. Laudable in their goals, these courses aimed to describe features of the Papua New Guinea constitution, the structure of local government, and the problems of economic development in outstation areas so that local people in small groups could think about and come up with their own ideas and interpretations. The training sessions were conceived in the best tradition of liberal education and were attended by some twenty young men from Gasumi Corners and adjacent settlements. These participants involved the most influential segment of the Christian community at Gasumi Corners— the generation of young men who aspire to follow in Keda's footsteps and embrace the world of Kiunga by means of the Catholic Church. Most of these up-and-comers have completed five or six years at Nomad Community School, understand rudimentary English, are eligible bachelors or young married men, have been baptized, remain regular churchgoers, and aspire to become prayer leaders.

As a requirement of the course, all instruction and conversation was conducted in English with no translation. Nonetheless, my hopes were raised when the instructional leader handed out copies of a cartoon that critiqued the "sponge theory of education": the drawing lampooned a pompous teacher who thought that all students who asked questions must be troublemakers. As the course proceeded, however, it quickly became a series of morning-to-dusk lectures by diocesan personnel about legal structure and ideals of development. Long lists of technical terms were written in English on large posters, from which they were dutifully and laboriously copied in school notebooks by those attending the class.[9] Interactive discourse was largely lost in the process.

Amid the pens scratching and concepts large with Western legalism and liberalism, how could I not think of Bourdieu's critique of arcane education, in which the structure of communication undermines its content of ostensible enlightenment?[10] A paradigm of authoritative pronouncement and subordinate passivity that shuttles between sitting in church and sitting in school was here recapitulated under the banner of promoting equality by well-meaning and genuinely committed teachers of contemporary liberalism. The schoolboys buried their difficulties of understanding by trying to write everything down. The fact of language inequality—an arcane and foreign spirit talk for the listeners, the language of enlightenment for the speakers—became a medium that was the message. Those in attendance copied and copied, listened but did not speak.

The latter part of the week's course promised to be more dynamic, including small-group sessions to discuss the possibility of specific development projects that the community might carry out. But in the groups I observed, no one had any ideas but the Catholic pastor. He suggested building something. No response. A nice new building. No response. A church. No response. A new Catholic church that could be built right next to the pastor's own house. No response.

The idea of cutting house posts for a new church had been roundly

resisted by the Gasumi community and particularly by its landowners during the preceding weeks. But the pastor's goal of building a bright new place
of worship was paramount. All the points of process that the course leaders
had been making—about group dynamics, participation of local people in
setting priorities, evaluating the problems and drawbacks of development
projects as well as their strengths—all of this had been copied down but
quickly disappeared with little sense of discontinuity or dissonance. The
pastor had discursive authority; he received passive expressions and nervous smiles and no opposition.

One young man finally suggested, mumbling, that it would be best
to wait a year before building a church, since community members were
working on some of their own houses just now. There was awkward silence
as the pastor admitted, yes, that it might be possible to wait—but he then
moved ahead with more concrete and immediate plans. There was uneasi-
ness and muffled schoolboy laughter when he suggested that local landowners should go straightaway and cut scarce hardwood house posts from
their land and carry them to the new church site. Ditto when he suggested
that some of the money for the church be raised by the Gasumi ward leader,
who was the father of one of the prayer-leader-hopefuls. Getting down to
business, the pastor said he wanted between one and two thousand kina
from the Gasumi ward leader, whose government allocation was supposed
to benefit the 400-odd people in his district, including those in bush communities as well as at Gasumi Corners. Notably lacking was discussion of
why the church needed to be moved or improved, what kind of building
would be appropriate, how the responsibility for supplying building materials could be equitably distributed, or how a roof and other materials might
be salvaged from the old church.

One local member was supposed to summarize the group's ideas for
the collected larger assembly, but no one showed interest. The pastor wrote
out the presentation as others looked on, but he still needed someone else
to present the results of the ostensible discussion group to the larger forum.
He quickly settled on the ward leader's son, suggesting that it would be
good for him to present the plan as "practice for the skills you will need if
you are chosen to go as a prayer leader for instruction in Kiunga." Visibly
uncomfortable, the young man took the points the pastor had written and,
at his instigation, recopied them into his own notebook:

- Church → Remove old church building to new location
- Talk with the landowners. Ask the landowners if they could allow us to
  cut sticks sport [supports] from their land.

- Ask the church members to contribute
- Ask our Councillor to help us with K1,000–K2,000 from council grants.
- Ask Bishop for additional funds—transport costs, labor costs.

The above interaction crystallizes a microsociology of power that subtly but with quick effectiveness undercut at the level of practice the most laudable principles. Its process is common in the work of development projects, NGOs, and other liberal initiatives the Third World over when and if they actually engage the experience of local people. In the present case, we also see maintained the chasm between a "bigheaded" Gasumi community and the principles of liberal development that condemn foot-dragging when it comes to enlightenment and, more concretely, to supplying labor and local materials to build a new church.

Nervous joking ensued among the young men as the larger meeting restarted. The ward leader's son followed his script, but with pained embarrassment. His English and confidence were compromised in equal proportion. The pastor prompted him to elaborate several points that he forgot or mispronounced until he mumbled over the finish line and immediately drank a half liter of water to quench his awkwardness. The course leader closed by noting how important it was to have grassroots ideas, and how the first contribution should come from local people.

These comments concluded the course, and course evaluations were handed out to those who had attended. Participants again confronted the labor of writing in English. They pored over the sheets for fifteen minutes until hen scratches appeared on their papers. The main evaluation question was, "How do you feel about this workshop?" To a man, the young men answered simply, "I feel happy." As servants of progress, how could they be otherwise?—especially if they aspired to Kiunga, much less to heaven.

Given this response, had my own spontaneous critique of the course been too strong? Was I simply being cynical and patronizing, not giving due respect to the freely expressed opinions of participants?

When I looked again at one young man conferring with the pastor for proper English phrasing as he wrote his answers on the evaluation sheet, I became convinced that there was a "structure of feeling," as Raymond Williams (1977) would call it, in which an expression of criticism by the young men would effectively be a vote against progress and modernity itself. The young men—the only ones from Gasumi Corners who can pretend to understand English and thus be eligible to attend the workshop—*were* happy. They were happy to be included in this course directed by people associated with the larger world of progress. They were happy to have been hosted with free lunches of rice and tinned fish and noodles for several days, the hard floor and the hard language notwithstanding. And despite their quick exit from the course and their complaints of sore backsides from sitting so long on the floor, they echoed these same sentiments to me afterwards: they were happy.

Did the appreciation and aspiration of participants undercut my own irrepressible criticism? Yes and no. The structure of Christian development is inherently conflicted. It resists control and yet feels responsible for this resistance and grateful for the efforts of those in power. In many ways, the path of becoming a Christian depends on this very vacillation; it is predicated upon it. Christianization is at heart an ebb and flow between routinized adherence and the waywardness and guilt that become the mandate for more fervent recommitment. In this jaw-boning process, resistance and ambivalence alternate with internalization and commitment. These emerge as complementary sides of Christianization over time. The cycle includes submitting oneself to harangues, being guilty, making expressions of faith, then feeling that the enterprise is too intrusive, having second thoughts, but also acceding to new demands in other contexts.

This dynamic of approach and avoidance and approach again is strongly evident among the young men in Gasumi Corners—those at the cutting edge of the local Catholic church. They want to fly to Kiunga and to do so through Christ. They appreciate the church, want to be upstanding young men within it, and would like to consider themselves good Christians. But they also joke crudely about girls, regale each other about drinking the beer that they can't obtain at Nomad, attend traditional feasts and dances, chafe at the long church services, and grouse at the pastor behind his back. In a world of conflicted motives and ambivalence, their commitment to Christianity and their resistance to it are closely linked. If moral change is a jagged process, the tension of forces that this change unleashes and pits against each other is itself one of its most important driving forces. It informs a historical and economic and spiritual dialectic, now progressive, now regressive and "backsliding," now reengaged as further stimulus for Christian progress and commitment.

The Moderate Majority and the Pastor in Charge

What about the churchgoing community as a whole, including the women, older men, and others? Beyond the context of church itself—and cases of sickness in the community—discourse about Christianity is not particularly developed in Gasumi Corners. Given the lack of greater local exegesis, attendance at church itself serves as an important index of Christian commitment. Church attendance varies from week to week, with individuals attending church or staying home depending on their personal inclination. In addition to absences due to sickness, some say that if they are angry about something or not in a good frame of mind—"not happy" (*obeagihe-da*)—they don't go to church. The underlying sense is that it is not good to worship God while having an irritable or recalcitrant disposition. Through systematic observation, nonetheless, it became evident that Catholics at Gasumi Corners do indeed attend church—"go to sing to God"— 60 percent or more of the time that they are able to do so.[11] This is a demonstrable reflection of their Christian commitment.

Attending church for an hour or two on Sunday is for many a notable and unambivalent weekly event. It links the community with a morally progressive institution, provides an important occasion for getting dressed in Western clothes, and provides one of the few opportunities for women and older persons to participate in a modern organization. As a cultural symbol of Gebusi aspirations, church is important: it is associated with development and the future, and it combines spiritual progress with the image of economic betterment and of a more modern style of life. In concrete material terms, the Catholic Church is also associated with Kiunga. And Kiunga, for Gebusi, is a kind of heaven on earth.

If, as he hopes to do, the lead Catholic pastor moves back to his natal home in Mountain Ok country, north of Kiunga, the people of Gasumi Corners will be genuinely sorry—and with good reason. He has dedicated most of his prime adult years to live on the outskirts of their community in this out-of-the-way place. He has brought a sense of forward direction, occasional material support, and service to people who have desired it. As an anthropologist who was there only intermittently, who am I to be jaded about his commitments? He has raised his children at Nomad; they and his wife speak Gebusi fairly well. He has suffered his own hardships and passed up economic and political opportunities that a man of his education could dependably have attained elsewhere. He suffers Gebusi passivity with calm demeanor, is philosophical about the limits to what he can accomplish, and maintains an offhanded style that leaves his harsh edge in the pulpit and pursues a milder manner outside of it. His preached exhortations are general warnings from God and rarely, anymore, focused attacks on specific activities or individuals in Gasumi Corners. He faces his own tensions as he negotiates his own resistances to Gebusi, just as they do with him. Between the pastor and his flock, a willing and mutual symbiosis has developed. That their relationship is not greatly interactive outside of church itself is part of the deal from both sides of the altar and not to be denigrated.

Christianity: Individuality

The wide range of Christian commitments in Gasumi Corners—from non-churchgoing to occasional participation to regular adherence to the commitment of the prayer leaders—underscores the individuality of Christianity at Nomad. Though people go to church together, their dedication to God is essentially personal. Pastors stress that Christianity demands personal commitment and that each individual is separately accountable to God on Judgment Day. Keda Segwa emphasized this in part of his own sermon:

> We should think of the story in the Bible about Sodom and his town.[12] Sodom found that his village wasn't good. This was the way we lived before, with our traditional customs up at old Gasumi, before Cyril found us. We fought and sang spirit séances and killed people for sorcery or thought people secretly sent parcel sorcery, and we fought over this. Okay, we started to listen to God, but only a few of us paid any attention. [. . .] But God is good, and he said, "Let's see if some people end up living good and some keep living bad." Okay, like with Sodom's people, we didn't want God and just wanted to stay as we were. But if even one or a few people believe, God won't forget us, he will remember those who are good when it's time to go to heaven. God did not destroy Sodom's town even though most people didn't believe. He only destroyed those who didn't believe. If only one or two believed and all the others didn't, they would still be saved.

Belief in personal as opposed to collective morality presents a major departure from the ethics of kin group and community responsibility that have been so strong among Gebusi and more generally in Melanesia. Christian ideology cuts across notions of collective reprisal and retribution. Even if one feels moved to take action, God sees your innermost thoughts and feelings; actions cannot be justified by kinship or collective responsibility. Acts of Christian adherence are themselves individual ones: deciding to go to church, praying, reading the Bible. There is no collective punishment or collective benefit in the eyes of God.

So, too, with baptism. Eligibility for baptism depends on the individual's record of attendance and commitment to the church. When the visiting priest or bishop comes to Nomad every year or two, each person eligible and wishing to be baptized is treated individually. As recounted by those from Gasumi Corners, this is a portentous event. The visiting cleric in his full vestments interviews each aspirant separately. He asks the candidate severely if he or she is sure he or she can live a good Christian life irrespective of what other people may do or say—in contrast to the beliefs and practices they have followed in the past. The person needs to be committed to God in his or her heart. This commitment carries with it Christian rules that must be maintained through interior discipline and personal will.

Christian individuality also has a larger institutional dimension: adults can choose among several Christian denominations at Nomad—or may eschew Christianity altogether. Though the Catholic Church looms largest in Gasumi Corners, some families prefer to attend one of the other major churches near the station: the Evangelical Church of Papua New Guinea (ECPNG) or the Seventh Day Adventist Church.[13] Personal choice is underscored by the decisions of one set of three full brothers: Keda, my old friend Yuway, and his younger brother Halowa. Though Keda is a principal member of the Catholic Church, Halowa has joined the Evangelical Church and Yuway worships on Saturday with the Seventh Day Adventists. There is no antagonism between the brothers over their respective decisions, which they attribute to the style and level of Christian commitment that each desires to pursue.[14] Though husbands and wives usually go to the same church (with the decision typically made by the husband), differing commitments can sometimes develop over time. One middle-aged woman who had gone to the Evangelical church with her first husband continues to go there even though her present husband has become a Catholic. Without controversy, they attend separate churches each Sunday.

Wider Churches, Nomad Christians

The Christian denominations at Nomad are all fundamentalist but they have slightly different emphases. Though 59 percent of the adults in Gasumi Corners are members of the Catholic Church, 22 percent belong to the Evangelical Church of Papua New Guinea, and 3 percent belong to the Seven Day Adventist Church. The remainder are nonchurchgoers. There is little prestige or stigma in belonging to one or another congregation, except that old women are well-advised to be church members somewhere.

The primary difference between denominations, as Gebusi see it, is their strength of restrictions and taboos. Catholics are viewed as the most lenient. Though Catholics admonish against fighting, drinking kava, and belief in alternative spirits, they are not in principle against traditional costuming or dancing. As festivity rather than "worship," traditional performances may be celebrated—as when a man and woman danced in indigenous costume for the visiting bishop. More stringent than the Catholics are the Evangelicals, who place a firm ban on spirit séances and on indigenous dancing in villages. Evangelicals also prohibit all smoking of tobacco. This is highly significant since sharing smoke from large bamboo pipes used to be a major feature of Gebusi male etiquette and camaraderie (Knauft 1987a).

The doctrines of the Seventh Day Adventist Church are the most restrictive. In addition to the taboos followed by the Evangelicals, SDA adherents are prohibited from eating smooth-skin fish and from consuming the flesh or any other part of a pig. This stricture has major repercussions, since large-scale feasts typically revolve around the cooking of one or more pigs and the distribution of pork. Even though Gebusi own few pigs relative to some other parts of Melanesia—only one pig for every seven persons[15]—raising and caring for an adult pig and/or piglets forms an appreciable part of women's responsibilities in many non-SDA households. The SDA ban on pork has further implications in that its members are effectively precluded from being exchange partners at major feasts. This further erodes the indigenous sense of relational personhood while highlighting the distinctive and individuated nature of Christian identity.

Seventh Day Adventists are enjoined to fast and stay in a state of atonement from Friday evening through Saturday evening each week. Related strictures prohibit watching or participating in sports activities, parties, or discos, particularly those that occur on Friday night, Saturday, or Saturday night. Even working in one's garden on Saturday is condemned; adherents should stay home after the church service and fast and pray to God. By contrast, Sunday should be spent glorifying God's name by coming to work in collective SDA projects, such as improving or beautifying the church, cutting grass in the church compound, maintaining its trails or grounds, or supplying food for church activities. Written records of church attendance and labor contributions are kept by SDA church leaders. Those wishing to be baptized must maintain a high level of compliance and participation in church activities to be eligible for membership. In all, SDA affiliation has a major impact on the weekly lifestyle of adherents.

Within the range of Christian variation at Nomad, then, Catholic belief is seen as relatively tolerant, the Evangelicals as more stringent, and the SDA church as the most severe. When I asked my old friend Yuway why he chose to join the SDA, he said he thought that Catholics and Evangelicals were too loose and "free" with their members. He wanted to worship a God who was strong and hard, who demanded more from people. In this sense, the harsh authority that can emanate from religious leaders seems, at least for some, to be viewed as a positive force. It is perhaps consistent that the highest-ranking government officer at Nomad, the area affairs manager, is a staunch member of the SDA church. Most of the school teachers and both policemen are evangelical Christians.

In all three churches, attendance is multiethnic and includes those who speak different local languages or, in the case of government em-ployees or other outsiders, communicate only in *tok pisin*.[16] Going to church thus puts one in contact with people of other ethnic and language groups. In this respect, churchgoing indexes a social as well as a spiritual sense of wider belonging and affiliation beyond one's residential community.

Fortunately for me, all three churches were open to outsiders; I was warmly welcomed at Evangelical and SDA services as well as the Catholic ones nearest to Gasumi Corners. I sensed little concern or possessiveness from members about my visiting each of these congregations in turn. Some-what to my surprise, the three denominations seemed to exhibit many more similarities than differences. All of them espoused strong core com-mitments to fundamentalist Christianity. All emphasized the acceptance of outside pastoral authority and downplayed spontaneous expression or charismatic experience of Christianity. In this respect, the more evangelical and "Second Coming" emphases of the ECP and SDA services, respectively, can be seen as extensions or refinements rather than contraventions of the Catholic's orientation. Collectively, these three denominations provide a broad ideological context for understanding Christianity at Nomad in addi-tion to rounding out its spiritual cartography. On a larger scale, each of these churches is linked beyond the Nomad Station to national and interna-tional networks of fundamentalist Christian support and influence.[17]

Adventists of the Seventh Day

Seventh Day Adventist services are as long and intense as a hot Nomad morning, lasting on Saturday for up to three hours or more, until the after-noon. The humble passivity of the congregation provides a seemingly self-conscious complement to the stern and accusatory harangue of the preacher. Simple, bleak messages may be inscribed through more than an hour of repetition and reelaboration as heads sink lower in humility and self-abasement. The horrors suffered by Jesus are often detailed, including his trials on the cross and his forty days in the wilderness. Against his suffering, the small inconveniences borne by Christians at Nomad pale in significance: atoning and attending services on Saturday, working for the church on Sunday, praying and avoiding temptation the rest of the week.

Knowing the Bible is a major concern for Seventh Day Adventists. Biblical emphasis is underscored by 45 minutes of scriptural instruction about halfway through the main service. For this teaching—a kind of sermon within a sermon—the congregation divides into sections and attends smaller lectures in one or another language—Bedamini, Gebusi, Samo, Kubor, or tok pisin—on a given set of scriptural passages. Possessing and learning to read and study the Bible during the week is emphasized, since without this ability Christian knowledge and commitment are compromised. The overall theme for one Sabbath was "Why We Need the Bible," summarized and paraphrased as follows:

> The Bible is *not* just the talk of the church leaders, but the talk of God himself. You must read the Bible in order to understand. All the words of the Book are hard for you to understand, but you must understand, you must read to understand. You must read, read in order to know. You must pray and read. All morning and afternoon. Then you will know and live forever. You must read to find the meaning and understand. You can't be tired of reading the Bible if you want to live forever. You have to read the Bible in the morning, in the afternoon, and at night. You have to understand the meaning well. If you don't, you don't have the spirit of God and you can't be fully recognized by God.

SDA doctrine emphasizes the importance of being saved without delay and maintaining a constant state of Christian readiness—because God's anger is coming soon.

> God has the power to remove your name from the book of life. This *will* happen if you are only a "branch" or a "leaf" without the fruit of Jesus.[18] If you get baptized, you have fruit, and you will grow. God sees this. But if you don't have tree fruit, God will burn you. If you don't know how to read the Bible, if you eat pork, if you don't go to church and observe the Sabbath, then God will hurt you. If you believe in SDA, you will come up from baptized water and will be saved. But if you try to keep *bisnis* [business or work] on Saturday, God will see this and will put you in the fire. If you are baptized and speak out the talk of God, if you become a leader in

the church, it will be different. You must have a life of learning and teaching the work of God. The choice is yours: Do you want to help Jesus, or do you want to help Satan? The choice is *yours!* Read Revelation 20:15.[19]

The importance of choice in this sermon underscores the role of individual discipline and commitment to SDA doctrine. There is special urgency to this message because God's judgment can come at any moment. Time is short; one cannot wait to become a devout Christian if one harbors any hope of being saved. As might be expected, the Second Coming of Christ and passages from Revelation are among the most important themes in SDA services. Predictions of exactly when the Second Coming would happen were never made definite, but there was little doubt that the end was near.

> In this year, 1998, this *pitpit* [annual food plant] will be finished. We are like this pitpit. There will be a change and our lives will be over. Maybe this year, maybe next year. We will only last a small time, like the pitpit. Nineteen ninety-eight is almost over now. When will Jesus come? Maybe before the year is over. Or maybe next year. But it will not be a long time. But we cannot wait until 1999 or another time. He may be coming NOW. Make a decision TODAY! You cannot wait until tomorrow or you will die. You must get ready quickly, and not be like your fathers, who waited and waited and just let things happen when they happen.

The importance of hurrying one's conversion to beat the passage of time emerges centrally in SDA doctrine. Other sermons addressed signs of the world's imminent end, as described in Revelation. Anxiety about maintaining one's soul in a state of readiness is also revealed in the elaborate series of weekly SDA activities and proscriptions, which stretch from Friday evening through Sunday, and sometimes on Wednesdays as well. As described at the end of the sermon passage above, this temporal anxiety contrasts markedly with the traditional disposition to "just let things happen when they happen." More generally, the passage of time itself becomes a moral problem in fundamentalist Christianity.

The idea that time presents a moral imperative for spiritual progress contrasts strongly with traditional notions of Gebusi temporality, discussed in chapter 1, in which time was basically circular, repetitive, and self-reproducing in nature. More generally, SDA anxieties reveal a larger feature of modern temporality, namely, that the passage of time should correspond with significant personal progress.

The individual's responsibility for his or her own spiritual development is importantly connected to SDA notions of time as a moral problem. As illustrated in the passage above and that which preceded it, religious discipline and the following of God's word is something that no one else can do for you. These themes were galvanized in the following sermon segment:

> No one can make you be angry or fight or be bad. They can try their best, but you wait until Jesus comes. If this man wants to go to disco or steal or be bad, you let him. He can do what he wants. But if you want to go to heaven, you need a clear idea of your way. God doesn't care if you are a man or a woman or a boy or a girl, an old person or a young person. He doesn't care. But he cares how you live and how you eat and how you work and how you sleep. He knows if you finish church on Saturday but then you go work in your garden and play ball and don't observe the Sabbath. We must be the good steward, we must know how to be a good boss. [. . .] You may think God doesn't see what you do and what is in your heart. But God knows, and he will judge soon when Jesus comes back.

In all, SDA doctrine draws together and highlights key dimensions of modern subjectivity: individual choice, personal responsibility, and the passage of time as a moral mandate for progress. Personal discipline and commitment supersede identity based on kinship, locality, and even gender while linking one instead to a wider community of Christians and especially to the kingdom of God. Viewed against predisposing local patterns of male domination and control, the idea of gendered equality before God helps explain why there are more than twice as many women as men in the large SDA congregation at Nomad on most Saturday mornings.[20] It is sometimes said in Papua New Guinea that church is for women what *bisnis* (business) is for men. For women at Mount Hagen, Stewart and Strathern (1998b: 140) suggest that, "[C]hurch activities may have altered the relative prestige that women hold within the society." At the same time, the leaders and authoritarian figures in most Melanesian churches are men, and this is certainly true of all three Christian denominations at Nomad.

The Evangelicals

The Evangelical Church of Papua New Guinea (ECPNG) affords a more celebratory style of Christianity at Nomad. Evangelical services swell with song and spiritual uplift. The long service is enlivened by hearty choruses of favorite hymns led by up to three guitar-playing leaders. Though strongly fundamentalist, its evangelism has an emotive cast, even if not charismatic. Like SDA, the Evangelical congregation is large, usually well over a hundred persons. Compared to the Catholics and even the SDA, a larger percentage of those present are literate, including many of the government workers and their families as well as sixth-grade leavers from local Samo, Bedamini, Pare, and Kubor populations. Among these ranks is also the single most literate man from old Gasumi, my friend Hawi Suaripi, who has lived for many years at the Nomad Station and is an active lay leader of the Evangelical church.

The evangelical service is in some respects more modern than those of the Catholic or SDA churches. From a Western perspective, the scriptural emphasis in the ECPNG seems more sophisticated and nuanced, even as it commonly evokes draconian images of the Second Coming and the need to be continually ready for Judgment Day. With their greater literacy, a wider range of congregation members emerge during the service to give scripture readings, say prayers, provide testimony, lead hymns, and give the sermon or message.[21] Each Sunday, the plan of the service was written on the church blackboard behind the table that serves as altar and pulpit. The responsibilities of congregation members for various parts of the service were carefully written on the board in large letters.

Personal testimonies sometimes dotted the service, including confessions or morality tales concerning events that transpired during the preceding week. That members of the congregation felt willing and able to stand up and speak publicly in front of others—invariably in tok pisin or Papuan English—provided a notable contrast between the Evangelical church and the other denominations at Nomad. Given their limited linguistic skills, however, Gebusi (with the exception of Hawi) did not participate in this fashion. Being able to speak publicly in a national tongue was simultaneously an icon of personal agency, a symbol of modernity, and an index of one's ability to interpret and apply the Bible to one's personal experience and social world. Most of those who spoke were government workers or members of their families. At one service, a woman stood up and said (in Papua New Guinea English):

> I would like to testify. I am a woman who likes to have things in their place. I get cross with my husband and my children if they don't keep things where they are supposed to be. Last night I wanted the broom. It was supposed to be in the cookhouse but it was in the big house. I got so angry that no one wanted to get it that I said, "The next one who takes the

broom away and leaves it in the wrong place, I am going to chop off your hands!" It seems like a small thing but it can burn in you like a big thing. But if you believe in Jesus you will cry for mercy. If you are still angry the next day, you have to ask Jesus for mercy to heal your anger. Why did I do this? I should have just forgiven it. Jesus may come any time. And people could die any time that you get angry at them; you might get angry at them and they could die and you would always remember that you were angry at them when they died. So you have no other road to heaven except through Christ.

Testimonials and confessions illustrate how dramatically Christian allegiance can be internalized by at least some church members. Complementing this theme is a strong and often strident emphasis on the horrors of sin and the dangers of "backsliding." The following passage is from a sermon by the main pastor:

We are backsliders! We are sinners, but we must overcome sin! I stayed seven years at the Bamu timber camp [which is rife with drinking and prostitution] and I had many temptations but never gave in to temptation. I never failed, I never ran away. I set up the radio, the school, the metal shop center. This is my testimony. Even though they tried to spoil my name, I never ran away.

The Lord's eyes are a mirror. We drink two bottles of beer. We look [lust] at a woman. God sees these things. And when we do these things, we let Satan enter our hearts. God wants us to run away from sin just like we would run away from a snake. [Screaming:] WHY DO WE LET SATAN INTO OUR LIVES? JESUS is our helper. We should let Jesus into our hearts, but we are listening to Satan, to Satan's talk. Christians are doing this today. Today we are being tested by God, like the Israelites. God killed 23,000 Israelites coming out of Egypt who weren't listening to the word of God, who were drinking kava, stealing, and fighting. If we don't throw these things away and confess, God will crush us. If you give one finger to Satan, he will take your whole body and your heart. So don't give even one finger to Satan! Satan will take your soul and drive you into the pit of fire! Satan kills the body, but if you let him do this, the Lord will kill your spirit!! So let us pray for forgiveness [starts a prayer . . .]

In some services, posters were used to dramatize the impact of sin. In one well-known series of posters, termed "Bel Bilong Man" ("The Heart of

Man"),[22] a poster of a dark heart closed to God is used to dramatize the opposition between Christian and traditional beliefs (see photo 10). Surrounding the dark heart, its snarling face, and its unused Bible are animals of the forest associated with traditional subsistence. Accompanied with horned devils with tails, the beasts include a cassowary, pig, frog, lizard, possum, rat, snake, bat, and the red bird of paradise. Segments of the pastor's interpretation follow:

> The bad bird of paradise is when you think falsely that you can own lots of nice things, have an easy life. But this leaves your heart dark and closed to God. Don't let Satan into your life! Satan will get control of you. If your heart is as dark as this poster, you must repent and change. Jesus wants to hear from you. He is willing to cleanse you with his blood. But the wages of sin are death. Let us confess our sins to one another so we can do good to one another. Look at this man, Satan is controlling his heart. The snake has Satan inside. The dog likes to fight. The frog is a liar. The cassowary eats the good fruit and spoils it.
>
> [The Gebusi translator, Hawi, adds:] They are all like osaw.

As graphically presented in this imagery, the features of traditional life in the forest—and the customs and beliefs that accompanied it—are associated with backwardness, darkness, and lack of spiritual enlightenment. These are configured as pagan and inimical to Christianity. For traditional Gebusi, these same beings—the cassowary, possum, lizard, and the red bird of paradise—were at once creatures of the forest and key incarnate forms of traditional *to di* spirits. The harmony of these spirits was literally embodied on the person of the decorated dancer at traditional rituals and feasts (see photo 21 and Knauft 1999: photo 9). As such, the Christian damnation of these images is transformative and even revolutionary from the perspective of traditional Gebusi cosmology.

The Manichean opposition between tradition and Christianity is thrown into relief by the beneficent and literally enlightened representation of salvation in the posters of Christian conversion used at Nomad (see photo 11). This appears to be a common feature of Christianity in Melanesia. The result, as LiPuma (2000: 230) describes it, is, "A moral divide . . . that is also a historical disenfranchisement of the past, and of course of the ancestors who inhabited this past." LiPuma's description of Christianity among the Maring echoes the situation among Gebusi. His account continues directly as follows:

The Maring's own past comes to be re-presented as an endless era of warfare and violence, pain and sickness, the poverty of stone tools and "bush"
clothes—what in "mission ideology" comes to those who live in sin and
darkness. But on the "new road" the ancestors are little more than mute relics; they have lost their ability to speak social truths and hence their divinity. By contrast, the Western God and his disciples now obviously possess
the truth, this exemplified by the superiority of their knowledge and its results.

As in the SDA church, the Evangelical homilies that expound upon
this opposition emphasize the imminence of Judgment Day and the need
to repent and be saved before it is too late. The sermon cited above concluded with the following passage:

[Shouting:] WE MUST NOT THINK THE FUTURE IS THE SAME AS TODAY!
We have to be *ready* for Christ. Tomorrow might be different. [. . .] Now we
only have a little time to live, and where we will end up, we do not know.
[. . .] Only God can know. [Yells:] HE WILL JUDGE US ALL!!

How do church members react to this invective? Their passive and
hunched or head-hung posture can combine many things: guilt, subordination, worthlessness, simple boredom, waiting, dawdling, or the barely sup-
pressed yawn. Where along this spectrum are the evangelical Christians
from Gasumi Corners? Decidedly toward the less educated and passive end
of the continuum.[23] This is consistent with their low literacy rate and remoteness from the Nomad Station prior to 1988.

The response of those from Gasumi Corners to one of the more forceful Evangelical sermons was indicative. The sermon provided a graphic account of recent natural disasters in Papua New Guinea—drought, volcanic
eruption, a tidal wave—which paralleled the tribulations of Revelation.[24]
The preacher—one of the teachers at the Nomad School—proclaimed that
the end of the world was clearly close at hand. He described how the antichrist would now reign until God's final triumph. His account swelled with
vivid references to the Papua New Guinea Defense Force, which would fly
over the rainforest in gunships and shoot those who had not already been
taken up to heaven during the first coming. Pursuing his premillennialist
theme, he emphasized that the devil's mark of "666" was encoded in the
Uniform Price Codes that are printed on manufactured goods such as
tinned fish or bags of rice (see Robbins 1997). Because computers were
"coming up everywhere," he said, they would certainly be used to provide

universal surveillance of people's whereabouts, that is, by tracking their price codes. Anyone who had a single tin of fish or bag of rice, even deep in the forest, would be tracked down by computer scanning devices that could detect these items. They would then be pursued and relentlessly shot and bombed from military helicopters: "So how important it is to give oneself to Christ *now?* The first ascension to heaven has already taken place!" At the end of the service, the lead pastor, who had been absorbing this narrative, became highly emotional and rushed to the altar to elaborate. He concluded his tirade by screaming, *"The antichrist is among us! We must be ready for the Rapture today!"*

While walking home to Gasumi Corners after the service, I asked my Gebusi friends what they thought of the sermon. The men had understood most of the details. Mostly, however, they thought the service was *long*—longer than usual because of the extended sermon. I asked if they were worried. Did they need to do anything special to avoid being killed by the helicopters? No, not really. They did not doubt the content of the message—they believed it entirely—but exactly when all this would happen simply didn't concern them. It would take place when God willed it, and no one knew when it would be. They felt comfortable rather than angst-ridden by their present level of Christian commitment. "We go to sing, and we've given up smoking tobacco," said one of the men. At the present moment, they had all just demonstrated their Christian commitment by attending the Evangelical service. Having done their part by going to church and observing the proper taboos, they were content to take their chances and let God and the angels take care of the rest.

Christian Influence as Limited Context

The mundane response of my friends to the cataclysmic forecast implies that though church is taken seriously in its own context, it does not overshadow other features of life in Gasumi Corners.[25] Surprisingly to me, this included a general attitude—among lay leaders as well as the rank and file—that there was nothing wrong in observing and attending traditional feasts, dances, and even initiations. These indigenous festivities are still held in a few outlying settlements that have not become Christianized. General statements were often made that these pagan rites would not be taken seriously, but when the time came, many from Gasumi Corners wanted to go and participate as visitors. For instance, my friend Keda Segwa, lay leader of the Catholic church, became a sponsor to one of the initiates at the distant settlement of Yulabi and spent many hours carving traditional arrows to give to this initiand. At the event itself, Keda whooped and hollered and plucked his bow string and attended the all-night singing and dancing. Some of the women at Gasumi Corners were similarly active. Before the event, one of them told me quite earnestly that they would not sing traditional songs at the initiation, since they were Christians and had been baptized. But she led the women's singing at the event and saw no problem in having done so.

Even leaders of the Christian churches are prone to accept secular re-presentations of traditional dances and costuming as special events at the Nomad Station. The area affairs officer, one of the staunchest members of the SDA church, arranged a special cultural show of indigenous costuming at Nomad. This show, which included scores of dancers from different villages and ethnic groups, was attended by a regional member of the national parliament and was supported with government prize money.

In practice, then, traditional dancing does not threaten fundamentalist Christianity at Nomad as long as it is performed as a secular spectacle and not as a form of worship. Sometimes, the strictures are even looser than this. At one of the initiations I attended in a remote village, one of the SDA lay leaders came to the event dressed as a customary ritual transvestite—festooned in red body and face paint, beads, feathers, a female skirt, and, in a modern touch, a brassiere stuffed with coconut shells to imitate breasts. This risqué costume is not just transvestitic, it makes the wearer a target for homoerotic teasing and joking. Indeed, it was said by some that ritual homosexuality had accompanied the rites of initiation, that is, that the male initiands of the host village had been orally inseminated to facilitate their masculine development.[26] Despite this context, the SDA man was subsequently at the front of his church, in shirt and tie, leading praises to God.

To call this contextual Christianity is partly accurate but also partly beside the point. In the moment, each experience appears genuine and honest. But the shift from one context to the other—from church to traditional ceremony—poses little problem for Gebusi and, indeed, for most Christians in and around the Nomad Station. Though the analogy may be slightly stretched, it is perhaps not that different from my neighbors here in Atlanta who might absorb a heartfelt Sunday sermon about sensitivity to others' pain and suffering and then go home and enjoy a rousing afternoon of bone-crushing football on TV.

What is the bottom line of Christianity's influence in Gasumi Corners and at Nomad more generally? At church, as ideology, the word of God weighs heavily. It is contextually adhered to and internalized. But how often, when, and where to worship remains a matter of individual choice. Most find it personally and spiritually important to attend church when convenient, accept a few basic religious rules, consider themselves Christian, and live the rest of their lives largely as they wish. This can include attending and participating in traditional rituals hosted at non-Christian settlements. The Christian injunctions taken most seriously are those that stigmatize spirit séances, sorcery, fighting, kava drinking, and the hosting of traditional initiations.

At first blush, the influence of Christianity around Nomad may seem like a spiritual transformation. At second blush, it may seem like a grudging acceptance in church and only selective acceptance outside of it. But in fact I think it is both of these linked together. Each alternative drives the other in a spiraling tension of seemingly opposed complementarity. The result is a jaw-boning dynamic whereby flashes of Christian commitment eventually congeal and cool. These may be followed by ho-hum attitudes and foot-dragging, which are then superseded by worries that one has been "backsliding" too much. Consciences are then salved through more active participation in church or helping the pastor with a significant task. Indeed, it becomes all the more important to go back to church and reassert one's Christian goodness after having strayed from church or having exposed oneself to traditional dancing. The fact that these activities are tacitly tolerated rather than irrevocably condemned places the onus of moral responsibility upon the self-monitoring and self-judgment of the individual.

In general terms, it may be suggested that Christian "conversion" is almost intrinsically partial. Amid self-questioning and continuing injunctions to repent and come back to God, it is hard to imagine how any degree of Christian commitment could avoid this oscillating dynamic. Dedication and lack of dedication are linked in a continuing cycle.

In Gasumi Corners, this pattern emerges most strongly among those who are most fully engaged with Christianity: the young men who aspire to be prayer leaders. They want to be spiritually modern and good—and to experience life in Kiunga by means of Christian education. But they crave the pleasures and indulgences of modernity far more than its sinless privations. They alternately commit themselves to church and bristle at its obligations, recoil from its strictures and then from their own resistance. Unless one appreciates this larger social dynamic, it is easy to either overrate or underrate the impact of Christianity in a place like Nomad.

Christian Modern

At Nomad, the progress of Christianity and becoming modern are practically one and the same. Church services get one dressed up in his or her best Western clothes. They encourage a general sense of weekly time and a bodily sense of temporal discipline. At a minimum, they require showing up on time for church and waiting patiently through the long service. They also encourage a new form of interior morality judged against the passage of time—the imperative to make personal and heartfelt commitments to God before time has run out. Christianity also inculcates the importance of a larger world beyond Nomad. This includes the universal authority of God, which is represented by educated leaders who have power and agency at Nomad. They speak authoritatively in tok pisin or English, and they can read and understand the Bible. They control the wealth that associates as if naturally with spiritual progress. And in the process, they connect with the wider Christian community that supports local churches at remote places like Nomad.

From a *Western* perspective, of course, fundamentalist Christianity appears *anti*-modern rather than modern. It proclaims an arbitrary end to time, the destruction of the world, the evils of too much wealth, and the duties of personal suffering and abnegation. Premillennial dispensationalism—the large tragedy and small rapture of humanity before its very end—is hardly a charter for general progress. In Western countries, Christian fundamentalism has often been reactionary. It is opposed to the notion that secular progress could continue, and it serves as an agonist rather than a champion of modernity.[27] In a place like Nomad, however, the sense of time and wealth and well-being that is associated with Christian fundamentalism seems very modern, economically appealing, and open-ended—relative, that is, to the cultural orientations and practical realities that preceded it.[28] Particularly in out-of-the-way places like Nomad, fundamentalist Christianity provides a powerful means of explaining not just the need but the *absence* of greater economic and spiritual progress under conditions in which these are most fervently desired.

Despite the lack of greater material means, fundamentalism provides a way to emulate a more modern style of life. This lifestyle is associated with knowledge of the outside world; increased awareness of money and manufactured goods; a high value placed on education and literacy; a sense of unidirectional time; the need for progress; individuated agency, discipline, and authority; and a notion of personal goodness based on self-consciousness and self-control. These features link rather than oppose the church to the worldview and political economy of other modern institutions at Nomad—the school, market, store, government office, health clinic, sports leagues, and fleeting opportunities for paid employment. Though mediated by existing patterns of kinship and community, life is perceived less as a collective journey and more as a course of individual self-fashioning (see Greenblatt 1984).

At subaltern places like Nomad, however, the monumental problem is that accepting modernity—including its Christian dimensions—undercuts rather than expands the personal agency of those who rest at the bottom of the hierarchy. What easily results is passivity and recessive agency rather than self-assertion. This description dovetails as if naturally with the perceived backwardness, isolation, and lack of entrepreneurial development in places like Nomad.

The link between Christian fundamentalism and becoming modern is broader than the practices of weekly church services. As in many parts of the so-called developing world, the influence of Christianity is at once deep and superficial, cosmic in implication and restricted in daily impact. Societies also vary. Some groups in Papua New Guinea, such as the Urapmin, discussed in chapter 5, have been swept up in waves of charismatic fervor. Others resist Christianity and encourage radical forms of traditionalism, as in the Kaliai cargo cults and among the Kwaio of the Solomon Islands.[29] In many cases, Christian beliefs intertwine with local-level politics, rivalries, kinship alignments, and ethnic identities.[30] Christian sects and denominations proliferate easily in contemporary Melanesia. Kiunga has forty-three churches. Daru, the tiny capital of the Western Province, has well over one hundred.

In the absence of economic development or access to money, spiritual development in one form or another easily becomes an even stronger imperative. The apocalypse moves closer to the present as if to compensate for the lack of alternative routes to a promised land of material reward. Though adherents hedge their bets and are wary of imminent endings, the image of risk and ultimate reward encourages notions of personal responsibility and self-discipline crosscut by subordination and culpability. At Nomad and other remote or impoverished places, these notions promote desire for personal progress in a world of limited opportunities controlled by others in power. In Gasumi Corners, Christianity works in a context of underdevelopment to emulate progress. A spiritual way of being modern, it pulls on Gebusi like the moon like the tide.

Chapter 7

School Bells and the Energy
of Hard Benches

It was only 6:25 in the morning, but they were already leaving
with the last crispness of the night air. I poked my head out
the door, my eyes squinting, but their small faces already
gleamed and laughed. They ran off and sometimes skipped
down the path on their way to school. It was always an hour
too early, I thought—not just for my own mental gears to do
more than creak, but the gong didn't sound until eight and it
was only a half-hour walk to Nomad. But they were always
there ahead of time. They had time to dawdle, perhaps to
wash off in the Hamam River along the way. More than that,
though, they went to be with pals accumulating along the
route and congregating happily on the school grounds well before the bell. They struck me as joyous in those dawns when I
dragged myself up and out to the Nomad market before eight.
As I walked through the school grounds, the boys would be
laughing while playing tag or marching arm and arm and singing some school song. The girls would be clustered more quietly at the other end of the school yard in subtler groups kibitzing, laughing, and playing. If you could see them, you'd also
see the angelic smiles. The idea of two hundred unsupervised
kids aged eight to sixteen might strike us as a cause for concern, but this didn't occur to the cheerful participants, nor, it
seems, to those in charge.

School for Being Modern, School for Ethnography

The ethnography of schooling brings to mind theories of education and social control, especially as applied to Western settings. For anthropology and sociology, investigation often foregrounds the pedagogical authority of the educational environment and the means by which students are socialized to reproduce existing structures of class and social inequality (e.g., Bourdieu and Passeron 1977; Willis 1977; Reed-Danahay 1996). Less commonly, an ethnographic study of schooling is combined with the study of contemporary social change among people from one or another world area. Despite some hopeful recent exceptions (Sykes n.d.; Stambach 2000; see also Liu et al. 2000), this general neglect is remarkable, since schooling is a monumental force for contemporary socialization and social change in most world areas.[1]

Over the course of even a year or two, the indoctrinations of school—for perhaps six hours a day, five days a week, nine months a year—can easily imprint social development and belief as much as did traditional instruction or initiation. The structure and dynamics of school strongly influence children's configuration of social relations, their sense of themselves as contemporary subjects, their relation to persons and images of authority, and the production of status or class relations within the community. The structure and availability of schooling articulates strongly with national projects and state or regional governments, which typically direct the course and management of education. Correspondingly, schooling is a key vehicle whereby regional or national identity is imparted to children.

In broader terms, schooling exerts a crucial influence on what it means or should mean to be a successful person in a contemporary world; socialization at school is central to the local construction of what it means to be modern (see Knauft in press a). Indeed, notions of progress versus backwardness are often pivotal to classroom ideology and practice. As Stambach (2000: 2) puts it in her ethnography of secondary education in rural northeastern Tanzania, "Schools provide one of the clearest and most illuminating windows into the complexities and contradictions of cultural change." In practical terms, "Schooling makes a profound difference in the ways people think about and organize their lives. It models changes in political organization, the division of labor, social stratification, economic exchange, and cultural differentiation" (ibid: 45).

All this seems self-evident, yet ethnographic focus on schooling remains the exception rather than the rule. Perhaps one reason is that schooling seems so "Western" and, by implication, either predictable or uninteresting to anthropologists. Little could be farther from the truth.[2] Exactly how and why children at Nomad bring so much energy and enthusiasm to school, how and why this energy gets transformed and pushed back onto itself in the classroom, and how and why the passivity of students intensifies despite the earnest and laudable efforts of committed local teachers— all this is worth examination. Of larger significance is how the fervent desire to engage the wealth and power of a larger world gets both internalized as image and virtually eliminated as real possibility.

The Nomad Community School

In 1998, the 204 students registered at the Nomad Community School reflected the populations of the seven ethnic groups that cluster in "corners" around Nomad. Biami [Bedamini] children provided 23 percent of the total, Kubor 21 percent, Samo 14 percent, Pare 14 percent, Gebusi 10 percent, Honibo 4 percent, and Oybae 2 percent. The final 12 percent came from yet other groups—children of Nomad government workers who come from more distant parts of the Western Province or the country. To call the school multicultural would be an understatement. Of the 204 students, the average ethnic group has only twenty-five pupils spread across six grades, and even the largest group, Biami,[3] has less than one-fourth of the total. Each group has its own tongue, and though some are mutually intelligible, the three major local language families are not. Starting with the first day of school in grade one, the language of instruction is English—in its distinctive Papua New Guinean style.

Nomad's diversity enshrines itself in a poster of the subdistrict's self-designated "Tribes" on the wall of the school office. Though youngsters cohere naturally with those from their own ethnic enclave or "corner" of Nomad, they also gather acquaintances and friends across ethnic lines. Teachers typically put children from different language backgrounds in adjacent seats so they will be forced to use English or tok pisin to communicate with their classmates. Though the training of a common tongue is incomplete, it does expose children to ethnic diversity on a daily basis. The variety of cultures in the Western Province and across Papua New Guinea as a whole emerges as a major topic during those segments of the school day devoted to social and community studies.

It was remarkable to me that students at Nomad did not polarize into competitive cliques or gangs. Fighting was a nonissue and never came up in complaints or in the laundry lists of problems that arose spontaneously at school meetings and in my conversations with teachers. None of the teachers worried that ethnic fights would break out among students, in contrast to those few but dramatic altercations among adults at the station. We will see why this is so in due course.

Children in and around Nomad want to be in school, and they want it badly. Despite a yearly school fee of ten kina per student—which parents grumble about mightily—all twelve of the boys and girls from Gasumi Corners who were aged roughly from nine to fourteen went to the Nomad School in 1998. For those close enough to attend, school is a major arena of socialization and status elevation. Like schooling in most parts of the world, education provides symbolic capital and the hope of a better life. At Nomad, the school experience offers the energy, pizzazz, and excitement of being together with over two hundred children—when the entire Gebusi population is only three times that number. It provides children a way to find out about a wider world, be part of life at the Nomad Station, wear Western clothes every day, play team sports during recess, learn a few things, experiment with new languages, interact with teachers who are powerful outsiders, fool around when teachers are out of the room, and be only a hundred yards from the station's airstrip, where the airplanes land and take off. School ushers in a new way to associate and identify with the various things that indicate progress, advancement, and being developed in a local world. Of course, the hard benches, hot days, and routine lessons take their toll over the years. Review of the scattered enrollment records indicated that a third to a half or more of the students drop out before grade six. But even if it is ultimately a hard and boring path of mental and physical discipline, school has plenty of fringe benefits. Overall, then, the experience of elementary schooling is enjoyed and looked back upon fondly afterwards.

If most children arrive by 7:30 in the morning to play and socialize, they don't get home until after four in the afternoon. Their one-hour noontime break doesn't leave enough time for many students—including those from Gasumi Corners—to return home for lunch. Many and perhaps most pupils don't eat much for nine or ten hours, excepting perhaps a handful or two of locally grown peanuts.[4] Despite this, energy levels stay surprisingly high, especially in the morning and even in waves during the afternoon. Hands shoot up like tendrils that must reach the sun in response to teachers' questions; the classroom easily explodes in cascades of response. That many students do not know the answer; that their shouts repeat or parrot the teacher or someone else's response, which may be wrong; and that there is supposed to be a link between personal knowledge and individual response—all this is effaced in collective excitement, in the vaunted identity of the Melanesian collective, here transposed from kin group or "tribe" to class in its most pedagogic sense.

The Setting for Sitting

The school compound and the structure of its days congeal the students into a mass. Take two hundred students aged between eight and sixteen, clump them into five or six grades of between forty and seventy each, then pack each group into a twenty-five by thirty-foot room for six hours every school day.[5] Equip the room with a blackboard, tin roof, rows of wobbly benches fashioned from plywood, and a couple of jerry-built tables. The upper grades, three through six, combine in two large classrooms that sport louvered windows and a lumber floor with only a few holes. The first and second graders get a dirt floor or one of split logs with gaping gaps, along with squares cut in the walls for windows. The forty-nine first graders get no benches or tables but are packed cross-legged on the floor, sitting in imaginary two-and-a-half foot squares for the many hours of instruction.

The school has a clock and a bell, but no fan to dull the hurt of the sun as it griddles the roof and bakes the students. Melted together, they shout so that their joy and restlessness and discipline and energy and modernity fuse into a collective mantra and sometimes mania that shuttles back and forth from laughing smiles to harder grimaces.

As the teachers lament, school materials are expectably deficient. Stacks of tattered primers line the classrooms, but there are seldom enough to go around and everyone wants a copy, so often they are not used. The reading texts tend toward simple Papua New Guinea town and village scenarios but also include a surprising number of Western fairy tales set in a Melanesian context. For me, the most revealing was a version of Hansel and Gretel. A boy named Gari and girl named Heni are forced by a nasty stepmother to work while their father is away. Their stepmother abandons the children in the forest, whereupon they are found by a nasty old witch. The witch cages Gari and prepares to eat him, but after Heni builds the cooking fire, she entices the witch near it and pushes her in. The witch then burns to death. The story ends as the children escape back to their loving father. This tale might seem quaint to Western sensibilities—until we realize that sorcerers and witches still exist in the mind of Nomad. Indeed, the copy of the primer that I borrowed to transcribe the story came from a girl of Gasumi Corners whose grandmother—still alive and well and living in her household—had been tied to a stake and tortured as a sorceress when her granddaughter was young.

As this incident illustrates, the ironies of cross-cultural pedagogy can mix modern fantasies with traditional realities. But more commonly, the process works the other way around: a real modernity from elsewhere incites fantasies that become local. Students easily project themselves into the experiences and possessions of a wider world of manufactured goods, houses, and exciting ways of living. This world brims with power and authority and literacy and travel, like that of the teachers who fly to Nomad from other towns or cities to teach those at the station about other places and countries, science and its products, and words and numbers that seem to produce this progress.

Students hear, imagine, and eventually recognize and internalize these realities, but their ability to express themselves, to speak and write in the terms of this wider world, remains limited. A growing chasm emerges between students' increasing ability to understand spoken and eventually written English and their much greater difficulty in actually speaking or writing it. The size of classes and the style of teaching impede students' ability to speak individually, while the structure of copied assignments and the shortage of notebooks undercut their writing skills. When a few new notebooks get handed out, students strain for them like chicks at feeding time. The difficulty of correcting work from so many students curtails the length and creativity of assignments, which stress recognition, copying, and rote memory of stock words and rules.

If social spirit endures despite regimentation, the latter is also pronounced. The school day is divided into segments that are each only 15 or 30 minutes in duration. By grade two, there are 23 subject areas enumerated and sequenced over the school day: (1) assembly; (2) listening; (3) oral expression; (4) talking [English]; (5) reading; (6) spelling/dictation; (7) written sentences; (8) USSR [Un-Structured Silent Reading]; (9) written composition; (10) handwriting; (11) radio broadcast instruction; (12) mathematics; (13) science; (14) health; (15) community life; (16) physical education; (17) expressive arts; (18) music; (19) block times—optional projects; (20) CRE [Christian Religious Education]; (21) community activities; (22) agriculture; and (23) sports.

Each of the four teachers compiles a massive notebook with his instruction plan for each subject for each class period of each day of each week. Entries for different subjects on different days of the school year emerge as follows:

8:30–8:45 Oral expression, Week 3, Tuesday. Objective: To answer questions about a picture and will participate in discussion. Display p. 23 of the flip chart "trade store." Ask questions.

8:45–9:00 Spelling, Week 5, Wednesday. Objective: To spell the words "glue," "true," "blue," "due," and will recognize a pattern in the words.

9:00–9:20 Talking drills, Week 7, Friday. Objective: by the end of the class, the student is able to correctly use the adjective "every" in sentence, e. g., "give me every piece of paper."

From entries to pages and into volumes, these handwritten sheaves collect over the school year as the official record of each day's work of each teacher. Most entries are copied almost verbatim from standard teaching manuals, but they must be written anew each day. As is the case for police record books, a blank column is put on the right side of the page for a visiting inspector, eventually, to thumb through and initial every page. Beyond official confirmation that the teacher is doing his job, this also "finishes" the book, which can never be used again. As a result, teachers must rewrite their entire corpus of lesson plans all over again each year, subject and day, chapter and verse. This time-eating task takes a significant portion of the teacher's day, and some of the instructors don't write that quickly. The task is typically slaved away at by the teacher during class while children drift through vague periods of individual activity or group study. Frequently, this becomes rote learning all around: the teacher copies his lesson plan from the previous year while the students are copying the instruction sentences he has written on the board.

Despite the officially regimented plan, intrusions reduce the time spent in actual instruction. The teacher may go to confer with other teachers, make a call on the station radio, take care of other business, or correct papers at the back of the room. When a teacher travels from Nomad on personal or official business in town or city, the remaining teachers must double up to cover his class. As the school day progresses, they flit back and forth between one classroom and another, giving instruction to one grade while the other is left to work on its own. If teachers leave for long periods, or altogether, the other teachers must pick up the slack. When I was there in 1998, the school had lost its fourth-grade teacher. As a result, the intrepid Mr. Salangau packed the thirty-one fourth graders in with his forty-eight fifth graders and taught a single crammed class of seventy-nine students for the entire year.

Time-consuming bureaucracy extends beyond the writing of lesson plans. In his record book, each teacher must copy not just the exam questions and proper answers but each student's separate answer to each objective test question. These spreadsheet tabulations are collected into large folios. Keeping records becomes a monumental task. Below, from second grade, are examples of questions from tests, which are generally given each Friday.

Science: Choose the right answer
- How do worms help improve the soil?
  (a) mix up soil (b) eat soil (c) water soil
- Do all insects have wings? (a) sometimes (b) yes (c) no

Health: True or False
- Never play with dynamite.
- Broken teeth makes us unhealthy.
- Bad manners make others happy.

English: Choose the best word for the space
- I ran home _____ it got dark. (a) after (b) before (c) when
- What does the cat do? (a) it meows (b) its mine (c) I came to school

In principle, the teacher's in-class paperwork and various departures dovetail with student's independent work or study. In the absence of homework, students use class time to work on assignments, read, write, compute, and study—at least in theory. In fact, the school day alternates between intense bursts of teaching activity and large doses of what I call "mulling."

Passing Time

Mulling is the unspoken contract between teacher and students about what can be done when the teacher is not in the room or is working at his table. It is the paste that holds the day together across the blank spaces between the teacher's words. Most periods of mulling begin with a period of respectful individual work that may last from thirty seconds to several minutes. Like a waking beehive, students then start buzzing with distractions that rise in verbal and physical expression. Some dawdle and gaze aimlessly, others copy each other's books or trade them. A few continue to work diligently, but most begin to socialize with those within several feet of themselves. The chatter rises to a hubbub like that of a nice restaurant rather than a wild party. The noise gets a shade louder, of course, when the teacher leaves the building, but even then, I was surprised (as I sat outside unnoticed) that the jabbering did not become a roar.

A few antics invariably break the surface—a pencil flips onto another student's table, a flung workbook lands on the floor, a student gets jostled "accidentally." Among the first graders, students might cluster and flow as a herd to one side of the classroom or the other to see what some classmate is doing or to look outside. But the unspoken rules were respected: no yelling, screaming, hurting another student, or damaging anything significant in the classroom. Talking and movement were acceptable, but wholesale disruption was not. The middle and upper grades internalized an additional injunction not to move more than ten feet or so from their work space when mulling. Roamers remained close enough to their seats to return normally when the teacher reemerged on the scene. I often mused what would happen to a fifty-student class of nine-year-old American children if left on their own for twenty minutes, half an hour, or longer. But at Nomad I could find no evidence of fighting, damage to property, or breaking higher decibels. Reciprocally, teachers gave students a wide berth for mulling, including when they were in the room writing lesson plans or doing paperwork. The contract appeared to be as firm as it was unwritten.

Perhaps because of this, Nomad teachers, like their students, were accommodating rather than aggressive. This ethos fits the cultural stereotype of southern lowlanders in Papua New Guinea as having a more relaxed and less aggressive lifestyle than the country's highlanders. It also flows from the low-key style in which the Nomad teachers led their classes. Teachers interacted with students more casually and less formally than many instructors in American schools. The tone of instruction was often conversational, communicating "by the way" rather through authoritative exhortations or the threat of punishment (which was rare). Allusive comments by the teacher about bad behavior typically found their mark. At other times, students were loudly told what to do. But even if this involved shouting over childish zeal—as it often did in the younger grades—it was rarely vitriolic. Many of the students listened, some were attentive, others looked dazed, and a few would continue to fool around quietly. As long as perhaps a third of the students were paying attention, this seemed acceptable.

As one might expect, the instructional style at Nomad places great emphasis on rote learning—and very little on individual expression. Singsong repetition is the rule, whether practicing the letter "o," subtracting three from five, spelling "garden," or knowing the capital of the Western

13. Teacher Jack Truman teaches counting to his forty-nine first graders at the Nomad Community School.

14. A girl from Gasumi Corners waits in hopes of selling her produce at the Nomad market.

15. A weekend rugby game between men of different ethnic groups in front of spectators at the Nomad Station.

16. Traditional séance singing is supplanted by evening performances of Gasumi string band singers, accompanied by guitars and s ukulele.

17. Drawing by a Nomad schoolboy who aspires to be a modern singer in the future.

18. A visiting man arrives in traditional costume at an initiation feast.

19. Hybrid costuming:
a man combines modern
and traditional decorations
at an initiation feast.

20. Women from Gasumi
Corners in modern dress at
an initiation feast.

21. An official wearing a Michael Jackson T-shirt judges a Gebusi dancer during the traditional costume competition at Nomad on Independence Day.

22. A man dressed as a traditional villager seeks in vain for help from a modern boss in a Nomad drama skit.

23. Nomad drama skit of the Second Coming of Christ and the death of bare-breasted heathen women. The angel Gabriel stands beside Christ, holding a trumpet.

24. Individual creativity in costume display competition at Nomad on Independence Day.

Province. Phrases and sentences are copied endlessly from the board and crammed into school workbooks. Answers are drilled and repeated in a rising chorus like an endless hymn of educational praise.

Though seldom analyzed by researchers, this style of schooling can be found the world over and is common in the many so-called developing countries burdened with low literacy rates, a paucity of educational resources, and a shortage of teachers—especially in rural areas. Among the Chagga of northeastern Tanzania, Stambach (2000: 112, 116) foregrounds what she calls the "ritualized effects of call/response and repetition," which pervade both verbal instruction and the extended tedium of copying from the blackboard. As is the case at Nomad, in the hills of Mount Kilimanjaro, and many places in between, education by means of tedious repetition has been bequeathed from earlier periods of colonial rule or missionary teaching.

Instruction is ultimately and invariably followed by examination. At Nomad, exams come like small dramas on Fridays. Though answers are easily cribbed from other students, pupils still have to judge whether the answer being copied is correct. Especially in the lower grades, there are squeals of delight or disgust when the teacher reads out the right answers after the test is over, but reactions seem to dissipate as quickly as they spontaneously arise. Overall tallies of student progress are religiously kept by the teachers, but there is little worry one way or the other among most students in the class. Gebusi children acknowledge that one or another student might have "a good head" in school, but what does it matter? There are no cumulative tests or year end exams to qualify for the next year of primary school. The community school at Nomad is radically democratic: each student whose family pays the ten kina school fee is automatically advanced to the next level, up to grade six. Many students do poorly on assignments and receive long strings of failing grades, but there is no sense that they will be failures in life as a result. And there is equality in the fact that almost everyone fails the high school entrance exams that mark the end of year six—the final grade of education of Nomad. At least among Gebusi from Gasumi Corners, no student has ever been admitted to Kiunga High School, and none seems destined to do so in the near future.

The Holy Grail of School on High

In the Western Province, high school is probably the most important gateway to achieving a richer and less parochial life. Children who have been to high school generally obtain wage-earning jobs that take them to other parts of the province or allow them to earn at least intermittent cash income in places like Nomad—as a government worker or assistant.[6] Parents know this. In some parts of Papua New Guinea that have a longer and more robust history of formal education, graduation from high school at grade 10 is itself a stressful way station. Only about one-quarter of those who graduate from high school pass the examinations that provide the advanced professional or university training to ensure a full-salary career. The bulk of high school graduates return to their village areas or pursue transient and often unsatisfying jobs in town or city (see Sykes 1999; Sykes, n.d.: chap. 5). Some regions of Papua New Guinea thus share the so-called "diploma disease" of many developing countries, in which secondary education provides symbolic prestige without enabling dependable employment and regular income.[7] In remote parts of the Western Province, however, standards of success are notably lower. From the perspective of those in the Nomad Subdistrict, which has no secondary education of its own, attending high school is a life-transforming experience that provides higher status and the likelihood of relative wealth.

Admission to Kiunga High School—the district's main boarding school for secondary education—is at once paradoxical and overdetermined. At one level, the procedure for acceptance is as objective as the decisions are important. A comprehensive admissions test is given to sixth graders to see whether they can qualify for the district high school. Mr. Ted Ano, the perceptive and low-key headmaster of the Nomad Community School, had served as a high school exam reader for the Western Province, and he did so again in 1998. His account of the process was revealing.

The admissions test is comprehensive and includes a variety of multiple-choice questions on "combined subjects" plus an English essay composition. To grade the exams of the province's students, five evaluators from different areas plus a central administrator fly to Daru, the tiny capital of the expansive Western Province. They stockade themselves in the town's one hotel—a dangerous place where drunken fights with weapons easily break out. Not coincidentally, the town is also known as the funneling point for drugs, guns, sex videos, and other contraband items coming into Papua New Guinea from Australia across the Torres Strait. Almost anyone with cash can bribe the security officers to get into the fenced hotel, which also hosts a regular flow of prostitutes. These women complement the lower-priced sex workers who service men for only two kina (U.S.$1) along the sewage-strewn beach of the town (see Hammar 1995, 1996). Given this larger context, the work of the examiners is surrounded with intrigue and danger. Adding potential injury to insult, local parents and officials can be highly intimidating to the visiting examiners: "My son better get into high school! If he doesn't, you should watch out for yourself!" Additional security guards are supposed to be hired at the hotel to protect the examiners during their stay.

The exams arrive by the thousands in large cartons, along with teacher evaluations for each student. Despite the large volume, each exam, including its multiple choice as well as its essay portion, is graded independently by each of the five evaluators. This hyper-duplication is designed to stop any favoritism. If the evaluators cannot agree about the essay portion of the exam, they call Port Moresby and ask for advice. The repetition of work, all done by hand, means the evaluators work nonstop for two weeks, typically from 8 A.M. to noon, from 1 P.M. to 4 P.M., and again after dinner from 7 P.M. to 10 P.M.

Despite this exercise in objectivity, many villagers are convinced that favoritism explains why the children of government officials so consistently gain admission to high school while their own children do not. They are both more and less than right. Mr. Ano explains that the most difficult parts of the exam for students are the math and especially the English essay portion, which typically consists of a story opening that the students must extend and complete on their own. Consistency of style and plausibility of plot as well as grammar, spelling, and punctuation are all considered in the evaluation. Finally, the teacher recommendations are assessed.

Though it is possible for a smart and diligent pupil from any village to score reasonably well on the objective portion of the exam, the overwhelming emphasis on rote learning and copied assignments comes at the expense of active expression in spoken or written English. Students get very little practice in free writing. Essays are seldom assigned in community schools and are difficult for teachers to grade appropriately, especially given the large size of their classes. Against this background, those who come from a home where English or pidgin is spoken, and where written works and styles of modern narrative are used or referred to, have a huge advantage when they take the exam. Knowing the importance of the exam, literate parents cultivate their children's test-taking ability. For village children, however, the language divide is too great to be easily breached. Hence the outcome: a fair evaluation reproduces the linguistic and class division between children of educated and wealthy parents and those of villagers. As such, the examination privileges a style of life and way of thinking predisposed by the education and literacy of parents (see Bourdieu and Passeron 1977; Bourdieu 1989).

Money matters form the final linchpin of high school enrollment. Though heavily subsidized by the government, the yearly fee for high school in Kiunga still amounts to K 300 plus K 100 for project fees for school activities—a total of about U.S.$200 per student per annum. To this is added the cost of traveling to and from Kiunga by air, plus return visits home at the end of semesters. These costs outstrip the resources of parents in Gasumi Corners. In practical terms, then, it is only those children of literate, wage-earning parents who have a chance of attending Kiunga High School.

Recessive Agents

Beneath the constraints of money and qualifications lies a subtler but no less significant impediment to education at places like Nomad: recessive agency among students. Modern pedagogy in out-of-the-way places uses discipline, repetition, and passive absorption rather than active or creative use of new knowledge. Pedagogy is formally marked by school bells and fifteen-minute or half-hour periods for children whose sense of time has previously been a diffuse and undifferentiated flow. Added to this is the discipline of sitting on hard benches or on the floor, hour after hour. Drill, drill, repetition, repetition among a class of forty, fifty, sixty, seventy, even eighty students. If the collectivity of the student mass is their refuge and enjoyment, it also ensconces their collective passivity—the sense that outsiders have knowledge and power and facts that pour into pupils like water into the school's leaky cistern, which can never be filled. Students may recall enough to do reasonably well on simple exams at the end of each week; they recognize and regurgitate items of knowledge. But how the pieces relate, how to ask a question or reflect upon an issue or express oneself actively or in narrative form is a different process. Such expression would be consistent with the verbal art of creative and dialogic assertion that attended the traditional spirit séance or the longhouse palaver—but these are inimical to instruction or transformation into English at school. What results is a gap of agency reflected in the difficulty of using modern knowledge to construct a narrative or assert a point of view. Beyond the specifics of knowledge, this gap of constructive agency separates teachers, pastors, aid post workers, and government officials from villagers.

I had great fun trying to breach this problem when I guest-taught classes in each of the six grades at Nomad Community School. At first I expected that my greatest constraints would be the fragmented time segments and lesson plans, but I quickly realized that the teachers gave me a lot of latitude—and could disappear for an hour or more after making some initial remarks. All of which worked out fine. Being demonstrative and something of a ham, I showed the students glossy photo essays that my parents had sent me from the *National Geographic*. I told them what it might be like to be a Tibetan pastoralist, a craft-seller in Oaxaca, a Navajo dancer, or raise ponies in the Shetland Islands. I showed them pictures of Atlanta, explained some features of living in the United States, taught a social studies lesson on Indonesia, showed them my first book on Gebusi, and described how I thought Nomad had changed since I had first been there in 1980. The students gave every indication of being interested, attentive, and in some cases captivated.[8] The kids seemed to love it, but when it came to saying much about themselves—indeed, saying much of anything that wasn't a collective repetition—they became tongue-tied. Students had a kind of tone deafness when it came to expressing themselves, being prompted to ask a question, or giving an opinion about anything not pre-answered through drill and repetition.

Part of their reluctance may have stemmed from my anomalous status as a tall, white American outsider. They may also have had difficulties understanding my meaning and intonation (though I took pains to talk slowly and to reexpress myself in tok pisin and in Gebusi as well as in Papua New Guinean English). It was only after repeated sessions with all grades—and after listening to teachers instruct their own classes—that I realized how deeply students had internalized a sense of recessive agency. I remember asking a fifth-grade class to name pictures by category and how difficult this was for them even though they knew the words. For them to speak individually was extremely hard. I gave three photos of flowers to one group of schoolgirls, and I knew that they knew what they were. I coaxed them with antics and pleasantries to say the word "flowers." They seemed to want to say it in the worst way, and they beamed as they squirmed, but none of them could speak. Finally, I gently leaned close so one of them could whisper it so very faintly in my ear: "flowers."[9]

The idea of standing out, of speaking out, of using words in writing or speaking in English—this is the difference in literate agency that forms the key dividing line between contemporary "success" and the status quo of village underdevelopment and subordination in the Nomad area. This is not just our own view of progress or knowledge, but what local people and students want most fervently. But it requires a transition from absorbing new knowledge to actively speaking, writing, and using a national language to manipulate the world in modern contexts.

In foreign or minority contexts, the slippage between educational goals and student performance is commonly attributed to differences in cultural or subcultural orientation. But Gebusi do not encourage social and verbal passivity among children and young adults. In the school setting, however, there is an active if unwitting socialization to absorb, be patient, and parrot without reflection. The activeness of this process becomes its very willing passivity, its respect for outside authority. This reduces spontaneous expression to areas outside or beyond the formal structure of education per se: mulling, recess, lunchtime, and the casual gathering of students before and after school.

Recuperative Moments

Lest my remarks appear overly critical, another side to community education should be mentioned: the benefits of school for the many, the commitment of the teachers, and the learning that does take place. What *does* take place at Nomad Community School is fairly remarkable. Take nine-year-old children from more than half a dozen ethnic groups and put fifty of them in a class. After six months, they can understand simple English and begin to write and use words and numbers. They relate to each other and maintain the discipline of the school day, have learned the protocols of call-and-response and mulling, and begin to feel that what goes on at Nomad Station is a comprehensible way of life.

After six years, these same students can understand English fairly well and can read and write a range of simple texts. They know a great deal about each other, their nation, and the regions of their country. They have rudimentary knowledge of health and hygiene, arithmetic, and English literacy. They relate socially and in a common tongue with others who do not share their kinship or ethnicity or specific background. They know how to sit still, how to mind the clock, and how to negotiate authority to carve out effective spaces of passive subversion. They write in and often treasure the school notebooks in which they record their assignments. By the end of sixth grade, these notebooks contain verbatim entries such as the following:

Written sentences Thursday
1. *The people in the Western Island of the Manus province make finely-woven hats and bags they use fibres from the leaf-buds of coconut trees.*
2. *In the Sepik people use river-grass fibre dyed in reds browns and greens to make mats and bags.*

3. *Weavers from Siassi Island also [use] coconut leaf bud fibre to make small bags for carrying betel-nut.*

Written Composition [All of the below was handwritten as if to duplicate an official form and its completion]
Application is made for the replacement of the attached Postal Order No.
　(a) 107 value　　　*(b) K20 for which the period of validity has expired.*
Applicant to complete in block letters:
　(c) Christian name:　*(d) Surname:*
　　DIDIGA　　　　*IMBO*

Didiga Imbo was one of my closest friends in Gasumi Corners. He had been a very good student through grade six, though he failed his high school exam. But he still kept and wrote in his school notebook. The fact that he could write was considered a positive skill in the community (as well as by me, when I now receive his letters!). He knows how to use a calculator and now helps to manage the local community store.

Education at Stake

In contemporary settings, education is vital. The three most successful men from Gasumi Corners are the three who, though not accepted to high school, managed to participate in post-elementary school training programs beyond Nomad that are supported by Christian organizations. Hawi Suaripi now lives at Nomad and serves as an airline agent (often unpaid) who keeps manifest and passenger lists for the Mission Aviation Fellowship airplanes when they land at Nomad. He is a leader in the Nomad Evangelical church. Keda Segwa, who we met in the previous chapter, is a lay leader in the Catholic church and ran a trade store in Gasumi Corners for several years. Abi Kasubia is the only one from Gasumi whose status has taken him outside the Nomad area to live; he held various jobs in and near Kiunga, and he now lives permanently with his family outside that town, residing with his daughter's husband.

At a lower educational level, schooling is starting to have a significant impact on girls as well as boys—and on the future of gender relations in Gasumi Corners. This is a recent development. Among married women from Gasumi Corners, only one out of 28 ever attended school.[10] By contrast, over half of the married men (11 of 21) have had some schooling, and a third of them (7 of 21) have completed more than one year. Among the 15 bachelors in Gasumi Corners, everyone has been to school—with an average of 4.5 years of schooling apiece. Though only one-third of the women in the equivalent category have been to school (2 of 6), schooling for girls as well as boys is now universal. In 1998, all seven of the girls aged nine to fourteen from Gasumi Corners—as well as all five of the boys— attended school. In the Nomad School as a whole, 36 percent of the students are girls (73 of 204), including 29 percent in the highest grade.

The ability of girls as well as boys to be exposed to English, to play team sports, to make friends from other corners of Nomad, and to know about life at the station constitutes a major change from previous generations of Gebusi. Among women beyond school age, for instance, only 12 percent (4 of 33) understand the national lingua franca of tok pisin, in contrast to 61 percent of the men (22 of 36), including almost all of the bachelors. This disparity is sure to change in future years, though women will likely remain much more reluctant than men to actively talk or express themselves in tok pisin or English. And if school fees are raised or become more onerous to pay, girls are likely to be the first to be taken out of school.[11]

Even among men who know English or tok pisin, it was surprising to me how seldom they spoke these languages and how painful it was for them to do so. At the Nomad Station as well as when interacting with the local pastor, it was common for Gebusi to *hear* tok pisin or English but to say little in response. It's not that speaking English is considered unimportant by Gebusi. One morning in Gasumi Corners, I overheard an endearing conversation: Gwabi, my next door neighbor, was gently instructing his two-and-a-half-year-old son how to say and understand simple English words: "house," "stone," "fire," "tree," and so on. Though Gwabi himself had only had one month of schooling as a teenager, and though his English was extremely limited, he recognized the importance of being able to speak in English and was attempting to pass on this sense to his son in whatever small way he could.

For me personally, the authority of English and the passivity it created in listeners was so great that I never felt comfortable speaking English or even tok pisin in Gasumi Corners. Walking home from school with children who I had just taught in English, my language shift to Gebusi came spontaneously and completely. To speak English or tok pisin conveyed monologue versus dialogue. Hence the irony that Gebusi are schooled to hear English and to engage a wider world but on terms that make them at once separate and passively divided from that to which they aspire. They are committed to school and appreciate the fact that it is close at hand even as they accept that none of them can duplicate its agency—nor breach the pearly gates of high school in Kiunga.

These impediments are yet larger for those who live farther afield than Gasumi Corners. By governmental principle, every major community in Papua New Guinea should have access to education. One might think that the Western Province could approximate this goal. With a sparse population of 133,400, the provincial government boasts a relatively high annual income of almost ten million kina a year a year from the royalties of the Ok Tedi gold mine, plus a number of other subsidies.[12] In the Nomad Subdistrict, ten schools in outlying communities complement the two school buildings at Nomad Station. However, only three of these ten other schools are staffed; the other seven are effectively closed. These closures include a beautiful new school made from sawn timber and complete with metal roof and glass-louvered windows in the Gebusi community of Yehebi, located with an airstrip eight miles south of Nomad on the south bank of the Sio or Rentoul River. The school stays empty for a simple reason: it has no teacher.

Teaching in rural areas is considered an arduous job in Papua New Guinea, as it is in most countries. Teachers are poorly and irregularly paid, and these problems are worst in the most remote areas. It is difficult to attract teachers to areas like Nomad unless they already have natal or marital ties to the area. If few of a locale's own students go to high school and manage to receive teacher training, the area becomes dependent on the trickle of outside teachers who are sympathetic but cannot be expected to stay more than short periods of time. As such, a vicious circle is engaged: few teachers, poor schooling, unqualified students, lack of educational advancement, and further difficulty attracting outside teachers.

Because it is flanked by a subdistrict station with a regular airstrip, radio, and Western-style houses (mostly left over from the Australian era), the school at Nomad continues to function. In 1998, one of the teachers was from the Pa ethnic group across the Strickland River; two of the three others were from towns or other, more developed parts of the Western Province. Even so, the school is approved and budgeted for *six* teachers, one for each grade, though it could attract only four. By the end of 1998, three of these men were attempting to transfer to other locations. The main stated discontents are lack of amenities and the difficulty of transport and communication. Another revealing complaint concerns "poor community support." Before unpacking this key issue, however, we need a better understanding of the teachers themselves.

The Courage to Teach

I was impressed with all of the teachers at the Nomad Community School. They seemed thoughtful, friendly, committed to their profession, fairly well educated, and sensitive to the problems of the school and its mandated structure of elementary education. And each of them enjoyed teaching children. I listened to them in and out of class, sometimes observed and sometimes not. All the instructors had been teaching for several years, but I would never have guessed their longevity. Mr. Ano helped open the Nomad Community School in 1976 before going off to teach at other schools in the province and recently returning to Nomad for a two-year term as headmaster. Mr. Truman, muscular and energetic, had been teaching for 27 years in all parts of the Western Province. A natural comedian, he enjoyed teaching the first graders best because he felt joy introducing them to school when they were so fresh to the experience: "At first, they are so frightened. And I don't speak any of their village languages. But you speak to them with your body before you speak with your tongue. At the beginning of the year it is hard to get them to make a sound. But just listen to them now! I can't shut them up!!" The following comes from one of his lessons in arithmetic (see photo 13):

> Okay, let's go to the NEXT question. You take your counting stones or sticks in front of you. You count out along with me on this. This question has a picture to follow, look at this!! Amanda has 13 eggs, THIRTEEN of them, LOOK, you can count them. All together! [Mr. Truman with class in exuberant chorus:] "ONE, TWO, THREE, FOUR, FIVE, . . . ELEVEN, TWELVE, THIRTEEN!" THIRTEEN of them. Now Amanda's bad dog comes along and EATS some of the eggs. Oh, bad dog. [Children swell with laughter.] The dog eats some of the eggs. He eats this one and that one and that one and that one and that one. He eats FIVE of the eggs. Count FIVE with me [in unison:] ONE, TWO, THREE, FOUR, FIVE . . . Now here is the QUESTION: HOW many good eggs does Amanda have LEFT?! She had THIRTEEN eggs and the dog ate FIVE, so how many does she have left now? Take your counting sticks or stones in front of you and take away FIVE of them. So how many are left?! . . .

The energy of teaching at Nomad was powerful, both in what it took and in what it gave back. But teachers consider it a major struggle to maintain this energy and commitment at a place like Nomad. More afternoons than I can remember, the teachers were drained from teaching and sank into what could be called professional depression. The days were long and the wages short. After mandatory deductions for insurance, taxes, and so on, take-home pay was just K 175 a fortnight, about U.S.$175 per month. Given the largesse of the government payroll and its budgets in Daru and Kiunga, this was hard to understand. Moreover, teachers' pay was often delayed months at a time; they called continually on the radio in attempts to dislodge their paychecks from one official or another. Adding to this injury, each teacher had to pay K 10 to the pilot when he landed in order to receive a paycheck. And with no bank at Nomad, none of the tiny trade stores at the station would cash a government check without imposing a large surcharge.

The school's budget was similarly strapped. In 1998, it was K 898 per quarter—less than U.S.$20 per student per year. In addition to supplies, teaching aids, year-end prizes, and everything else, the budget had to cover air freight for everything brought in at the rate of one kina per kilogram. Unsurprisingly, teachers often felt pressed to supplement the school budget with their own meager salaries.

Finances at Nomad create a byzantine path since most expenditures are made by proxy in the town of Kiunga by whatever government official happens to be traveling there. Funds must be lent, items bought and retained and kept in good condition by the recipient, change received back from the sale, and reciprocity rendered to the person who conducted the transactions—including the cost of air freight and other intangibles associated with the work of conducting this business on behalf of someone else. Tracking these convolutions and their unanticipated results adds greatly to the overall logistics of paperwork as well as leaving loopholes for funds to slip through the cracks even when all parties are well-intentioned.

The bureaucracy of finance compounds that of keeping lesson books, exam spreadsheets, and attendance records. The walls of the Nomad School office are covered with official documents, charts, and memos, including two elaborate administrative flow charts that include boxes and arrows replete with ID numbers and functions and duties and codes for the "administrative structure"—that is, the four teachers of the Nomad School. A list of the school's difficulties was written by the teachers during a staff meeting for their annual report:

> Nomad Community School action plan.
> Basic purpose:
> To improve the standard of the school by repairing the school buildings, imposing
>   tougher rules, making teachers prepare advance programming so that the
>   children will have good education which will make them useful members of
>   the community.

Related to this:

Problems—in no particular order

(1) Attendance; (2) Behavior; (3) Health/clothing; (4) Basic materials;
  (5) Furnitures, e.g., desks; (6) Classrooms (poor condition); (7) Disturbances
  by moving public [people going through school grounds]; (8) Lack of parents'
  support; (9) Lack of fencing for the school grounds; (10) Staff shortage and
  poor teacher housing; (11) Possibility of theft and break and enter at
  the school; (12) Pay problems: teachers not paid; (13) Cashing checks;
  (14) High food prices [for store goods]; (15) School subsidy not forthcoming;
  (16) Inspection [inspectors do not arrive to certify teacher planning
  books]; (17) Transportation—cost of airfares going very high; (18) DMT
  [district management team] meeting ["This depends on one man, and he is
  an Idi Amin type. There should be a committee, but he takes all the
  money."]; (19) Lack of school funds; (20) Social problems; (21) Mailing
  system [no incoming mail except as physically collected while visiting Kiunga];
  (22) Multigrade teaching not paid [no pay increment for teaching a double
  class]; (23) Hardship allowance [not forthcoming]; (24) Boarding allowance
  [not forthcoming]; (25) Gazette not published [no public listing of teaching
  jobs for purposes of application or transfer; teaching positions are allocated
  through word of mouth and cronyism].

Some of these problems were highlighted for the country as a whole in one of Port Moresby's two daily newspapers, *The National,* in a 1999 article titled "Lack of teachers deprives students of education."

> The status and salaries of teachers leave much to be desired. The failure of inspectors in some provinces to do their work denies teachers the opportunity for promotion and causes deep dissatisfaction. The real situation with teachers in remote or isolated schools is ignored, which adds to the problems. Allowances for remote teacher payment are gazetted but not paid. No wonder remote schools are abandoned and the teachers leave.

Given all this, I was amazed these four instructors worked as conscientiously as they did, notwithstanding the time they gave over each day to student "mulling." Like teachers in most places, those at Nomad persevere out of raw commitment plus the enjoyment of educating children. With understated pride, Mr. Ano reminisced one day about the students he had taught over the years, including a number who were now teachers themselves. As headmaster, he is highly mindful of the school's bureaucratic, financial, material, and logistical limitations. But he continues after a quarter century with a dedication that balances cynicism with humor and self-effacement. One Sunday I started back to Gasumi Corners from the station and found Mr. Truman, the veteran first-grade teacher, cutting the school yard—larger than two football fields—with the school's rotary push lawnmower. The grass was five inches high and it was about 100 degrees. He tried to make light of the situation: "This is grassroots education!"

The Backward Slide and the Forward March

Schooling at Nomad is beset by a deep sense of being behind the curve, of being bypassed and left behind by what is more modern. As part of this malaise, teachers and government officials easily slip from their awareness that the station needs more resources to a more disparaging view: that people in the Nomad area are backward, unappreciative, and ultimately deserve the lack of development that besets them. This perception emerges in cycles of disgruntlement between teachers or administration officers and villagers.

At one outlying school, disagreements escalated until the one teacher was ousted by the local community on the grounds that he had been overbearing and dictatorial. In response, the provincial board of education decided to "teach the villagers a lesson" by not sending any teachers to the school for several years; the school was closed.[13] Even at Nomad, the difficulty of living in a poorly supplied station can easily lead to projecting fault onto the local community. This persists despite the fact—as teachers widely acknowledge—that Nomad is a safer and more friendly place than most towns and cities in Papua New Guinea. It has few problems of discipline at school, affords garden land that is readily lent to teachers, and sells fresh produce cheaply at the local Nomad market. Teachers also note that they can be active social leaders at Nomad and regular players on the Nomad sports teams. Notwithstanding these attractions, the dominant perception remains that Nomad is a backward and uninviting place to live. In this respect, the spiritual and moral shortcomings emphasized by Christian teaching combine with logistical problems and the desire for material amenities associated with life in towns or cities.

Amid these difficulties, the school and the churches work to promote mental and moral progress for a local populace that is seen as backward and in need of enlightenment. Educational and religious agendas are closely linked. Christian education is taught as a regular subject at the Nomad School, sometimes by the local pastors themselves. This instruction is facilitated by school use of Bible comics, which combine literacy training and graphic illustrations of scriptural stories. In church, reciprocally, school teachers are the most frequent and effective preachers at the Evangelical services. Both school and church emphasize the importance of literacy, disciplined learning, individual responsibility, and personal progress directed by the written and verbal authority of those in charge. Two of the three churches have a blackboard behind the altar, where sermon themes and scriptural passages are written and diagramed to instruct the congregation concerning the sermon.

Church and school also share common patterns of socialization. From a young age, children learn to sit and fidget quietly during the long church service—and then to punctuate their wait by rote singing of religious hymns. These experiences provide a model for students' longer hours of passive listening and mulling at school—punctuated by energetic repetition of call-and-response refrains. The link between socialization in church and in school is further reinforced in later instruction—the rote learning of Christian education classes, on the one hand, and the tedious professional training courses that teachers and government officials are periodically subject to, on the other. For those at the bottom of the hierarchy, however—schoolchildren and parishioners—the frustrations of leadership from above are easily redirected onto themselves—that they should take greater responsibility for their own lack of enlightenment.

Radio Blues

The school incident that prompted greatest discussion and concern—and which redirected blame directly onto the villagers—was the theft of the two school radios. Complete with cassette player and loudspeakers, these boom boxes are the icon of modern identity for young men. Boom boxes constitute key symbols of both wider understanding and modern recreation in places like Nomad. They boast modern radio personalities. They reference a larger world through confident intonations of English and tok pisin. And they croon the modern music that combines sexual allure with a style of life based on travel and commodities.

The radios in question also symbolized modernity for the Nomad Community School. Beyond tapes and music, the radios provide national education programs that are broadcast in English for different grades at set times each morning. These broadcasts constitute a regular and prized part of the daily curriculum at the Nomad School.[14] Additionally, the radios are an important instrument of nationalism.[15] In principle, the broadcasts bring together all the students in the country of a particular age and grade level. Nationalism is also reinforced by the theme song of Papua New Guinea, which is broadcast frequently and sung by students. The song boasts a silky Melanesian male vocalist, a glittering chorus, guitars, a catchy tune, and production values consistent with those of a top music and marketing firm from Sydney. The lyrics flow as follows:

> In our land of a thousand tongues, brothers and sisters old and young, unite our spirits so we speak as one. We have to learn to live together side by side. We have to learn to give each other dignity and pride. The strength to be one people, one nation, one country, P.N.G.
>
> [Spoken by Melanesian children as the chorus hums in the background:] We, the people of Papua New Guinea, pledge ourselves united in one nation. We pay homage to our cultural heritage, the source of our strength. We pledge to build a democratic society based on justice, equality, respect, and prosperity for our people. We pledge to stand together as one people, one nation, one country. God bless Papua New Guinea! [All singing loudly:] [. . .] Unite to be one people, one nation, one country: P.N.G.!!!"

This catchy and rousing tune is well-conceived for collectivizing listeners by linking local cultural pride with unity and national progress. In the mix, ethnic diversity becomes fully consistent, rather than in tension, with national integration, on the one hand, and the democracy of Western-style government, on the other. So successful and popular is this song that I have heard twenty year olds break out singing along with its broadcast. It is particularly fitting that this message arrives by radio, the machine of fluent English and pidgin instruction as well as musical modernity.

Against this background, the theft of the two radios at the Nomad Community School struck at the heart of the school's mission. This theft became the dominant agenda item at the semiannual Nomad Community School meeting, which, however, did not take place until almost three months after the theft. Sixty-three adults attended, including thirty men and thirty-three women. In fully democratic spirit, everyone who wanted to speak was allowed to do so. This opportunity was taken up by many of the senior men from the station, often at length.

Quickly, the discourse became a harangue against the extended Nomad community and its associated settlements. Repeatedly, the larger community was referred to as "no good and bigheaded" (*ples kamap bikhet no-gut*). This epithet carries the connotation of being noncompliant and conceited—insistent, selfish, and needlessly angry. This resonated with comments that Nomad was an impulsive and unappreciative place, backward and bushy. Nomad was a rotten place. People refused to respect authority. No wonder development wouldn't come to them! This was followed by statements about the moral depravity that had allowed the radios to be stolen in the first place. Everyone was exhorted to look unrelentingly until they were found (even though they had been taken almost three months before). There was little discussion of who the thief could have been, how the radios might be replaced, or how to improve security at the school. Remedies and redress were vague. At issue was the moral culpability of the community as a whole, which had insufficiently supported the school. The larger problems of the school were not caused by the government or teachers, but were the community's own fault. In his calm way, Headmaster Ano underscored the seriousness of this theft. He stated matter-of-factly that "teachers will not want to stay at a place like Nomad if the community doesn't support the school. For a community with a bad reputation, no new teachers will come and the school will close."[16]

As the discussion widened, it linked moral condemnation to a more general explanation of why Nomad stays so undeveloped and so poorly supported by the government. Speakers dramatically emphasized that if important things like school radios are lost, the government won't want to invest in such a "bad place." One even opined that airplanes wouldn't come to the airstrip if the radios weren't returned. The reasoning here was that if the flow of goods to Nomad dwindles beyond a critical level, there would be no reason for planes to land at the station. (This comment had special impact since the local airline had just raised the cost of air freight to Nomad by 60 percent.) "It is YOU who must get it back," yelled one man emphatically. "You must check *everywhere,* Samo, Biami, Kubor, Gebusi, all the corners and bush places. Check all the big boys. We must find this."

The meeting was a four-and-a-half-hour marathon. At many points, the speeches evoked the guilt-ridden invective of Nomad church services. In both cases, the shortcomings of the community included backwardness, sin, and bigheadedness. By contrast, the modern wealth that alternately attracts and reflects status and authority was contrasted with the absence of goodness and morality. If the church measured shortcomings against modern divinity, the school articulated these moral failings with the local failure of educational and economic progress. These were linked as two sides of the same coin.

Ultimately, the drama of the stolen radios was as much about the perception of Nomad as a backward and undeveloped place as it was about finding the thief or obtaining recompense. About a month later, one of the radios was found and returned, though it was broken. Everyone denied knowing who the original thief had been, and the matter was dropped with little fanfare. The goal had not been to find and punish the perpetrator but to publicize a collective condition of unworthiness. In the process, parents of children at the Nomad Community School were reinforced in the belief that lack of development was their own fault.

Imagining the Future

Toward the end of my stay at Nomad, I sponsored a draw-a-picture contest for the school children to portray "what you want to be in the future." I had accepted my inability to get the students to talk about their school experience, even in private, and so wondered whether their artistic representations would be more revealing. Had students internalized a sense of limitation or failure? Or had their desire to be modern held sway despite all frustrations to the contrary? Their graphic answers were striking and definitive. Emerging in bright color and filling the page were student drawings of themselves as airplane pilots, machine operators, teachers, soldiers, nurses, policemen, and even a TV technician, scientist, professional actor, and rock singer. The students were enthusiastic about the project. Hardly speaking, they stopped me on the trail to the Nomad Station to show me their wonderful works-in-progress. Some made several full-scale drafts before turning in a final picture.

Adult roles of modern power and command captivated the boys: almost half of them (31 of 46) drew pictures of themselves as members of the police or the P.N.G. Defense Force. Another 22 percent projected themselves as an airplane or helicopter pilot—usually uniformed and standing next to or sitting inside the colorful aircraft they flew. One boy wanted to be Moses and another wanted to be in heaven. Of the sixty-four drawings the boys submitted, only three were "traditional": two boys portrayed themselves in traditional dance costumes, and a third as a fisherman (but wearing blue jeans and a cowboy hat).

Girls' responses were almost equally modern. Over one-fourth (11 of 40) wanted to be a trained nurse and another quarter (10 of 40) envisioned themselves as teachers. One-eighth (5 of 40) of the girls portrayed themselves in the Defense Force, and another eighth simply wanted to be "a woman"—dressed in a pretty Western dress, but with a face that often had no mouth. One-tenth (4 of 40) portrayed themselves in heaven, and one girl aspired to be a doctor and another a pilot. The only traditional drawings were one girl who drew herself as an old woman in traditional dress, and another who drew herself fetching water.

The energy, color, and aspirations of these drawings makes me wish I could reproduce all of them for readers to see. Though some are copied from schoolbooks, many are intricately designed and wonderfully creative. The agency that I had found missing in student discourse and writing was conveyed through their imaginative drawings of a modern future.

Of course, the reality is that almost none of these children will realize their dreams of becoming a policeman or pilot or nurse or teacher. Some of the government workers' children will end up with education and paid employment, but precious few among the rest have a realistic chance of this. With no roads and no real employer in the Nomad Subdistrict except the government itself, education and Christianity are the effective routes upward. The practical result for villagers is not a material world of being modern, but its desire, fantasy, and aspiration. The emulation of this imagined modernity emerges through the local construction of a vernacularly modern style of life.

Given this outcome, what social result does the school produce? Perhaps it was best symbolized by what happened at the end of the prize contest. The teachers divided the prize money into tiny units and spread it among a wide range of drawings from the various grades. Finding a number of additional entries that I also wanted to reward—including more by girls and some "traditional" ones—I added more funds and extended the list of awards. The result was that a large number of students each received less than one kina as recognition. They still considered this to be an honor and a major recognition. Packed into a single classroom, the entire school cheered as the members of the school oversight committee called each artist forward to receive prize money and have his or her drawing shown to the school. The energy was electric—but few of those called forward could bear to look up. Most of them shuffled and looked at the ground, embarrassed. Asked, they were unable to speak.

Ultimately, the longing to be modern and successful is as high as its required agency is missing. The school cultivates both sides of this paradox, just as the lament about the stolen school radios increases the community's desire to attain what is good and modern while decrying and internalizing its inability to do so.

The Meaning of Meeting

School at Nomad, in the best spirit of neoliberalism and progressivism, fuels the imagination and the fantasy of being successful in a future modern world. Yet the structure and practical result of its educational dynamic, notwithstanding the school's committed and well-intentioned teachers, is to promote a recessive agency in students' speaking and writing that is not just refractory to the hoped-for world but directly antithetical to its effective appropriation. As in so many rural settings in developing countries, the structure of well-meaning education—the endless sitting, listening, and copying—produces by its structure the very things it would seem to oppose in principle and in personal intent.

This pattern is structural and cannot be blamed on teachers' laziness or incompetence. It does not limit itself to students but reproduces itself in the duties and meetings of staff members. The teachers at Nomad feel justifiably crushed by the demands of sitting and copying reams of work for the sake of bureaucratic justification. The evaluators of the high school entrance exams stagger under this same ethic, duplicating fivefold the massive work of grading the efforts of all high school applicants in the Western Province. As discussed in the previous chapter, a structure of laborious listening and copying pervades the Catholic development courses given at Nomad as well as their prayer leader courses in Kiunga, just as it did the police education course taken by Constable Gobi in Tabubil, alluded to in chapter 4. The area affairs officer at Nomad confided a similar exhaustion to me when he flew back to Nomad from a provincial budget meeting—carrying a weighty stack of memos, forms, and new procedural protocols to apply for funds that would probably never arrive. The paperwork for ever-changing procedures has become massive and requires interminable hours of new rote learning.

Amid the difficulties of bureaucracy in the Western Province emerges an escalating pattern of ever-newer reform initiatives—each of which requires its own new instructional meetings, paperwork, and guidelines for ever-more-complicated policies and bookkeeping. In 1998, these initiatives included a government decentralization initiative, several new changes in budgetary policy and procedure, and a new national school reform plan, funded by the Australian Agency for International Development. All of these projects stress local empowerment and are based on neoliberal principles. But all these initiatives, like the students at the Nomad Community School, are prone to burnout, despair, and passivity. The problems of recessive agency—of being reduced to passive listening and copying, and being blamed for the problems in the system—are linked directly to bureaucratic attempts to "fix" the problem of local disempowerment. The result is a new round of yet more ostensibly new and improved bureaucratic programs and guidelines and policies. Progressive as these may be in principle, they end up aggravating the problems of red tape and recessive agency that are ostensibly being addressed, including among staff members.

Particularly at the local level, the weight of passive absorption is compounded by self-criticism, guilt, and the never-ending feeling of being backward and inadequate for a modern world. In a Christian country like Papua New Guinea—and perhaps especially in remote places like Nomad—these sentiments easily articulate with the fundamentalism that makes local failing a personal sin caused by lack of personal discipline, motivation, and effort. Hence it is that the Nomad Community School meeting so eerily echoes church invective—the long moral harangue, the masculine preaching about personal responsibility for sin and failure, and the sense that those who fail have themselves to blame.

For students at Nomad, this takes place in the larger context of a school that they leave aside in their teenage years, at the end of grade six. It imprints village children with fantastic possibilities and ultimately dashed hopes of modern success. They nonetheless look back upon school as a largely positive experience. It provides energized exposure to a way of modern life beyond their home settlement. Like the young men at the conclusion of their Christianization course, discussed in the previous chapter, they would mostly claim to be appreciative and happy about their experience at school, notwithstanding the active passivity it creates by way of modern engagement.

Chapter 8

The Corners in the Round

Institutions and historical trends do not make a life. As Clifford Geertz once said, "No one lives in the world in general." The changing lives of Gasumi Corners emerge from their history to twine with modern institutions, but they cannot be reduced to features such as school, church, police, government bureaucracy, and so on. As crucial as such institutions now are for contemporary anthropology, they need to be put in the context of people's broader experience. Most Gebusi have sporadic contact with the police, selective if poignant exposure to Christianity, and half of the adult men and almost all of the adult women have had little or no experience of schooling. Although these are cutting edges of change, they are far from fully determining life in contemporary Gasumi Corners. This is true in most of Papua New Guinea and indeed in most countries of the so-called developing world: institutions and other engines of modern change have an impact that is at once crucial and incomplete.

More broadly, the occurrence of change and the products it produces do not seem easily predictable by either the intrusions of a modern world or resistances against it. This simple point is sometimes neglected by our most prominent theoreticians of modern change—whether they focus on economic development, the impact of the global on the local, or the persistence of local culture despite the appearance of modern engagement. As ethnographers have often shown, it is important to know and feel the daily rounds of elsewhere—even if and especially when they do not fit our existing categories of change or stasis. It is hence a good idea to have daily patterns of Gebusi experience fresh in mind before moving toward ethnographic and theoretical generalizations. This more rounded view dovetails with my own field experience, which was based in Gasumi Corners and focused on the lives and activities within its four hamlets as much as it did on events and institutions at the Nomad Station.

◆ ◆ ◆

The first sounds of the morning were usually schizoid. Twelve feet to one side, in the house next door, young wife Oip would grapple with making food and building a fire while her little boy was hungry and cranky and still sleepy. Twenty feet to the other side, in one of the men's houses, her husband, Gwabi, would be lounging with some of the other men, sleeping in or having a quiet smoke as they recovered from a late-night palaver the evening before. Half an hour later the kids would be fed and those old enough to go would be off to school. Everyone else would wander around slowly, clearing their heads of fog as the mist rose in the forest clearings around them.

Once the day gets rolling, a tradition of flexible time and activity intersects with the expected events and activities for that day of the week. Monday through Friday, when children and young teenagers are at school, adults talk casually over cooked bananas before beginning whatever gardening or foraging or domestic activity they plan for the day. For activities in the forest or in the settlement itself, planning is almost as loose, unstructured, and relaxed as it was in 1980–82. Sit around talking and enjoy a slow morning for an hour or more, especially if rain has come in. Wander off to cut some bananas or fetch some firewood. Talk and smoke some more. Go off for the more strenuous work of digging a garden or processing sago or hunting, perhaps for several days in the forest. Tasks can easily be changed, and the weather also makes changes of plan without warning—and sometimes more than once in a day—baking now, pouring then, rivers rising or falling, mud everywhere or caking to hardpan.

Flexibility for adults also extends to the Nomad Station—the freedom to see what is going on at the government office, the market, the weekend ball games, to see if there are goods in the tiny family trade stores, or just wander around and "go for a spin" (*spin degra*). The young bachelors have the greatest freedom; they can stay where they want, sleeping here or there, visiting, clowning, working, schmoozing, aspiring to flirt. Women are more constrained, but they have their own choices and often go off in their own groups, including to the Nomad market on Tuesday and Friday mornings. Their lives are less constrained than they were before by either fear of tribal violence or the sexual jealousy of husbands. Almost unthinkable in 1980, now young married women sometimes even go off with kin to enjoy feasts in other villages while their husbands stay behind.

Amid the apparent laissez-faire, gardens get cut and planted, food is gathered or harvested, houses are built, children are raised, village feasts are prepared for, relatives are visited, and so on. Gebusi have always had a low-labor subsistence regime, and this easy past also informs their present. Rough-hewn gardens easily sprout with the suckers of bananas and other produce, some of which may be sold at the Nomad market. Cleared land yields one crop or two at most; after that, the ground lies fallow for years while sites are claimed from other timberland. Except for sporadic weeding, little effort is needed once trees are cut and the seedlings planted. Most plots have the luxury of being unfenced, including the large gardens of sweet potato that sprout on much of the land surrounding Gasumi Corners—since the community's pigs are kept on the other side of the Kum River.

Further afield is the forest, seemingly endless in all directions and even more thinly settled than it was before. With no roads, its stately timber remains intact. The quiet solace and broad abundance of the forest remain vital for Gebusi, providing serenity and relaxation as well as food and materials for living. A smile of cool air welcomes the family under the canopy—a little vacation from life in the village.

Added to the options of the forest and the village, of course, are those of the church, school, and other institutions we have not yet encountered, such as Nomad's twice-a-week market, its sports team competitions, evening entertainment at the Nomad Station, and the Nomad health clinic. These and other attractions enlarge the variety of life and the array of potential activities and experiences.

Fashioning Lives in Gasumi Corners

Gebusi lifestyles shuttle between Corner, forest, and the Nomad Station. Do Gebusi have more choices than before? In many ways, they do. There are choices of church, market, sports, going to the forest or taking a "spin" to the Nomad Station, of participating or not participating in special events—feasts, parties, Independence Day, and so on. Both individually and collectively, the people of Gasumi Corners fertilize their hopes with the choices they make. Their options remain traditional as well as modern; one can pursue a life of gardening and hunting in the forest and minimize exposure to modern features and influences. Even men who explore modern roles and institutions may later retire to a more traditional life—as is common throughout much of rural Melanesia.

This variety has an important gendered dimension: women and men have different exposures to the outside world. Though over half the men of Gasumi Corners have been to Kiunga (19/33, 57.6%), the same is true of only about one woman in seven (5/33, 15.2%). As discussed in the previous chapter, few women can understand tok pisin or English. Women do go to church, however, and they participate in the Nomad market. Girls go to school along with the boys, and younger women easily go to video night and other activities at Nomad, plus dancing disco in their own community.

Given these developments, indigenous and more contemporary alternatives almost intrinsically emerge as figure and ground for each other—and for women as well as men. This tension continues as practices deemed traditional continue to morph but fail to catch up with the promises of being modern. In the process, people are confronted with a variety of potential activities and roles: student, sports player, churchgoer, prayer leader, string band performer, disco dancer, and so on. Within this enlarging context, indigenous capacities—being a good hunter or dancer or gardener—take on increasingly contrastive status vis-à-vis alternatives that emerge as more modern.

My friend Wobebiay, son of a dead spirit medium, is now a strong and robust man. Quickly bored with school and reticent by nature, he had little education but is physically adept and has become an excellent hunter and skilled house builder. A few years ago, Wobebiay walked all the way to Kiunga to see the town. He earned substantial money working as a manual laborer when an oil exploration team hired workers to cut transects through the forest. Wobebiay's cash dissipated quickly upon his return to Gasumi Corners, however, and he has since resumed a traditional lifestyle, including rejection of Christianity. As a visitor at one of the recent initiations, he performed in full traditional costume and was the most stunning of the dancers.

Wobebiay's life course contrasts with the budding manhood of Anagi, son of the elected councillor of Gasumi Corners. A graduate of sixth grade, Anagi is an avid sportsman and captain of the Gasumi rugby and soccer teams. He has also emerged as a prayer leader at the Catholic church, labors to read and write, and was recently chosen to fly to Kiunga and attend a church instruction course. He returned from this modern trip to town with a new pair of cleated sports shoes and a boom box, which is a pride of Gasumi Corners. Anagi is dapper by Nomad's standards and has already won the heart of a girl from a neighboring community. Though neither Anagi nor Wobebiay have "sisters" who could be enjoined to gain them brides in sister-exchange, Anagi, who is still a late teenager, recently married his girlfriend without paying significant bridewealth. In such cases, the strength of the woman's desire to stay with the man—sometimes against the wishes of her own relatives—can be a determining factor. Wobebiay, on the other hand, has failed to attract a wife and is still a bachelor, despite passing well into his mid-twenties, beyond the age by which a man should be married (see Knauft 2001).

Though many features inform the contrast between Wobebiay and Anagi, their differing relationship to modern values and lifestyles helps explain their divergent outcomes when it comes to attracting a wife. In this respect, the impetus to be modern is a powerful force exerted through personal choice by women as well as men.

Penny-ante Production

Much of what happens in Gasumi Corners can be traced as parts of a weekly cycle. We can begin with Monday mornings on alternate weeks, which are designated as a time of community work. This collective labor usually entails clearing grass and intruding brush from the paths that connect the four hamlets of Gasumi Corners and link them to Nomad. The work is sometimes paid for by the elected ward leader, who gets a yearly allocation of between 750 and 1,000 kina from the provincial government for infrastructural maintenance in Gasumi Corners and several other communities. Not everyone works, of course—some are off in the bush or just recalcitrant on any given Monday. But those who don't work don't get paid on those occasions when money is handed out. And the ward leader entreats those who don't work on one occasion to do their part at a later time.

Tuesday mornings are for market, as are Fridays. For Gasumi Corners, the Nomad market helps distinguish the present from the early 1980s, when the community lived in the bush and was too distant to participate. Now, however, Nomad is only a half-hour's walk away. Twice a week, women laden with produce trudge out of Gasumi Corner before 7 A.M. Predictably, the market also draws from those in Nomad's other corners: Samo, Honibo, Biami, Pare, and Kubor. Like the community school, then, the Nomad market is a multiethnic scene; Gebusi comprise only about one-sixth of those present.

Perched above a graceful bend in the Nomad River, the marketplace boasts an expansive roof that shelters half a dozen broad tables and, on market mornings, a bustling flock of a hundred and fifty or so sellers, buyers, and onlookers. Vendors take over the market tables on the side or corner of the market that is closest to the community from which they have come. They spread their food and plunk themselves behind, in front, or underneath the tables, while the few potential buyers and many nonbuyers roam around. The food is fresh and clustered in mounded piles. No signs or negotiations are necessary, since the general size of food piles and price for each is standardized. On a good morning, the market becomes a cornucopia that spawns a vigorous whirl of socializing and inspection, though general activity far exceeds actual buying. Quality plantains and sweet potatoes are the staple food items. Depending on the season, other foods for sale include bamboo shoots, breadfruit seeds, Tahitian chestnuts, coconuts, pitpit, taro, yam, forest greens, papayas, sugar cane, sago, and introduced crops such as peanuts, pineapple, squash, corn, cucumbers, and an English variety of potato. Most purchases—excepting the casual purchase of peanuts for twenty toea—are made by the few station workers and particularly by their wives.

I became interested enough in the Nomad market to keep systematic records for all the sellers from Gasumi Corners who showed up on any of 25 different market days. Over nine-tenths of the sellers were women (285/313, 91.1%). A similar pattern characterized the other ethnic groups; as is common in Melanesia, women are the primary sellers at food markets. Especially for those who come from remote areas, it is hard to overestimate this gendered significance. Unheard of in 1980, women from Gasumi Corners are now agents in monetary transactions. Typically unaccompanied by husbands or brothers,[1] they regularly carry food to the Nomad Station, sell food to male or female buyers from the station or from other ethnic groups, and have primary control over the money obtained—at least to begin with.[2]

More broadly, the ability to sell food at Nomad has influenced the community's own subsistence as well as becoming an important aspect of its identity. Previously, sweet potatoes were a rare and insignificant food, but now they are raised in large quantities using mounding techniques introduced by agricultural officers. These nutritious tubers are now frequently eaten in Gasumi Corners and are a significant component of their feasts—as well as being sold at the Nomad market. The association of sweet potatoes with being more modern dovetails with residents' statements that government workers' desire for sweet potatoes was the reason they began cultivating them in larger numbers at Gasumi Corners.

The growing of sweet potatoes has also affected the raising of pigs. Pigs eat sweet potatoes with a vengeance, but the fencing of gardens is an arduous task that Gebusi have always avoided. To safeguard their tubers, the residents of Gasumi Corners now keep the 18 pigs that belong to community members on the other side of the broad Kum River, just a few minutes from their hamlets. The elimination of pigs from the hamlets of Gasumi Corners is taken as a positive modern development in another sense as well, since pigs used to foul the village with feces and by rooting in the mud following rains, as well as being a general nuisance. The absence of pigs is seen to make settlements cleaner and more hygienic as well as protecting root crops.[3]

In addition to sweet potatoes and pigs, the Nomad market has also influenced the raising of specialty crops such as peanuts, pineapples, squash, and corn for sale at the station. In addition, domesticated pigs may be butchered and their pork sold at the market, though the number of pigs raised is too small and their social value too high for this to happen frequently (see Minnegal and Dwyer 1997). The desire to sell surplus food does, however, impact Gebusi foraging, since those coming back from the forest may return with extra net bags filled with bamboo shoots, Tahitian chestnuts, greens, or other food for sale at the market.

How much economic impact does the Nomad market have in Gasumi Corners? On an average market day, 11.4 women from the community go as sellers—plus fractionally less than one man. Of the 34 teenage or adult women in Gasumi, this means that a bit over one-third go to sell produce on a given market day. Large net bags heavy with tubers and bananas and other produce are lugged to market every week, but women from Gasumi Corners sell less than half (49.8%) of the items they bring. And prices are extremely low. A sizable pile of sweet potatoes—fourteen or so large tubers weighing about ten pounds—sells for one kina (U.S.$0.50). A large haulm of bananas (also about 10 pounds) sells for 2 kina, while a plump bunch of sweet bananas fetches a mere 20 toea (U.S.$0.10). Many other items, such as peanuts, bamboo shoots, Tahitian chestnuts, and greens, are also sold in 20 toea units. For U.S.$5, one could buy a whopping 50-pound assortment of different kinds of quality foods. But few have money to spend and demand is low, determined largely by a few government workers and their sparse disposable income. Despite the labor involved, the average yield for a woman who makes a selling excursion to the Nomad market is only K 1.20 (U.S.$0.60). Over 20 percent of those women who bring produce

(68/313 = 21.7%) sell nothing at all. And food left unsold must either be taken back to Gasumi or simply given away for free, since the fixed unit/fixed cost system of market selling does not allow vendors to reduce their prices in an attempt to sell their food.

For women, carrying heavy net bags of produce to market, waiting, and returning takes an entire morning—in addition to the labor of growing and harvesting the food, or foraging it from deeper in the forest. If one were to calculate the money earned per calories of energy exerted in producing and marketing the food, the yield would be frighteningly low. The uneconomical nature of marketing is underscored by the exorbitant price of the few foods and other items available for purchase at the tiny Nomad trade stores. A one kilo bag of rice or a single tin of low-grade mackerel costs about K 3.00. Either of these items costs the entire proceeds of almost a month of the average woman's sales at market.[4] Yet, women are easily pressured by men to use market money for these very items—tinned fish or rice—to be used in village feasting.

Added to these economic costs are social ones. Selling food at the market puts women in a passive role vis-à-vis buyers. With initially high hopes for the best produce they have, women wait patiently for two or two and a half hours and usually sell less than half and many times none of what they have brought. With so many sellers and so few purchasers, it is decidedly a buyer's market. Given the fixed-price system of marketing, there is virtually no verbal interaction between buyers and sellers. So the women wait and wait (see photo 14). They often seem unhappy that their efforts are not more productive and are visibly disheartened or embarrassed by the sizable public display on the selling table of their unsold produce as the market proceeds.

Despite the passive and uncomfortable wait, marketing has tenacious cultural value. Women keep coming week after week. This underscores the extreme importance of earning money, however little. The desire for money persists and intensifies as its source remains out of reach. As in school and church, however, women's participation in the market results in recessive agency: the willing desire to put oneself in a condition of passivity, waiting, and subordination to those with more modern power in the hopes of becoming more modern, however slightly.

Of course, the market also provides other less tangible benefits than earning small amounts of money. It remains a place of energy and gossip and information. The market is also the place where a government official shouts public announcements about special activities or developments at the station. Some women walk to market for the occasion even if they have nothing to sell. The same is true of the occasional man and especially un-married bachelors, who often come after the market has started and hang around its periphery smoking and socializing. But women remain physi-cally and symbolically at the center of the market as a modern institution—even if they do not sell very much.

Of Sports, Waiting, and Watching

Saturday and Sunday afternoons provide the occasion for ball games at the Nomad sports field, which is now an important part of male community culture. Gasumi Corners has its own rugby and soccer teams comprised of school graduates and young adult men plus a few others from Nomad, who complete the squad. They also compete in volleyball and darts. On Saturday and Sunday afternoons, the "Gasumi Youths" pair off in rugby, soccer, and sometimes other sports against teams from another corner of Nomad—one of the six teams comprised of Samo, Kubor, or Bedamini; the one Pare team; or the team comprised of those living at the Nomad Station itself (see photo 15). The matches are orchestrated by a Youth Organization Committee at the station. Each team chooses a captain and pays nominal dues to defray the costs of the organizing committee, the referees and timekeeper, and those who periodically keep the field and the goal posts in repair.

Beyond the games themselves, the sports contests are important for spectatorship. The men from Gasumi Corners are regular supporters of their local team, and they walk to the station and wait for the matches in which their team plays. This waiting often takes much or most of the day, since the time schedule for beginning a given match is undependable and often delayed. It is not uncommon for Gebusi men to sit and watch four or six or even eight complete games of soccer and rugby from midday until dusk on Saturday and Sunday, including contests that may occur after their own team has finished its matches. Over the hours of watching the games, an almost couch-potato mentality develops among the observers. In this man-ner, almost all the men and boys from Gasumi Corners spend a large part of each Saturday and Sunday afternoon watching a lengthy series of sports matches on the Nomad ball field.

Amid the waiting and watching, sports spectatorship allows men from different communities and ethnic groups to associate lightly with each other. Though each community's spectators tend to stay on "their" side or corner of the field, there is no demonstrative rooting or defined space for one or another group of supporters. Men occasionally wander over and shake the hands and smoke or otherwise visit with someone they know from another community along the sidelines. Unlike the traditional male etiquette of welcoming visitors with frontal display and attentiveness, those sitting nearby do not focus on each other but have their relationship mediated by the common "third" that absorbs their gaze for such long periods of time: the action on the field. This shared attention allows space for intermittent comments and interaction while circumventing any expectation of giving or receiving anything. Like a stretched elastic band, this allows sociality across a larger cultural space while thinning its dynamics. Men easily shift their location among the spectators and may wander off or walk home alone. As such, sports spectatorship provides a modern form of unobligated social association, individualistic in nature and accompanied by long periods of waiting and silence.

In selected ways, the same is true of the players on the field. As opposed to the traditional ritual fights that pit visitors and hosts against each other as enemies over a specific social dispute, sports matches depersonalize competition between opposing sides and allow them to play without grievance and walk away impersonally when the contest is over. In ritual fights, by contrast, enmity was physically expressed by attacking with long sticks but then reconciled by the snapping of fingers and the sharing of food—so that a positive social relationship between the sides was actively reestablished.[5]

Sports competition presents a more modern dynamic. On the field, competition is managed to domesticate both the expression of antagonism and the possibility of future relationship. Interaction is governed by rules of play that are carefully overseen and effectively enforced by officials. It was striking to me in this remote place that sports games were officiated by referees with whistles, line judges with flags, and a timekeeper who sounded the siren on the station's airhorn to signify the beginning and end of periods of play. Government workers usually served as the referees, and during many hours of watching, I never saw or heard of their officiating being disputed. Like the authority of the pastor or the teacher or the policeman, then, the judgment of the referee—the icon of modern authority—was final and beyond challenge.

In selected respects, sports at Nomad are almost the realization of a dream of early patrol officers: that rugby or soccer competition between enemy groups could replace their rivalry in warfare. Gebusi do sometimes worry that fights might break out between the teams—particularly when the Bedamini team is losing. But there was only one small ethnic altercation among the matches during my stay. In the larger and more populous parts of Papua New Guinea, by contrast, sports competitions can carry distinct risk of fighting, and matches may be curtailed or the season canceled as a result.[6]

Due largely to their own disinclination, women from Gasumi Corners seldom watch men's sports competitions.[7] They do, however, attend as supporters if and when their daughters play in the one women's soccer game, held on the main field on Saturday and again on Sunday. For the most part, the women who play in these matches are wives or older daughters of government officers; they have learned to play team soccer at an elementary or high school elsewhere in the province. As more girls graduate from the Nomad School, however, it is likely that more of them will play sports and that there will be more women's sports teams. The adult women of Gasumi Corner said almost uniformly that they had no objection to girls playing soccer and that they would go to Nomad to watch if their own daughters played.

That organized sports now form a significant part of Gasumi social life came as a complete surprise to me. I was surprised not just by the level of interest and the caliber of play—which was very good—but by the strong internalization of rules, organization, spectatorship, and sportsmanship. At the end of the day when energy and sunlight had expended themselves, the crowd would disperse to its respective corners of Nomad. The men from Gasumi Corners would occasionally reminisce in a low-key way about the best and especially the most comic plays of the day, but little mention was made of the score or of winning or losing. While embarrassing to talk about defeat, it was also improper to gloat over victory or encourage winners to be higheaded. As such, the games appeared to have a sportsmanlike conclusion.

Rounding out the Week from Nomad

In addition to the market on Tuesday and Friday, and sports games on Saturday and Sunday, the residents of Gasumi Corners occupy themselves with church for a significant part of either Saturday or Sunday morning. Since Christianity has been discussed at length in chapter 6, there is no need to comment further here except to note that church services and other church-related activities anchor the weekly calendar and provide the most widely shared activity of modern institutional affiliation and cross-settlement association. In complementary fashion, for older children, weekdays bring daylong attendance at the Nomad Community School.

Though schooling does not directly involve adults, it does exert a significant impact on the weekly structure of community activity. Families of
school children typically make sure that at least one parent—usually the
mother—is at home by late afternoon to feed the children and sleep in
the house with them at night. A family with school-aged children thus has
difficulty going to the forest for extended periods when school is session;
departure for sago processing and foraging in the bush must now be managed with this constraint in mind. It is always possible to pull one's children
out of school for a day or a week. But having paid the K 10 school fee,
parents are reluctant to do this, and they can be quite upset if their children
skip school on their own. As such, the school at Nomad exerts an indirect
influence on the extent and configuration of weekly subsistence and foraging activities—and is probably influential in reducing the percentage of
nights spent away from the settlement by 15 percent since 1980–82.[8]

For residents of Gasumi Corners—and especially teenagers—Friday
and Saturday evenings hold the possibility of special entertainment at Nomad. Every few weeks, one or another of the government workers arranges
a "video night" at the station. The event can draw upwards of two hundred
people, who sit packed on the floor of Nomad's large community hall. Beginning at perhaps 9 P.M., children pay a mere 10 toea and adults 20 toea
to watch random videos that an enterprising official has brought back from
Kiunga to show through a VCR-TV powered by the station's old diesel generator. The films are a bizarre mix of C-grade shoot-em-up army combat
movies, syrupy Christian songfests, rugby matches in Australia, and poorly
plotted Hollywood films of the 1970s or '80s that few in the audience understand. Almost all the videocassettes are in English except P.N.G.'s answer
to MTV music videos, which combines English and tok pisin. The entire
array of videos is shown idiosyncratically back-to-back until the Nomad
power supply is abruptly curtailed at midnight—in the middle of whatever
happens to be running at the time. Video night usually draws a hefty crowd
from all ethnic groups around the station. Estimating from a rough head
count, about 65 percent of those present are boys, 20 percent girls, 10 percent adult men, and 5 percent adult women.

Like the market, school, church, and sports events, video night exposes villagers and wide-eyed youngsters to a larger sample of people in the
Nomad community. It also exposes them to assorted representations of a
world that seems strange and potentially violent but one that is nothing if
not rich, powerful, and full of fancy gizmos and pretty faces and well-
dressed bodies in all sorts of modern activities. Viewing all this, the audience is passive, eager to see and absorb what they can even when the film's

content and meaning is beyond them. Video nights are avidly attended when money can be spared to cover the entrance fee. In addition to young-sters, older people go when they wish, and a few of the bolder widows in Gasumi Corners have taken a shine to video night. According to my house-hold interviews, every child and adult in Gasumi Corners has been to video night at Nomad at one time or another.

A more adventurous and enticing possibility for young unmarried men is attending a disco in another corner settlement at Nomad, also held sporadically on a Friday or Saturday night. These discos at Nomad usually require a small entrance fee and entail the playing of Papua New Guinea cassette music (national "string bands," rock and roll, and so forth) from a full-volume boom box in a cleared area where Western-style fast-dancing can take place. On occasion, a local string band may also perform live mu-sic. For those from Gasumi Corners, discos are particularly charged because a small smattering of single women from other villages, communities, and ethnic groups may be present. The prospect of meeting and perhaps even dancing with one of these women is hugely alluring, but young men have to conquer their embarrassment to actually go to the disco, much less ask a young woman to dance. This assertion of individual agency in a modern intersexual context outside of Gasumi Corners is highly problematic. As I observed, the bachelors can become virtually paralyzed with fear and un-able to continue when they get within earshot of the music after intending to go to an openly advertised disco held in another corner community of Nomad. Married women and even unmarried teenage girls from Gasumi Corners are discouraged from going to such discos, since it is considered racy and improper to court the possibility of dancing with unknown men. Open discos under government oversight at the Nomad Station, however, are somewhat more acceptable, if only to watch or to dance with same-sex friends. In fact, the dancing of young men with their peers, and of women with other women, is by far the most common type of dancing at discos.

Recessive Results

Collectively, the activities and institutions of Nomad have become a major and ongoing part of Gebusi social life. Church, school, market, and sports are all substantial and important parts of the normal social week, in addi-tion to video night or a public disco at the station on an intermittent basis. To these influences are added the direct influence of government officers, police, and the Nomad health clinic, which is freely visited when community members are sick and by women during pregnancy and for childbirth.[9] Though the social dynamics of the Nomad health clinic were beyond the scope of my time and energy to effectively investigate, I did spend enough time there to realize its structural similarity to many contexts discussed above. These features included increased interaction with those from other communities; worries about appearing backward or insufficiently progressive; subordination to outsiders in authority; the importance of waiting for services, knowledge, and judgment of those in control; and a sense of individual responsibility or culpability in responding or failing to respond to the directives given. Together, these features inform Gebusi's practical engagement with what it means to be modern at Nomad.

In none of the contexts considered above have Gebusi been pressured or coerced; Gebusi themselves have taken an active and sometimes very strong initiative to engage and be part of modernizing institutions and practices such as church, school, market, sports, the health clinic, and video or disco nights. More generally, those from Gasumi Corners have moved next to the Nomad Station of their own volition. Yet, their actions have put them in a positions of willing passivity, of protracted and patient waiting, of marked subordination, and of objective payoffs that are minimal or highly deferred relative to their hopes and expectations.[10]

All this betokens recessive agency that engages modern activities and institutions through a cultural and subjective impetus of modern subordination. Because this engagement stresses personal responsibility for being "backward," the result is not to discourage Gebusi from attempting to become more modern, but rather to intensify their passive subordination in an ongoing attempt to achieve its elusive promise.

Another Side to the Coin?

If the institutions and activities associated with Nomad exert a powerful influence on subjectivity, activity, and agency, they do not exhaust Gebusi social experience or cultural orientation. As alluded to at the beginning of this chapter, modern influences do not completely determine activities and interactions in Gasumi Corners itself, nor in the forest or at feasts, dances, and initiations held at other settlements. In all of these contexts, a model of recessive agency does not apply to Gebusi—at least not to the same extent that it does in the institutional contexts considered above and in previous chapters.

A key question is thus posed: What is the relative significance and relationship between so-called modernizing contexts—the activities and institutions of progress authorized by outsiders—and those under greater control by Gebusi themselves? More generally, this question pertains in different cultural and historical contexts to local peoples in many developing countries.

♦ ♦ ♦

Late afternoons are casual times in Gasumi Corners. Families mill about, socialize, and share portions of food. Children still play with that casual and unfettered abandon that seems to know few bounds of age or temperament. Adults enjoy watching toddlers wobble about—tender entertainment toward the end of the day.

As was always true for Gebusi, men's talk and stories and jokes continue to drift past dusk and relax into evening, sometimes continuing late into the night. Nowadays, tales and banter are more apt to revolve around trade goods and money, current goings on in Gasumi Corners and at the Nomad Station than they are to address traditional lore or tales of danger in the forest. As mentioned in chapter 1, the scale of conversation is smaller and less intense, more common among an extended family than among the men of the settlement as a whole.

Songs of Rousing Sadness

Among Gebusi, the evening entertainment of spirit séances has been fully replaced by other kinds of music. Should one be fortunate enough to have a machine with working batteries, the cassette player/boom box now easily attracts male attention after dark. Men's shouts of sadness and longing can rise up with cassette music somewhat like they used to in the all-night séance. Alternatively, a home-grown "string band" singing group of teenage and young adult men, accompanied by guitar, may sing into the night while men in the settlement listen and socialize (see photo 16). Rather than chanting with the to di spirits of old, the string band songs hybridize séance-style chanting with beautiful new harmonies and the tonalities and rhythm of guitar accompaniment. Popular and widely sung, string band songs are occasionally recorded on cassette and shared among the ethnic groups of the Nomad area.

Spanning themes from the traditional to the modern, string band songs are highly diverse. Some of them almost evoke the sexual enticement of the to di spirit women in séances of old, for instance:

Going, coming, going, coming
A man, from where has he come to marry [me]?
Here, drink this good breast; you're not sleeping.
Having slept, who will marry [me]?

A much larger number of songs, however, mix themes of melancholy and
sexual attraction with modern themes of travel or going to school:

I go to school
I look at my friend from before
She looks at me and I look at her,
her eyes fill with tears
Why did you come to play with me?

Or the following:

Woman, *wantok*[11]
Your thoughts that you planted in me, you can't plant them in another
    man.
You write a letter to me at Elabea [a place in the New Guinea highlands]

Many songs evoke travel to distant places or stress nostalgia for home, as
per below:

But for my mother [I would go].
My father went, my father went to the company [for wage labor]
He went, oh sorrow.
I would go, too.

Other songs commemorated particular occasions.[12] Plaintive and haunting,
like haiku in song, string band songs resonate through escalating repetition
and overlaid harmonies. Spine-tingling shouts and expostulations would
sometimes erupt from the male audience, though with nowhere near the
fervor or frequency of emotion as in traditional spirit séances.[13]

As was true in séance singing, string band songs employ dense poetic
imagery that frequently draws on arcane or obscure references, sometimes
from foreign languages. But in perhaps 40 percent of the string band songs,
references and words from foreign languages were so obscure that a wide
range of informants—often including the singers themselves—could not

supply any significant meaning. Some songs were sung largely or wholly in Kubor or Bedamini, which are largely unintelligible to most listeners, and others incorporated song lines said to come from Highlands languages. Other songs presented a hybrid mix of words from different languages and places. Some were sung entirely or almost entirely in tok pisin, and these were palpably modern in content, including some that were nationalistic. The following song in tok pisin was sung for Independence Day celebrations but remains popular throughout the year:

P.N.G., Papua New Guinea
Prime minister of all of us: Somare [the nation's first prime minister],
His power made
Our independence.
It came up
Received in 1975,
United men and women together.

In a few ways, string band singing provides an updated replacement of spirit séances—but it does not in many others. The songs develop a roughly similar aesthetic of melancholy and longing through haunting melodies and harmony. Both kinds of song can be laced with sexual or romantic allusions heightened by a degree of referential obscurity. Both forms have been sung by young men to a male audience at night, and both can be responded to with hyperbolic and intentionally humorous "anger." In my opinion, the singing and harmony of string band songs are at least as beautiful as that of traditional spirit séances.

But string band singing is not the same as traditional singing in a range of crucial respects. Most importantly, string band singing is simply for enjoyment; it has no divinatory function and is not a way to communicate with spirits (see photo 17). No sicknesses are diagnosed, no sorcery inquests generated, no hunting expeditions foreseen, no sorcery suspects indicted, no executions generated. Likewise, string band singing cannot divine the whereabouts of lost pigs or divine the outcome of fish poisoning. Though the entertainment aspect of the traditional séance has been in some ways retained, its divinatory purpose as well as its spiritual and cosmological significance have been effectively eliminated. Additionally, string band singing is not as frequent as séance singing and does not last as long as a séance—perhaps three or four hours instead of a songfest that lasts all night until dawn. Its emotional energy is also significantly less, and string band singing does not generate the energy or pyrotechnics of traditional spirit séances, during which men would scream, display wildly, throw things, or frolic in bodily banter and hysterical humor. The emotional contrast between a spirit séance and a string band performance is a bit like that between going wild at a rock concert and appreciating a jazz band in a restaurant lounge. Most of all, however, the practical efficacy and cosmic agency of string band singing—its ability to articulate spirituality, on the one hand, and to influence concrete social action, on the other—is but a pale shadow of traditional spirit séances.

Guns in the Forest

For those of Gasumi Corners, the flow of weekly activity is more flexible than can be described in a brief synopsis. Choice is great. Older women in particular may have little occasion to visit Nomad except for the occasional market. For men, hunting wild pigs and cassowaries is still what draws them most to the deep forest. The forest is if anything more sparsely inhabited by people than it was in 1980–82.[14]

Hunting is actively pursued by about one-third of the men at Gasumi Corners and it raises significant interest among the rest. Though smaller game can be pursued with an ax, bush knife, or whatever else is at hand, a major hunting trip for wild pigs and cassowaries employs one of Gasumi Corner's two old shotguns whenever possible.[15] A bolt of social electricity surges through the village when word comes that a game animal has been taken. The news means food and festivity and excitement. Even though the owner of the dead animal may now choose to take its meat to the local market (where it will quickly sell), social pressure is still strong enough that the animal is usually cooked and shared in the community. As such, hunting continues to be a collective benefit as well as a triumph of men.

A major hunting expedition takes several arduous days of searching for game deep in the bush and risks not only an empty-handed return but shooting and missing—or being wounded by the charging animal. Shotgun cartridges are extremely valuable; each of them is an individually owned and prized possession. The animal killed does not belong to the hunter, but to the owner of the shell that killed it. This puts the masculine skill of the hunter very much on the line—along with his social relationship to the cartridge owner. A "hit" means the owner gets to distribute a major game animal; a "miss" means the loss of the valuable "arrow," as shotgun shells are called. To go hunting tests one's social relations as well as one's skill with modern weaponry.

Festive Punctuation

Though Gebusi social life is an endless permutation of life in the forest, life at Gasumi Corners, and activities at the Nomad Station, the occasion that still commands the greatest energy and attention in the settlement is the holding of festive events. In their contemporary form, village feasts articulate the forest, Gasumi Corners, and the Nomad Station. Putting on a feast begins with preparatory work in the forest and the garden; men chop sago palms and women process the pith. The resulting sago starch—wet and heavy in bags weighing fifty or sixty pounds—must be carried to the Kum River, where it can be taken by canoe to within a short walk from Gasumi Corners. The processing and transport of sago for a major feast occupies many weeks of backbreaking labor, predominantly by women. In addition to sago, most feasts in Gasumi Corners now also include large quantities of steamed sweet potatoes. Planning a large feast thus also means planning and planting one's gardens well in advance.

Firewood must also be procured in large quantities, and this is not an easy task given the scarcity of fallen tree limbs near Gasumi Corners. Many bushels of cooking leaves and other cooking implements must also be obtained and carried back to the village. Additional food is always needed, including greens and coconuts or Tahitian chestnuts to cook with the sago. For a particularly large feast, men from the host community may also kill one or more domesticated pigs and cook the meat in large sago packets placed over coals.

Work in the forest is important for those attending the feast as visitors as well their hosts. For any major feast—and especially if meat is being served—the hosts are reciprocated in direct exchange with net bags of dried wild pig, cassowary, or fish. Extensive hunting in advance is thus practically required for major visitors. Between this and other chores and activities, both the hosts and the guests are dispersed deep in the forest for several weeks prior to a major feast. It is hence the climactic food giving that brings them out of relative isolation and into the large-scale sociality and festivity of the host settlement.

The "Nomad Station" component of contemporary feasts includes food, especially tinned fish and rice, bought and carried back by the hosts from one of the tiny trade stores at Nomad. Still considered an expensive luxury, tinned fish and rice are nonetheless an obligatory dimension of feasting at Gasumi Corners and in other communities close to Nomad. The hosts pool their paltry cash reserves to buy overpriced items at local Nomad trade stores. Given the need for at least twenty or thirty kilos of rice and a case or two of tinned fish, a major feast ends up having a monetary cost of between K 150 and K 300. By Gebusi standards, this is an enormous sum. It can be noted, for instance, that the entire yearly proceeds for a Gasumi woman at the Nomad market averages only K 40. For men to earn money, there is nothing that approximates regular wage labor or cash crops for export—just the odd job cutting grass around the Nomad Station, which is transient work and poorly paid.[16]

Perhaps consistent with a growing emphasis on trade-store food, feasts in Gasumi Corners easily draw a larger and more diverse group of visitors than they did in the past. Acquaintances and distant relations from other corners of Nomad may attend, and even a government official or two may come. Major gifts of meat are reserved for close in-laws and those in relations of exchange, who bring bags of dried meat from game animals hunted in the forest in reciprocity. But well beyond this circle, a large number of people can come just for the festivity of the event, a bit of starchy food, and an evening of entertainment. This last, predictably, is more variable than it used to be. The entire structure of feasting now challenges the hosts to be more modern—to dress up in nicer clothes, to supply more store-bought foods, and to arrange for recorded music from a boom box.

From Ritual Feast to Party

In 1980–82, ritual feasts entailed a traditional dance in which one or more beautifully costumed male dancers from visiting villages performed to the beat of their long drums and to the accompaniment of women's plaintive singing (see Knauft 1999: photo 9; compare the present volume, photo 21). Though such dances are still held in more distant settlements—and though a few young men from Gasumi Corners may still dress up and dance at these events—traditional dancing has become rare at Gasumi Corners and in most Gebusi settlements. This change is reflected in the very word used to describe feasts. These are no longer "*gigobra*" or "*habra*," the traditional terms for "dance-feast." Rather, the celebratory feast is now a "party" (*fati* in tok pisin).

Almost by definition, a "party" entails disco music, sometimes also accompanied by a string band. The commercial cassette music that blares from the local boom box is mostly a blend of rock music and string band vocals by Papua New Guinea national groups. The tapes can be bought at Kiunga for about K 10 apiece and are in hot demand, along with batteries to power the cassette player. Beyond music, the great attraction of the disco is, of course, its occasion for Western-style fast dancing—and when discos are held as part of feasts, no gate fee is charged. Dancing invariably occurs outside in the evening.

Though the first dancers are tentative—like those at a junior high school dance in the United States—the event gains energy as the evening wears on. The holding of a party disco involves young women quite integrally, and this is key to the allure and attraction of the occasion. This contrasts to the traditional Gebusi dance, which centered around the stately drumming of costumed male dancers. Perhaps because of the charged nature of modern dancing for those who are older, prepubescent school children are the most active and unabashed disco dancers, particularly during the earlier parts of the evening. About three-quarters or more of the dancing is between same-sex partners who are simply friends and enjoy the beat of the music.[17] Older teenagers join in a bit later and also tend to dance primarily with same-sex friends. But the most alluring activity is cross-sex dancing between individual pairs of teenage boys and girls. Though straightforward in outward demeanor, these pairings are charged with suggestion. Married persons almost never dance disco, and especially not with someone of the opposite sex, even with their own spouse.

Unless the boom box or the batteries give out, dancing continues all night until dawn. Indeed, the slang term for a disco dance is to "go six to six," that is, to continue dancing from six at night to six in the morning. This affords the possibility for romantic intrigue, though the casually watchful eyes of everyone present make it difficult for couples to slip away for more than a minute or two of furtive conversation. The stigma and social repercussions of being charged with or caught in premarital sexual intercourse makes this a highly risky option that teenage boys and girls are extremely careful about.

Though the indigenous dance, string band, and "disco" appear as opposed options along a scale from tradition to modernity, they may complement or overlap with each other during a party. For the large feast commemorating my departure from Gasumi Corners in 1998, all three of these were held. Visitors and hosts floated easily from the main house, where a small traditional dance was held (partly for my sake), to the village clearing outside, where the disco was in progress, or off to the side, where the string band sang. As if to reflect the increasingly differentiated nature of Gebusi social life, all three of these entertainments occurred simultaneously—a virtual three-ring circus of entertainment. Though some of those present watched the traditional dance—especially the senior men and women—the bulk of those present, including most of the young adults and almost all the children, were either watching or dancing disco. The push of social energy certainly lies with disco dancing as the wave of things to come at feasts and "parties" in places like Gasumi Corners. It should be added that because beer and spirits are generally unobtainable at Nomad, drunkenness is not yet a problem at Gebusi parties.[18]

Since party-goers usually sleep a good portion of the day following the festivities, parties are typically held on Friday nights so as not to compromise attendance at church on Sunday morning or children's attendance at school on weekdays. As such, parties are integrally woven into the regular weekly calendar.

From Male Initiations to Modern Art

The staging of parties in places like Gasumi Corners is contextualized by developments in more distant and traditional settlements. Remote long-house villages are themselves beginning to adopt more "modern" types of festivity. But their large traditional ceremonies—especially the climactic feasts of the male initiation—continue to be magnets of social interest and excitement among all Gebusi, including those from Gasumi Corners. Two of the most talked-about events during my six months at Gasumi Corners were the two male initiations held in relatively traditional Gebusi settlements whose members had not yet converted to Christianity. Though these locations were somewhat distant, a number of people from Gasumi Corners traveled to attend as visitors, as did I. At each occasion, two young men from Gasumi Corners danced as visitors in full traditional costume. One of these young men was Sayu, depicted in the opening vignette of this book.

On entering the host villages, my first impression was the rush of a time machine to the past. In both initiations, the traditional longhouse, costuming, and public ceremony were similar in structure to what I had experienced during the initiation at Yibihilu seventeen years earlier. My photographs of the dancers and of the initiates in 1998 were almost identical to those taken in 1981 by my wife, Eileen Cantrell. However, a number of the preparatory rites for strengthening the initiates—including the wearing of heavy bark wigs tied into the scalp—were dispensed with in both recent cases (compare Knauft 1999: photo 5). The intensity of male camaraderie and the powerful displays of warrior aggression were also much tamer than in 1981, though the overall scale of the events in 1998 was augmented by a significant number of nonrelatives and onlookers from various corners of Nomad as well as by visitors from the station itself.

Based on circumstantial evidence, it seems plausible that at least some traditional homosexual practices were followed prior to one of these initiations: some of the initiands had probably been inseminated orally by adult men.[19] However, in great contrast to 1981, homoeroticism played a quite minor part in the proceedings. Costumed display and food-giving were highlighted while the emphasis on public joking and sexuality—both heterosexual and homosexual—was reduced.

Consistent with this change, the dramatic dancing of young Gebusi women in beautiful red bird-of-paradise costumes has now virtually ceased in even the most remote settlements. Nowadays, women, including those in distant locations, are far more interested in dressing up in colorful Western clothes than in painting themselves red and baring their breasts (see photo 20). Those few older women who did dance traditionally would sometimes wear or paint bras on their bosoms. Likewise, the women's singing that accompanies men's dancing at traditional feasts was desultory and on the decline in 1998 even in remote settlements.

This gendered change dovetails with altered forms of entertainment staged by visitors during the night. While selected visitors may provide traditional dancing, others come to the initiation ceremonies with guitar and ukulele for string band singing or with boom boxes to play cassette tapes. These developments are not shunned by the host villagers but are rather welcomed as ways to increase the festivity of the event. Indeed, the staging of string band music as well as traditional dancing is prearranged by the organizers of the initiation, who invite visitors to perform. Generally speaking, the traditional goal of drawing visitors from other settlements to the initiation has expanded; the event is now something of an open invitation to a range of modern visitors and influences from the vicinity of the Nomad Station.

This mix of traditional and modern was strongly reflected in visitors' costuming, which ranged dramatically from fully traditional—elaborate feathers, body paint, and leaves (see photo 18)—to snappy Western clothes that might include a white shirt, hat, dungarees, and sunglasses in the night. Between these extremes were mix-and-match combinations: a headdress on top of a hat, traditional face paint along with bright Western shirts or plastic flower decorations. It was hard to imagine better examples of cultural hybridity (see photo 19).

If Gebusi initiation in distant settlements continues as a traditional rite of passage, it is also becoming a modern costume party accompanied by diverse festivities. Increasingly, the public presentation of initiates and the celebration of their manhood is being encompassed by a different mode of aesthetic presentation. Self-decoration is becoming less a means of sedimenting and symbolizing one's social relationships in the community and more a fashion of decontextualized bodily art among people who may not otherwise know each other.

The growing separation of bodily art from traditional identity for many Gebusi articulates with the fact that the young men of Gasumi Corners will never be initiated. The last male initiation in Gasumi was a highly hybrid and compromised affair held in the early 1990s. Since then, a new cohort of young men has come of age but not been initiated; they are now in their twenties and getting married. Some if not most or all in this new generation of young men have not been told about traditional practices of male insemination and ritual homosexuality (see Knauft 2001). They attend and view the initiation in distant settlements as an increasingly historic display that they do not completely understand. By contrast, young men from Gasumi Corners gain their own adulthood in significant part by going to school, becoming a member of a local church, participating in team sports, and developing a locally modern style of life.

The Art of Independence Day

The cutting edge of change between personal identity and bodily costume emerges at the Nomad Station on Independence Day. As part of the festivities, villagers dress up in traditional garb for elaborate dance competitions. They later adorn themselves in full costume to perform buffoonish skits that mock their traditional practices. Many parts of Papua New Guinea now hold cultural shows in which participants dress and dance in traditional costuming. These shows range from local affairs to national competitions and even international engagements, where the winners are sponsored or invited to perform in Australian or Southeast Asian cities. At the bottom rungs of this competitive pageantry are places like Nomad, where the winners are given a few kina in prize money and perhaps the unrealistic hope of performing in a town or city. But the Nomad area remains distinctive for the intricacy and diversity of its decorative traditions.

For some, the display of traditional costuming is not just a thing of the past, trotted out for the touristic gaze of officials and others at the Nomad Station on Independence Day. For many others, however, traditional dancing is a decontextualized reenactment—a "folklore" they do not otherwise perform in other contexts. Many performers no longer dance or get initiated in their own villages but do so exclusively for public presentation on Independence Day. In Gasumi Corners, there was talk of dressing up a young man and having him perform as an initiate at the Nomad festivities—even though he had never been initiated. Likewise for Gebusi villages where young men *had* been initiated, the scale of their display was augmented for public viewing at Nomad by dressing up boys as young as six or seven years of age in the yellow striping of a preparatory initiation costume. In the villages themselves, however, this adornment was never used for boys this small and is being increasingly dispensed with even for older boys and teenagers. In short, the modern divorce between transient costuming and deeper ritual identity is occurring even in the most traditional Gebusi villages.

This divorce has its own modern benefits. Each of Nomad's several ethnic groups has its own distinct and splendid variations upon dance costuming and initiation display. These differences have always been a source of fascination. This is reflected in the traditional custom of inviting dancers from distant communities to perform at major feasts and initiations (Knauft 1985b). Expanding this tendency on a modern scale, the Nomad Independence Day festivities organize and schedule a wide array of costuming styles, performance genres, and individual decorations from groups affiliated with different parts of the subdistrict (see photo 24). Collectively, these displays are quite remarkable. Drawing a crowd of more than a thousand spectators, they dwarf the size of any indigenous gathering or event (see Knauft in press b). Recognizing the larger attraction of these performances, the area affairs manager followed the Independence Day festivities by organizing a special cultural show of Nomad costuming and related festivities on October 27–30, 1998. To publicize the event he invited dignitaries from the Western Province and arranged for a national video crew to record the performances for rebroadcast on Papua New Guinea TV. Though the camera crew missed its plane, the national M.P. for the Middle Fly District arrived and was welcomed on the Nomad airstrip by traditional dancers. The pageantry of Independence Day was then revisited on a yet larger scale with over fifty dance groups and displays.

Both at Independence Day and at cultural shows, the audience for traditional dance performances is multiethnic, including officials and those from all local language groups. A large crowd rings the performance area, which is marked out on the lawn or ball field adjacent to the Nomad Subdistrict office. Performances are judged by officials (see photo 21) and small amounts of prize money are awarded to performers after the conclusion of the festivities. As well as monetizing the display of traditional ritual, this puts traditional performance under the authoritative judgment of outsiders, who are now deemed qualified to rate its aesthetic and bodily merit.

These developments are not resisted by Gebusi or others in the No-mad area—far from it. Villagers fully embrace the idea of presenting their costumes, dances, and initiation displays for a wider official audience—however distinct this may be from the historic rituals that took place in their own settlements. The possibility of earning a little money serves as a large additional incentive. The display of indigenous costuming at Nomad has become so important that remote villages that still practice initiations now orchestrate their ritual calendar so their climactic rites and perfor-mances occur in August or early September. This allows participants to eas-ily get dressed up in their costumes again and perform for prize money on the lawn of the Nomad Station on September 16. In the process, ritual per-formance is decontextualized from the ritual structure and meaning that previously housed it. Costumes were previously seen at night in the long-house. Lit by resin torches held by kin and friends, they signaled a transi-tion or a celebration of status for those in the community. Now, by contrast, they parade in the light of day for official judging next to the government station before a multiethnic audience on the holiday of national indepen-dence. Significant numbers of those performing do not otherwise use or qualify for their adornments. This is no way minimizes the remarkable art-istry, splendor, and festive enjoyment of cultural performances at Nomad. At the same time, these displays provide a key means of redefining tradi-tions and putting them within an acceptably modern frame of reference.

The Biggest Party

Independence festivities at Nomad are more than a celebration of indige-nous costuming; they are a high point of the year, a party for everyone. Though smaller celebrations for Independence Day dot other parts of the subdistrict, those at Nomad are by far the largest. They attract well over a thousand people and last several days. Some visitors walk for three days to see the festivities, perform their own costumed dances, and stay with rela-tives in one or another of Nomad's corners. Festivities are augmented by dozens of rugby, soccer, and other matches, including ones between vis-iting teams. All-star contests pit the "A," "B," and "C" teams from Nomad against corresponding squads from Mougulu, the largest outpost in Beda-mini country, a long day's walk away.

Other competitions range from the athletic to the humorous. They include sprint and cross-country races, climbing a greased pole, holding one's breath under water, chopping wood, playing tug-of-war, blindfolded women trying to split pawpaws, pillow fighting on a beam, drinking hot tea, starting a fire with a traditional bow drill, and archery for accuracy and for distance. Impromptu booths emerge on the perimeter of the Nomad sports fields to attract customers with boom-box music and to sell them food or other items. A few tables of ring-toss gambling are even tolerated. Energy is high, with the festive spirit of a county fair. In the afternoon and especially in the evening, string band competitions are followed by public "discos" at the station (where there's no gate fee), and the music attracts great throngs of young dancers and onlookers, many of whom gyrate until the power goes off at midnight.

Surprisingly—and fortunately, in my opinion—there is no public drinking. Though young men yearn to get drunk, there are no places to buy beer. Liquor licenses have not been approved and the major airline, Mission Aviation Fellowship, will not accept it as cargo. Alcohol cannot be obtained except by government employees for private and personal consumption, and most officials at Nomad are Christians and abstainers. As a result, the drinking and fighting that often plague parties and festivities in some other parts of Papua New Guinea have not afflicted Nomad, at least as of 1998.[20]

Perhaps the most ethnographically significant feature of Independence Day festivities at Nomad—in addition to their multiethnic dancing, sports games, discos, and string band concerts—is the performance of "dramas." Most of these skits enact practices and beliefs that are dead or dying out, self-consciously presenting tradition as a thing of the past (see Knauft in press b). Performed at night, the skits enact customs such as chopping trees with a stone ax, making a fire with a bow drill, singing traditional séances, doing magic for fish poisoning, fighting with bows and arrows, and, notably, holding death inquest divinations and carrying out mock executions of sorcery suspects. Performed with clever buffoonery and rife with slapstick comedy, the skits make a farce of traditions at the same time that they illustrate them. Even though the costumes donned by performers are often beautiful and meticulous, the stupidity and clumsiness of the performers' actions claim center stage.

Villagers in the large audience, for their part, are presented by their own compatriots with a strong and self-conscious sense that their collective past is primitive, superstitious, and backward. From a contemporary point of view, however, these customs emerge as truly funny and humorous. Hundreds of people throng to the performances to see what flashes from the past will come alive, how creatively their foibles will be portrayed, and how effective the parodies will be. If the past has now become history, this history is now comfortable enough to not require heavy-handed disparagement. Rather, it provides a story of playful primitivity that easily measures its past against the progress of the present.

As if to clearly frame their enactment within modern brackets, each set of performers bows to the audience in formal unison—to the front, to the back, to the left, and to the right—both before and after their skit. Lest any children, government officials, or others fail to understand the belief or custom depicted, one of the performers explains its "meaning" to the audience through a battery-powered bullhorn. Each performance is rated by a panel of judges—teachers and pastors from Nomad—on five criteria:

- respect (the etiquette and skill of bowing to each direction in unison before and after the performance)
- introduction (the point or meaning of the skit, and how well this is delivered)
- dressing (costuming)
- interest (how interesting and funny the performance is, including the strength of audience reaction)
- timing (whether the drama uses time effectively but stays within a 10–12 minute limit)

Officials not only judge the performance but how effectively local people make fun of their traditions. And yet, the dramas are not a command performance of self-loathing for official benefit. Rather, they emerge as rich, spontaneous, and acute expressions of local humor as historical comedy (see Errington and Gewertz 1995: chap. 3). They are avidly watched and greatly enjoyed by villagers, who come from near and far, for hours into the night.

As an anthropologist, part of me was sad to see this self-mocking of tradition. Rich songs, spells, cosmology, and vitality were here reduced to so much buffoonery and slapstick—but the skits *were* very funny, often uproariously so. The humor of both presenting and good-naturedly poking fun at tradition was here a fine art, not just for the audience but also for me as ethnographer. I fought back tears of deep laughter that mixed appreciation for these rich comedies with nostalgia born from my own vivid memories of these same customs being practiced very much for real just sixteen years earlier.

For me, the most dramatic skit was that of sorcery divination and execution, staged by my friends from Gasumi Corners. The spirit medium of the skit was played by Yamda Wasep, a Catholic prayer leader and son of a former spirit medium. The person accused of sorcery in the skit—who blubbered so humorously while being "tortured"—was Uwok Hawalkiayl, an older man who when young had slain three persons for sorcery but who has since become an earnest church supporter. The man in the skit who "killed" Uwok with a huge blow was none other than Ubole Koy, the former spirit medium whose sickness prompted the execution of a suspected sorceress at Yehebi in the 1980s. As mentioned in chapter 5, Ubole has since given up spirit mediumship, moved to Gasumi Corners to avoid sorcery, and become an evangelical Christian.

To me, the skit portrayed the degree to which sorcery inquests and executions are considered a thing of the past in Gasumi Corners. Rather than a prominent current threat, they lie increasingly in a historical realm of buffoonish primitivity. I was also reminded that among all that is lost with tradition, not all of this loss is regrettable. As Gebusi themselves assert, they now enjoy the benefits of a largely nonviolent way of life.

Other skits parodied the clumsy singing of spirit séances, the failure of magical spells, the silliness of indigenous origin myths, and even mocked the beautiful Gebusi dance costume, which was previously thought to incorporate the reincarnated forms of the upper- and lower-world spirit figures on the body of the dancer. In one skit, the stunning adornment of the traditional dancer was used to mock indigenous fish-poisoning practices. As I myself observed in 1981, a dancer in full costume danced in stately fashion along the river to woo the poisoned fish to the surface. In the skit, these beliefs and the role of the dancer were made farcical: the men playing the "fish" in the skit snapped at the dancer and scared him so much that he drummed in a frenzy and pranced around wildly until he eventually ran out of the performance area entirely.[21] Here we have not just the playful satire of selected customs but a renunciation of traditional cultural beliefs and practices at a deeper level. The Gebusi dancer in full costume had previously been the cultural symbol of stately beauty, allure, and spiritual integrity. In the skit, however, this dignified embodiment of spiritual and human harmony has become a slapstick figure of clumsy buffoonery.[22]

Modernity Presented

Though most of the skits at the Nomad show were farces of tradition, a few provided revealing and important commentaries on social change and contemporary development. Of the forty-two dramatic skirts presented over two nights, fourteen fell loosely into this latter category.[23] Here we find dramas of "first contact," in which weak and cowardly villagers are corralled by strong and confident patrol officers (played by villagers). Other skits portrayed traditional ignorance concerning trade goods, as when the doltish bushman cooks unopened rice in an empty plastic bucket on a blazing fire—only to panic in awe as it erupts in a molten blaze. More modern dramas included the enactment of Bible stories. These morality plays instruct how sin leads to hell and damnation while piety allows resurrection on Judgment Day; dancers and fornicators die while the virtuous are saved. The Bible verse that informs each Christian skit is prominently recited and written on a poster—for instance, "The immoral woman. Proverbs 7: 6–27." From a traditionalist perspective, it seems nothing short of expectably amazing to see a white-robed black Jesus dramatically "kill" wayward sinners and drive them from the stage (see photo 23). In one sense, this action presents the second coming of traditional sorcery inquests, as mentioned in chapters 5 and 6 above. Sin becomes a general form of sorcery writ large—and made modern in the process. Those who are damned can still be killed with terrible vengeance, but by the ultimate executioner, God.

As drama, however, even Christianity's wrath did not outrun the mirth of some performers. In one skit, the devil's wry dance was greeted by audience applause while the sword-wielding Gabriel was left in the shadows and the other actors looked glum. As if to celebrate sin, three dramas were just dances by women to the music of a boom box. Two of these sported maidens who had conquered their embarrassment to dance barebreasted with flowers in their hair, as if to combine the temptations of modern arousal with those of more traditional allure.[24] In another drama, men and boys leapfrogged across the stage, careening over each other, exuberant, brushing against the audience, and finally fleeing the stage.

How should we view all this pantomime and play? As a trashing of tradition? Or as a jest with no rest, a skewer that strikes all targets, the Nomad fair as the world of Rabelais?[25] The dramas at Nomad are certainly all of these in some measure. But their strongest motivation, I think, is a welling desire to transcend the past and move instead into a modern future. The process isn't always utopian. Three of the skits played with modern life itself. In one, antic school graduates ignored their former teacher (one "Masta Bruce"!) and went off to explore the power house generator at Nomad. Engrossed in play, the boys in the skit ended up being electrocuted, one by one in turn, by the forbidden machine that enticed them. The message seemed clear: modernity's attractions are powerful but dangerous. Without learning and discipline, they can be shocking.

Another creative skit presented a young man dressed in rags searching for a job in Kiunga. He finally received work and was paid a few toea by a white-shirted boss who sported sunglasses, a hat, a suitcase full of money, and security guards who flanked him on either side. The boy's chores were mindless: he picked up trash all day and then cut grass with a small pair of scissors. Quickly bored, he worked in a desultory manner. Meanwhile, the boss became inert in his luxury, stretched, and decided to take a walk— leaving his stash of money behind. Seeing his chance, the nimble youth sprang to life. Stealing the suitcase and its cash, he bolted away before the boss's security guards could react. The boss then returned. Discovering his loss, he searched but failed to find the boy. In a final twist, the boss then pulled out his gun and shot his two security guards to death for failing to protect his wealth.

Incisive and clever, the skit suggests that modern work is controlled by wealth and can result in poverty and malice. You have to be quick and grab for yourself, ignore the risks, and hope to survive. No one is really above reproach. Indeed, it is the boss who becomes an evil murderer as a result of his financial loss. But the boy has also been tainted; he becomes a criminal *raskol,* that is, one of those who are widely acknowledged to be among the greatest elements of social disruption and impediments to so-called modern progress in contemporary Papua New Guinea (see, for example, Goddard 1992, 1995).

A third and final skit portrayed a poor unclothed villager begging medicine from a Western-style man for his sick son (see photo 22). The latter, dressed in a white shirt, sunglasses, and a large cowboy hat, was intent on reading his newspaper. Though the villager spoke clear English ("I need medicine for my son!") the man in authority failed, or refused, to understand. The villager then fought with his wife; she pointed to their sick son and refused to believe that worthwhile results could come from her husband's efforts to find a modern cure. But the village man in the skit was undeterred. He explored and found a magical machine (a card table covered by a tablecloth that was draped to the ground). To his joy, objects put under the table came out after shaking and tumult as transformed prizes of Western manufacture. A coconut bowl shoved under the card table returned as a shining 10-gallon metal pot. But his wife remained angry and forlorn, comforting their sick son. After much ambivalence, the village man finally decided to take his son and put him bodily into the machine. The boy crawled under the draped table and the "machine" shook and rattled mightily until the boy was eventually spit out. He now emerged as a grown and modern product: a strapping young man with a fancy backpack and the latest Western clothes. His father and mother leaped to him in joyous conclusion, covering him in hugs as the performance ended.

This skit played quite effectively with the underlying spirit and sensibility that I think affects many village men. For those who risk engaging them, the things that are modern are marvelous, despite all their frustrations. Even if a person in authority is sometimes a hindrance, and even if women at home can be skeptical, the perseverance of local men in a world of modern wonders should ultimately produce amazing results. These results are not just ones of material transformation but of healthy growth and modern personhood. Ultimately, the modern subject is produced through manufactured objects to become a figure of true accomplishment.

This is not the only view, of course. Modern as risky, modern as ambivalent, modern as wonderful—all these are depicted in the Nomad dramas. But the thread that seems to tie them together—the parody of the past, the ambivalence of the present, and the utopia of the future—is the underlying desire to create a more modern and progressive way of life. Though the critiques and farce of Nomad dramas sometimes target new as well as traditional things, the tension between them reveals a directional sense of historical progression—from the reality of backwardness to the hope of progress, from a past of sin to the potential of modern success. The overall message draws upon the most prevalent performances: to reject a shackled past and seek a progressive future.

Past in the Present, Present Beyond the Past

Gebusi freely choose to be more modern as they expose themselves to church, school, market, sports, and the health clinic. That is, they associate themselves willingly with the goods, organization, forms of knowledge, and modes of subordination associated with a contemporary Western world. As Gebusi engage these institutions they internalize strictures of discipline, time, and a sense of their own recessive agency in modern institutional contexts. Part of the way modernity expands—perhaps its most important path—is not by economic necessity but through internalized notions of personal progress and "advancement" that make becoming modern a moral imperative. This imperative quickly becomes sedimented through institutional constraints and the cultural as well as economic need to approximate a more enlightened lifestyle. Hence the irony that Gebusi's local engagement with becoming modern is at the same time so volitional and so highly constraining, so agentive and yet so replete with recessive agency as villagers sit quietly with discipline in school, church, at official meetings, at the market, by the ball field, and on video night.

This process filters diffusely into the fields of action that Gebusi themselves control. It is still possible to live in the village and orient to the forest and toward tradition—but this is not the favored or desired choice, including for most of those living in outlying villages. Forms of Gebusi expression that include contemporary singing, dancing, feasting, and ceremonies shade increasingly from traditional ritual to modern party. The performances of villagers at Nomad on Independence Day vividly reveal the willing extension of these trends. Ritual identity becomes decontextualized as public display—a monetized performance judged by officials and distanced from identity based on ritual accession and personal meaning. Traditional art, performance, and custom are framed in brackets that make them historical even as they are, in some ways, more publicly splendid than ever. As customs are reinvented and recontextualized, they change from being relatively unmediated practices and beliefs to being self-conscious constructions in historical time vis-à-vis a modern present. By this means, indigenous culture becomes neotradition.

Amid this change, as if an afterthought, sorcery inquests and the execution of sorcerers are increasingly associated with the past, seen as archaic and primitive. They are no longer a current reality nor even much of a neotradition in Gasumi Corners, but rather something to be reenacted across the divide of time—a safely parodic past. Comfortably back in the present, the vestiges of sorcery merge into the larger category of sin, just as the need for retribution pales before the desire for economic wealth, spiritual progress, and a more enlightened style of life. The modern side of this equation is underwritten variously by God, pastors, teachers, government officials, and persons with money. As the dramatic skits of the villagers demonstrate, such influences are open to various interpretations and need not be consistent with each other. But they do resonate in different ways with themes that emphasize the backwardness of the past, the progress of the future, the importance of individual responsibility, and the desire to be wealthy and have a locally modern style of life. In this sense, the dramas at Nomad reveal themselves as creative constructions of a vernacular modernity.

Chapter 9

Subaltern Modern

For people in diverse world areas, becoming modern is not a diffuse intellectual process. As is evident in previous chapters, a locally modern style of life has emerged among Gebusi in the following respects:

- increased exposure to people from other communities in ways that individuate and depersonalize social interactions;
- temporality associated with directional progress—against which the passage of time becomes a moral and subjective threat to development;
- emphasis on personal responsibility and increasing assessment of individual weakness, failure, or lack of material well-being along a yardstick of betterment and advancement;
- cultural as well as social pressure to accept authority figures associated with the knowledge and power of an outside world; and
- passive waiting for knowledge and judgment in contexts where these are imparted by modern authorities.

These developments contrast markedly with both Gebusi patterns of life in 1980–82 and, more generally, with patterns of Melanesian social living and belief as portrayed in the ethnographic record.[1] These changes have been striking and relatively sudden among Gebusi, but versions of them are widespread among many peoples as they experience modern institutions and their authoritative agents. These engagements do not produce similar outcomes; becoming locally modern has highly different results among Gebusi than it does elsewhere, including in other parts of Papua New Guinea.[2] Yet, this process is not so locally relative as to escape the desire for modern success. Associated with this is often the practical pressure to accept the contextual authority of an external "boss" who controls modern goods or values—the government official, employer, preacher, development program officer, teacher, and so on. In Papua New Guinea, the attempt to gain modern wealth *without* submitting one's efforts to the directives of one or another of these authorities has become practically the defining feature of being a criminal *raskol*, who are widely stigmatized.[3]

The key feature that motivates these developments and links them together is a strong and unrelenting desire for the commodities and cash associated with a Western style of life. That the fruits of this development are largely unobtainable for people such as Gebusi does not retard, and may intensify, the process of social change. Agents of modern institutional change need not be personally exploitative or malicious; they can have de facto superiority and dominance in an economic and structural or ideological sense.

The process of becoming locally modern through contextual subordination articulates with but is not the same as that described by classical theorists of modernity such as Durkheim, Marx, Tönnies, Simmel, or Weber, nor those forwarded by more contemporary analysts such as Michel Foucault, Marshall Berman or David Harvey.[4] As Max Weber would remind us, the motives and outcomes of modernity, like those of capitalism, are likely to change over time and depend on cultural context. In this regard, it can be noted that all the above theorists focused on a Western or at least urban process of becoming modern as opposed to that which perpetuates modern subordination in non-Western cultural contexts.[5]

Sub-mission

At Nomad, the cultural sentiments and institutional patterns of becoming locally modern are tangible and prominent in the churches, in school, at government offices, at the health clinic, in the sports leagues, at the market, and in the staging of official cultural shows and national celebrations. As the previous chapters illustrate, Gebusi have become recessive agents in

many of these contexts. Not coincidentally, this trend is especially prominent in settings that place the greatest emphasis on personal progress and
responsibility for failure—church, school, and the market. At the same
time, Gebusi submission stems in significant part from their own volition
rather than from political coercion or the pressure of economic intrusion.
It is perhaps all the more internalized as a result.

Why does this occur? In one respect, Gebusi interactions extend their
longstanding sense of being less powerful than outsiders. First they were
human fodder for Bedamini raids. Then they were welcome subordinates of
the *pax Australiana* that pacified Bedamini but left their own communities
largely intact. More recently, they have become willing residents near a
postcolonial Nomad Station that provides a new dominant culture at their
doorstep. In some of these respects, Gebusi are unusual, maybe even exceptional. Where local people have their own robust histories of social, political, and cultural power—of territorial and social success, much less of political enlargement or local empire—the kinds of passivity and recessive
agency one finds among Gebusi are often less pervasive.[6]

In this regard, the recessive agency of Gebusi in modern contexts may
fit with other highly disenfranchised or fourth-world peoples under conditions
of geographic remoteness and heightened political decentralization (Bodley
1999).[7] At the same time, the sociocultural and political history of Gebusi
sheds important light on processes that occur more widely in contextually
specific and less generalized forms—especially when people engage external
agents and institutions designed to make them more developed, enlightened,
or democratic. This is not to deny or ignore the many ways that people resist
or subvert outside influences. It is rather to realize that these responses are not
always overriding and that they may be compromised over time by deeply
internalized desires for change as well as by external constraints.

Many people around the world do not resist modernizing intrusions
as pervasively or wholeheartedly as anthropologists and critical analysts
sometimes imply. People often seek out and sometimes actively submit
themselves to these developments—even when they come with a high cost
of changing previous ways of life. In this respect, current work in anthropology and critical theory needs to be more attentive to the contemporary desires and motivations of local people. Amid burgeoning desires in many
rural areas for manufactured goods and a cultural lifestyle that foregrounds
them, it is common to find local people adopting forms of recessive agency
in specific contexts of modernizing institutions and experiences even when
they have not been coerced and when benefits are marginal or negligible
relative to the time and effort expended.

Reciprocally, these contexts tend to individuate local clients and then trump them through an ideology of knowledge-as-power that encourages them to subordinate not just their actions but their way of thinking about themselves. A palpable and forceful dynamic of passivity and waiting often attends the interaction of local people with agents of modern institutions—government officials and bureaucrats, educators, clerics, health care workers, and development officers. Even apart from being lectured or disparaged, the boredom of enforced patience has its own effects. And as Horkheimer and Adorno (1972: 148) emphasized, "Anyone who doubts the power of monotony is a fool."

This perspective draws upon critical understandings of modern social life that have been widespread in various guises since the development of Western social sciences in the nineteenth century. For Durkheim (1964), social passivity could stem from modern anomie; for Marx (1964), it could result from lack of consciousness about social relations that alienate a person from the fruits of his or her modern labor. Both of these approaches and many others considered passivity to be a negative result rather than an assertive social force. But recessive agency can easily be more than a reactionary result; it often becomes an active social force in its own right. This development is not adequately explained as passive or tacit resistance against becoming modern—as suggested by critical theorists as diverse as James Scott (1985, 1990) and Michel de Certeau (1984). Its passivity can be personally willed and actively internalized as an important dimension of becoming modern in a local way.

Neotradition

In most societies, including Gebusi, many aspects of social life are domestically determined and lie outside the formal control of modernizing institutions and external authorities. Circumstances at home or within a residential community may at first blush seem distant or safe from these influences. For Gebusi, these domestic contexts include interactions in Gasumi Corners, in the forest, and when visiting traditional settlements. Given these alternatives, one might be tempted to consider Gebusi practices of contemporary feasting, aesthetic performance, or subsistence activity as beyond or outside the influence of institutions such as the church, school, market, government administration, and so on.

Over time, however, these environments are themselves recontextualized—as they have been for Gebusi during the last two decades. In cultural as well as social terms, activities in the village or in the forest no longer afford a self-sufficient way of life. Instead, they are increasingly configured as the complement to modern institutional engagements. Because customs of so-called tradition and those of becoming modern provide the figure and ground for each other, they become mutually defining and cannot be isolated. The ongoing influence of recent developments on traditional ways of life is emphasized by Gebusi themselves when they say they are exchanging their previous customs for those that are "new" and could help them "come up" in a larger world.

In the process, customs considered "traditional"—such as community feasting or dancing in indigenous costumes for official judging on Independence Day—are revaluated and reinvented.[8] The result is an ongoing development of neotraditions that are strongly influenced by standards of being more modern. Indigenous practices are updated: they are made more acceptable within a contemporary frame of reference while retaining the sense that they are under local control and consistent with local traditions.

In this sense, one cannot escape from modern desires and institutions by simply going back to the village or the forest. The practices undertaken in these contexts are in a dialogue of cultural power between the present and the past. Even as this mediation continues unabated (how could the idea of becoming more progressive or developed persist without a corresponding fear of sliding toward the past?), the desire to be successful in a contemporary world exerts a tidal pull on developments over time. As illustrated in Gebusi skits of tradition at the Nomad cultural show, the past is now cited as a problem, something to be judged against the present and the hoped-for progress of the future. In this regard, the assessment of customs as "traditional" is itself linked to modern development and to a new sense of historical self-consciousness. Among Gebusi, these sensibilities contrast markedly with traditional notions of repetitive time and cyclical repetition, as discussed in chapter 1.

This does not mean that contrary and resistant responses are absent, even among Gebusi. We can note the snickers of prayer leaders behind the pastor's back, the "mulling" behavior of students in school, the creative combination of Western and indigenous clothing at Gebusi "parties," and those few skits at Independence Day that mock aspects of becoming modern itself. These features could be foregrounded to create a different and more optimistic if less critically acute understanding of cultural change among peoples such as Gebusi. Cultural hybridity and local resistance have been widely emphasized by anthropologists in recent years. As part of this strong emphasis, however, the way that outside values and inequalities are internalized within the dynamics of local cultural change has often been downplayed. As I have tried to show in the present work, local initiatives are not always polarized against those from the outside. In further studies, research might go beyond either of these perspectives. It would be useful to have a more nuanced understanding of how the internalization of modern values and inequalities becomes strongly self-perpetuating, on the one hand, and yet always incomplete and contested, on the other.

From both sides of this coin, it is obvious that modern changes do not present a glowing path of material improvement, social progress, or global convergence. As Bourdieu (2000) has stressed, a cost-benefit calculus of material gain can be highly discrepant with the cultural realities whereby people pursue the seductions of a modern world. The process of becoming locally modern is highly refractory to the assumptions made by classic theories of modernization.[9] What explains this discrepancy is the inequality underpinned by images and ideologies of modern material success. The fantasies, beliefs, and values incited by these ideologies are underscored by the remarkable willingness of people like Gebusi to subject their way of life to social and cultural change. Gebusi have not been subject to land alienation, resource expropriation, taxation, forced labor, systematic imprisonment, colonial decimation, forced religious conversion, or significant economic development. But the imagination of social and material progress can be strong and ever more intense in the relative absence of economic reinforcement.

Sorcery Revisited

Gebusi patterns of direct reciprocity and exchange have not been completely swept away as the people of Gasumi Corners become locally modern. But as we have seen, they do become contextualized, compromised, and reduced in scale, scope, and social salience. Thus, for instance, Gebusi sorcery beliefs are not completely a thing of the past even though they are but a pale reflection of their former self. General beliefs in spiritual malevolence still exist, and in some cases these may still be vaguely associated with particular individuals, but fervent belief in sorcery and retribution against suspects are culturally associated with the past. This association is increased by the regular and encompassing context of church, school, market, sports, and the other activities and events associated with life in the extended Nomad community. Against this frame of reference, retribution against sorcery has become anachronistic. This view was clearly represented by those from Gasumi Corners in their parody of a traditional sorcery inquest at the Nomad cultural show.

Amid larger patterns of change, it is only in a restricted sense that the demise of spirit séances caused the decline of Gebusi sorcery retributions. Certainly, Gebusi spirit séances were the primary means of identifying sorcery suspects and a principal way of galvanizing collective violence against them. And Gebusi spirit mediumship is now defunct; this dimension of indigenous spirituality has not been resuscitated. Its echoes are seen in contemporary forms of expression that have effaced its divinatory and dialogic function: singing the praises of God in church, and providing entertainment through string band music. As discussed in chapter 5, spirit mediumship in Gasumi Corners was not eradicated by external mandate and was not subject to Christian invective. Rather, it fell into decline because Gebusi found it inimical to their new style of life and less important than going to church, on the one hand, and developing more modern forms of musical enjoyment, on the other. That the Catholic pastors did not know the true significance of séance singing and that curing through spirit mediumship is still officially encouraged by their church underscores the point. Ultimately, the decline of spirit mediumship and of sorcery retributions are both part of more encompassing changes.

As discussed in chapter 5, the decline of traditional sorcery beliefs and retributions dovetails with the emergent belief that personal malice is an aspect of sin or Satanic evil. Correspondingly, the responsibility for taking retribution against sorcery and against sin more generally rests with God. This occurs either at the judgment day of one's individual death, or in the general apocalypse of the Second Coming, which will collectively purge sorcerers and other evil persons. Gebusi now consider themselves individually responsible to avoid being sinful and to go to church. Since the large majority of them have given up sorcery accusations, the remainder are unable to take collective action or gain community support for it, even if they feel highly aggrieved. Reciprocally, people take steps such as going to church to reduce the chance that they will be either attacked by a sorcerer or thought to be one themselves. Even those most strongly associated with the practice of sorcery—old women—can demonstrate their commitment to goodness by being baptized and attending church regularly.

Gebusi have bridged the difference between older beliefs in sorcery and newer beliefs in sin and Satanic evil by expanding the category of the traditional Gebusi osaw spirit—the bogeyman figure who was vaguely associated with the underworld. Increasingly, Gebusi no longer know whether a sickness has been caused by sorcery or not. This absolves them and in practice precludes them from investigating the cause of sickness or who might be responsible for it. In a larger sense, then, the demise of retribution against Gebusi sorcerers has been overdetermined by the various ways—prominently but by no means exclusively related to Christianity—that Gebusi have identified with the ostensibly more progressive and modern style of life associated with the Nomad Station.

Alternative Historical Outcomes

Under different conditions, the process of becoming modern could have turned out otherwise for Gebusi. With an alternative twist of cultural and modern engagements, local sorcery beliefs could have ended up as a robust neotradition rather than being relegated to the realm of vestigial custom. This could potentially have occurred, for instance, if the historical conditions of Gebusi engagement with colonial influence had been more disruptive or if the postcolonial police had been more aggressive or violent in accusing suspected sorcerers themselves. As dislocations and inequalities proliferate, beliefs in sorcery can transmute into resentment—and the perception of resentment—against those who are more successful in a modern world. For instance, Karen Sykes (n.d.: chap. 5) shows how Papua New Guinean high school students may be plagued by sicknesses associated with the jealousy of others as they prepare to take their culminating exams. In many parts of Melanesia, sorcery has been deeply associated with power in both modern and traditional contexts.[10] Modernization of sorcery beliefs is also highly developed in many parts of Africa and other areas of the world, as mentioned in chapter 2 (see Geschiere 1997; Comaroff and Comaroff 1993). If Gebusi are unusual in largely avoiding this trend in the present, this outcome may result from their history of political subservience and the distinctive way sorcery has been treated by the Nomad police, as discussed in chapter 4. This illustrates the importance of considering each circumstance in its vernacular context and not reducing it to either the spread or the subversion of a generalized modernity.

Depending on how the wheel of fortune turns, it is not impossible that Gebusi themselves could resuscitate sorcery beliefs and accommodate them with new definitions of what it means to be modern or neotraditional. If the Ok Tedi gold mine shuts down and if the Western Province is unable to replace its subvention with national funds or those from development agencies, outstations such as Nomad could lose support. In a worst-case scenario, the government station and airstrip at Nomad could close, along with its school, health clinic, and market.

More generally, as hopes for economic development persist or increase, reality can easily move in the opposite direction. Given the rising hope of modern rewards, indeed, it is increasingly important for anthropologists to engage what Ferguson (1999) calls the "ethnography of decline" in various world regions and circumstances. Frustration and resentment can readily intensify, including in ways that draw upon sorcery beliefs. Even under conditions of seeming stasis or improvement, escalating images or fantasies of progress can make existing conditions seem increasingly unpalatable.

If Gebusi beliefs in sorcery are ever resuscitated, however, they would certainly be reinvented in new guises that reflect the influence of Christianity and the impact of modern lifestyles associated with government workers and others at the Nomad Station. One can see just such a trajectory in places such as the northern province of South Africa, considered by Jean and John Comaroff (1999; cf. 1991, 1993, 1997). In this region, Christianization and colonial modernization have since articulated with long-standing beliefs to spawn retributions that swell with neomodern vengeance against suspected witches or sorcerers. Among Gebusi, resentment and disillusionment would have to be much greater than is presently the case for such a pattern of violence to develop (especially given the degree to which they now internalize a sense of personal culpability for sickness and failure). But given the monumental changes in Gebusi society and culture during the last two decades, it would be foolhardy to preclude unanticipated developments in an uncertain future.

The point to be drawn here is not that local circumstances are refractory to predictable understanding, much less to the analysis of how people become locally modern. It is rather that detailed local ethnography of contemporary and historical circumstances continues to be crucial. In a changing world, the ethnographic enterprise is important not simply to document ever-new developments. Nor, on the other hand, should it subserve the notion that old patterns stay the same while only appearing to change. Cultural transformations do occur, as the history of Gebusi amply attests. And many of these changes fit widespread trends of becoming locally modern, as discussed at the outset of this chapter (see Knauft in press a). The point is that contemporary ethnography can provide new insight about larger trends while also understanding how historical and cultural factors produce different outcomes in specific cases.

Agency That Isn't?

Among Gebusi, the process of becoming modern has included active subordination to figures of modern influence as well as the redefinition of remaining traditional practices within a contemporary frame of reference. Accordingly, one of the concepts that has emerged in this book is "recessive agency": willingly pursued actions that put actors in a position of subordination, passivity, and patient waiting for the influence or enlightenment of external authority figures. As an aspect of becoming locally modern, recessive agency is contextual rather than generalized, and it occurs more in some societies than in others. It becomes especially prominent as local actors in marginal circumstances engage themselves with modern institutions and their agents. In academic study, however, the dynamics of recessive agency tend to be neglected both by modernization theories, which emphasize entrepreneurial action, and cultural resistance theories, which foreground patterns of subversion or counterassertion.

It should be stressed that, in highlighting this aspect of social action, my purpose is not to disparage local conduct or those who pursue it. To the contrary, my goal is to expose and undercut the neoliberal assumption that contemporary developments produce a narrow range of self-interested behaviors—or counterbehaviors. Conditions of marginality and structural disempowerment easily produce results that are at odds with our academic assumptions about how people should act—or resist. And if Gebusi choose to be passive in certain contexts as their ticket to the church, the school, the market, and so on, who am I to criticize them?

The deeper issue here is our Western construction of self-assertion as a motivating force of social action. As many anthropologists have noted, Western notions of agency privilege the prevalence if not the moral goodness of an individual, autonomous, and energetic personal actor. This assumption stems from Western notions of personhood, identity, and personal progress more than from universal patterns of human relationship or social status. Yet, such assumptions often inform theories that derive from positivist sociology or global economics, on the one hand, and those that stress critical resistance against hegemony, modernization, and globalization, on the other. Such assumptions have been effectively critiqued in relation to Melanesian notions of personhood by Marilyn Strathern (1988, 1999) and others, who stress the importance of social relationality as an alternative to Western individuality.

Having clarified this point, however, it remains true that Western styles of agency are often associated with modern institutions and are often used to evaluate local activities in very different cultural contexts. Insofar as these intruding standards are influential or internalized, they can influence the way local people evaluate and judge their own behavior—even when they cannot effectively emulate the styles aspired to due to economic and linguistic impediments. In this sense, modern agency is what Gregory Bateson (1972) might call a proposition whose validity depends on belief in it. The various chapters of this book have documented how the values that Gebusi absorb at church, in school, at the market, and on the sports field now place a high value on individual responsibility and principled self-discipline. A moral imperative arises for individual progress through self-fashioning in a world of diverse choices and alternatives. In the process, new expectations are formulated and the process of choosing a life course is made problematic in new ways. Along the lines of analysis suggested by Foucault (e.g., 1983, 1984, 1988), this could be construed as the subjective dimension of becoming locally modern.

The catch is that the kinds of actions that indicate success in modern arenas—holding a wage-earning job, being able to pass school examinations, knowing how to read and preach the Bible, or being able to make a cash profit in local economic activities—are made unattainable at places like Nomad by the recessive agency that is a practical requirement for engaging these modernizing contexts in the first place. Though a sense of personal responsibility and culpability may be internalized, the capacity for more assertive agency is typically precluded, especially in the context of modern institutions and activities.

This general dynamic is one of the ways that so-called development works to enforce inequality: it fosters a sense of personal responsibility to be materially successful while undercutting the authoritative agency that would make this possible in modern institutional contexts. In this sense, the ideological work of becoming modern easily promotes the illusion of opportunity while ensuring the reproduction of status inequality (see Bourdieu 1984). As developments at Nomad illustrate, this structural pattern can be ironically prominent even when local agents of modern institutions—teachers, police, government officials, pastors, health clinic workers, and others—are uncommonly honest, committed, and in principle respectful of local customs. Many well-intended interventions or development programs sponsored by NGOs and related agencies produce similar results in developing countries.

The larger point, then, is not to relegate the modern response of non-Western peoples to the realm of "passivity"—as if people like Gebusi become recessive agents due to some personal or collective deficiency. Rather, it is to acknowledge how the structure of so-called modernization has social and ideological features that produce this result under conditions of socio-political, economic, and cultural marginality.

From a Western perspective, recessive agency may seem like "agency that isn't"—the lack of agency altogether. But people like those in Gasumi

Corners take strong initiative and often go to great lengths to put themselves in a situation of "active passivity" at church, school, or market. These
contexts are actively sought out and pursued by Gebusi themselves. That
this dynamic may persist and intensify despite being relatively unsuccessful
in material and economic terms underscores its subjective and cultural dimension. What it provides is a sense of being modern by cultural association through subordinate inclusion.

Locally Modern

The term "modernity" has been used in many different ways and can mean
different things depending on how it is defined.[11] But whatever we want to
call them, forces of extralocal influence and interconnection that started
to become global with the rise of Western capitalism are here to stay, including in Melanesia (Foster 1999). These influences are highly cultural as well
as political and economic.

The present work illustrates both how variable the process of becoming locally modern can be and how larger trends can be revealed by considering emergent patterns of social interaction and inequality. Melanesian
cultural diversity is justifiably renowned and has attracted great anthropological interest over the decades (Knauft 1999). Given the extent of contemporary changes, it would be an empirical as well as a theoretical blunder
to expect hundreds of Melanesian cultural orientations to have a singular
relationship to current developments, much less to expect them to con-
verge toward a similar result. More broadly, a range of recent work by ethnographers has emphasized the diverse ways that people in different world
areas develop a local sense of what it means to be modern (see chapters in
Knauft in press c).[12]

Some features of contemporary social change do emerge as common
in many world areas. These include increased and increasingly impersonal
exposure to people from other communities, increasingly disembedded and
decontextualized social relationships, emphasis on individual choice and responsibility, and an increasing mandate for material and moral progress
marked against the passage of unidirectional time. In the present case, these
features flow inductively from the ethnographic specifics of Gebusi's actions
and choices over the last two decades—as well as articulating with a range
of classic research on the historical emergence of modernity in Western societies. But developments among Gebusi also underscore how the process of
becoming modern has different inflections in non-Western areas. In particu-

lar, ideologies of becoming modern can cultivate subordination in the context of institutions controlled by external authorities. As the Gebusi illustrate, this can occur even in the absence of major economic development or political coercion. Substantiating this pattern has entailed an ethnographic description of local change and contemporary circumstance across a variety of social and institutional settings at Nomad. These developments have had specific implications for Gebusi but they may have larger implications for considering contextual conditions of contemporary change and inequality among marginalized peoples elsewhere.

Summarily expressed, the present work illuminates how institutions and activities associated with becoming modern are locally engaged. Among Gebusi, these engagements increase social subordination to outsiders while not affording local people the agency or objective opportunities likely to produce economic or social success. Given the influence of modern institutions such as the church, school, market, and sports leagues, Gebusi have reframed and hybridized their previous customs in ways that are increasingly neotraditional. Belief in sorcery has diminished, and practices such as spirit séances and the taking of violent retribution against sorcery suspects have virtually disappeared. Dancing in indigenous costume is increasingly reframed as a historical enactment to be judged by government officials, and local feasts or "parties" articulate with modern styles of commodity acquisition and disco dancing. In some domestic situations, modern styles of asserting dominance that are associated with Nomad and its institutions are locally reproduced.

Considering cultural change as a process of becoming locally modern provides an interactive way to think about the impact of contemporary institutions in local areas while allowing us to understand outcomes that are refractory to theories of modernization, resistance, or cultural relativism. In the process, our attention is drawn to cultural and subjective dynamics as people become enmeshed in larger fields of power and inequality.

The goal, always difficult, is to keep the cultural construction of change in touch with large-scale patterns of influence, on the one hand, and the lived experiences and meanings of local people, on the other. Broader critical awareness requires a greater appreciation of how peoples and cultures change, sometimes quickly, but without losing their humanity. One of ethnography's strongest assets has been its careful portrayal of human experience through the sustained enterprise of living richly with others. This remains at least as true under contemporary conditions as it ever was in the past.

Afterword

On the day of leaving, I had no shame. The morning started rainy, and I hoped it would continue so the plane wouldn't come. I didn't care that my few boxes were already sealed up and everything else given away. But eventually the drops lessened and I moped with everyone else in collective sorrow to the airstrip. Though Sayu, Didiga, and I were flying off to Kiunga, I was leaving all my other friends behind.

I started choking up well before the plane emerged from the flat horizon. I knew it would happen, just like it had during the previous three days, as I gave things away to so many good friends: I fought back the tears, but they kept coming. I had known the people of Gasumi so well before and now again at the end of eighteen years, first when they were children or young adults and now, a generation later, with their own children in their place. We all know it will be years, at best, before I can return again. Their place is so very remote, the rigors of living there so exacting and hard on my middle-aged body. My obligations back home are packed full in a whole other life, including my wife and son and parents who miss me. My Gebusi friends know this. Those who were middle aged and older know as well that I will probably never see them again; they will be dead by the time I will be able to return. Despite other changes, their lives stay all too short.

I couldn't think of my camera that last day but took pictures that were more indelible. As I moved down the sorrowful line of those gathered to say their good-byes to me, I forced myself to peer into the face and linger on the eyes of each person from Gasumi Corners. Snapping their fingers in the best and most forthright traditional manner, I burned into my mind the living image of each of these important and unique persons, to never forget their exquisite humanity. They reflected my look with tear-streaked faces, fighting their own reflex to turn away. I sobbed along with them, oblivious to onlookers and people from the station, a six-foot bald-shaven white guy crying with a crowd of villagers.

I lost it when I came to Yuway. Along with Swamin, Hawi, and another clan-mate, Yuway had led us on our very first patrol in 1980. He had been my most sensi-tive and caring helper when I was first learning the Gebusi language. He was my best friend during that first fieldwork, one of the young men I helped sponsor for initiation, and one of the nicest and most decent people I have ever known. Now a staunch convert to the Seventh Day Adventist Church, Yuway had become a forward-looking older man with two of his four children pushing toward adulthood. I looked into his eyes and suddenly blurted out, "Oh friend, friend, when will I ever see you again?!" His wisdom was greater than mine. With a weepy and yet dignified smile, he told me, "I'll see you later, in heaven."

I don't remember much after that. The plane loaded and taxied and turned to take me away in the dampness. My last sight at the end of the airstrip was Yuway. He had walked down to the end of the path, all alone, waiting to catch that very last wave from me through the airplane window, and I from him. Then I sailed away toward the heavens of Kiunga while Yuway awaited his own.

Who can deny the world of change in cultures? Or that richness of humanity that lives on despite all that would suppress it?

Notes

Prelude

1. In his historical study of Western temporality, Koselleck (1985: 279, 285) stresses how modern notions of time, which emerged toward the end of the eighteenth century, enlarged the difference between experience and expectation so that a generic sense of progress emerged, along with a complementary notion of "history in general"—against which progress was assessed. As discussed by Foucault (1984: 32–50), notions of "Enlightenment" developed in a distinctive way during this same period, as illustrated in the work of Immanuel Kant. These developments presaged the nineteenth-century tendency of Westerners to think increasingly about becoming different from what they had ever been or could predictably become on the basis of past traditions. As Foucault (1984: 39) notes more generally, "Modernity is often characterized in terms of consciousness of the discontinuity of time: a break with tradition . . ."

Of course, what Foucault (ibid.) describes as a distinctive "attitude of modernity" can entail quite different consequences for people with different cultural backgrounds.

2. E.g., Comaroff and Comaroff 1991, 1992, 1997; Ong 1987, 1999; cf., Appadurai 1996.

3. E.g., Sahlins 1985, 1995, 2000; M. Strathern 1988, 1991, 1999; see Englund and Leach 2000.

4. For example, see Sahlins (1995) versus Obeyeskere (1992); compare the assertions of Englund and Leach (2000) and its attendant critical commentaries.

Chapter 1

1. Concerning direct reciprocity systems in Melanesia, see A. Strathern 1982; Godelier 1982, 1986; Godelier and Strathern 1991; Lindenbaum 1984; see, more generally, Lévi-Strauss 1969.

2. See A. Strathern 1971; Meggitt 1974; Lederman 1986; see also Wormsley 1987.

3. Some persons executed were said by Gebusi to have caused the sickness-death of more than one victim.

4. See A. Strathern 1992, 1993; Meggitt 1977: chap. 9; see also Ward 2000.

5. See Roscoe 1999; Kulick 1991, 1993; concerning raskols in towns and cities, see Goddard 1992, 1995; Hart Nibbrig 1992; see also Sykes 1999.

6. See Gaonkar 1999; Dussel 1993; Rofel 1999; Donham 1999; Chatterjee 1997; Prakash 1998; Larkin 1997; Knauft in press b; Lichtblau 1999; see also Appadurai 1996.

7. Concerning the gendering of modernity in Melanesia, see Knauft 1997. Compare more generally, Massey 1994; Gibson-Graham 1996; Freeman 2001; Felski 1995; Marchand and Runyan 2000.

8. In 1980–82, 68 percent of true Gebusi brothers-in-law (wife's brother/sister's husband) lived together in the same settlement (Knauft 1985a: 28). In 1998, the rate of coresidence was 50 percent within each hamlet of Gasumi Corners and 75 percent within Gasumi Corners as a whole—that is, three-quarters of men's living true brothers-in-law lived somewhere in Gasumi Corners. Persistence of traditional coresidence was yet stronger with respect to maternal uncle or *bap* relationships (true mother's brother/sister's son or mother's brother's son/father's sister's son in this Omaha kinship system). In 1980–82, true *bap* coresided in the same settlement 47 percent of the time, while in 1998 this rate of coresidence was 40 percent within each hamlet of Gasumi Corners and 80 percent within Gasumi Corners as a whole.

9. In 1980–82, Yibihilu and its three main hamlets formed a four-settlement community of 115 persons, with an average individual settlement size of 28.75 inhabitants and a range from sixteen to fifty-two persons. In 1998, this population's new settlement of Gasumi Corners had a community size of 121 divided into four hamlets or "subcorners" that averaged 30 persons and had individual populations ranging between eighteen and forty-two persons. This size and organization are highly consistent with earlier patterns.

The owners of the specific land parcel on which Gasumi Corners is built belong to three Gebusi clans that support having a large, semiaggregated, multiclan community on a portion of their land. This disposition is traditional. Gebusi clans have always been very small, and land has never been scarce. The owners of the land on which a longhouse was built invariably desired to attract a larger and more socially, ritually, and militarily viable group. As such, they often invited residents from clans related by fictive siblinghood and affinal or maternal affiliation. The longhouse settlement of Yibihilu and its outlying hamlets, where I resided from 1980 to 1982, had this character, and its descendant community of Gasumi Corners now mirrors its organizational structure. The current residential system is likely to be increasingly under stress in future decades, however, as garden land and forest resources in the immediate proximity of the Nomad Station are progressively depleted. Under traditional residence patterns, habitation sites were shifted every few years, resulting in a general recycling of lands in alternate generations. The desire of increasing numbers of Gebusi to stay within easy walking distance of Nomad for school, church, market, and sports may cause problems further in the future. Added to this is a slow but steady population growth.

10. Concerning place names, the 1980 settlement of Yibihilu and its wider community were both labeled "Gasumi" in patrol reports. In fact, the actual village of Gasumi had been disbanded during the 1970s, after which some of its residents combined with others to build the new village at Yibihilu. However, patrol officers retained the older name for the new village during the 1980s. When Gebusi from the Yibihilu com-

munity moved near Nomad in the late 1980s, they kept the official name "Gasumi" and, in the process, indicated their historical ties to the earlier community.

11. The greatest threat of logging in the Nomad Subdistrict lies to the south of Gebusi, across the Rentoul or Sio River, where tiny populations of Oybae and Kabasi peoples occupy very large tracts of virgin rainforest. Concerning logging in Papua New Guinea's Western Province and in Melanesia more widely, see Brunois 1999; Schieffelin 1995; Wood 1996, 1997, 1999; Barlow and Winduo 1997; Filer 1997; Filer with Sekhran 1998.

12. Sleeping location data were collected for the 133 days between July 17 and November 26, 1998 for each of the seventy-three adult and young men and women of Gasumi Corners. (This population fluctuated slightly due to one death and a small amount of out- and in-migration.) The resulting 9,720 data entries were distributed as follows:

- sleeping in primary residence, 69.7 percent (6,775 of 9,720 person/nights)
- sleeping in a forest subsistence house, 15.5 percent (1,511 of 9,720 person/nights)
- sleeping at the forest pig-house complex, 1.3 percent (126 of 9,720 person/nights)
- sleeping at another settlement outside of Gasumi Corners, 9.0 percent (878 of 9,720 person/nights)
- sleeping at another hamlet within Gasumi Corners, 3.8 percent (371 of 9,720 person/nights)
- sleeping in Kiunga (or another town or city), 0.6 percent (59 of 9,720 person/nights)
- total sleeping away from primary residence, 30.3 percent (2,945 of 9,720 person/nights)

Data collection would not have been possible without the following research assistants: Didiga Imbo, Anagi Agi, Yamda Wasep, Keda Segwa, Howe Uwok, and Gilayo Dedagoba.

13. Data collection was facilitated by my ability to speak Gebusi, by being a longstanding acquaintance, and by living in Gasumi Corners during the entire six-month field period. Genealogies and residential and mortality data for Gebusi were updated from records kept from 1980 to 1982. Residence in Gasumi Corners was supplemented by trips to Nomad for part of the day several times a week and by a number of major trips into the full rainforest, including to attend feasts and initiations at distant settlements. In addition to Gebusi, school teachers, government officials, and church pastors welcomed my presence and helped me obtain both participant observation data and documentary information from official records.

Linguistically, my fieldwork was conducted in the Gebusi vernacular when in Gasumi Corners and while with Gebusi people in other contexts and settlements. At the Nomad Station, my conversations took place in a mixture of tok pisin and what may be called "Papua New Guinea English." (Since I did not use tok pisin during my first fieldwork in 1980–82, I acquired basic competence through language drills with a tok pisin instruction manual and associated cassette tapes before leaving for the field in 1998.) Though Nomad school children understood simple English in instructional contexts, I found myself switching spontaneously back to Gebusi as soon as I left the school grounds. Likewise in Gasumi Corners, my use of tok pisin (or English) was largely limited to words or phrases pertaining to modern circumstances that were difficult to convey in Gebusi. Though a number of the younger men understood tok pisin completely, my ability to converse in Gebusi was better than my ability to communicate in tok pisin, and I was also averse to the socially exclusive and asymmetrical linguistic agency that tends to accompany speaking in pidgin.

Notes compiled during the six months of fieldwork included 425 word-processing files comprising six megabytes of straight text plus some fifty tabular data files. Data collection was greatly facilitated by a notebook computer and rechargeable battery powered by two solar panels. This system was also used to recharge a highly portable microcomputer that I carried when outside Gasumi Corners. Electronic data collection was supplemented by sound recordings made with portable and microcassette tape recorders and by some 2,700 photographic slides taken with a N-70 Nikon camera outfitted with a 28–200mm zoom lens.

14. Concerning Gebusi male homosexuality, see Knauft 1986, 1987b, 2001; see also Herdt 1992. As documented by my wife and colleague, Eileen Cantrell, Gebusi women did not engage in homosexual relations, either ritually or nonritually.

15. Gebusi women often associated in female groups, both in the longhouse settlement and in the forest. They were not as domestically constrained as women in many parts of the New Guinea highlands. Nonetheless, married Gebusi women remained subject to the decisions of husbands, who would not hesitate to beat them if they felt their masculine authority was being questioned or if they thought their wives were acting in a flirtatious manner toward unrelated men. During 1980–82, approximately half of the marriages at Yibihilu involved at least one instance of wife beating that was severe enough to attract widespread public attention. Most of the other marriages, however, seemed relatively harmonious, including peaceful understandings between husbands and wives concerning their respective activities and standards of female behavior. The relationships of perhaps one-quarter of the couples seemed actively congenial in this respect. Perhaps one-quarter of the marriages could thus be characterized as chronically conflicted, one quarter as distant and sometimes conflicted, and one-quarter as typically congenial but occasionally tense.

In 1998, by comparison, major cases of wife beating came to public attention for four of the seventeen married couples in Gasumi Corners. Since the duration of this fieldwork was only six months, as opposed to twenty-two months in 1980–82, it seems likely that the incidence of major wife beating in Gasumi Corners would have been as great as or greater than it had been in the village of Yibihilu sixteen years earlier if field research had been undertaken for a comparable period of time.

16. Commonly, women's money is used to buy rice or tinned fish, which augments the food that men otherwise present to kin and visitors at intersettlement feasts. This extends the traditional pattern in which bulk food that has been produced or processed by women—such as sago starch and greens—is presented with great fanfare to visitors by the men of the host community.

17. Concerning the comparative anthropology of time, including lineal and non-lineal codifications, see Lee 1977; Hughes and Trautmann 1995; Gell 1992; Greenhouse 1996; see also Gould 1987. For an alternative interpretation of cyclical time in a Melanesian society, see Scaglion 1999.

18. Gebusi live in a complex climatic zone at the confluence of three weather systems. The timing of rain, relative dryness, and cloudy weather is difficult to predict. In many years, the weather does not follow a cycle of predictable seasons. At six degrees south latitude, there is also little seasonal solar variation.

19. Patterns of traditional Gebusi tobacco sharing and hospitality etiquette are discussed in Knauft (1987a).

20. This trend had begun in 1980–82 but is now much more pronounced.

21. At Gasumi in 1980–82, with its longhouse and compact family dwellings, there had been a total of 5,234 square feet of roofed living space for fifty-two residents—an average of 100.7 square feet per person. In my hamlet of Gasumi Corners in

1998, by contrast, there were thirteen dwellings with various functions for a population of twenty-eight persons—a total of 4,884 square feet or 174.4 square feet per person. In addition, the hamlet had built another substantial settlement in the forest at Harfolobi, which provided another 2,037 square feet, for an overall total of 6,921 square feet, or 247.2 per person. (Though temporary settlements in the bush were common in 1980–82, none were the size of Harfolobi.)

22. For purposes of meeting in Gasumi Corners, most men and boys crowd into the largest of the men's raised sleeping houses in the settlement. Typically, this space is not large enough to hold a traditional dance, and it also lacks a traditional ground-floor cooking section, where women would otherwise be able to congregate as part of the event.

23. See Godelier 1986, Godelier and Strathern 1991.

24. The Nomad Station was built on no-man's land along the border of three tribal groups: Gebusi, Samo, and Honibo. Weak claims to part of this land have been made by a remnant Gebusi clan, whose lone male survivor has received nominal compensation.

25. The Ok Tedi gold and copper mine, which helps support the Western Province government, likely will be closed down by 2010—due to decreasing yields and extensive ecological damage caused by the flow of mine sediments into the Fly River system, well to the west of Nomad. Though large-scale gold and gas/petroleum projects are set to come on line in the future, most of them are located in areas of Papua New Guinea outside the Western Province. As such, the longer-term future of Nomad is uncertain. Because the station is a subdistrict headquarters with a large and level airstrip that has been in continuous operation since 1963, continuation of its basic services is likely, however. The level of government commitment and upkeep will drop, though, if provincial funds generated by the Ok Tedi mine are not replenished by Australian or other development agencies or national sources (see Banks and Ballard 1997).

26. See Mauss (1967 [1925]); M. Strathern (1988); Knauft (1999: chap. 2).

27. The importance of waiting can be pronounced even or especially in the absence of an outside presence altogether, as illustrated for the Kubo, further north of the Gebusi, by Dwyer and Minnegal (1998).

28. Concern with "agency" has burgeoned in anthropology and critical sociology since the work of Anthony Giddens during the 1970s and 1980s (e.g., Giddens 1979, 1984). In Giddens's theory, agency was a means by which the social action of individuals influenced the operation of larger social structures. Reciprocally, structural forces influenced social action. As such, a mutually interactive or recursive relationship was held to exist between agency and social structure, even though, as Giddens stressed, the results of social action often had structural consequences that were unintended by the actors. As emphasized by Sherry Ortner (1984), Giddens's theory of social action—along with Pierre Bourdieu's critical theory of practice (1977)—helped put issues of individual action, motive, and consciousness back into sociological and anthropological models that had been overweighted with structural determinants while neglecting the lived experience of social actors (see Knauft 1996: chap. 4). Selected theoretical issues concerning "agency" are addressed in the concluding chapter of the present book (see also Knauft 1995). The presently relevant point is that notions of agency in social theory have often smuggled in Western notions of active individualism that may be at variance with the construction of agency in alternative cultural contexts (e.g., Hobart 1990; Povinelli 1995; Rumsey 2000; see Keane 1997).

29. Dwyer and Minnegal (1999: 380) note, "Among Bedamuni by 1996, tobacco smoking both by individuals and as a greeting ceremony was common, initiations occurred somewhere within Bedamuni territory nearly every year, and séances were held by some communities." Intriguingly, Dwyer and Minnegal contrast the "conservatism" of Bedamini with the "flexibility" of the neighboring Kubor, to their northeast. Like the Gebusi, the Kubor are few in number (450), have low population density, and were militarily unsuccessful against the more populous and warlike Bedamini. Not coincidentally, Kubor have in recent years been extremely solicitous of outside influence, and they have gone to great lengths in a futile attempt to attract outside wealth in the absence of local economic development (see Dwyer and Minnegal 1998; Minnegal and Dwyer 1997). Similarly to Gebusi but in contrast to Bedamini, Dwyer and Minnegal (1999: 380) state of the Kubor, "By 1995 few individuals smoked tobacco or shared it with others, and the ritual performances referred to appeared to have been abandoned."

Dwyer and Minnegal's own argument relates the contrast between Kubor and Bedamini to greater restrictiveness concerning land and resources among the Bedamini, who have a much higher population density (up to $10/km^2$) than the Kubor ($0.4/km^2$)—or the Gebusi ($2.6/km^2$). In several respects, this is a materialist complement to my own line of reasoning: in the present ethnographic context, higher population density among Bedamini has gone hand in hand with larger group size, local military strength, greater resistance to and antagonism toward colonial and then postcolonial authorities, and greater retention of indigenous customs.

30. At the time of my fieldwork, K 1.00 was equal to approximately U.S.$0.50.

31. Among the four men (of ten) who did give bridewealth, the payment ranged from K 60 to K 200, with an average of K 140. In two of the ten first marriages, a pig was given. No second marriages in Gasumi Corners were accompanied by either bridewealth or the giving of a pig.

32. Remote outstations in Papua New Guinea can suffer significantly when services deteriorate. By the early 1990s, Roscoe (1999: 181) notes of the Yangoru Station of the East Sepik Province, "The *kiaps* [patrol officers] were gone, but so too were the agricultural officer, the small civil service presence, the post office, and the bank. The Yangoru Health Centre's health-maintenance officer had 'run away,' and the Centre itself was kept open only by the valiant efforts of a few local nurses. Some police, whose presence people now desired, were still in residence, but their personnel were apt to disappear after just a month or two of service."

33. See also Comaroff and Comaroff 1991, 1997. Many ethnographers have had an understandable fear that as local peoples move away from traditional customs, they exchange their cultural heritage for modern developments that are culturally flat and personally unsatisfying. Anthropology's hallmark has long been its appreciation of cultural diversity and its celebration of practices that subvert the assumptions of the modern West. This has been nowhere more true than in the anthropology of Melanesia (see Knauft 1999). In late modern ethnography, this trend continues as ethnographers search for new and hybrid forms of subversion or irony that resist the march of capitalist "progress."

34. See Knauft in press a; Rofel 1999; LiPuma 2000; Piot 1999; Ferguson 1999; Schein 2000; Donham 1999; see also earlier work by Comaroff and Comaroff 1991, 1993, 1994.

35. The reinvention or redefinition of tradition has been an important general issue in the anthropology of the southwestern Pacific during the last two decades. See Keesing and Tonkinson 1982; Keesing 1992; Jolly and Thomas 1992; White and Lindstrom 1993; Jolly 1994; White 1991; Errington and Gewertz 1995, 1996. See, recipro-

cally, from the perspective of the colonial encounter, Thomas 1991, 1994, 1997; see also, more generally, Comaroff and Comaroff 1992.

Chapter 2

1. By contrast, there are other parts of Melanesia where practicing parcel sorcery and becoming known as a sorcerer have a long and robust tradition. See, for instance, Fortune 1932; Young 1983; Munn 1986; Forge 1970; Stephen 1987; for a brief overview, see Glick 1973. The Australian colonial authority established laws outlawing the practice of sorcery, and the Papua New Guinea legal system has continued this prohibition. One anthropologist, Michele Stephen (1994), apprenticed herself to a renowned sorcerer from the Mekeo of the south Papuan coast and learned most of his stock in trade. This would have been impossible among Gebusi: The traditional rate at which Gebusi executed those accused of sorcery made attempting it, or being suspected of practicing it, one of the last things a person would contemplate. Though it is theoretically possible that Gebusi denials cover a hidden practice—"thou dost protest too much"—it was our firm impression, over years of living there and endless conversations and more deaths and sorcery inquests than we care to remember, that parcel sorcery, like assault sorcery, was practically if not totally nonexistent.

2. In the interim before this divorce, Silap was married jointly to Tosi's daughter and to Boi, his first wife and mother of Sayu.

3. The details of these homicide figures are discussed in Knauft (1985a, 1987c), but it is worth noting here that these deaths include every deceased individual in eighteen Gebusi clan genealogies. Since the average number of *non*-homicidal deaths per time period is relatively constant in this sample, there is little reason to suspect that violent deaths have been disproportionately remembered for earlier time periods.

Students have sometimes asked whether some deaths believed by Gebusi to result from sorcery have been convincingly described to me as if they were homicides. Though this is theoretically a problem, it was easy in the field to use case accounts and crosschecking to distinguish homicidal deaths, in the Western sense of the term, from natural deaths believed caused by sorcery. Potential confusion was quickly dispelled when I asked what happened after the death, what happened to the body, who was accused of sorcery, and what divinations were held. (I asked about all these issues for each death, regardless of cause.) When a sorcerer was executed, the body was simply eaten or buried and there was no sorcery accusation following the killing. Persons executed for sorcery were also marked linguistically by attaching the suffix "-*faym*" (hit/killed) to the name of the deceased, and there was little taboo on mentioning this name. If the death was due to illness caused by sorcery, this reference could not be used. Death by sickness was also clearly indicated by the occurrence of divinations, spirit séances, and other inquests arranged to identify the sorcerer. Even in the rare absence of these procedures, Gebusi would discuss the type of sorcery deemed responsible for the sickness-death and explain why no divinations were held. Information about each death was independently cross-checked with informants from at least two clans to ensure that discrepancies about basic facts were resolved.

4. Homicide rates of other societies relative to Gebusi are tabulated in Knauft 1987c and Knauft 1985a: Appendix E.

5. Specific calculations for Gebusi homicide rates are provided in Knauft 1985a: 376–79 and 1987c.

6. For Hewa, see Steadman 1971: 215; cf. 1985. For Etoro, see Kelly 1993: 550.

7. See Meggitt 1977: 110; Heider 1979: 106; Hallpike 1977; Koch 1974; Barth 1971: 175; see generally, Knauft 1999: chap. 3.

8. See Knauft (1987c) for an empirical review and comparative analysis of the social ethos of violence in extremely decentralized societies from different world areas.

9. E.g., Watson 1971; A. Strathern 1971; Koch 1974; Hallpike 1977; see Knauft 1993 concerning the societies of the south coast of New Guinea.

10. Concerning Gebusi spirit séances, see Knauft 1985a: chap. 11, 1989. See Sørum 1980 regarding spirit séances among the neighboring Bedamini people.

11. The following text is paraphrased and condensed from transcripts of several sorcery accusations tape-recorded during 1980–82.

12. Once when Silap ran amok, my wife and I suggested to villagers that he should be tied up until he returned to normal. They agreed and tried to restrain him, but the attempt backfired—he bit through his bonds, was still possessed, and emerged more violent than ever. Villagers said he was a wild animal when possessed and could not be constrained.

13. Gebusi initiation rites are considered in Knauft 1987b; 1999: 79; n.d. Male initiation rites and fertility practices among the neighboring Bedamini people have been discussed by Sørum 1982, 1984.

14. The ability of Gebusi to downplay their suffering never ceased to amaze me. A year and half before my fieldwork in 1998, Gebusi had been subject to a devastating El Niño drought that had caused severe food shortages. All but the largest rivers dried up, leaves fell off many of the rainforest trees, and a number of Gebusi would have starved except for relief supplies flown in to the airstrip at Yehebi, in southern Gebusi territory. When I arrived a year and a half later, however, Gebusi—along with their environment— had rebounded so completely from the drought that I would hardly have known about it at all except for my previous knowledge of the crisis in New Guinea from colleagues and international press reports. Gebusi were quite willing to discuss their hardship during the drought, but they did so in a matter-of-fact way that seemed devoid of psychological scars or lingering distress. I never once heard the drought discussed spontaneously by Gebusi among themselves. My firm impression was that this was simply because the drought was no longer relevant to their present daily concerns. In cultural terms, Gebusi seemed to be very well adjusted to handling stress without reliving it or suffering aftershocks. As such, they appear to be surprisingly resistant to the syndrome of post-traumatic stress disorder (PTSD) that has been developed in our models of psychic distress.

15. Though exact population figures for the Nomad Subdistrict are unobtainable, 1995 census books had, by November 1998, been returned for ten of the subdistrict's twenty-four wards. These books seem quite accurate for the communities covered and include a good distribution of wards from all major ethnic groups in the Nomad Subdistrict. Assuming that the population tabulated in these books, 3,760 persons, is equivalent to 10/24 of the population, then the total population of the Nomad Subdistrict was close to 9,024 in 1998. This figure is close to the rough estimate of between eight thousand and ten thousand inhabitants that is commonly used in official reports. It thus seems a reasonable population estimate.

16. Even if twice as many homicides are still kept from government awareness as those which are publicly known, the homicide rate would be just 33 per 100,000—extremely low by historical standards in the Nomad area.

17. Could the passive acceptance of outsiders' authority by Gebusi have been undertaken as an effective means of reducing their own suffering and death? This line of reasoning resonates with Gebusi positive acceptance of colonial efforts to pacify their Bedamini neighbors, on the one hand, and their sense of benefiting from the social and institutional influences of the Nomad Station in more recent years, on the other.

However, the Gebusi experience of violence and suffering is culturally distinctive and at odds with this logic. Gebusi did not personally identify with the suffering of sorcery suspects. Since the sorcerer was considered heinous and inhuman, the killing of the person accused was seen as a major benefit to the community, excepting only his or her closest kin. There seemed to be little guilt or anxiety about having executed a sorcerer—nor worry that one would personally be accused of sorcery, since beliefs in the objective validity of sorcery inquests were so strong. It was only as people became elderly that they began to realize that one could be indicted by the spirits and found guilty through divination without having practiced sorcery. As such, identification with or fear resulting from the suffering caused by sorcery executions was not widely shared in Gebusi society.

Second, it is hard to explain why the most actively pursued subservience of Gebusi to outside authorities occurred when violence had already dropped significantly during the 1990s, since suffering from violence was greatest during the 1960s and before.

Third, the greatest and most prevalent suffering for Gebusi is that caused by debilitating and lethal illnesses. The incidence of sickness-deaths has been reduced in only a small and equivocal manner in recent years. By contrast, it was intrinsic to indigenous Gebusi beliefs that vengeance against sorcerers was the *consequence* and *not* the *cause* of suffering. In this respect, the cultural logic of Gebusi sorcery is just the reverse of the functionalist argument.

Finally, the functionalist reasoning at issue does not fit well with comparative evidence from elsewhere. In many if not most comparative cases where local violence has been intense—including the violent scapegoating of those in the community—the perpetrators of violence tend to resist rather than embrace the idea that they should stop their actions in order to reduce suffering. The persistence of endemic local violence and suffering in many world areas—and the staunch resistance of perpetrators to being stopped by outsiders—presents a compelling counterexample to the functionalist hypothesis on a comparative global basis.

Ultimately, then, functionalist explanations of violence reduction tend to be tautologous: they explain the outcome by its de facto result rather than by its preceding causes. Of course, it is theoretically possible for people to consciously decide to seek means of reducing their level of violence by submitting themselves to the authority of outsiders. This could be considered a positive outcome, the causes of which could be empirically investigated (along with the potential drawbacks of the new power relations that result from submission to outside authority). But in human societies, this chain of events does not seem to be common; it would need to be empirically demonstrated and cannot be easily assumed on the basis of post-hoc reasoning.

18. Concerning contemporary sorcery or witchcraft, see for Melanesia: Stephen 1987, 1994; Stewart and Strathern 1998b, 1999; Strathern and Stewart, 1999: 86–92; Stürzenhofecker 1995, 1998; Zelenietz and Lindenbaum 1981; for Africa: Comaroff and Comaroff 1993, 1998; Geschiere 1997; MacGaffey 2000; for South Asia: Kapferer 1997; for Southeast Asia: Watson and Ellen 1993; for England: Luhrmann 1989; for Latin America: Taussig 1980; 1987; for Caribbean Voodoo: Métraux 1972; Hurston 1990; Rigaud 1985; Laguerre 1990.

19. See Strathern and Stewart 1999: 86–92; Stewart and Strathern 1998. Modern killing of sorcerers in Papua New Guinea has been documented among the Ankave of the Anga-speaking region, where two women were killed and mutilated in 1987 and 1990 after being accused by a sorcery hunter (Lemonnier 1998: 297).

20. See Comaroff and Comaroff 1999; MacGaffey 2000: 16; Nitibaskara 1993.

21. Nitibaskara 1993: 130–32; see more generally, Watson and Ellen 1993.

Chapter 3

1. The principal people and places referred to in this chapter are as follows:

Agi: a patrol officer's houseboy who married a Gebusi woman, stayed on at Nomad, and founded a nearby Gebusi settlement with his in-laws.

Agiwa Corner: Previous Gebusi settlement on the outskirts of Nomad, named after Agi.

Basowey: Accused as the ogowili sorcerer responsible for Boi's death; killed by Doliay.

Boi: wife of Silap, then second wife of Doliay; mother of Sayu; resident of Harfolobi.

Bruce: husband to Eileen; anthropology graduate student and resident of Yibihilu, 1980–82; resident of Gasumi Corners, 1998.

Cyril Afenang: Lay pastor of the local Catholic church.

Doliay: second husband of Boi; killer of Basowey; imprisoned at Port Moresby for six years.

Eileen: wife to Bruce; anthropology graduate student and resident of Yibihilu, 1980–82.

Gasumi (original): Old village site upstream where some of the parents and grandparents of members of Yibihilu originally lived.

Gasumi (mid-1970s through 1985): government name for the village of Yibihilu.

Gasumi Corners: Amalgamated residential cluster of the descendants of the Yibihilu community, including those who moved to Harfolobi and Agiwa Corner. A thirty-minute walk south of Nomad and an eight-minute walk from the Kum River.

Hadeagum: wife of Doliay.

Harfolobi: upstream locale inhabited as a permanent settlement for about three years following the breakup and abandonment of Yibihilu.

Hogoswimam: spirit medium living near Harfolobi, whose sickness prompted the accusation of six bogay sorcerers.

Kusabi: natal community of Boi.

Nomad Station: government patrol post founded, along with its airstrip, in 1962–63. Primary source of outside influence and only point of outside entrance to Gebusi and surrounding groups.

Sayame: Elderly childless spinster accused as a bogay sorcerer and nearly burned to death by the people of Yulabi. Fled with her relatives to Gasumi Corners.

Sefomay: resident of Harfolobi; accused of bogay for Hogoswimam's death; jailed for this reason.

Silap: cofounder of Yibihilu longhouse; wife of Boi; father of Sayu; friend to Uwok.

Sirigubi: natal community of Basowey.

Swamin: spirit medium of Yibihilu; later moved to Agiwa Corner.

Tosi: woman of Yibihilu accused of bogay in the death of Hiali, Silap's brother. Clan relative to Sayame, who later moved in with Tosi's descendants at Gasumi Corners.

Uwok: cofounder of Yibihilu longhouse; friend to Silap; moved to Agiwa Corner; became an early Catholic convert.

Yehebi: settlement south along the Sio River inhabited by the descendants of Kusabi. Situated next to an airstrip constructed by an American fundamentalist missionary in the late 1980s.

Yibihilu: settlement overlooking the Kum River; founded by Uwok and Silap; residence of Bruce and Eileen from 1980 to 1982; disbanded upon Silap's death in 1985.

2. In 1982, one of the national officials at Nomad boasted with bravado how his fist helped bring out the truth when cases of local sorcery were brought to his attention.

3. The fact that these women are regular churchgoers and that their identity has become a matter of official police record at Nomad also serves to protect them.

4. Since Basowey wasn't a member of Boi's settlement or community, it was difficult to kill him on the spot; he had many relatives from the Sirigubi community who

were not in sympathy with the accusation and would have tried to take immediate revenge if Basowey had been attacked. Such dynamics help explain why sorcery executions less frequently take place between communities and are more likely against persons from the same community as the person who died from sickness.

5. Some of Basowey's supposed anger had been indirectly due to me. When Eileen and I left Yibihilu in 1982, we left behind a house full of items for the Gebusi we knew best. In order to ensure an equitable distribution, we gave each major item—a metal patrol box, metal tool, pot, or piece of equipment—to a specific person or publicly announced who should receive it upon our departure. We didn't have time, however, to specifically apportion the smaller and less valuable goods. I don't remember what we ended up slating for Basowey, but it couldn't have been much; we only saw him once every month or two, and he wasn't among our circle of close friends and associates. Shortly after we left in 1982, however, he apparently heard about the distribution of goods from our house and came to claim a share. Gebusi said he became particularly insistent that a certain towel that we had left behind should belong to him. Others overruled him, however, and he got nothing. He seldom ever visited Yibihilu after that, affiliating with his natal village of Sirigubi instead. His lingering anger over not receiving our towel was later said to be one reason he had resorted to sorcery.

6. Doliay's account continued as follows:

The village headman, Imbo, asked me why I had come to Harfolobi. I said I had just killed a man. Imbo was very angry at first, saying, "Why did you do that?!" [The killing caused great complications not only with the government but with Basowey's now-furious relatives in Sirigubi.] I told him how angry I was and how it was only right to take revenge for Boi's death. So Imbo became happy. It was almost dusk by this time. But we all agreed that everyone from Harfolobi should go down to Nomad right away [so no one would be left vulnerable to attack by men from Sirigubi].

We took our bows and arrows and got most of the way to Nomad, but we were still in the forest when it got dark. Carrying firebrands, we saw another firebrand in the distance and told the women and children to run and hide. We stood together, Imbo, Sabol, Uwok, Yuway, Uwano, and me. We asked who it was; we thought it was a person from Sirigubi wanting to shoot and take revenge. But it was Agi, our councillor, my initiate sponsor. "Don't shoot!!," he said. So we didn't shoot. He asked if I was going to run and hide in the forest. "No," I said, "I am going to Nomad."

They wanted me to sleep at the Nomad Station that night, but I wanted to sleep in my own house [for the last time]. They insisted I sleep at Nomad, but I wanted to sleep at my own house [and wouldn't mind fighting even if Sirigubi people did come down] and so I did. In the morning I went to the station house. The police asked me, "Did you kill that man?" "Yes I did," I said. "Are you prepared to work [do years of prison work]?" "Yes, I am," I said. The police were not angry with me, but became my supporters. [The police believe in assault sorcery and were glad the sorcerer had been killed.] They took their shotguns and put shells in them and aimed them out against people from Sirigubi in case any of them came to attack me at the station. But the Sirigubi people never came, they were too scared of the Nomad police. The police became my supporters. When it was time for them to eat, they left and let me stay on my own. They even gave me a shotgun with a shell in it in case the Sirigubi people came to try to kill me while they were gone eating.

The police called by radio and an airplane came. The police took their rifles and stood by and I got into the plane. The plane first went to Lake Murray and then to Obo and then landed in Kiunga. I slept in a jail cell that night in Kiunga. The police there were not angry at me. They thought it was good that I was a man and didn't try to run away but came right to the police and was willing to work [to do prison work to atone for the crime]. They thought it was good that the assault sorcerer was dead. They said I was a good man, and they went to the store and with their own money bought me ten sticks of Mitrus tobacco and biscuits and things to eat. I stayed in Kiunga for two weeks before my trial. Then I went to prison at Bomana in Port Moresby for six years.

7. The text of Doliay's reference letter follows:
Corrective Institutional Services
Staff Training College
P.O. Box 6373
BOROKO

22nd April 1993

TO WHOM IT MAY CONCERN

REFERENCE: OLISOP GOBALE

The abovementioned person has been under direct observation for the past four (4) years engaged in catering duties at the College Mess.

For the period he spend with us we've found him to be a hard working man requiring very little supervision from his supervisors.

He has showed his initiative and certain degrees of creativeness in his daily tasks and will certainly continue to do so in any catering tasks he will embark on in the future.

I won't hesitate to recommend him for any catering duties in what ever Department he wishes to seek employment.

Signed,

SAMSON I. KISSA
SENIOR MESS SUPERVISOR

8. Concerning visuality, darkness, and Christian enlightenment among prisoners in the Bomana prison, see Reed (1999).

Chapter 4

1. See Schieffelin and Crittenden 1991.

2. Despite or perhaps because of their aloofness, patrol officers remained a model of strength, power, and beneficial wealth—as well as being angry and scary. In one Gebusi folktale, the patrol officer can be reached by a villager only by going through one door after another in almost infinite regress inside the government station house. The timid Gebusi visitor summons up courage and knocks and knocks and is admitted through each entrance in turn. Finally seen, the officer is huge, with thighs as big as tree trunks and a nose as big as a housepost. Though burly and blunt, he is also generous. In the tale, the officer gives the visitor piles of money and clothes in exchange for mere bags of sweet potatoes (Knauft 1996: 211–16).

3. For a compelling historical account of the Papua New Guinea colonial police, see Kituai 1998.

4. The procedures for obtaining the check itself are remarkable, as revealed in the official correspondence [spelling unchanged]:
Department of Western Province; Division of Primary Industry; P.O. Box 5; Daru
17 April 1997

Our ref WPD/8-014-3:caa

CIRCULAR INSTRUCTION NO: DAL-03/97

SUBJECT: FINANCIAL CONTROL PROCEDURES

This financial control procedures are extraction from the financial management manual and application of duties and responsibilities as stipulated in both the Financial Management manual and the Fly River Provincial Government Acts.

This procedures therefore does not in any way over-rides the two financial acts. It is intended only to drive the financial working mechanism to apply brakes where unprofessional dealings have been allowed, thereby the Government's financial reputation among the communities and business world have been damaged.

To amend this damages, the following procedures would need to be followed to have control over unauthorised expenditures, thus bringing the government to a sound Financial Controls and return of the confidence with business customers within the province and the Nation at large.

THE PROCEDURES
Although there are thirteen (13) difference steps to be followed before the actual cheque is paid to the payee . . .

If every authorised person who has a part to play in this process does his or her part correctly, and adhere to one another's advice, as required in this process, there should not be any set backs for prompt payments been made to our suppliers and there by avoiding officers accusing one another for nonpayments of claims in time, or causing over-draft in the accounts.

. . . .

So let's follow the lay out procedures and ensuring that it is done and followed correctly.

For your adherence and correct application of the procedures

(Signed) Babalela Kalama; Principal Advisor

WESTERN PROVINCIAL ADMINISTRATION. FINANCIAL CONTROL PROCEDURES SYSTEMS APPROACHES:

STEP 1: Project or a service is identified for implementation by the Division/Sector

STEP 2: Initial Preparation—Quotations /Pre–Qualification Tenders. Principal Advisors, District Managers, Provincial / District Managers, Administrative Officers or appointed Requisition Offices to get quotations for that particular project or service.

STEP 3: Check for availability of funds with Provincial Treasurer or Provincial Finance Officer:
Check (A) funds on cash fund certificate (CFC); (B) funds in bank; (C) funds in cash money market projections; (i) if funds available then proceed on to the preparation of requisition/tenders call for the service or project (ii) if no funds available, no pre-commitments should be made either in writing or verbally to clients

STEP 4: If funds are available as in item 3i, then proceed on with the following:
(a) Requisitions and General Expense forms raised (FF3 and FF4); (b) Tender Board Meeting

STEP 5: Requisition Officers to refer all prepared documents to the Office of Principal treasurer / Provincial Finance officer to check on the availabilities of funds: (A) Cash Fund Certificates (CFCs); (B) Daily Cash Money Market Projections; (C) Cash in Bank (actual)

STEP 6: If cash available in 5(a) (b) and (c) refer claims for Financial Delegates' signature. After the Financial Delegate as signed, claims are referred back to the Provincial Treasurer/Provincial Finance Officer for reconfirmation on the availability of funds in the Bank (actual).

STEP 7: If funds available in the bank (actual) the Provincial Finance Officer shall counter sign the voucher either at the top or the bottom of the original claim as approved or authorisation being granted for payment to proceed. Any claim without the countersignature of the Provincial finance Officer shall be returned unpaid to the Requisition Office.

STEP 8: ACTION ONE: On receipt of the claim, the Examiner shall register the claim in the claim register book with number.
ACTION TWO: On receipt of claims by Account Clerk /Examiner from the Provincial finance Officer or the Division, the Examiner shall: (A) examine the claim for correctness (Vote No., Signature for Requisition Officer, Financial Delegates); (B) check for funds availability on Cash Fund Certificate; (C) check for signature of Provincial Finance Officer as authorised claim for payment.

NOTE:
If during the cause of examination, the Examiner detect errors in the claim or one of the items in STEP 8. . . the particular claim shall be immediately returned to the Provincial Finance Officer for checks, examination, investigations or referal to originating Division /Requisition officer.

STEP 9: If the claim is in order at STEP 8, it should be refered to the Certifying Officer for certification before payment.

STEP 10: After certification of the claim, the Examiner/Certifying Officer should refer the claims to Data Manager/Computer Operators for cheque drawing

STEP 11: After the cheques have been drawn, the Account Clerk/Examiner to collect; (A) original vouchers; (B) cheques drawn; (C) Cash sheets. These documents should then be refered to Provincial Finance Officer

STEP 12: The Provincial finance Officer, on receipt of the above documents as in STEP 11; (A), (B), (C) shall check all documents for correctness. If all the documents are in order; then the Authorising Officer shall sign the Cash Sheet as indication of approval granted for despatchment of the cheques to the originating Divisions.

STEP 13: After authorisation of the cheques for despatchment the Account Clerk shall collect, paid vouchers, cash sheets and cheques and do the following: (A) register the cheque number and amount in the register against the original claim registration entry; (B) Divisional Clerks to sign both on the cash sheet and on the registration book as indication of receipt of payment; (C) Vouchers plus the Cash Sheets to be given to the Filing Clerk for filling in their consecutive number order.

FINAL NOTE: The Divisional Clerks after collection of cheques, do the same as in STEP 13:(a), No cheques should be paid out for the Office Of Treasury or Provincial Finance Office to the payees. Cheques should be paid to payees from originating Divisions.

Payees to sign on the originating Divisional register book as an indication of receipt of payment.

5. By contrast, the Pare people across the river benefited from a very good local mission school that, before its expatriate missionary departed, educated the two men who later became the Nomad policemen, along with a number of others.

6. Roughly half the police book "occurrences" concern the populous Bedamini people, east of the Gebusi. Others concern the Samo and Kubor peoples, north of Gebusi, and the Pa, to their west across the Strickland River.

7. Other complaints fill out the remaining quarter of the "occurrences": improper firearm (confiscation of homemade or broken rifle), 13 = 4.6 percent; murder (including sorcery cases apparently listed as murder), 10 = 3.5 percent; insult, 10 = 3.5 percent; trespassing, 8 = 2.8 percent; false report, 4 = 1.4 percent; compensation dispute, 4 = 1.4 percent; marijuana use, 4 = 1.4 percent; liquor selling (there are no liquor licenses at Nomad), 3 = 1.1 percent. The remaining offenses include a single case each of gambling and of unlawful detention of a person, and two cases each of suicide, infanticide, misuse of government funds, public discharge of a firearm, armed hold-up, arson, and land dispute. Relative to some other parts of Papua New Guinea, it is notable that compensation and land dispute cases are rare. This reflects the relative lack of land pressure and of traditional compensation payments in the Nomad area.

8. Some of the westernmost villages in the Nomad Subdistrict can be reached by motorized dinghy, but these boats are often unavailable, prone to break down, and must be rented and gasoline obtained and paid for in any event.

9. Money for travel supplies and to recompense villagers for food and lodging can be requested from the local-level government (which has its own substantial bureaucracy at Nomad), but funds are worse than tight and seldom forthcoming.

10. In John Kolia's imaginative novel *Without Mannerisms* (1980), for instance, almost half of the plot concerns a fictitious scheme to relocate Papua New Guinean convicts to the Nomad area because the region has less fighting and a smaller population than other parts of the country (see especially Kolia 1980: 132–33, 168–69).

11. This perception of the Nomad police may be more accurate among Gebusi, Samo, and Kubor than it is for Bedamini, who often see Mr. Gobi and Mr. Haga as partial to their traditional enemies. The Pa people are across the Strickland River from Gebusi and are not seen as direct political or cultural competitors to them.

12. The distinction between police and soldiers was not always clear from the drawings.

13. See Liria (1993) concerning the questionable actions of the Papua New Guinea Defense Force during the Bougainville rebellion.

14. See Roscoe 1999; Goddard 1992, 1995; Hart Nibbrig 1992; see also Dinnen 2001; Dinnen and Ley 2000.

15. In Papua New Guinea, it is noteworthy that reports of police brutality can be made public and that charges of excessive force can be brought against police officers. Lawyers and judges sometimes take such charges quite seriously. The reporting of these incidents in the national newspapers indicates significant press freedom in Papua New Guinea. In short, awareness of police problems suggests a more active and vocal public sphere of debate in Papua New Guinea than in many developing countries.

16. See Dinnen and Ley (2000) and Dinnen (2001) for reviews of current patterns of violence in Melanesia.

Chapter 5

1. This case parallels the attack on female sorcery suspects in Gasumi for causing the sickness of the spirit medium Hogoswimam in 1988, as described in chapter 3. In both cases, the attack occurred before the spirit medium was fatally ill, and in both cases he recovered. Though it was somewhat unusual for sorcery suspects to be attacked or killed prior to the sickness-death of their ostensible victim, these exceptions reflect the traditional importance of the spirit medium to his community.

2. By contrast, 65 percent of married women (13/20) and 60 percent (12/20) of married men or widowers in Gasumi Corners have been baptized.

3. For more details about the empirics of Gebusi homicide and sorcery attribution by sex and age category, see Knauft 1985a: chap. 5 and 1985a: 406n5.

4. The relative increase of ogowili attributions is also spurred by changes in the way sicknesses are treated in Gasumi Corners. Since the Nomad health clinic is only a half-hour's walk away, medical treatment is readily sought. Though the benefits of this intervention are typically marginal—an incomplete dose of antibiotic or antimalarial pills—they can provide a transient feeling of improvement and the knowledge that modern efforts are being used by outsiders in an attempt to cure the sickness. The sick person can rally, at least briefly, even if his or her condition later becomes all the more grave. This pattern was evident in both of the fatal illnesses in Gasumi Corners in 1998. This temporary reprieve undercuts the notion that the ill person is dying from a long, relentless illness—which is associated with parcel sorcery. When the sick person eventually does die, there is also a greater chance that they have been out and about in the community during the weeks preceding their death—as was the case with Uwano. This increases the postmortem assessment that the person has died from a quick and decisive attack by an assault sorcerer (*ogowili*) rather than from parcel sorcery (*bogay*). In the past, by contrast, the diagnosis of bogay was reinforced prior to death by the spirit medium in spirit séances. Once the affliction was diagnosed as bogay, the person typically internalized his or her condition as hopeless. He or she seldom left the house, lost appetite, sometimes stopped eating food altogether, and waited to die. With the decline of spirit séances, however, this dynamic has been undercut. Currently, the cause of illness cannot be attributed until death has already taken place, at which time a diagnosis of ogowili becomes relatively more likely.

5. This union did not preclude the marriage of the spirit medium to a human Gebusi woman. In this sense, Gebusi mediums could be married polygamously to a human wife and a spirit wife.

6. See Barker 1990; Errington and Gewertz 1995: chap. 4.; Jebens 1997; LiPuma 2000: chap. 5; Whitehouse 1998; Lattas 1998: chap. 8.

7. E.g., Robbins 1995, 1998a, 1998b; Robbins et al. 2001; Robin 1982.

8. See, similarly, Schieffelin 1981a, 1981b, cf., 1996; Brunois 1999; Lemonnier 1998.

9. The goal of understanding the relationship between subjective motivation and social result was the key basis for Max Weber's (1958, 1978) analysis of world religions, through which he developed the notion of ideal types.

10. See Foucault 1985, 1986.

Chapter 6

1. This statement is excerpted from the sole sermon given by a villager during my fieldwork at Nomad and at Gasumi Corners. It was delivered in Gebusi and translated by me from a tape recording.

2. Increased access to Western clothing is one of the most visible material changes among Gebusi since 1982. Every few months, an enterprising official or broker manages to have a large bale of used clothes flown in and its contents sold to villagers at nominal prices.

3. According to Mr. Afenang, the Catholic diocese had tried to use converts from other parts of the Western Province to bring Catholicism to Nomad but only the "mountain boys" from the Mountain Ok area had the tenacity and commitment to live for long periods and establish the church in this remote place.

4. In the pidgin original, this theme is rendered as *Yumi olgeta i mas traim hat long stap trupela disaipel bilong Jisas Kraist.* The sermon is loosely based on Jesus' parable of the narrow door, Luke 13:22–30.

5. Kava is a local intoxicant produced by pounding and emulsifying the root of *Piper mythesticum.* Widely used in lowland Melanesia and Polynesia, kava (*ti*) was drunk by Gebusi at most ritual dances and occasionally at spirit séances and other social gatherings, where it produced soporific effects and was sometimes accompanied by vomiting (Knauft 1987a; see also Lebot et al. 1992). The Catholic pastors at Nomad campaigned strongly against the use of kava, and, as a result, its consumption has been almost eliminated at Gasumi Corners. This eradication has been medically beneficial, since Gebusi processed kava by chewing and spitting it into a common bowl, from which it was collectively drunk. The copious salivary mixture was a ready conduit for the transmission of diseases such as tuberculosis, influenza, and other pulmonary ailments. A similar medical benefit could presumably have been effected by chewing and mixing the plant individually, since it has no known detrimental properties itself. Kava has reportedly become a niche-market product in the United States and has been sold for drinking in so-called "kava bars" in Seattle and selected other cities along the U.S. West Coast as well as in the Pacific islands.

6. This Christian message seems to be based on Luke 17: 7–10:

Jesus said, "Suppose one of you has a servant ploughing or minding sheep. When he comes back from the fields, will the master say, 'Come along at once and sit down?' Will he not rather say, 'Prepare my supper, fasten your belt, and then wait on me while I have my meal; you can have yours afterwards'? Is he grateful to the servant for carrying out his orders? So with you: when you have carried out all your orders, you should say, 'We are servants and deserve no credit; we have only done our duty.'"

7. Nonchurchgoers typically explain their disinclination by saying that they don't wish to be subject to the constraints of the pastors and that church services are long and boring. This explanation parallels the statements of converts who miss church services due to periodic disinclination.

8. The Catholic Diocese at Kiunga is run and supported by the Montfort Catholic Mission of Canada and is staffed by French Canadian priests and sisters, overseen by an expatriate bishop who also resides in Kiunga. In addition to their residences and church and vocational training facility in Kiunga, the Montforts also have a conference and training center there.

9. A small sample of these text items are as follows:

Integral Human Development: (1) Making efforts to achieve IHD of everyone; (2) Education based on mutual respect and dialogue; (3) Encouragement of new methods; (4) Improving health standards; (5) Recognition of family units; (6) Applying P.N.G. ways in development

National sovereignty and self-reliance: (1) Commitment to National Goals; (2) Plan according to the Goals and Principals; (3) Promotion of interdependence and unity;

(4) Government control of economy; (5) Control and access foreign resources; (6) Government control and participation in economy; (7) Use of local skills and resources; (8) Respect and recognize sovereignty of P.N.G.

10. See Bourdieu 1988, 1989; Bourdieu and Passeron 1977; Bourdieu, Passeron, and Saint Martin 1996.

11. I observed who among the forty baptized Catholics in Gasumi Corners was present during twelve Sundays sampled between July 7, 1998 and November 22, 1998. The number of persons who could have attended was adjusted slightly over this period due to one death and a few residential relocations.

In absolute terms, church attendance was 43.5 percent of what would have been theoretically possible (201/462), with almost equal figures for men (43.4%) and women (43.6%). The main range of variation was among the young men; for aspiring prayer leaders, attendance was 57.7 percent (26/45), but among those four young men who were baptized but not interested in becoming prayer leaders, attendance was but 18.8 percent (9/48). Attendance figures are contextualized by the fact that members of Gasumi Corners sleep in the forest for subsistence purposes or while visiting at another location 30.3 percent of the time, as discussed in chapter 1. Even if this figure is reduced for overnight visits in another of the subhamlets within Gasumi Corners (3.8%), this means that more than one-quarter of the time (26.5%), the average member of Gasumi Corners is not within feasible walking distance of church. Given this reduction, the maximum effective attendance rate would be approximately 73.5 percent. Against this figure, the absolute attendance rate of 43.5 percent is approximately three-fifths (59.2%) of what would be practically possible. This figure does not take into account cases of sickness or infirmity that make church attendance impossible or inadvisable.

12. See Genesis 18:16–33.

13. The Catholic church is within a 10-minute walk from Gasumi Corners. The Evangelical and Seventh Day Adventist churches are within a 30–45 minute walk and are considered easily accessible to those in Gasumi Corners.

14. In some areas of Melanesia, by contrast, there is rivalry or social antagonism between more "mainline" religious groups and locally entrepreneurial charismatic or Pentecostal sects (Jebens 1997). The absence of this conflict at Nomad could be due to the fact that, in practice, all three Christian denominations are strongly fundamentalist.

15. In 1998, the 121 inhabitants of Gasumi Corners kept 18 semidomesticated pigs. This is typical for Gebusi more generally.

16. Though the Catholic church adjacent to Gasumi Corners is attended primarily by the members of this community, it is also attended by a few non-Gebusi Catholics from other corners of Nomad or from the Station itself, including two of the station's nurses.

17. The spread of evangelical Protestant, Seventh Day Adventist, and Catholic practices at Nomad is clearly related to the international spread and growing global influence of fundamentalist Christianity (see Hefner 1993; van der Veer 1996; Vasquez 1998; Willaime 1992; CNRS 1999; Fath 2000; see more generally Cox 1995; Poewe 1994; Weber 1979; Hexham and Poewe 1997). In the present case, these linkages are largely beyond the awareness of Gebusi and would take us beyond the scope of the present account. Works concerning fundamentalist or charismatic Christianity in Melanesia have proliferated in recent years, including especially Robbins et al. 2001; Robbins 1995, 1998a, 1998b, 2001; Schmid 1999; Stewart and Strathern 1997, 2000; Jebens 1997; Eves 2000; see also earlier work by Barker 1990; Boutilier et al. 1978; and

Trompf 1991. A review of the types of Western authorship that have emerged in the anthropological study of Melanesian Christianity has been supplied by Douglas (2001).

18. This passage appears to be based on John 15:1–10.

19. Revelation 20:15 reads, "The lake of fire is the second death; and into it were flung any whose names were not to be found in the roll of the living."

20. Among the men and women of Gasumi Corners who attend the SDA or ECP churches, 71 percent are women (12/17). By contrast, men make up a slight majority among the Catholic adherents (22/40, 55%). Nonchurchgoers from Gasumi Corners are also predominantly men (7/11, 64%), and all of the four women who do not go to church are married to nonchristian husbands. Two of these women attend church when their husbands are absent.

21. During the seven Evangelical services I attended, only one sermon was given by the main paid pastor. On some occasions, this pastor was gone from Nomad on official church business; on other occasions, he was present but delivered only a punctuating prayer or harangue, or helped lead the singing.

22. I thank Joel Robbins for bringing the published version of these posters to my attention (see Evangelical Church of Papua New Guinea 1991).

23. The principal exception is my deeply evangelical friend Hawi Suaripi. Orphaned and having attended a missionary school even prior to our first arrival in 1980, Hawi nonetheless lived during the early 1980s in traditional Gebusi style. He was initiated in 1981 and was an active participant in men's camaraderie, sorcery inquests, and funeral fights (see Knauft 1999: photos 4 and 7). During the 1980s, however, Hawi moved permanently to the Nomad Station and became a staunch Christian. He became deeply involved with the church after he recovered from a debilitating series of headaches. He attributed his improvement to fervent worship and divine intervention.

24. Gebusi themselves suffered severely during the El Niño drought of 1996–97. Gardens withered to almost nothing, and all but the largest rivers dried up. Gebusi grew weak, and some of them would probably have died from starvation except for supplies of rice and cooking oil flown in by Australian relief organizations to the airstrip at Yehebi, to their south. (Due to bureaucratic difficulties, almost no food aid relief was flown in to the Nomad airstrip.) The severity of the drought in the Nomad area is confirmed by Allen and Bourke's (1997) comparative regional assessment.

25. This pattern of appreciating but not actively responding to millennial predictions appears to be common in Melanesian Christianity. As Bashkow (2000) emphasizes for the Arapesh, dramatic visions of an imminent apocalypse may be appreciated as a riveting story but not result in changes of personal activity. Based on his work among the Urapmin, Robbins (2001) makes a helpful distinction between the charismatic immediacy of intense but relatively brief millenarian fervor and the temporal and social shift that allows for a calmer form of "everyday millenarianism" the majority of the time.

26. This is not to say that the SDA man was a homosexual participant but rather that his costume was both homoerotic and symbolic of insemination practices that were carried out as part of the initiation (see Knauft 2001; in press b; 1987b).

27. See Weber 1979; Sandeen 1970; Marsden 1980.

28. In an African context see, similarly, Donham 1999: chap. 5.

29. See Lattas 1998; Keesing 1982, 1992.

30. E.g., Errington and Gewertz 1995: chap. 4; Jebens 1997.

Chapter 7

1. From the field of education studies, see Fuller and Clarke 1994; Raudenbush et al. 1993; and Curtin and Nelson 1999. Gould (1993) provides a useful overview of relevant cross-cultural literature published prior to 1993. Concerning Papua New Guinea, general overviews of education include Monsell-Davis 1998 and Bray 1984. The emerging work of Sykes (1999, n.d.) on secondary education and generational tensions in insular Papua New Guinea is particularly important.

2. For an interesting example in an Islamic context, see Lambek 1993: chaps. 1–2.

3. The self-attributed name of this ethnic group, "Bedamini," was referred to in chapter 1 and in selected other passages. The government name for this group, which has solidified over the years in official contexts, is "Biami." I use this latter term when referring to the group in an institutional context and retain the former term when referring to them as an indigenous people.

4. Students occasionally cache bananas in the tall grass by the airstrip and cook them at noon, but such stashes can be pilfered by others while classes are in session and there is no place to store food at school. The children of station workers are lucky to go home for lunch. But the other students mostly go without and relax near the school or swim in the adjacent Nomad River during the noontime break.

5. The school day affords a half hour for recess, a noontime break of one hour, and time outside at the end of the day for "agriculture," which usually means working in the school garden or tidying up the school grounds. Classes must have at least thirty-five students to merit a teacher; if they do not—or if there are not enough teachers—two grades combine into a single giant class.

6. The hiring of local high school graduates by government and business enterprises is directly or indirectly increased by royalties received by the province from the Ok Tedi gold and copper mine, north of Kiunga. In addition, the number of high school graduates from the Western Province is not large relative to more populous parts of Papua New Guinea, where the educational system is often more well developed.

7. Concerning "diploma disease" in Third World contexts, see Gould 1993: 152–54. For a theoretical discussion of diploma inflation in relation to economic and class disempowerment—in the French educational system—see Bourdieu 1984: 132–56.

8. Both for fun and communication, I compared phrases or concepts in simple English, tok pisin, and Gebusi. That I could speak a vernacular language that many of them could not generated particular excitement.

9. In another class, I followed the outline of an outmoded primer when teaching students about Indonesia. I explained the standard facts that would be tested at the end of the week: population size, capital, geography, major industries, language, religion, and so on. The students seemed highly attentive. As the class period continued, however, I realized they were spending more and more time laboriously copying things down. Finally, I saw from scanning their workbooks that many students had slowly copied down the category names without having noted their Indonesian substance. The words "Official name," "Population," "Capital," "Language," and so forth had been copied line by line without content words written beside them. A few of the most committed students did finish writing the content after the various categories—even staying into recess to complete the task. But most of the others never got beyond the categories themselves. Education was not a process of learning and using substantive information so much as retaining the discipline of categorical imposition.

10. The one adult woman with schooling who lives in Gasumi Corners is not Gebusi and has an unusual background. In-married from the Pa-speaking group across the Strickland River, she went to school because her mother was imprisoned for killing her younger brother as an infant. Effectively orphaned, the girl was raised by an uncle who lived at the Nomad Station.

11. Because Gebusi girls typically marry during their mid-teens—as opposed to the late teens or early twenties for boys—girls who begin schooling at age nine or ten may also have their education cut short by marriage prior to completing grade six. This also increases the perception that money spent on schooling for girls is not as important as for boys—since girls are likely to get married in short order after they leave school.

12. In the 1990 census, the population of the Western Province was tabulated to be 110,420, and there has been an estimated annual growth of 2.3 percent since that time (Temu 1997: 6). Concerning royalty figures from the Ok Tedi mine, see Temu 1997, part 2, p. 3.

13. Likewise, when Nomad's previous area affairs manager—the station's top officer—was charged with improprieties and forced to leave, his replacement was told that if the people at Nomad did not appreciate his new leadership, the province would not send any more replacements for his position. "They said to me, 'If you leave Nomad for good, just lock the door and take the station key with you. We won't be sending anyone else. They don't deserve it.'" Though such threats may be rhetorical, they raise the real threat of government neglect and periodic absences in local administrative positions.

14. The school radio broadcasts vary widely, from vapid Western fairy tales for the first graders to insightful dramas about the stresses of town living for the more advanced students.

15. Radio provides a key means of encouraging and reinforcing a sense of national citizenship. In the Pacific, the relationship of mass media to nationalism is an important area of current research (e.g., Foster 1995, 1996/97; see also Otto and Thomas 1997). In this sense, radio usage greatly extends the nation-building impact of print media, as emphasized by Anderson (1991; see also Spitulnik in press).

16. In particular, Mr. Ano read a letter written two months previously by the school district superintendent to the chair of the Nomad School Board of Management. I was encouraged to copy it:

> I am in receipt of BREAK AND ENTER letter submitted to me . . . Two (2) radios have been reported stolen, one from the School office and the other from the Headmaster's House. This is very unacceptable action especially to whoever is responsible. Now school has no radios for School Broadcasts. I instruct the following to take place. Immediately convene Special Board of Management meeting next Month (June) and discuss the following:
> - Community to fully involve in identifying the culprits,
> - Community, with *no* condition, to avoid stealing from the school,
> - Teacher staff (teachers) may *leave the school* should this practice continue.
> - School may be *understaffed* and *subsequent suspension/closure*
> - The community must *appreciate* and *support* the existence of that school.
> - Have the matter reported to the Police.
>
> Please have this instruction executed and post me a copy of the minutes.
> (signed) G. LALIMO (MR), DISTRICT EDUCATION SUPERINTENDENT
> cc: Headmaster—Nomad Community School
> cc: District Manager—Nomad, W.P.

Chapter 8

1. Women invariably go to market as a group. Given traditional patterns of same-sex communalism, I never heard of a man from Gasumi Corners getting angry at a wife or daughter for having gone to the market (or pressuring her not to go) despite the fact that husbands typically stay behind. Women remain in a group and tend to be their own best collective defense against the flirtations or innuendos of other men.

2. In practical terms, husbands gain effective control over market proceeds if they accumulate over time.

3. In 1998, the 121 residents of Gasumi Corners owned five large, eight medium, and five small pigs, in addition to several piglets. As in 1980–82, the pigs are semidomesticated; they forage in the forest at will during the day and come back periodically to be fed by their human owners. In the present arrangement, the pigs wander back in late afternoon to the "pig house" on the far side of the Kum River in order to eat the sweet potatoes, pawpaws, and occasional cooked bananas that the women ferry across the river and feed them daily. Given the breadth of the river, the pigs cannot easily swim across to root in the gardens and create a nuisance in Gasumi Corners, which is a major benefit to the community. In the early 1980s, by contrast, semidomesticated pigs often foraged for food in the village, rooted in the mud that pervaded the settlement after rain, and tried with occasional success to get into houses. Pig feces, often mixed in mud, were a regular and obnoxious part of the village landscape to villagers and anthropologist alike—and they easily transmitted diseases via dirty hands and grimy fingernails. After leaving the field in 1982, I was diagnosed as having blood concentrations of an internal cystic disease, fortunately asymptomatic, thought to have been transmitted in this manner. Concerning the traditional and changing significance of semidomesticated pigs in the Strickland-Bosavi area, see Kelly 1988; Dwyer 1989; Minnegal and Dwyer 1997; see also Minnegal 1999.

4. It takes two and a half market sessions for the average woman to earn K 3.00—averaging K 1.20 per session. A woman attends only one-third of the market days, on average, or about three of nine market days per month. A K 3.00 item thus costs five-sixths of the average woman's monthly proceeds.

5. See Knauft 1985a: 250–53; 1987a.

6. In Port Moresby, I saw one TV news story about a final championship match in which some of the players attacked a referee for favoritism after a crucial ruling. The video clip showed the referee losing his temper, chasing down one of the attackers, and pummeling him until the inevitable brawl ensued. Though such altercations are not typical of sports throughout Papua New Guinea, it is notable how absent they are from competitions at Nomad between groups that have been tribal enemies.

7. In the latter stages of my fieldwork, this sexual division of leisure provided me a convenient way to interview and talk casually with Gebusi women in the absence of men—since all of the latter would typically be at the Nomad ball field and gone from the village on weekend afternoons. This opportunity was ethnographically important since a range of topics were difficult for me as a male ethnographer to raise with women in the presence of men.

8. As mentioned in chapter 1, Gebusi slept away from their main settlement 44.7 percent of the time in 1980–82 and 30.3 percent of the time in 1998. Schooling constraints are now partly accommodated by the fact that men or women often go to the forest in same-sex groups. A woman with school-age children may tend gardens near Gasumi Corners while her husband is on an extended hunting trip with other men.

Conversely, her husband may stay in the settlement gardening or building houses while his wife is in the deeper bush processing sago with other women.

9. Concerning the equivocal results of health care at the Nomad health clinic, see the penultimate section of chapter 2 and note 4 in chapter 5.

10. This generalization is perhaps least true of sports matches, at which Gebusi along with others are the main agents and focus of attention on the field. Relatedly, however, sports events are an arena in which the stakes do not include an attempt to gain knowledge or material reward from an external source. Thus, for instance, sports participants are not engaged in the pursuit of money, divine spiritual redemption, education, or health care, which tend to be dispensed under the authoritative control of modern institutions and agents.

11. *Wantok* is a tok pisin term for persons who speak the same natal language.

12. The following song was sung to welcome me back to Gasumi Corners:

Father mother, father mother
A big man comes finally back here
We all lived at the Gasumi place
Thank you truly for staying with us again,
Bruce.

13. In both cases, arousal reflects the emotional force of the song upon the listener and the power of the performance (see Schieffelin 1976, 1979; Feld 1982).

14. Despite a gradual increase in overall population, the accumulation of people in and around Nomad and Yehebi has decreased the population in other forest areas and especially in the thinly settled area south of the Rentoul (Sio) River. This latter area, a day and a half walk from Gasumi Corners, is a prime area for hunting. It also borders a prime tract of rainforest that may be subject to timber extraction by logging companies in future years.

15. One of these shotguns was supplied to the people of Gasumi by me in 1981 and is still in use.

16. Adding to these difficulties is the fact that the feast-sponsoring unit is smaller than it used to be. Gasumi Corners no longer sponsors feasts as a whole; rather, these events are organized by just one of its hamlets at a time, comprising between 20 and 40 persons. The other hamlets of Gasumi Corners attend as "visitors." This pattern reflects the more differentiated nature of social life in Gasumi Corners as opposed to life in the community's previous upstream village of Yibihilu in 1980–82.

17. I have no evidence or innuendo that homosexual partnerships are encouraged by or reflected in same-sex dancing; homosexual attraction is, at most, a latent aspect of same-sex disco dancing among Gebusi. From all indications, Gebusi men and boys in places like Gasumi Corners no longer engage in same-sex intercourse or related homosexual activity (see Knauft 2001).

18. Selling beer at Nomad is effectively illegal because no one holds a liquor license and police take action against violators. The largest air carrier of supplies to Nomad, the Mission Aviation Fellowship, considers alcohol use to be unchristian and refuses to accept beer or liquor as cargo.

The current situation at Nomad contrasts with that in many towns, cities, and highly populated rural areas of Papua New Guinea, where disruption from alcohol use can be pronounced and sometimes endemic (see Marshall 1982; Wormsley 1987). As discussed in Knauft 1987a, earlier experiences of Gebusi with alcohol suggest that similar patterns could erupt at Nomad if and when larger quantities of beer or other spirits are made available. Young Gebusi men are highly aware and keenly desirous of drinking alcohol—based on stories and transient personal experiences in Kiunga or other parts of the Western Province.

19. Information was equivocal, but the comments of trusted informants along with a passing display of one initiate with his "mentor" suggested to me that some homosexual activity persisted. Some senior informants, however, opined that the homosexual aspects of the initiation had been entirely dispensed with. Concerning Gebusi male homosexuality, see Knauft 1986, 1987b, 2001; see also, for the Bedamini, Sørum 1984, and more generally, Herdt 1992, 1999.

20. See note 18.

21. The skit in question played on traditional beliefs on a number of levels. Gebusi believed that the "poison people" (ti os) inside the derris root routed the fish from their longhouses at the bottom of the river—causing them to flee to the surface in fright. In 1980–82, Gebusi abetted and symbolized this process by setting a small raft of sticks alight and floating it downstream along with the poison. This was thought to scare and disorient the fish, just as Bedamini used to do to Gebusi when they set fire to the roofs of Gebusi longhouses in traditional predawn raids. When the fish broke the surface, the Gebusi dancer was believed to further paralyze them with his beauty, making them easy prey for Gebusi men in the water, who scooped them up in large numbers.

In the skit, the actors built an enormous bonfire to scare the fish. The dancer danced so close to it that his tail plumage started to smolder and he danced in a clumsy manner to the river, where the fish started snapping at him. Between the fire and the fish, the dancer started banging his drum in a speedy chop-chop manner while jumping up and down as fast as he could. This made an effective travesty of the slow and melancholy bounce-step of the traditional dancing aesthetic. The young fish catchers, for their part, leaped and clawed in the clumsiest of manners in order to grab the fish. Adding to the confusion, the distraught and careening dancer "inadvertently" drummed directly into the ear of one of the fish catchers. The latter jumped out of the "river" and pursued the running dancer as his smoking dance skirts trailed behind him. At this point, the fire in the skit began exploding dramatically with the popping of bamboo tubes that had been placed in it in a futile attempt to intimidate the fish. These loud reports sent the actors and dancers fleeing from the scene in all directions and sent the audience, for its part, into fits of laughter as the skit ended.

22. Only in one skit, by contrast, was the traditional Gebusi dance costume portrayed in a positive fashion. This exception revalued tradition in a highly revealing manner by creating a yet darker and dimmer past preceding it. In this creative performance, the traditional dancer in costume was portrayed not as an indigenous figure but as an emergent one who arrived on the scene to counteract and dispel an even earlier period of incest and sin. This "prequel" to indigenous tradition involved the dramatic portrayal of a "pre-traditional" time that was, as far as I am aware, not part of any indigenous local cosmology. In the skit, this original condition of humanity was portrayed by a darkly muddied and disheveled old man with long, unruly hair. This man was accompanied by black-painted young boys who engaged each other repeatedly in wild pantomimes of promiscuous heterosexual intercourse (to the great humor of the audience, of course). It was as counterpart and agonist against this state of neo-original sin that the traditional dancer then appeared in the skit. Dancing dressed in splendor and with his outstretched drum as a stately force, he emerged on the scene triumphantly to supplant and dispel this prior state, driving the actors of the dim past to the corner of the performance area and then drumming them off stage.

Here we have the other side to a simple rejection of indigenous tradition, namely, the creative reconfiguration of a neo-tradition that salvages parts of its former self by presenting traditional dancing as progressive and enlightened relative to a yet earlier alternative. There is a striking parallel between the role of the traditional dancer in this skit and the role of God in some of the Christian skits in which God appears at Judgment Day to kill traditional sinners and drive them from the stage. In the skit presently described, then, a partially recuperative interpretation of traditional dancing was made possible by reinventing it as a historically "progressive" moment relative to an even more primitive and backward state that preceded it.

23. Of forty-two "dramas" presented, twenty-three were parody enactments of traditional customs, five were first-contact stories, five were Christian morality tales, four were about modern (secular) life, three were performances of women dancing to boom box music, one was a physical drama (bounding leapfrogs), and one was a unique hybrid.

24. None of these women were Gebusi.

25. See Bakhtin 1968; see also Knauft 1996: chap. 6.

Chapter 9

1. Social connectedness and a deep sense of social relationality have been repeatedly stressed in the ethnography of Melanesia (see Strathern 1998; Knauft 1999: chap. 2; see also Mauss 1967).

2. See Wardlow in press; Foster in press; LiPuma 2000; Gewertz and Errington 1999.

3. See Roscoe 1999; Sykes 1999.

4. See Durkheim 1964; Marx and Engels 1964, 1976; Weber 1958; Tönnies 1957; Simmel 1978; Foucault 1984; Berman 1982; Harvey 1989.

5. Though not specifically attending to non-Western contexts, the perspectives of critical theorists such as Gramsci (1971) and Horkheimer and Adorno (1972) become important in this regard. Concerning Gramscian theory in cultural anthropology, see Knauft 1996: chap. 6.

6. This characterization may apply to significant parts of the New Guinea highlands, which have been characterized by the aggressive leadership of big-men or great men (see Sahlins 1963; Godelier 1986; Godelier and Strathern 1991; Roscoe 2000; see also Knauft 1999: chap. 3). In the Nomad area, this characterization applies to some extent to the Bedamini, Gebusi's larger and more aggressive neighbors (see chapter 1, note 29 above).

7. Well-known case studies from other world areas include Comaroff and Comaroff 1992, 1994; Tsing 1993.

8. Concerning the invention of tradition in Melanesia, see chapter 1, note 35 above; compare more generally Hobsbawm and Ranger 1983.

9. Concerning classic modernization theory, see Rostow 1952, 1960, 1963, 1971; contrast Arndt 1987.

10. E.g., Zelenietz and Lindenbaum 1981; Stephen 1994; Young 1983; Forge 1970; Fortune 1932.

11. See above p. 4, cf. the critique by Englund and Leach 2000; Donham in press; contrast Knauft in press a.

12. See also Rofel 1999; Donham 1999; Piot 1999; Ferguson 1999; Schein 1999, 2000; LiPuma 2000; Comaroff and Comaroff 1991, 1993, 1997; Chatterjee 1997; Larkin 1997.

References

Allen, Bryant J., and R. Michael Bourke
    1997 Report of an Assessment of the Impacts of Frost and Drought in Papua New Guinea. Australian Agency for International Development. Report on Phase 1, October; Report on Phase 2, December.

Anderson, Benedict
    1991 *Imagined Communities: Reflections on the Origin and Spread of Nationalism,* rev. ed. London: Verso.

Appadurai, Arjun
    1996 *Modernity at Large: Cultural Dimensions of Globalization.* Minneapolis: University of Minnesota Press.

Arndt, Heinz W.
    1987 *Economic Development: The History of an Idea.* Chicago: University of Chicago Press.

Bakhtin, Mikhail M.
    1968 *Rabelais and His World.* Cambridge: MIT Press.
    1986 *Speech Genres and Other Late Essays.* Austin, Tex.: University of Texas Press.

Banks, Glenn, and Chris Ballard, eds.
    1997 *The Ok Tedi Settlement: Issues, Outcomes, and Implications.* National Center for Development Studies, Policy Paper #27. Canberra: Australian National University Press.

Barclay, R. E.
    1970–71 Official Correspondence for Patrol Report No. 10. Nomad Subdistrict Office, Western Province, Papua New Guinea.

Barker, John, ed.
    1990 *Christianity in Oceania: Ethnographic Perspectives.* Lanham, Md.: University Press of America.

278   References

Barlow, Kathleen, and Steven Winduo, eds.
    1997   *Logging the Southwest Pacific: Perspectives from Papua New Guinea, Solomon Islands, and Vanuatu.* Special issue of *The Contemporary Pacific,* vol. 19, no. 1.

Barth, Fredrik
    1971   Tribes and Intertribal Relations in the Fly Headwaters. *Oceania* 41:171–91.

Bashkow, Ira
    2000   Confusion, Native Skepticism, and Recurring Questions about the Year 2000: "Soft" Beliefs and Preparations for the Millennium in the Arapesh Region, Papua New Guinea. *Ethnohistory* 47:133–69.

Bateson, Gregory
    1972   *Steps to an Ecology of Mind.* New York: Ballantine.

Bauckham, Richard
    1993   *The Theology of the Book of Revelation.* Cambridge: Cambridge University Press.

Baudelaire, Charles
    1970 [1863]   *The Painter of Modern Life and Other Essays.* London: Phaidon.

Berman, Marshall
    1982   *All That Is Solid Melts into Air: The Experience of Modernity.* New York: Penguin.
    1992   Why Modernism Still Matters. In *Modernity and Identity.* Edited by Scott Lash and Jonathan Friedman, pp. 33–58. Oxford: Blackwell.

Bodley, John H.
    1999   *Victims of Progress.* 4th ed. Mountain View, Calif.: Mayfield.

Bourdieu, Pierre
    1977   *Outline of a Theory of Practice.* Cambridge: Cambridge University Press.
    1984   *Distinction: A Social Critique of the Judgement of Taste.* Cambridge: Harvard University Press.
    1988   *Homo Academicus.* Stanford: Stanford University Press.
    1989   *La Noblesse d'État.* Paris: Les Éditions de Minuit.
    1990   *The Logic of Practice.* Stanford: Stanford University Press.
    2000   *Les Structures Sociales de l'Économie.* Paris: Seuil.

Bourdieu, Pierre, and Jean-Claude Passeron
    1977   *Reproduction in Education, Society, and Culture.* London: Sage.

Bourdieu, Pierre, Jean-Claude Passeron, and Monique de Saint Martin
    1996   *Linguistic Misunderstanding and Professorial Power.* Stanford: Stanford University Press.

Boutilier, James A., Daniel T. Hughes, and Sharon W. Tiffany, eds.
    1978   *Mission, Church, and Sect in Oceania.* Ann Arbor: University of Michigan Press.

Bray, Mark
    1984   *Educational Planning in a Decentralized System: The Papua New Guinean Experience.* Port Moresby: University of Papua New Guinea Press; Sydney, Australia: Sydney University Press.

Brunois, Florence
    1999   "In Paradise, the Forest Is Open and Covered in Flowers." In *Expecting the Day of Wrath: Versions of the Millennium in Papua New Guinea.* Edited by Christin Kocher Schmid, pp. 111–30. Boroko, NCD, Papua New Guinea: National Research Institute, Monograph #36.

Cantrell, Eileen M.
    1998 Woman the Sexual, a Question of When: A Study of Gebusi Adolescence. In
          Adolescence in Pacific Island Societies. Edited by Gilbert H. Herdt and Stephen
          C. Leavitt, pp. 92–120. Pittsburgh: University of Pittsburgh Press.

Certeau, Michel de
    1984 *The Practice of Everyday Life*. Berkeley: University of California Press.

Chatterjee, Partha
    1997 *Our Modernity*. Lecture to the South-South Exchange Program for Research
          on the History of Development (SEPHIS) and the Council for the
          Development of Social Science Research in Africa (CODESRIA). Rotterdam:
          Vinlin Press.

CNRS
    1999 *Le Pentecôstisme: Les Paradoxes d'une Religion Transnationale de l'Émotion*.
          Archives de Sciences Sociales des Religions, no. 105. Paris: CNRS.

Comaroff, Jean, and John L. Comaroff
    1991 *Of Revelation and Revolution, Volume One: Christianity, Colonialism, and
          Consciousness in South Africa*. Chicago: University of Chicago Press.
    1999 Occult Economies and the Violence of Abstraction: Notes from the South
          African Postcolony. *American Ethnologist* 26(2): 279–303.

Comaroff, John L., and Jean Comaroff, eds.
    1992 *Ethnography and the Historical Imagination*. Boulder, Colo.: Westview.
    1993 *Modernity and Its Malcontents: Ritual and Power in Postcolonial Africa*. Chicago:
          University of Chicago Press.
    1997 *Of Revelation and Revolution, Volume Two: The Dialectics of Modernity on a
          South African Frontier*. Chicago: University of Chicago Press.

Cox, Harvey G.
    1995 *Fire from Heaven: The Rise of Pentecostal Spirituality and the Reshaping of
          Religion in the Twenty-First Century*. Reading, Mass.: Addison-Wesley.

Curtin, T. R. C., and E. A. S. Nelson
    1999 Economic and Health Efficiency of Education Funding Policy. *Social Science
          and Medicine*. 48(11):1599–1611.

Dinnen, Sinclair
    2001 *Law and Order in a Weak State: Crime and Politics in Papua New Guinea*.
          Honolulu: University of Hawaii Press.

Dinner, Sinclair, and Allison Ley, eds.
    2000 *Reflections on Violence in Melanesia*. Canberra, Australia: Asia Pacific Press.

Dirlik, Arif
    1999 Is There History After Eurocentrism?: Globalism, Postcolonialism, and the
          Disavowal of History. *Cultural Critique* 42:1–34.

Donham, Donald L.
    1999 *Marxist Modern: An Ethnographic History of the Ethiopian Revolution*. Berkeley:
          University of California Press.
    In press. On Being Modern in a Capitalist World: Some Conceptual and
          Comparative Issues. In *Critically Modern: Alternatives, Alterities, Anthropologies*.
          Edited by Bruce M. Knauft. Bloomington: University of Indiana Press.

Douglas, Bronwen
    2001 From Invisible Christians to Gothic Theater: The Romance of the Millennial
          in Melanesian Anthropology. *Current Anthropology* 42(5): 615–50.

Durkheim, Émile
  1964 *The Division of Labor in Society*. New York: Free Press.
  1965 *The Elementary Forms of the Religious Life*. New York: Free Press.

Dussel, Enrique
  1993 Eurocentrism and Modernity. *boundary 2*, 20:65–74.

Dwyer, Peter D.
  1989 *The Pigs That Ate the Garden: A Human Ecology from Papua New Guinea*. Ann Arbor: University of Michigan Press.

Dwyer, Peter D., and Monica Minnegal
  1998 Waiting for Company: Ethos and Environment among Kubo of Papua New Guinea. *Journal of the Royal Anthropological Institute* 4:23–42.
  1999 The Transformation of Use-Rights: A Comparison of Two Papua New Guinean Societies. *Journal of Anthropological Research* 55:361–83.

Edgerton, Robert B.
  1992 *Sick Societies: Challenging the Myth of Primitive Harmony*. New York: Free Press.

Englund, Harri, and James Leach
  2000 Ethnography and the Meta-Narratives of Modernity. *Current Anthropology* 41: 225–48.

Epstein, A. L.
  1984 *The Experience of Shame in Melanesia*. RAI Occasional Paper no. 40. London: Royal Anthropological Institute.
  1999 Tolai Sorcery and Change. *Ethnology* 38:273–95

Erikson, Kai T.
  1966 *Wayward Puritans: A Study in the Sociology of Deviance*. New York: John Wiley.

Errington, Frederick K., and Deborah Gewertz
  1995 *Articulating Change in the "Last Unknown."* Boulder, Colo.: Westview.
  1996 The Individuation of Tradition in a Papua New Guinea Modernity. *American Anthropologist* 98:114–26.

Escobar, Arturo
  1995 *Encountering Development: The Making and Unmaking of the Third World*. Princeton, N.J.: Princeton University Press.

Evangelical Church of Papua New Guinea
  1991 *Bel Bilong Man* ["The Heart of Man," in tok pisin, with illustrations]. Lae, P.N.G.: Evangelical Brotherhood Church. National Library of Australia ISBN 0–909172–20–X.

Eves, Richard
  2000 Waiting for the Day: Globalization and Apocalypticism in Central New Ireland, Papua New Guinea. *Oceania* 71:73–91.

Fath, Sébastien
  2000 From One Convert to Hundreds of Millions: The Pentecostal Paradox in an Age of Secularization (20th Century): A Sociohistorical Overview. Paper presented at the conference, "Recent Forms of Christianization in Oceania, Africa, Asia, and Latin America." École des Hautes Études, Paris.

Feld, Steven
  1982 *Sound and Sentiment: Birds, Weeping, Poetics, and Song in Kaluli Expression*. Philadelphia: University of Pennsylvania Press.
  1995 From Schizophonia to Schismogenesis: The Discourses and Practices of World Music and World Beat. In *The Traffic in Culture: Refiguring Art and*

Anthropology. Edited by George E. Marcus and Fred R. Myers, pp. 196–226. Berkeley: University of California Press.

Felski, Rita
1995   *The Gender of Modernity.* Cambridge: Harvard University Press.

Ferguson, James
1999   *Expectations of Modernity: Myths and Meanings of Urban Life on the Zambian Copperbelt.* Berkeley: University of California Press.

Filer, Colin, ed.
1997   *The Political Economy of Forest Management in Papua New Guinea.* National Research Institute of Papua New Guinea, Monograph #32. Port Moresby: National Research Institute; London: International Institute for Environment and Development (IIED).

Filer, Colin, with Nikhil Sekhran
1998   *Loggers, Donors, and Resource Owners.* International Institute for Environment and Development, UK (IIED) and the National Research Institute, Papua New Guinea. Nottingham, U.K.: Russell Press.

Fitzpatrick, P.
1970–71. Patrol Report No. 10. Nomad Subdistrict Office, Western Province, Papua New Guinea.

Forge, Anthony
1970   Prestige, Influence, and Sorcery: A New Guinea Example. In *Witchcraft Confessions and Accusations.* Edited by Mary Douglas, pp. 257–75. London: Tavistock.

Fortune, Reo F.
1932   *Sorcerers of Dobu: The Social Anthropology of the Dobu Islanders.* London: E. P. Dutton.

Foster, Robert J.
1996/97   Commercial Mass Media in Papua New Guinea: Notes on Agency, Bodies, and Commodity Consumption. *Visual Anthropology Review* 12(2):1–17.
1999   Melanesianist Anthropology in the Era of Globalization. *Contemporary Pacific* 11(2):140–59.
In press.   Bargains with Modernity in Papua New Guinea and Elsewhere. In *Critically Modern: Alternatives, Alterities, Anthropologies.* Edited by Bruce M. Knauft. Bloomington: Indiana University Press.

Foster, Robert J., ed.
1995   *Nation Making: Emergent Identities in Postcolonial Melanesia.* Ann Arbor: University of Michigan Press.

Foucault, Michel
1979   *Discipline and Punish: The Birth of the Prison.* New York: Vintage.
1983   The Subject and Power. In *Michel Foucault: Beyond Structuralism and Hermeneutics,* 2nd ed. Edited by Hubert L. Dreyfus and Paul Rabinow, pp. 208–26. Chicago: University of Chicago Press.
1984   *The Foucault Reader.* Edited by Paul Rabinow. New York: Pantheon.
1985   *The Use of Pleasure.* Vol. 2 of *The History of Sexuality.* New York: Vintage.
1986   *The Care of the Self.* Vol. 3 of *The History of Sexuality.* New York: Vintage.
1988   Technologies of the Self. In *Technologies of the Self: A Seminar with Michel Foucault.* Edited by Luther H. Martin, Huck Butman, and Patrick H. Hutton, pp. 16–49. Amherst: University of Massachusetts Press.

Freeman, Carla S.
    2001   Is Local:Global As Feminine:Masculine? Rethinking the Gender of
           Globalization. *Signs* 26(4): 1007–37.

Fuller, Bruce, and Prema Clarke
    1994   Raising School Effects While Ignoring Culture?: Local Conditions and the
           Influence of Classroom Tools, Rules, and Pedagogy. *Review of Educational
           Research,* 64(1):119–57.

Gaonkar, Dilip Parameshwar
    1999   On Alternative Modernities. *Public Culture* 11:1–18.

Geertz, Clifford
    1973   Deep Play: Notes on the Balinese Cockfight. In *The Interpretation of Cultures:
           Selected Essays.* By Clifford Geertz. New York: Basic Books.
    1995   *After the Fact: Two Countries, Four Decades, One Anthropologist.* Cambridge:
           Harvard University Press.

Gell, Alfred
    1992   *The Anthropology of Time: Cultural Constructions of Temporal Maps and Images.*
           Oxford: Berg.

George, Kenneth M.
    1996   *Showing Signs of Violence: The Cultural Politics of a Twentieth-Century
           Headhunting Ritual.* Berkeley: University of California Press.

Geschiere, Peter
    1997   *The Modernity of Witchcraft: Politics and the Occult in Postcolonial Africa.*
           Charlottesville: University of Virginia Press.

Gewertz, Deborah, and Frederick Errington
    1999   *Emerging Class in Papua New Guinea: The Telling of Difference.* Cambridge:
           Cambridge University Press.

Gibson-Graham, J. K.
    1996   *The End of Capitalism (as we knew it): A Feminist Critique of Political Economy.*
           Oxford: Blackwell.

Giddens, Anthony
    1979   *Central Problems in Modern Social Theory: Action, Structure, and Contradiction in
           Social Analysis.* Berkeley: University of California Press.
    1984   *The Constitution of Society: Outline of the Theory of Structuration.* Berkeley:
           University of California Press.
    1990   *The Consequences of Modernity.* Stanford: Stanford University Press.

Ginzberg, Carlo
    1980   *The Cheese and the Worms: The Cosmos of a Sixteenth-Century Miller.* New
           York: Penguin.

Glick, Leonard B.
    1973   Sorcery and Witchcraft. In *Anthropology in Papua New Guinea.* Edited by H.
           Ian Hogbin. Melbourne, Australia: Melbourne University Press.

Goddard, Michael
    1992   Big-Men, Thief: The Social Organization of Gangs in Port Moresby. *Canberra
           Anthropology* 154:20–34.
    1995   The Rascal Road: Crime, Prestige, and Development in Papua New Guinea.
           The Contemporary Pacific 7:55–80.

Godelier, Maurice
    1982   Social Hierarchies among the Baruya of New Guinea. In *Inequality in New*

Guinea Highlands Societies. Edited by Andrew J. Strathern, pp. 3–34. Cambridge: Cambridge University Press.

1986   *The Making of Great Men: Male Domination and Power among the New Guinea Baruya.* Cambridge: Cambridge University Press.

Godelier, Maurice, and Marilyn Strathern, eds.
1991   *Big Men and Great Men: Personifications of Power in Melanesia.* Cambridge: Cambridge University Press.

Gordon, Robert, and Mervyn J. Meggitt
1985   *Law and Order in the New Guinea Highlands.* Hanover, N.H.: University Press of New England.

Gould, Stephen Jay
1987   *Time's Arrow, Time's Cycle: Myth and Metaphor in the Discovery of Geological Time.* Cambridge: Harvard University Press.

Gould, W. T. S.
1993   *People and Education in the Third World.* Harlow, Essex, U.K.: Longman.

Gramsci, Antonio
1971   *Selections from the Prison Notebooks.* Edited by Quintin Hoare and Geoffrey Nowell-Smith. London: Lawrence and Wishart.

Greenblatt, Stephen J.
1984   *Renaissance Self-Fashioning: From More to Shakespeare.* Chicago: University of Chicago Press.

Greenhouse, Carol J., ed.
1996   *A Moment's Notice: Time Politics Across Cultures.* Ithaca, N.Y.: Cornell University Press.

Gupta, Akhil
1998   *Postcolonial Developments: Agriculture in the Making of Modern India.* Durham, N.C.: Duke University Press.

Hallpike, Christopher R.
1977   *Bloodshed and Vengeance in the Papuan Mountains: The Generation of Conflict in Tuade Society.* Oxford: Clarendon Press.

Hammar, Lawrence
1995   Crisis in the South Fly: The Problem with Sex and the Sex Industry on Daru Island, Western Province, Papua New Guinea. Ph.D. diss., Department of Anthropology, Graduate Center, City University of New York.

1996   Bad Canoes and *Bafalo:* The Political Economy of Sex on Daru Island, Western Province, Papua New Guinea. *Genders* 23:212–47.

Hardt, Michael, and Antonio Negri
2000   *Empire.* Cambridge: Harvard University Press.

Hart Nibbrig, Nand E.
1992   Rascals in Paradise: Urban Gangs in Papua New Guinea. *Pacific Studies* 15(3): 115–34.

Harvey, David
1989   *The Condition of Post-modernity: An Enquiry into the Origins of Culture Change.* Cambridge: Blackwell.

Hefner, Robert W., ed.
1993   *Conversion to Christianity: Historical and Anthropological Perspectives on a Great Transformation.* Berkeley: University of California Press.

Heider, Karl G.
    1979   *Grand Valley Dani: Peaceful Warriors.* New York: Holt, Rinehart and Winston.
Herdt, Gilbert H.
    1999   *Sambia Sexual Culture: Essays from the Field.* Chicago: University of Chicago
           Press.
Herdt, Gilbert H., ed.
    1992   *Ritualized Homosexuality in Melanesia,* rev. ed. Berkeley: University of
           California Press.
Hexham, Irving, and Karla O. Poewe
    1997   *New Religions As Global Cultures: Making the Human Sacred.* Boulder, Colo.:
           Westview.
Hobart, Mark
    1990   The Patience of Plants: A Note on Agency in Bali. *Review of Indonesian and
           Malaysian Affairs* 24:90–135.
Hobsbawm, E. J., and Terence Ranger, eds.
    1983   The *Invention of Tradition.* Cambridge: Cambridge University Press.
Horkheimer, Max, and Theodor W. Adorno
    1972   *Dialectic of Enlightenment.* New York: Continuum.
Hughes, Diane O., and Thomas R. Trautmann, eds.
    1995   *Time: Histories and Ethnologies.* Ann Arbor: University of Michigan Press.
Hurston, Zora Neale
    1990   *Tell My Horse: Voodoo and Life in Haiti and Jamaica.* New York: Perennial.
Irving, John
    1978   *The World According to Garp: A Novel.* New York: E. P. Dutton.
Jebens, Holger
    1997   Catholics, Seventh Day Adventists, and the Impact of Tradition in Pairundu
           (Southern Highlands Province, Papua New Guinea). In *Cultural Dynamics of
           Religious Change in Oceania.* Edited by Ton Otto and Ad Borsboom, pp. 33–
           43. Leiden: KITI V. Press.
Jolly, Margaret
    1994   *Women of the Place: Kastom, Colonialism, and Gender in Vanuatu.* Chur,
           Switzerland: Harwood Academic.
Jolly, Margaret, and Nicholas Thomas, eds.
    1992   *The Politics of Tradition. Oceania* 62(4):241–354.
Kapferer, Bruce
    1997   *The Feast of the Sorcerer: Practices of Consciousness and Power.* Chicago:
           University of Chicago Press.
Keane, Webb
    1997   From Fetishism to Sincerity: On Agency, the Speaking Subject, and Their
           Historicity in the Context of Religious Conversion. *Comparative Studies in
           Society and History* 39:674–93.
Keesing, Roger M.
    1982   *Kwaio Religion: The Living and the Dead in a Solomon Island Society.* New York:
           Columbia University Press.
    1992   *Custom and Confrontation: The Kwaio Struggle for Cultural Autonomy.* Chicago:
           University of Chicago Press.
    1996   Class, Culture, Custom. In *Melanesian Modernities.* Edited by Jonathan
           Friedman and James G. Carrier, pp. 162–82. Lund Monographs in Social
           Anthropology #3. Lund, Sweden: Lund University Press.

Keesing, Robert M., and Robert Tonkinson, eds.
1982   Reinventing Traditional Culture: The Politics of Kastom in Island Melanesia. Special issue, Mankind 13:297–399.

Kelly, Raymond C.
1988   Etoro Suidology: A Reassessment of the Pig's Role in the Prehistory and Comparative Ethnology of New Guinea. In Mountain Papuans: Historical and Comparative Perspectives from New Guinea Fringe Highlands Societies. Edited by James F. Weiner, pp. 111–86. Ann Arbor: University of Michigan Press.
1993   Constructing Inequality: The Fabrication of a Hierarchy of Virtue among the Etoro. Ann Arbor: University of Michigan Press.

Kirsch, Stuart
1996   Return to Ok Tedi. Meanjin, December, pp. 657–66.
1997   Is Ok Tedi a Precedent? Implications of the Lawsuit. In The Ok Tedi Settlement: Issues, Outcomes, and Implications. Edited by Glenn Banks and Chris Ballard, pp. 118–40. Canberra: Australian National University Press.

Kituai, August Ibrum
1998   My Brother, My Gun: The World of the Papua New Guinea Colonial Police, 1920–1960. Honolulu: University of Hawaii Press.

Knauft, Bruce M.
1985a   Good Company and Violence: Sorcery and Social Action in a Lowland New Guinea Society. Berkeley: University of California Press.
1985b   Ritual Form and Permutation in New Guinea: Implications of Symbolic Process for Sociopolitical Evolution. American Ethnologist 21:321–40.
1986   Text and Social Practice: Narrative "Longing" and Bisexuality among the Gebusi of New Guinea. Ethos 14:252–81.
1987a   Homosexuality in Melanesia. Journal of Psychoanalytic Anthropology 10:155–91.
1987b   Managing Sex and Anger: Tobacco and Kava Use among the Gebusi of Papua New Guinea. In Drugs in Western Pacific Societies: Relations of Substance. Edited by Lamont Lindstrom, pp. 73–98. Lanham, Md.: University Press of America.
1987c   Reconsidering Violence in Simple Human Societies: Homicide among the Gebusi of New Guinea. Current Anthropology 28:457–500.
1989   Imagery, Pronouncement, and the Aesthetics of Reception in Gebusi Spirit Mediumship. In The Religious Imagination in New Guinea. Edited by Gilbert H. Herdt and Michele Stephen, pp. 67–98. New Brunswick, N.J.: Rutgers University Press.
1990   Melanesian Warfare: A Theoretical History. Oceania 60:250–311.
1993   South Coast New Guinea Cultures: History, Comparison, Dialectic. Cambridge: Cambridge University Press.
1995   Agency in Cultural Anthropology in the Mid-'90s: A Commentary. Presented at the annual meeting of the American Anthropological Association, Washington, D.C.
1996   Genealogies for the Present in Cultural Anthropology. New York: Routledge.
1997   Gender Identity, Political Economy, and Modernity in Melanesia and Amazonia. Journal of the Royal Anthropological Institute 3:233–59.
1998   How the World Turns Upside Down: Changing Geographies of Power and Spiritual Influence among the Gebusi. In Fluid Ontologies: Myth, Ritual, and Philosophy in the Highlands of Papua New Guinea. Edited by Laurence R. Goldman and Chris Ballard, pp.143–61. Westport, Conn.: Bergin and Garvey.

1999   *From Primitive to Postcolonial in Melanesia and Anthropology*. Ann Arbor: University of Michigan Press.

2001   Whatever Happened to Ritual Homosexuality?: The Incitement of Modern Sexual Subjects in Melanesia and Elsewhere. Plenary address at the third annual conference of the International Association for the Study of Sex, Culture, and Society. Melbourne, Australia, October 1.

In press a   Critically Modern: An Introduction. In *Critically Modern: Alternatives, Alterities, Anthropologies*. Edited by Bruce M. Knauft. Bloomington: Indiana University Press.

In press b   Trials of the Oxymodern: Public Practice at Nomad Station. In *Critically Modern: Alternatives, Alterities, Anthropologies*. Edited by Bruce M. Knauft. Bloomington: Indiana University Press.

In press c   *Critically Modern: Alternatives, Alterities, Anthropologies*. Edited by Bruce M. Knauft. Bloomington: Indiana University Press.

n.d.   Relating to Women: Female Presence in Melanesian "Male Cults." In *The Unseen Characters: Women in Male Rituals of Papua New Guinea*. Edited by Pascale Bonnemère. Under review.

Koch, Klaus-Friedrich
1974   *War and Peace in Jalemo: The Management of Conflict in Highland New Guinea*. Cambridge: Harvard University Press.

Kolia, John
1980   *Without Mannerisms, and Other Stories*. Boroko, P.N.G.: Institute of Papua New Guinea Studies.

Kosellek, Reinhart
1985   *Futures Past: On the Semantics of Historical Time*. Cambridge: MIT Press.

Kulick, Don
1991   Law and Order in Papua New Guinea. *Anthropology Today* 7:21–22.
1993   Heroes from Hell: Representations of "Raskols" in a Papua New Guinea Village. *Anthropology Today* 9:9–14.

Kunze, Michael
1987   *Highroad to the Stake: A Tale of Witchcraft*. Chicago: University of Chicago Press.

Laguerre, Michael S.
1990   *Voodoo and Politics in Haiti*. New York: St. Martin's.

Lambek, Michael J.
1993   *Knowledge and Practice in Mayotte: Local Discourses of Islam, Sorcery, and Spirit Possession*. Toronto: University of Toronto Press.

Larkin, Brian
1997   Indian Films and Nigerian Lovers: Media and the Creation of Parallel Modernities. *Africa* 67:406–40.

Lattas, Andrew
1998   *Cultures of Secrecy: Reinventing Race in Bush Kaliai Cargo Cults*. Madison: University of Wisconsin Press.

Lebot, Vincent, Mark Merlin, and Lamont Lindstrom
1992   *Kava: The Pacific Drug*. New Haven, Conn.: Yale University Press.

Lederman, Rena
1986   *What Gifts Engender: Social Relations and Politics in Mendi, Highland Papua New Guinea*. Cambridge: Cambridge University Press.

Lee, Dorothy D.
1977   Lineal and Non-lineal Codifications of Reality. In *Symbolic Anthropology*. Edited by Janet L. Dolgin, David S. Kemnitzer, and David M. Schneider, pp. 151–64. New York: Columbia University Press.

Lemonnier, Pierre
1996   The Good Pastor, the Satanic Anthropologists, and the Law: Individual Agency and Collective Resistance to Mission Power among the Southwestern Angans. Paper presented at the annual meeting of the European Society for Oceanists, December 13–15. Copenhagen.
1998   Showing the Invisible: Violence and Politics among the Ankave-Anga (Gulf Province, Papua New Guinea). In *Common Worlds and Single Lives: Constituting Knowledge in Pacific Societies*. Edited by Verena Keck, pp. 287–307. Oxford: Berg.

Lévi-Strauss, Claude
1969   *The Elementary Structures of Kinship*. Boston: Beacon.

Lichtblau, Klaus
1999   Differentiations of Modernity. *Theory, Culture, and Society* 16:1–30.

Lindenbaum, Shirley
1984   Variations on a Sociosexual Theme in Melanesia. In *Ritualized Homosexuality in Melanesia*. Edited by Gilbert H. Herdt, pp. 337–61. Berkeley: University of California Press.

LiPuma, Edward
2000   *Encompassing Others: The Magic of Modernity in Melanesia*. Ann Arbor: University of Michigan Press.

Liria, Yauka Aluambo
1993   *Bougainville Campaign Diary*. Melbourne, Australia: Indra Publishing.

Liu, Judith, Heidi A. Ross, and Donald P. Kelly
2000   *The Ethnographic Eye: Interpretive Studies of Education in China*. New York: Falmer.

Luhrmann, Tanya M.
1989   *Persuasions of the Witch's Craft: Ritual Magic in Contemporary England*. Cambridge: Harvard University Press.

MacGaffey, Wyatt
2000   *Kongo Political Culture: The Conceptual Challenge of the Particular*. Bloomington: Indiana University Press.

Maggi, Wynne R.
In press   *Our Women Are Free: Gender and Ethnicity in the Hindu Kush*. Ann Arbor: University of Michigan Press.

Marat, Allan
1987   The Official Recognition of Customary Responses to Homicide in Papua New Guinea. D. Phil. thesis, University of Oxford, Oxford, England.

Marchand, Marianne H., and Anne Sisson Runyan, eds.
2000   *Gender and Global Restructuring: Sightings, Sites, and Resistances*. New York: Routledge.

Marsden, George M.
1980   *Fundamentalism and American Culture: The Shaping of Twentieth-Century Evangelicalism: 1870–1925*. Oxford: Oxford University Press.

Marshall, Mac
    1982 *Through a Glass Darkly: Beer and Modernization in Papua New Guinea.* Boroko,
          Papua New Guinea: Institute of Applied and Economic Research.

Marshall, Will, and Mike Head
    2001 Papua New Guinea Government Under Siege after Police Kill Three
          Protestors. Sydney *Morning Herald,* June 29 [Australian on-line edition].

Marx, Karl
    1964 *Economic and Philosophic Manuscripts.* New York: International Publishers.

Marx, Karl, and Friedrich Engels
    1964 *The Communist Manifesto.* New York: Monthly Review Press.
    1976 *The German Ideology,* 3d rev. ed. Moscow: Progress Publishers.

Massey, Doreen
    1994 *Space, Place, and Gender.* Cambridge: Polity Press.

Mauss, Marcel
    1967 [1925] *The Gift.* New York: W. W. Norton.

Mead, Margaret
    1956 *New Lives for Old: Cultural Transformation, Manus, 1928–1953.* New York:
          William Morrow.

Meggitt, Mervyn J.
    1974 "Pigs Are Our Hearts!": The *Te* Exchange Cycle among the Mae Enga of New
          Guinea. *Oceania* 44:165–203.
    1977 *Blood Is Their Argument: Warfare among the Mae Enga Tribesmen of the New
          Guinea Highlands.* Palo Alto, Calif.: Mayfield.

Métraux, Alfred
    1972 *Voodoo in Haiti.* London: Deutsch.

Minnegal, Monica
    1999 Rereading Relationships: Changing Constructions of Identity among Kubo of
          Papua New Guinea. *Ethnology* 38:59–80.

Minnegal, Monica, and Peter D. Dwyer
    1997 Women, Pigs, God, and Evolution: Social and Economic Change among
          Kubo People of Papua New Guinea. *Oceania* 68:47–60.

Monsell-Davis, Michael
    1998 Education and Rural Development. In *Modern Papua New Guinea.* Edited by
          Laura Zimmer-Tamakoshi, pp. 315–32. Kirksville, Mo.: Thomas Jefferson
          University Press of Truman University.

Munn, Nancy D.
    1986 *The Fame of Gawa: A Symbolic Study of Value Transformation in a Massim
          (Papua New Guinea) Society.* New York: Cambridge University Press.

The National [daily newspaper of Port Moresby, Papua New Guinea]
    1999 Lack of Teachers Deprives Students of Education. July 16 [newspaper web
          page].

Nicholas, Isaac
    2000 Investigations into "Police Killings" Underway: Wakon. *The National*
          (daily newspaper of Port Moresby, Papua New Guinea), August 2
          [newspaper web page].

Nitibaskara, Ronny
    1993 Observations on the Practice of Sorcery in Java. In *Understanding Witchcraft
          and Sorcery in Southeast Asia.* Edited by C. W. Watson and Roy F. Ellen.
          Honolulu: University of Hawaii Press.

Obeyesekere, Gananath
    1992   *The Apotheosis of James Cook: European Mythmaking in the Pacific.* Princeton,
           N.J.: Princeton University Press.
Ong, Aihwa
    1987   *Spirits of Resistance and Capitalist Discipline: Factory Women in Malaysia.*
           Albany: State University of New York Press.
    1999   *Flexible Citizenship: The Cultural Logics of Transnationality.* Durham, N.C.:
           Duke University Press.
Ortner, Sherry B.
    1984   Theory in Anthropology since the Sixties. *Comparative Studies in Society and
           Culture* 26:126–66.
    1995   Resistance and the Problem of Ethnographic Refusal. *Comparative Studies in
           Society and History* 37:173–93.
Otto, Ton, and Nicholas Thomas, eds.
    1997   *Narratives of Nation in the South Pacific.* Amsterdam: Harwood Academic.
Piot, Charles
    1999   *Remotely Global: Village Modernity in West Africa.* Chicago: University of
           Chicago Press.
Poewe, Karla O., ed.
    1994   *Charismatic Christianity As a Global Culture.* Columbia: University of South
           Carolina Press.
Povinelli, Elizabeth A.
    1995   Do Rocks Listen?: The Cultural Politics of Apprehending Australian
           Aboriginal Labor. *American Anthropologist* 97:505–18.
Prakash, Gyan
    1998   A Different Modernity. Manuscript.
Randolf, R. E.
    1973   Area Study Report. Nomad Subdistrict Office, Western Province, Papua New
           Guinea.
Raudenbush, Stephen W., Suwanna Eamsukkawat, Ikechuku Di-Ibor, Mohammed
Kamali, and Wimol Taoklam
    1993   On-the-Job Improvements in Teacher Competence: Policy Options and Their
           Effects on Teaching and Learning in Thailand. *Educational Evaluation and
           Review* 15: 279–97.
Reed, Adam
    1999   Anticipating Individuals: Modes of Vision and Their Social Consequences in
           a Papua New Guinean Prison. *Journal of the Royal Anthropological Institute* 5:
           43–56.
Reed-Danahay, Deborah
    1996   *Education and Identity in Rural France: The Politics of Schooling.* Cambridge:
           Cambridge University Press.
Rigaud, Milo
    1985   *Secrets of Voodoo.* San Francisco: City Lights Books.
Robbins, Joel
    1995   Dispossessing the Spirits: Christian Transformations of Desire and Ecology
           among the Urapmin of Papua New Guinea. *Ethnology* 34:211–24.
    1997   666, or Why Is the Millennium on the Skin?: Morality, the State, and the
           Epistemology of Apocalypticism among the Urapmin of Papua New Guinea. In
           Millennial Markers. Edited by Pamela J. Stewart and Andrew J. Strathern, pp. 35–
           58. Townsville, Australia: Centre for Pacific Studies, James Cook University.

1998a   Becoming Sinners: Christian Transformations of Morality and Culture in a Papua New Guinea Society. Ph.D. diss. Department of Anthropology, University of Virginia.

1998b   Becoming Sinners: Christianity and Desire among the Urapmin of Papua New Guinea. *Ethnology* 37:299–316.

2001a   Secrecy and the Sense of an Ending: Narrative, Time, and Everyday Millenarianism in Papua New Guinea and in Christian Fundamentalism. *Comparative Studies in Society and History* 43(3): 525–51.

2001b   Whatever Became of Revival?: From Charismatic Movement to Charismatic Church in a Papua New Guinea Society. *Journal of Ritual Studies* 15:79–90.

Robbins, Joel, Pamela J. Stewart, and Andrew J. Strathern, eds.
2001   *Charismatic and Pentecostal Christianity in Oceania. Journal of Ritual Studies*, vol. 15, no. 2.

Robin, Robert W.
1982   Revival Movements in the Southern Highlands Province of Papua New Guinea. *Oceania* 52:320–43.

Rofel, Lisa
1999   *Other Modernities: Gendered Yearnings in China after Socialism.* Berkeley: University of California Press.

Rosaldo, Renato
1980   *Ilongot Headhunting, 1883–1974.* Stanford: Stanford University Press.

Roscoe, Paul
1999   Return of the Ambush: "*Raskolism*" in Rural Rangoru, East Sepik Province. *Oceania* 69:171–83.

2000   New Guinea Leadership As Ethnographic Analogy: A Critical Review. *Journal of Archaeological Method and Theory* 7:79–126.

Rostow, Walt W.
1952   *The Process of Economic Growth.* New York: W. W. Norton.

1960   *The Stages of Economic Growth: A Non-Communist Manifesto.* Cambridge: Cambridge University Press.

1963   *The Economics of Take-off into Sustained Growth.* New York: St. Martin's.

1971   *Politics and the Stages of Growth.* Cambridge: Cambridge University Press.

Rumsey, Alan
2000   Agency, Personhood, and the "I" of Discourse in the Pacific and Beyond. *Journal of the Royal Anthropological Institute* 6:101–15.

Sahlins, Marshall D.
1963   Poor Man, Rich Man, Big-Man, Chief: Political Types in Melanesia and Polynesia. *Comparative Studies in Society and History* 5:285–303.

1985   *Islands of History.* Chicago: University of Chicago Press.

1992   Economics of develop-man in the Pacific. *RES* 21:12–25.

1995   *How "Natives" Think: About Captain Cook, for Example.* Chicago: University of Chicago Press.

2000   *Culture in Practice: Selected Essays.* New York: Zone Books.

Sandeen, Ernest R.
1970   *The Roots of Fundamentalism: British and American Millenarianism 1800–1930.* Chicago: University of Chicago Press.

Scaglion, Richard
1999   Yam Cycles and Timeless Time in Melanesia. *Ethnology* 38:211–25.

Schein, Louisa
    1999   Performing Modernity. *Cultural Anthropology* 14:361–95.
    2000   *Minority Rules: The Miao and the Feminine in China's Cultural Politics*. Durham,
           N.C.: Duke University Press.

Schieffelin, Edward L.
    1976   *The Sorrow of the Lonely and the Burning of the Dancers*. New York: St. Martin's.
    1979   Mediators As Metaphors: Moving a Man to Tears in Papua New Guinea. In *The
           Imagination of Reality: Essays in Southeast Asian Coherence Systems*. Edited by
           Alton L. Becker and Aram A. Yengoyan, pp. 127–44. Norwood, N.J.: Ablex
           Publishing Company.
    1981a The End of Traditional Music, Dance, and Body Decoration in Bosavi, Papua
           New Guinea. *Cultural Survival*, 7:1–22.
    1981b Evangelical Rhetoric and the Transformation of Traditional Culture in Papua
           New Guinea. *Comparative Studies in Society and History* 23:150–56.
    1995   Attitudes toward Logging on the "Great Papuan Plateau." ASAONET Bulletin
           Board <ASAONET@UICVM.UIC.EDU>. September 13.
    1996   Evil Spirit Sickness, the Christian Disease: The Innovation of a New Syndrome
           of Mental Derangement and Redemption in Papua New Guinea. *Culture,
           Medicine, and Psychiatry* 20:1–39.

Schieffelin, Edward L., and Robert Crittenden, eds.
    1991   *Like People You See in a Dream: First Contact in Six Papuan Societies*. Stanford:
           Stanford University Press.

Schmid, Christin Kocher, ed.
    1999   *Expecting the Day of Wrath: Versions of the Millennium in Papua New Guinea*.
           Boroko, Papua New Guinea: National Research Institute, Monograph #36.

Scott, James C.
    1985   *Weapons of the Weak: Everyday Forms of Peasant Resistance*. New Haven,
           Conn.: Yale University Press.
    1990   *Domination and the Arts of Resistance: Hidden Transcripts*. New Haven, Conn.:
           Yale University Press.
    1998   *Seeing Like a State: How Certain Schemes to Improve the Human Condition Have
           Failed*. New Haven, Conn.: Yale University Press.

Simmel, Georg
    1978   *The Philosophy of Money*. London: Routledge and Kegan Paul.

Smith, Michael French
    1994   *Hard Times on Kairiru Island: Poverty, Development, and Morality in a Papua
           New Guinea Village*. Honolulu: University of Hawaii Press.

Sørum, Arve
    1980   In Search of the Lost Soul: Bedamini Spirit Séances and Curing Rites. *Oceania*
           50:273–96.
    1982   The Seeds of Power: Patterns of Bedamini Male Initiation. *Social Analysis* 10:
           42–62.
    1984   Growth and Decay: Bedamini Notions of Sexuality. In *Ritualized
           Homosexuality in Melanesia*. Edited by Gilbert H. Herdt, pp. 318–36. Berkeley:
           University of California Press.

Spittler, Russell P.
    1994   Are Pentecostals and Charismatics Fundamentalists?: A Review of American
           Uses of These Categories. In *Charismatic Christianity As Global Culture*. Edited
           by Karla Poewe, pp. 105–16. Columbia: University of South Carolina Press.

Spitulnik, Debra
    In press   *Media Connections and Disconnections: Radio Culture and the Public Sphere in
            Zambia.* Durham, N.C.: Duke University Press, forthcoming.

Stambach, Amy
    2000   *Lessons from Mount Kilimanjaro: Schooling, Community, and Gender in East
            Africa.* New York: Routledge.

Steadman, Lyle B.
    1971   Neighbors and Killers: Residence and Dominance among the Hewa of New
            Guinea. Ph.D. diss., Department of Anthropology, Australian National
            University, Canberra.
    1985   The Killing of Witches. *Oceania* 56:106–23.

Stephen, Michele
    1994   *A'aisa's Gifts: A Study of Magic and the Self.* Berkeley: University of California
            Press.

Stephen, Michele, ed.
    1987   *Sorcerer and Witch in Melanesia.* New Brunswick, N.J.: Rutgers University
            Press.

Stewart, Pamela J., and Andrew J. Strathern
    1998a   Money, Politics, and Persons in Papua New Guinea. *Social Analysis* 42:132–
            49.
    1998b   Witchcraft, Murder, and Ecological Stress: A Duna (Papua New Guinea)
            Case Study. Centre for Pacific Studies Discussion Paper No. 4. Townsville,
            Australia: James Cook University of Northern Queensland.
    1999   Feasting on My Enemy: Images of Violence and Change in the New Guinea
            Highlands. *Ethnohistory* 47:645–68.

Stewart, Pamela J., and Andrew J. Strathern, eds.
    1997   *Millennial Markers.* Townsville, Australia: Centre for Pacific Studies, James
            Cook University.
    2000   *Millennial Countdown in New Guinea. Ethnohistory,* vol. 47, no. 1.

Strathern, Andrew J.
    1971   *Rope of Moka: Big-Men and Ceremonial Exchange in Mount Hagen, New Guinea.*
            Cambridge: Cambridge University Press.
    1982   Witchcraft, Greed, Cannibalism, and Death: Some Related Themes from the
            New Guinea Highlands. In *Death and the Regeneration of Life.* Edited by
            Maurice Bloch and Jonathan Parry, pp. 111–33. New York: Pergamon.
    1992   Let the Bow Go Down. In *War in the Tribal Zone: Expanding States and
            Indigenous Warfare.* Edited by R. Brian Ferguson and Neil L. Whitehead,
            pp. 229–50. Santa Fe, N.M.: School of American Research Press.
    1993   Violence and Political Change in Papua New Guinea. *Pacific Studies* 16(4):
            41–60.

Strathern, Andrew J., and Pamela J. Stewart
    1999   *Curing and Healing: Medical Anthropology in Global Perspective.* Chapel Hill:
            University of North Carolina Press.

Strathern, Marilyn
    1988   *The Gender of the Gift: Problems with Women and Problems with Society in
            Melanesia.* Berkeley: University of California Press.
    1991   *Partial Connections.* Sabage, Md.: Rowman and Littlefield.
    1999   *Property, Substance, and Effect: Anthropological Essays on Persons and Things.*
            London: Althone.

Stürzenhofecker, Gabriele
  1995 Dialectics of History: Female Witchcraft and Male Dominance in Aluni. In
        *Papuan Borderlands: Huli, Duna, and Ipili Perspectives on the Papua New Guinea
        Highlands*. Edited by Aletta Biersack, pp. 287–313. Ann Arbor: University of
        Michigan Press.
  1998 *Times Enmeshed: Gender, Space, and History among the Duna, Papua New
        Guinea*. Stanford: Stanford University Press.

Sykes, Karen
  1999 After the "Raskol" Feast: Youths' Alienation in New Ireland, Papua New
        Guinea. *Critique of Anthropology* 19: 157–74.
  n.d.   Making the Generation Gap: Postcolonial Education and Political
        Consciousness. Manuscript.

Taussig, Michael
  1980 *The Devil and Commodity Fetishism in South America*. Chapel Hill: University
        of North Carolina Press.
  1987 *Shamanism, Colonialism, and the Wild Man: A Study in Terror and Healing*.
        Chicago: University of Chicago Press.

Temu, Andrew I.
  1997 *Administrative and Financial Brief for the New [Western Province Provincial]
        Government*. Daru, Western Province, Papua New Guinea.

Thomas, Nicholas
  1991 *Entangled Objects: Exchanges, Material Culture, and Colonialism in the Pacific*.
        Cambridge: Harvard University Press.
  1994 *Colonialism's Culture: Anthropology, Travel, and Government*. Princeton, N.J.:
        Princeton University Press.
  1997 *Oceania: Visions, Artifacts, Histories*. Durham, N.C.: Duke University Press.

Tönnies, Ferdinand
  1957 *Community and Society (Gemeinschaft und Gesellschaft)*. East Lansing:
        Michigan State University Press.

Trompf, Gary W.
  1991 *Melanesian Religion*. New York: Cambridge University Press.

Tsing, Anna L.
  1993 *In the Realm of the Diamond Queen: Marginality in an Out-of-the-Way Place*.
        Princeton, N.J.: Princeton University Press.

Tuzin, Donald F.
  1997 *The Cassowary's Revenge: The Life and Death of Masculinity in a New Guinea
        Society*. Chicago: Chicago University Press.

van der Veer, Peter, ed.
  1996 *Conversion to Modernities: The Globalization of Christianity*. New York:
        Routledge.

Vasquez, Manuel A.
  1998 *The Brazilian Popular Church and the Crisis of Modernity*. New York:
        Cambridge University Press.

Wanek, Alexander
  1996 *The State and Its Enemies in Papua New Guinea*. Nordic Institute of Asian
        Studies Monograph #68. Richmond, Surrey, England: Curzon.

Ward, Michael
  2000 Fighting for *Ples* in the City: Young Highlands Men in Port Moresby, Papua
        New Guinea. In *Reflections on Violence in Melanesia*. Edited by Sinclair
        Dinnen and Allison Ley, pp. 223–38. Canberra, Australia: Asia Pacific Press.

Wardlow, Holly
   2000   Passenger Women: Gender, Sexuality, and Agency in a Papua New Guinea
          Modernity. Ph.D. diss., Department of Anthropology, Emory University.
   In press   "Hands-Up"-ing Buses and Harvesting Cheese-Pops: Gendered Mediation
          of Modern Disjuncture in Melanesia. In Critically Modern: Alternatives,
          Alterities, Anthropologies. Edited by Bruce M. Knauft. Bloomington: University
          of Indiana Press.

Watson, C. W., and Roy F. Ellen, eds.
   1993   Understanding Witchcraft and Sorcery in Southeast Asia. Honolulu: University
          of Hawaii Press.

Watson, James B.
   1971   Tairora: The Politics of Despotism in a Small Society. In Politics in New
          Guinea. Edited by Ronald Berndt and Peter Lawrence. Nedlands: University
          of Western Australia Press.

Weber, Max
   1958   The Protestant Ethic and the Spirit of Capitalism. New York: Free Press.
   1978   Economy and Society: An Outline of Interpretive Sociology. Edited by Guenther
          Roth and Claus Wittich. Berkeley: University of California Press.

Weber, Timothy P.
   1979   Living in the Shadow of the Second Coming: American Premillennialism, 1875–
          1925. New York: Oxford University Press.

White, Geoffrey M.
   1991   Identity through History: Living Stories in a Solomon Islands Society. Cambridge:
          Cambridge University Press.

White, Geoffrey M. and Lamont Lindstrom, eds.
   1993   Custom Today. Anthropological Forum 6(4).

Whitehouse, Harvey
   1995   Inside the Cult: Religious Innovation and Transmission in Papua New Guinea.
          Oxford: Clarendon.
   1998   From Mission to Movement: The Impact of Christianity on Patterns
          of Political Association in Papua New Guinea. Journal of the Royal
          Anthropological Institute 4:43–63.

Willaime, Jean-Paul
   1992   La Précarité Protestante: Sociologie du Protestantisme Contemporain. Geneva:
          Labor and Fides.
   1999   Le Pentecôstisme: Contours et Paradoxes d'un Protestantisme Émotionnel.
          Archives de Sciences Sociales des Religions 105:5–28.

Williams, Raymond
   1973   The Country and the City. New York: Oxford University Press.
   1977   Marxism and Literature. New York: Oxford University Press.

Willis, Paul
   1977   Learning to Labour: How Working-Class Kids Get Working-Class Jobs.
          Westmead, U.K.: Saxon House.

Wolf, Eric R.
   1999   Envisioning Power: Ideologies of Dominance and Crisis. Berkeley: University of
          California Press.

Wood, Michael
   1996   Logs, Long Socks, and the "Tree Leaf" People: An Analysis of a Timber
          Project in the Western Province of Papua New Guinea. Social Analysis 39:83–
          117.

1997   The Makapa TRP As a Study in Project Failure in the Post-Barnett Era. In *The Political Economy of Forest Management in Papua New Guinea.* Edited by Colin Filer, pp. 84–108. London: IIED; Boroko: NRI.

1999   Rimbunan Hijau versus the World Bank and Australian Miners: Print Media Representations of Forestry Politic Conflict in Papua New Guinea. *Australian Journal of Anthropology* 19:177–91.

Wormsley, William E.

1987   Beer and Power in Enga. In *Drugs in Western Pacific Societies: Relations of Substance.* Edited by Lamont Lindstrom, pp. 197–217. Lanham, Md.: University Press of America.

Young, Michael W.

1983   *Magicians of Manumanua: Living Myth in Kalauna.* Berkeley: University of California Press.

Zelenietz, Marty, and Shirley Lindenbaum, eds.

1981   *Sorcery and Social Change in Melanesia. Social Analysis,* no. 8. Adelaide, Australia.

Index